Sabine De Knop and Gaëtanelle Gilquin (Eds.)
Applied Construction Grammar

Applications of
Cognitive Linguistics

―

Editors
Gitte Kristiansen
Francisco J. Ruiz de Mendoza Ibáñez

Honorary editor
René Dirven

Volume 32

Applied Construction Grammar

Edited by
Sabine De Knop
Gaëtanelle Gilquin

DE GRUYTER
MOUTON

ISBN 978-3-11-057852-2
e-ISBN (pdf) 978-3-11-045826-8
e-ISBN (EPUB) 978-3-11-045618-9
ISSN 1861-4078

Library of Congress Cataloging-in-Publication Data
A CIP catalog record for this book has been applied for at the Library of Congress.

Bibliographic information published by the Deutsche Nationalbibliothek
The Deutsche Nationalbibliothek lists this publication in the Deutsche Nationalbibliografie;
detailed bibliographic data are available on the Internet at http://dnb.dnb.de.

© 2016 Walter de Gruyter GmbH, Berlin/Boston
This volume is text- and page-identical with the hardback published in 2016 .
Typesetting: RoyalStandard, Hong Kong
Printing and binding: CPI books GmbH, Leck

♾ Printed on acid-free paper
Printed in Germany

www.degruyter.com

Table of contents

List of contributors —— vii

I Introduction

Gaëtanelle Gilquin and Sabine De Knop
Exploring L2 constructionist approaches —— 3

II Constructionist approaches to L2 learning and teaching

Thomas Herbst
Foreign language learning is construction learning – what else? Moving towards Pedagogical Construction Grammar —— 21

Sabine De Knop and Fabio Mollica
A construction-based analysis of German ditransitive phraseologisms for language pedagogy —— 53

Minchang Sung and Hyun-Kwon Yang
Effects of construction-centered instruction on Korean students' learning of English transitive resultative constructions —— 89

Gaëtanelle Gilquin
Input-dependent L2 acquisition: Causative constructions in English as a foreign and second language —— 115

III Crosslinguistic applications of constructionist approaches

Francisco José Ruiz de Mendoza Ibáñez and María del Pilar Agustín Llach
Cognitive Pedagogical Grammar and meaning construction in L2 —— 151

Alberto Hijazo-Gascón, Teresa Cadierno and Iraide Ibarretxe-Antuñano
Learning the placement caused motion construction in L2 Spanish —— 185

Annalisa Baicchi
The role of syntax and semantics in constructional priming: Experimental evidence from Italian university learners of English through a sentence-elicitation task —— 211

Paolo Della Putta
Do we also need to unlearn constructions? The case of constructional negative transfer from Spanish to Italian and its pedagogical implications —— 237

IV Constructing a constructicon for L2 learners

Bert Cappelle and Natalia Grabar
Towards an n-grammar of English —— 271

Hans C. Boas, Ryan Dux and Alexander Ziem
Frames and constructions in an online learner's dictionary of German —— 303

Lisa Loenheim, Benjamin Lyngfelt, Joel Olofsson, Julia Prentice and Sofia Tingsell
Constructicography meets (second) language education: On constructions in teaching aids and the usefulness of a Swedish constructicon —— 327

Index —— 357

List of contributors

Annalisa Baicchi
Università degli Studi di Pavia,
Italy
annalisa.baicchi@unipv.it

Hans Boas
The University of Texas at Austin, USA
hcb@mail.utexas.edu

Teresa Cadierno
University of Southern Denmark,
Denmark
cadierno@sdu.dk

Bert Cappelle
Université de Lille – CNRS, France
bert.cappelle@univ-lille3.fr

Sabine De Knop
Université Saint-Louis Brussels,
Belgium
sabine.deknop@usaintlouis.be

Paolo Della Putta
Università di Modena e Reggio Emilia,
Italy
paolo.dellaputta@unimore.it

María del Pilar Agustín Llach
University of La Rioja, Spain
maria-del-pilar.agustin@unirioja.es

Ryan Dux
The University of Texas at Austin, USA
ryandux@utexas.edu

Gaëtanelle Gilquin
Université catholique de Louvain –
FNRS, Belgium
gaetanelle.gilquin@uclouvain.be

Natalia Grabar
Université de Lille – CNRS, France
natalia.grabar@univ-lille3.fr

Thomas Herbst
Friedrich-Alexander-Universität
Erlangen-Nürnberg, Germany
thomas.herbst@fau.de

Alberto Hijazo-Gascón
University of East Anglia,
United Kingdom
a.hijazo-gascon@uea.ac.uk

Iraide Ibarretxe-Antuñano
University of Zaragoza, Spain
iraide@unizar.es

Lisa Loenheim
University of Gothenburg, Sweden
lisa.loenheim@svenska.gu.se

Benjamin Lyngfelt
University of Gothenburg, Sweden
benjamin.lyngfelt@svenska.gu.se

Fabio Mollica
Università degli Studi di Milano,
Italy
fabio.mollica@unimi.it

Joel Olofsson
University of Gothenburg, Sweden
joel.olofsson@svenska.gu.se

Julia Prentice
University of Gothenburg, Sweden
julia.prentice@svenska.gu.se

Francisco José Ruiz de Mendoza Ibañez
University of La Rioja, Spain
francisco.ruizdemendoza@unirioja.es

Min-Chang Sung
Seoul National University, South Korea
potamin3@snu.ac.kr

Sofia Tingsell
University of Gothenburg, Sweden
sofia.tingsell@svenska.gu.se

Hyun-Kwon Yang
Seoul National University, South Korea
yhkeun@snu.ac.kr

Alexander Ziem
Universität Düsseldorf, Germany
ziem@phil.hhu.de

Introduction

Gaëtanelle Gilquin and Sabine De Knop
Exploring L2 constructionist approaches

1 The need for an Applied Construction Grammar

The notion of Construction Grammar (CxG) covers a wide range of theoretical models (see Hoffmann and Trousdale (2013: 109–252) for an overview), all of them sharing the central tenet that constructions are the basic units of language. The interest for constructionist approaches to language started with Fillmore, Kay, and O'Connor's (1988) seminal paper on *let alone* and received its first book-length treatment in Goldberg's (1995) *Constructions: A Construction Grammar Approach to Argument Structure*. In this book, Goldberg describes constructions as conventionalized form-meaning pairs characterized by non-compositionality. In her later book *Constructions at Work: The Nature of Generalization in Language* (Goldberg 2006), the property of non-compositionality no longer constitutes a necessary condition to recognize constructions, as long as these structures are entrenched, i.e. characterized by frequency. In the last few years, CxG has gradually grown into a powerful descriptive and processing model which is now well-accepted in the scientific world, as attested by the organization of international events focussing on different issues related to CxG, as well as the publication of monographs and edited volumes describing the advantages (and limitations) of the constructionist models and the new insights they have provided, in English and more recently in other languages (see among others Fried and Östman 2004; Östman and Fried 2005; Fischer and Stefanowitsch 2007; Stefanowitsch and Fischer 2008; Lasch and Ziem 2011, 2014; Bouveret and Legallois 2012; Boas and Gonzálvez-García 2014).

Current research within the framework of CxG has mainly adopted a theoretical or descriptive approach, focussing on the principles of CxG, comparing it with other linguistic theories (e.g. valency theory, cf. Herbst and Stefanowitsch 2011; Welke 2011), describing specific constructions (e.g. the well-known caused motion construction or the ditransitive construction), or illustrating some of the CxG principles at work in constructions in different languages (e.g. Boas 2010; De Knop, Mollica, and Kuhn 2013). One perspective that has been relatively neglected up to now is the more applied perspective, and especially the question of how language acquisition and pedagogy can benefit from a CxG-based approach. Child language acquisition fares slightly better in this respect. Probably under the impetus of usage-based models of CxG, which hold that constructions gradually emerge from actual usage events and that language is thus learned inductively, the processes underlying the acquisition of a first language have received some attention in the literature (e.g. Goldberg, Casenhiser, and Sethuraman 2004; Tomasello 2006; Diessel 2013). Second and foreign language (L2) acquisition and teaching, on the other hand, have not been the focus of many CxG-based studies so far.

Among the few authors who have tackled L2 acquisition from a CxG point of view, Liang (2002, quoted in Goldberg 2006) is probably one of the earliest examples. Her study is a replication of Bencini and Goldberg's (2000) sentence-sorting experiment, which showed that American students favour construction over verb when sorting sentences (argument structure constructions) into different groups according to their overall meaning. Liang's (2002) subjects are not native speakers of English, but Chinese learners of English. Not only does it appear that the Chinese learners do sort by construction, but it also turns out that constructional sorts vary along with language proficiency: the more proficient the learners, the more likely they are to use constructional meaning as the main criterion for sorting the stimulus sentences. Gries and Wulff (2005) propose another replication of Bencini and Goldberg (2000) with advanced German learners of English. Their results, which are very similar to those obtained by Liang (2002) for the most advanced Chinese learners, indicate a preference for construction-based sorting over verb-based sorting. In fact, the foreign language learners appear to rely even more heavily on constructional sorts than the native speakers in Bencini and Goldberg's (2000) experiment, an outcome that could suggest that constructions are even more crucial for non-native speakers than for native speakers when it comes to the interpretation of sentences. Gries and Wulff's (2005) study also includes a sentence completion task and a (native) corpus analysis, both of which confirm the relevance of "attributing an ontological status to constructions for non-native speakers of English" (Gries and Wulff 2005: 182). In 2009, using the same combination of psycholinguistic evidence (acceptability rating task and sentence completion task) and corpus linguistic evidence (from native corpus data), Gries and Wulff provide additional support for the ontological status of constructions for German learners of English, this time exploring complementation constructions rather than argument structure constructions. Valenzuela Manzanares and Rojo López (2008) adopt a similar approach: they combine a replication of Bencini and Goldberg's (2000) experiment, an acceptability judgment task and a corpus analysis to demonstrate the psychological reality of constructions for yet another learner population, namely Spanish learners of English. What is particularly interesting about their methodology is that, unlike Gries and Wulff, they supplement the native corpus analysis with the investigation of learner corpus data, on the basis of which they examine learners' performance, identify their phraseological preferences, and also create anomalous stimulus sentences for the acceptability judgment task. These studies are important because they provide converging evidence that learners from different mother tongue (L1) backgrounds and different proficiency levels have some mental representation of various constructions, just like native speakers. This, of course, is a sine qua non for a constructionist approach to second and foreign languages: if non-native speakers do not (and cannot) have constructions, then a theoretical framework relying on constructions as the basic building blocks of language cannot be suitable for the description and analysis of an L2, while from a teaching point of view, "if constructions were not a psychologically real category, learners would profit very little from their inclusion in any learning materials" (Eddington and Ruiz de Mendoza 2010: 230).

Once the existence of constructions in L2 has been demonstrated, their use by learners can be analysed. Strictly speaking, since CxG models tend to consider that all language consists in constructions (morphemes, words, phrases, idioms, etc.), all previous investigations of L2 can be said to contribute to our knowledge of the L2 constructicon. However, we are interested here in studies that explicitly adopt a CxG approach and take advantage of the strengths of the theory to gain a better understanding of the processes underlying second language acquisition and foreign language learning. Gilquin's (2015) study of phrasal verbs, for example, starts from the CxG view that constructions exist at different levels of abstraction and form networks in the constructicon. It examines the use of phrasal verbs by French-speaking learners of English at three levels, from the more abstract to the more specific: the phrasal verb "superconstruction", the structural patterns [V Prt], [V Prt OBJ] and [V OBJ Prt] (where V = verb, Prt = particle, OBJ = object), and the lexically specified phrasal verbs. A comparison of (spoken and written) learner corpus data with a native baseline reveals that it is at the intermediate level, that of the structural patterns, that learners seem to be the most successful and thus, presumably, have best internalized the construction. Among other methods of analysis, the study relies on the technique of collostructional analysis, which measures the interaction between words and constructions (Stefanowitsch and Gries 2003). This technique, which reconciles CxG and (quantitative) corpus linguistics, has been applied in other investigations of L2 constructions, for example verb-argument constructions (Ellis and Ferreira-Junior 2009a), causative constructions (Gilquin 2012), or gerundial and infinitival constructions (Martinez-Garcia and Wulff 2012). Ellis and Ferreira-Junior (2009a: 203) note that, for verb-argument constructions, native collexeme strength, i.e. the strength of association between the constructions and the verbs occurring in them, as calculated by a collostructional analysis, "is a very strong predictor of NNS [non-native speaker] acquisition". This comment underlines the relevance of collostructional analysis for second language acquisition, but even more importantly, it shows that, beyond a simple description of non-native language, a CxG-based approach also makes it possible to predict and/or explain certain features of the interlanguage. A case in point is the presence of L1 traces in the use of L2 constructions, due to transfer from the L1 to the L2. Martínez Vázquez (2008) thus finds out that caused motion constructions, which are typical of satellite-framed languages (like English) but not verb-framed languages, occur more and with more diversity in the English essays of learners with a satellite-framed L1 than in those of learners with a verb-framed L1. Similarly, Römer, O'Donnell, and Ellis (2014), examining the responses to generative free association tasks, attribute differences between native and non-native English verb-argument constructions to language transfer and typology: "learners whose L1 is satellite-framed (and hence typologically similar to English) produce more verbs that correlate more closely with those produced by L1 English speakers than speakers whose L1 is verb-framed" (Römer, O'Donnell, and Ellis 2014: 967). Such phenomena are due to the fact that, when learning an L2, learners come with their own constructicon, which may interfere with the L2 constructicon. All this goes to show that second language acquisition, unlike first language acquisition, "involves processes of construction and *re*construction" (Ellis 2013: 366; emphasis original). These processes are determined by factors like construction frequency, form, function, and the interactions between these elements (Ellis 2013: 368ff.). Some of these factors are further investigated in two special issues of journals edited by Collins and Ellis (2009) and by Ellis and Cadierno (2009).

The authors of several of the above-mentioned studies briefly discuss some teaching implications of their findings. Thus, it is suggested that L2 instruction should "acknowledge the pervasiveness of constructions more than it currently does" (Römer, O'Donnell, and Ellis 2014: 967), that the description of constructions in teaching materials should better reflect actual usage (Martinez-Garcia and Wulff 2012: 240), that learners should be made aware of typical associations between words and constructions (Martinez-Garcia and Wulff 2012: 241) as well as differences between L1 and L2 constructions (Römer, O'Donnell, and Ellis 2014: 967), or that teachers defining the objectives of their teaching or preparing exercises for their students should use the results of CxG studies of interlanguage to "determine the stage of the students' learning process, locate their main problems and establish their needs" (Valenzuela Manzanares and Rojo López 2008: 223). While such suggestions are typically found in the conclusion section, as a kind of afterthought, a few publications are entirely devoted to the issue of applying CxG to language teaching, e.g. Wee (2007) or Holme (2010a, 2010b). Holme (2010a) stresses the important role of teaching in a CxG-based view of second language acquisition. Since, according to CxG (and usage-based models in general), constructions are generalized from the different instantiations that are encountered in language, generalizations might be more difficult to make for non-native speakers, who get exposed to fewer instantiations. Teaching, therefore, should compensate for this low exposure and implement strategies that encourage learners to generalize (Holme 2010a: 126). This could involve the repeated exposure to – and noticing of – various instantiations of a construction in different contexts, through the use of texts that "recycle new tokens of previously taught constructions" (Holme 2010a: 127). These educationalists who believe in the power of CxG for language teaching particularly emphasize the potential of "scaffolding" (Wee 2007: 29; Holme 2010a: 127). Their claim is that, starting from the use of a pathbreaking verb in a construction, learners can discover (or be made to discover) how the pathbreaking verb alternates with other verbs, how the construction relates to other constructions that the learner is familiar with (in the target language or in another language, including the mother tongue) – e.g. constructions that are embedded within the construction or represent a semantic extension of it – and how the productivity of constructions can be exploited for creative purposes. In other words, students should learn to "conceptualise the new through the known" (Holme 2010b: 362). Gradually, thanks to the presentation of language material "in a meaningful and logical, systematically structured way" (Pavlović 2010: 85), they should be able to build networks of constructions that will help them store constructions more efficiently in their mental constructicon and retrieve the information more rapidly. This approach is all the more interesting as it can be applied to "language elements of all shapes and sizes" (Hinkel 2012: 4), since CxG is a "uniform model of grammatical representation" (Pedersen and Cadierno 2004: 155) that recognizes constructions at all levels of language. Most of these pedagogical suggestions, though perfectly sensible from a theoretical point of view, have not been tested with real students, and we know very little about their possible teaching effectiveness. One exception to this is Holme's (2010b) description and evaluation of two CxG-based pedagogical interventions in a secondary school. By comparing the results of a pre- and post-test among the experimental group of students who participated in the pedagogical interventions and a control group who did not, he shows that the experimental group improved their score significantly more than the control group. This study thus provides modest but encouraging evidence that constructionist approaches have a role to play in the classroom.

    This literature review shows that the main issues related to L2 applications of CxG have been tackled, namely the ontological status of constructions, the analysis of their use and acquisition, and the pedagogical implications of a constructionist approach to second language acquisition and foreign language learning. However, given the small number of publications to date, the findings are necessarily limited – in terms of research questions, constructions, languages or learner populations investigated – which makes it difficult to draw wide-ranging and reliable conclusions about the relevance of CxG for second language acquisition research. Yet, the above studies, by providing interesting insights into the learning and teaching of constructions, have demonstrated the potential of using CxG for applied purposes. What is needed at this stage, therefore, is a continued and collaborative effort to pursue research in this field, which we will refer to as "Applied Construction Grammar" and which, adapting Pütz's (2007: 1139) definition of Applied Cognitive Linguistics, we will define as the acquisitional and pedagogical implications of Construction Grammar in second/foreign language teaching and learning. The present volume is a first attempt at bringing together different contributions that explore the various aspects of Applied Construction Grammar. In the next section, we present the volume and describe the main issues related to second language acquisition, foreign language learning and teaching that are addressed in its eleven chapters.

2 Main issues in second language acquisition, foreign language learning and teaching

The aim of this volume is to offer a collection of studies applying CxG (and CxG-inspired approaches) to relevant issues in second language acquisition, foreign language learning and teaching. As "[c]onstructions form a structured inventory of a speaker's knowledge" (Ellis and Ferreira-Junior 2009b: 370), it will come as no surprise that the contributions to the volume all take "constructions" as a starting point for their studies. However, the notion of construction is used and defined in various and more or less general ways in the volume. Most chapters follow Goldberg's (1995, 2006) definition and agree that constructions are form-meaning mappings. Goldberg's (1995) early defining property of constructions as having to be non-compositional does not represent an obligatory characteristic of the constructions as described in the volume. Entrenchment in a specific language is what primarily defines them. The volume offers a detailed description of a variety of constructions, mainly in English (resultative construction, caused motion construction, causative construction, subjective-manipulative construction, dative alternation), but also in other languages: the German ditransitive construction, the Spanish and Danish caused motion construction, the Spanish planned future periphrasis [*ir a* + infinitive] ('*go to* + infinitive') and iterative periphrasis [*volver a* + infinitive] ('*return to* + infinitive'), or the Swedish [X *och* X]

('X *and* X') construction. Like cognitive linguistics and other usage-based models of language, CxG can be seen as a "data-friendly" theory (Janda 2013: 2), and the last few years in particular have seen a greater reliance on empirical evidence among constructionists. Accordingly, all the studies brought together in this volume use some sort of data. Some of these come from corpora representing naturally-occurring language, either L1 production or L2 production; in some cases the corpus data are merely used to illustrate certain phenomena, but in other cases they constitute the foundation on which the whole analysis is built. Experimentation is also used as a source of data and includes sorting tasks, (picture-based or video-based) description tasks, translation tasks and priming experiments. This empirical orientation helps improve the reliability of the claims made.

The volume is divided into three main sections. The first one deals with constructionist approaches to L2 learning and teaching. The four chapters in this section examine how L2 use and acquisition appear through the CxG looking glass, and what consequences this can have for language teaching. In the second section, the focus is on crosslinguistic applications. The comparison between languages lies at the basis of the four chapters making up the section. However, this comparison is not an end in itself, but a way of gaining deeper insights into second language acquisition/foreign language learning, most notably through the idea of constructional transfer. The three chapters of the last section deal with the construction of constructicons for learners, i.e. databases of constructions meant to help learners acquire the main constructions of a language. Despite this neat division into three sections, it should be noted that there is a certain degree of overlap between the topics they cover, with, for example, teaching suggestions being found in the crosslinguistic applications, and crosslinguistic issues arising in the description of constructicons. In what follows, we identify some of the more specific topics that are discussed across the volume.

2.1 Learners' constructions

If constructions are the basic units of language, then the question can be asked whether language learners have constructions in their L2 and, if so, how they acquire them, and whether these constructions are acquired in the same way by native and non-native speakers or by non-native speakers from different mother tongue backgrounds. In her empirical study of the dative alternation, which replicates Hare and Goldberg's (1999) experiment, Baicchi provides some evidence that Italian learners of English do have constructions in their L2, even in cases where the construction does not have any counterpart in the L1 constructicon (cf. double-object construction and fulfilling construction, which are not part of the Italian language). De Knop and Mollica come to a similar conclusion with their sorting experiment of phraseological ditransitive constructions. In their study they observe that French- and Italian-speaking learners of German intuitively prefer to sort literal and phraseological ditransitive constructions according to their structure, rather than according to the verb type, the valency of the verbs or the lexemes used in these constructions. This seems to suggest that constructional templates are present in learners' interlanguage.

However, due to typological differences, languages may have different constructions and different constructional properties, as illustrated by Ruiz de Mendoza Ibáñez and Agustín Llach's contrastive analysis of the resultative, caused motion and subjective-manipulative constructions in Spanish and English. Hijazo-Gascón, Cadierno, and Ibarretxe-Antuñano also highlight the typological differences between placement caused motion constructions in Danish and Spanish, which are realized with a placement verb and a satellite in Danish, while in Spanish only a general *put*-verb is required. Such differences are likely to affect learners' representations of the constructions in the L2 and lead to possible transfer effects, as outlined in the next section.

2.2 Transfer of L1 constructions to L2

If we postulate cross-linguistically different constructions due, among other things, to typological differences, we may wonder whether constructions are transferred from L1 to L2 and whether certain constructions are more prone to transfer than others. Della Putta's study of the difficulties encountered by Spanish speakers when trying to express planned future and iteration in Italian (which cannot use the literal equivalents of the Spanish constructions) reveals that L1 constructions can indeed be transferred to L2. Della Putta even goes one step further by claiming that some L1 constructions function as an obstacle to the learning of an L2, which leads him to develop several teaching activities to "unlearn" the L1 constructions. Similarly, Hijazo-Gascón, Cadierno, and Ibarretxe-Antuñano observe possible traces of transfer (including semantic transfer) in Danish learners' use of the Spanish placement caused motion construction.

Yet, we are also reminded that transfer is by no means systematic. Hijazo-Gascón, Cadierno, and Ibarretxe-Antuñano point out that their Danish learners use fewer particle tokens in the Spanish placement caused motion construction than the native speakers, despite the fact that the Danish construction frequently includes a particle. As for De Knop and Mollica, they note that learners are not always able to select the correct meaning of ditransitive phraseologisms, even when the L1 and the L2 use the same image (e.g. the image of the shoulder to express rejection in German and Italian). These cases of non-transfer, as explained by the authors, could be due to learners' perceptions of the L1 and L2 constructions (cf. Kellerman's (1978) concept of psychotypology).

2.3 Constructionist view on L2 acquisition

CxG belongs to the usage-based approaches which emphasize that languages are learnt from usage, through abstraction and generalization. As pointed out in Herbst's chapter, such generalizations are arguably more difficult to make in L2 acquisition because of the smaller amount of input received by non-native speakers. On the other hand, Herbst notes that the presence of similar generalizations in the L1 may have a facilitative effect for learners. As will be shown in Section 2.4, teaching may also counterbalance learners' input-poor environment.

Not all learners live in an input-poor environment, however. A distinction can be drawn between learners who mainly learn the target language through instruction (i.e. with a limited amount of input) and those who acquire the language in a natural environment. Gilquin compares the use of English causative constructions by two groups of students representing these different acquisition contexts and shows that students with more exposure to naturally-occurring language tend to have a more native-like knowledge of the constructions. The amount of input also seems to influence the level at which learners generalize: a more abstract level for learners who receive more input and a lower, more concrete level for learners who receive less input and more instruction.

Another observation is that light verbs are central to the learning of constructions. The chapters by Gilquin and by Hijazo-Gascón, Cadierno, and Ibarretxe-Antuñano show that learners' constructions tend to be characterized by over-reliance on such verbs, and in particular the high-frequency verb *make* in English causative constructions and the general placement verb *poner* ('put') in Spanish placement caused motion constructions. Sung and Yang demonstrate that light verbs facilitate the learning of the constructions in which they occur. The use of these verbs could thus be the first step in the acquisition of constructions, a step that is necessary before more specific verbs can gradually come to be associated with the constructions.

2.4 CxG-inspired teaching strategies

Some of the contributions start by expressing dissatisfaction with the traditional teaching methodology as applied in certain teaching manuals. According to

Loenheim et al., Swedish L2 textbooks and study aid materials tend to neglect semi-general patterns and fail to capture the productivity and variability of constructions. In his analysis of Bavarian teaching manuals, Herbst draws a similar conclusion after observing that the terminology is not clear and sometimes even obsolete, and that some examples are contradictory. Dictionaries are of little help as they rarely provide information about the constructions in which words typically occur. Cappelle and Grabar stress that foreign language teaching is in dire need of an inventory of frequent constructions which can be considered relevant when learning an L2 (see Section 2.5). A major problem in traditional teaching methodology seems to be the (commonly used) dichotomy between lexicon and grammar, which entails that learners and teachers can either gain knowledge about words as listed in dictionaries/lexicons, or structural knowledge as described in grammar books. Only few teaching materials combine both knowledge areas in a constructive way.

With the demonstration of the ontological status of constructions in the L2, and hence their psychological reality for learners, Baicchi claims that it is highly advisable to introduce constructions in language pedagogy. According to Herbst, linguistics, and more specifically CxG, could help determine what to teach and how to teach it. For him, the most important asset of CxG is that it provides a cognitive perspective that is compatible with other approaches like corpus linguistics or foreign language linguistics, with which it shares many central concerns. This affinity makes CxG an ideal theory for language teaching applications. Taking a contrastive point of view, Ruiz de Mendoza Ibáñez and Agustín Llach suggest that pedagogical grammarians should provide learners with user-friendly versions of the generalizations that they should ultimately arrive at, and that these generalizations should be contrasted with their counterparts in the learners' L1. The authors themselves develop some very concrete pedagogical activities in their chapter, based for example on inferential activity and construction-based meaning composition.

Sung and Yang offer supporting evidence for the effectiveness of CxG-inspired pedagogical interventions. Using a translation task as a pre- and post-test, they show that Korean learners of English who have received construction-centred instruction improve their score more than learners who have received form-centred instruction. It also appears from their experiment that teaching a construction may positively affect the learning of directly related – and more basic – constructions, a point which is taken up again in the next section.

2.5 Elaboration of a constructicon

One of the characteristics of CxG is that it does not view constructions in isolation, but as forming networks or, as Ruiz de Mendoza Ibáñez and Agustín Llach call them, families of constructions. Taking advantage of this, De Knop and Mollica study ditransitive phraseologisms starting from the literal ditransitive constructions. The relation between the phraseological and the literal constructions is motivated by inheritance links defined in CxG. Such links can be exploited for teaching purposes, as suggested by Ruiz de Mendoza Ibáñez and Agustín Llach, who recommend teaching constructions in relation to other similar constructions (e.g. the English caused motion construction and its sister resultative constructions). The above-mentioned study by Sung and Yang demonstrates that the teaching of the transitive resultative construction can help improve learners' knowledge of other related constructions, especially the caused motion construction, which directly dominates the transitive resultative construction in the hierarchical network of argument structure constructions.

Using a large corpus from which part-of-speech n-grams are automatically extracted, Cappelle and Grabar aim to compile a list of the most frequent grammatical patterns in English and the lexical items commonly found in these patterns. The authors regard this list as the basis of an "n-grammar", in which abstract patterns are described, illustrated, and practised through, e.g., "chop and change charts". As for the chapters by Boas, Dux, and Ziem, on the one hand, and Loenheim et al., on the other, they describe the elaboration of a constructicon for German and Swedish, respectively. More precisely, Boas, Dux, and Ziem introduce the so-called German Frame-Based Online Lexicon (G-FOL), a frame- and construction-based resource relying on the principles of FrameNet. G-FOL seeks to provide English-speaking learners of German with useful lexical and grammatical information, as illustrated in the chapter for grooming events. German constructions and their "constructional elements" are described and exemplified by means of corpus sentences, and comparisons with their English equivalents are presented. Like Boas, Dux, and Ziem, Loenheim et al. see in the elaboration of their Swedish constructicon (SweCcn, also connected to FrameNet) a way of bringing together the general rules of grammar and the concrete lexical expressions of dictionaries. Through what they call constructicography, they hope to bring a constructional perspective to language education and to open up the possibility of developing construction-based teaching materials.

3 Conclusion and outlook

Combined with the already existing literature reviewed in Section 1, the contributions to this volume underline the advantages of approaching second language acquisition and foreign language learning and teaching from a constructionist point of view. Besides confirming the existence of constructions in learners' minds, Applied Construction Grammar can improve the description of learners' use of constructions, provide theoretical insights into the processes underlying their acquisition (e.g. with reference to inheritance links or transfer from the L1), or lead to novel teaching practices and resources aimed to help learners make the generalizations that native speakers make naturally from the input they receive. It will probably come as a relief to certain readers that adopting such a perspective does not necessarily mean that one has to do away with former beliefs or pedagogical materials and start something completely new. On the one hand, Applied Construction Grammar appears to be compatible with other frameworks, such as corpus linguistics or contrastive linguistics, as well as, obviously, the general theory of cognitive linguistics and all usage-based models. On the other hand, small adjustments are sometimes sufficient to make one's approach to L2 acquisition and teaching, if not truly constructionist, at least CxG-inspired, as suggested by Herbst's seven principles for Pedagogical Construction Grammar.

At the same time, it must be admitted that there is still a great deal of research to be carried out if we want Applied Construction Grammar to grow into a mature and fully-fledged discipline. Many more constructions, groups of learners and contexts of acquisition will have to be examined before a comprehensive constructionist theory of L2 acquisition can be developed. This will require more and new types of experimentation and corpus analyses, which might involve access to data that are perhaps not yet available, like for example dense longitudinal corpora representing several learner populations that would make it possible to chart the emergence of constructions in L2 acquisition (cf. Ellis 2013: 377). In terms of teaching, rigorously controlled classroom experimentation will be essential before we introduce CxG across the board in our schools. If they turn out to be efficient (for certain groups of learners), CxG-based pedagogical interventions will have to be created, and then probably refined as theoretical developments continue to be made. The conservative forces of the publishing industry will also have to be overcome if we are to make CxG-inspired teaching materials widely available (see Herbst's chapter) – even if we must recognize with Littlemore (2009: 173) that "we have a long way to go before we can produce suitable materials to introduce learners to L2 constructions and the relationships between them in a realistic, systematic and learnable manner". From a more theoretical viewpoint, it would be worth investigating whether the other models of CxG are as suitable as the Goldbergian model mainly considered here for applied purposes. It might be that, after such an investigation, the field of Applied Construction Grammar should be renamed "Applied Construction Grammars".

The above shows that many aspects of Applied Construction Grammar remain to be explored. However, the clear potential of the field augurs well for the future.

More synergy between CxG and second language acquisition/foreign language teaching is likely to bring them mutual benefit: second language acquisition and foreign language teaching can develop their theoretical insights about L2 learning and propose new ways of teaching languages, while CxG can test the plausibility of its theories through the confrontation with more applied issues. We hope that this prospect, as well as the example of the contributions collected in this volume, can encourage both constructionists and L2 acquisition/teaching specialists to dig deeper into Applied Construction Grammar and foster its development for our and our students' benefit.

References

Bencini, Giulia M. L. & Adele E. Goldberg. 2000. The contribution of argument structure constructions to sentence meaning. *Journal of Memory and Language* 43(4). 640–651.

Boas, Hans C. (ed.). 2010. *Contrastive studies in construction grammar*. Amsterdam & Philadelphia: John Benjamins.

Boas, Hans C. & Francisco Gonzálvez-García (eds.). 2014. *Romance perspectives on construction grammar*. Amsterdam & Philadelphia: John Benjamins.

Bouveret, Myriam & Dominique Legallois (eds.). 2012. *Constructions in French*. Amsterdam & Philadelphia: John Benjamins.

Collins, Laura & Nick Ellis (eds.). 2009. *Input and second language construction learning: Frequency, form, and function*. Special issue of *The Modern Language Journal* 93(3). 329–429.

De Knop, Sabine, Fabio Mollica & Julia Kuhn (eds.). 2013. *Konstruktionsgrammatik in den Romanischen Sprachen*. Frankfurt am Main: Peter Lang.

Diessel, Holger. 2013. Construction grammar and first language acquisition. In Thomas Hoffmann & Graeme Trousdale (eds.), *The Oxford handbook of construction grammar*, 347–364. Oxford: Oxford University Press.

Eddington, David & Francisco Ruiz de Mendoza. 2010. Argument constructions and language processing: Evidence from a priming experiment and pedagogical implications. In Sabine De Knop, Frank Boers & Antoon De Rycker (eds.), *Fostering language teaching efficiency through cognitive linguistics*, 213–238. Berlin: Mouton de Gruyter.

Ellis, Nick. 2013. Construction grammar and second language acquisition. In Thomas Hoffmann & Graeme Trousdale (eds.), *The Oxford handbook of construction grammar*, 365–378. Oxford: Oxford University Press.

Ellis, Nick & Teresa Cadierno (eds.). 2009. *Constructing a second language*. Special section of *Annual Review of Cognitive Linguistics* 7. 111–290.

Ellis, Nick & Fernando Ferreira-Junior. 2009a. Constructions and their acquisition. Islands and the distinctiveness of their occupancy. *Annual Review of Cognitive Linguistics* 7. 187–220.

Ellis, Nick & Fernando Ferreira-Junior. 2009b. Construction learning as a function of frequency, frequency distribution, and function. *The Modern Language Journal* 93(3). 370–385.

Fillmore, Charles J., Paul Kay & Mary Catherine O'Connor. 1988. Regularity and idiomaticity in grammatical constructions: The case of 'let alone'. *Language* 64(3). 501–538.

Fischer, Kerstin & Anatol Stefanowitsch (eds.). 2007. *Konstruktionsgrammatik: Von der Anwendung zur Theorie*. Tübingen: Stauffenburg.

Fried, Mirjam & Jan-Ola Östman (eds.). 2004. *Construction grammar in a cross-language perspective*. Amsterdam & Philadelphia: John Benjamins.

Gilquin, Gaëtanelle. 2012. Lexical infelicity in English causative constructions. Comparing native and learner collostructions. In Jaakko Leino & Ruprecht von Waldenfels (eds.), *Analytical causatives. From 'give' and 'come' to 'let' and 'make'*, 41–63. München: Lincom Europa.

Gilquin, Gaëtanelle. 2015. The use of phrasal verbs by French-speaking EFL learners. A constructional and collostructional corpus-based approach. In Sabine De Knop & Fanny Meunier (eds.), *Learner corpus research, cognitive linguistics and second language acquisition*. Special issue of *Corpus Linguistics and Linguistic Theory* 11(1). 51–88.

Goldberg, Adele E. 1995. *Constructions. A construction grammar approach to argument structure*. Chicago & London: The University of Chicago Press.

Goldberg, Adele E. 2006. *Constructions at work. The nature of generalization in language*. Oxford: Oxford University Press.

Goldberg, Adele E., Devin M. Casenhiser & Nitya Sethuraman. 2004. Learning argument structure generalizations. *Cognitive Linguistics* 14(3). 289–316.

Gries, Stefan Th. & Stefanie Wulff. 2005. Do foreign language learners also have constructions? Evidence from priming, sorting, and corpora. *Annual Review of Cognitive Linguistics* 3. 182–200.

Gries, Stefan Th. & Stefanie Wulff. 2009. Psycholinguistic and corpus-linguistic evidence for L2 constructions. *Annual Review of Cognitive Linguistics* 7. 163–186.

Hare, Mary & Adele E. Goldberg. 1999. Structural priming: Purely syntactic? In Martin Hahn & Scott Stones (eds.), *Proceedings of the 21st annual meeting of the cognitive science society*, 208–211. London: Lawrence Erlbaum Associates.

Herbst, Thomas & Anatol Stefanowitsch (eds.). 2011. *Argument structure – Valency and/or constructions?* Special issue of *Zeitschrift für Anglistik und Amerikanistik* 59.

Hinkel, Eli. 2012. Innovative and efficient construction grammar. *Selected papers from the 21st international symposium on English teaching*. English Teachers' Association, Republic of China (ETA-ROC), Taipei. Available at http://www.elihinkel.org/downloads/innovative-efficient-grammar.pdf (last accessed on 10 August 2015).

Hoffmann, Thomas & Graeme Trousdale (eds.). 2013. *The Oxford handbook of construction grammar*. Oxford: Oxford University Press.

Holme, Randal. 2010a. Construction grammars: Towards a pedagogical model. *AILA Review* 23. 115–133.

Holme, Randal. 2010b. A construction grammar for the classroom. *IRAL* 48. 355–377.

Janda, Laura A. 2013. Quantitative methods in *Cognitive Linguistics*: An introduction. In Laura A. Janda (ed.), *Cognitive linguistics: The quantitative turn. The essential reader*, 1–32. Berlin: de Gruyter.

Kellerman, Eric. 1978. Transfer and non-transfer: Where are we now? *Studies in Second Language Acquisition* 2. 37–57.

Lasch, Alexander & Alexander Ziem (eds.). 2011. *Konstruktionsgrammatik III. Aktuelle Fragen und Lösungsansätze*. Tübingen: Stauffenburg.

Lasch, Alexander & Alexander Ziem (eds.). 2014. *Grammatik als Netzwerk von Konstruktionen – Sprachwissen im Fokus der Konstruktionsgrammatik*. Berlin & Boston: Walter de Gruyter.

Liang, Junying. 2002. How do Chinese EFL learners construct sentence meaning: Verb-centered or construction-based? M.A. thesis, Guangdong University of Foreign Studies.

Littlemore, Jeannette. 2009. *Applying cognitive linguistics to second language learning and teaching.* New York: Palgrave Macmillan.

Martinez-Garcia, Maria Teresa & Stefanie Wulff. 2012. Not wrong, yet not quite right: Spanish ESL students' use of gerundial and infinitival complementation. *International Journal of Applied Linguistics* 22(2). 225–244.

Martínez Vázquez, Montserrat. 2008. Constructions in learner language. *Círculo de Lingüística Aplicada a la Comunicación* 36. 40–62.

Östman, Jan-Ola & Mirjam Fried (eds.). 2005. *Construction grammars: Cognitive grounding and theoretical extensions.* Amsterdam & Philadelphia: John Benjamins.

Pavlović, Vladan. 2010. Cognitive linguistics and English language teaching at English departments. *Facta Universitatis, Series Linguistics and Literature* 8(1). 79–90.

Pedersen, Johan & Teresa Cadierno. 2004. Construction grammar and second language acquisition: A cognitive understanding of language in a contrastive perspective. In Hans Lauge Hansen (ed.), *Disciplines and interdisciplinarity in foreign language studies*, 151–167. Copenhagen: Museum Tusculanum Press.

Pütz, Martin. 2007. Cognitive linguistics and applied linguistics. In Dirk Geeraerts & Hubert Cuyckens (eds.), *The Oxford handbook of cognitive linguistics*, 1139–1159. Oxford: Oxford University Press.

Römer, Ute, Matthew Brook O'Donnell & Nick C. Ellis. 2014. Second language learner knowledge of verb-argument constructions: Effects of language transfer and typology. *The Modern Language Journal* 98(4). 952–975.

Stefanowitsch, Anatol & Kerstin Fischer (eds.). 2008. *Konstruktionsgrammatik II: Von der Konstruktion zur Grammatik.* Tübingen: Stauffenburg.

Stefanowitsch, Anatol & Stefan Th. Gries. 2003. Collostructions: Investigating the interaction of words and constructions. *International Journal of Corpus Linguistics* 8(2). 209–243.

Tomasello, Michael. 2006. Construction grammar for kids. *Constructions* Special Volume 1. Available at http://www.constructions-journal.com.

Valenzuela Manzanares, Javier & Ana María Rojo López. 2008. What can language learners tell us about constructions? In Sabine De Knop & Teun De Rycker (eds.), *Cognitive approaches to pedagogical grammar: A volume in honour of René Dirven*, 197–230. Berlin: Mouton de Gruyter.

Wee, Lionel. 2007. Construction grammar and English language teaching. *Indonesian Journal of English Language Teaching* 3(1). 20–32.

Welke, Klaus. 2011. *Valenzgrammatik des Deutschen: Eine Einführung.* Berlin: Walter de Gruyter.

II Constructionist approaches to L2 learning and teaching

Thomas Herbst
Foreign language learning is construction learning – what else? Moving towards Pedagogical Construction Grammar[1]

Abstract: It is argued in this article that linguistics has a contribution to make to the teaching and learning of foreign languages. Using examples from textbooks of English used at German schools, it is shown that there are areas in which categories of traditional grammar are employed in an unreflected and unhelpful way. The article sets out to show that the framework of usage-based and constructionist approaches combined with corpus linguistic analyses could result in more adequate and much simpler descriptions of the linguistic facts and outlines a few general principles of a Pedagogical Construction Grammar.

Keywords: cognitive linguistics; construction; construction grammar; corpus; foreign language teaching; grammar; traditional grammar; tense; terminology; usage-based; valency; vocabulary

1 Linguistics and foreign language teaching

There are no particularly obvious parallels between managers of national football teams and linguists, but they have one thing in common: they are faced with millions of people who think they know better. While football managers can at least convince the fans by winning matches, linguists are in a much more difficult position because there is no comparable measure of success. And even if there were, nobody would care very much (because there are no fans either). As linguists, we will just have to accept the fact that the general public doesn't grant us the same amount of expertise in our field that they would to a neurologist, an archaeologist or a nuclear physicist. At the same time there seems to be more general awareness and recognition of progress in many sciences than there is in language studies. If a 21st century schoolbook for physics were to say that the elements out of which the different substances of

---

[1] I would like to thank Sabine De Knop, Susen Faulhaber, Gaëtanelle Gilquin, Kevin Pike and Peter Uhrig as well as two reviewers for their helpful comments on an earlier version of this chapter.

the world consist include water and fire, there would be a public outcry. But of course, no physics books would say any such thing. If 21st century teaching materials for the English language say that the parts of speech sentences are made up of include prepositions and conjunctions, most people will accept this as one of the facts of the English language. If students are taught that one must distinguish between a gerund and a participle in English and fail to see the difference, they tend to think that (English) grammar is difficult (and best be ignored) or that they are too stupid to understand English grammar (and thus had better ignore it). It would not occur to them that it is neither their fault nor that of the language, but that the blame is to be put entirely on a rather strange way of talking about the English language.

It is extremely difficult to change established patterns of thinking in any area. From what we know, during the times of Kopernikus, Kepler and Galilei scholars and laypeople were not exactly enthusiastic to accept that a view of the cosmos in which the earth revolves around the sun may be more appropriate than a view according to which the sun describes a squiggly course around the earth. In the case of language studies, few are prepared to make a comparable effort. And fewer even would be prepared to put their money on it. But this is precisely what is needed. Just imagine some (theoretical) linguists arrived at the conclusion that the established distinction between adverbs, prepositions and conjunctions is not particularly appropriate to the description of present-day English and were to subsume words such as *here*, *in* and *since* under one class and call them all prepositions, what chance would they have to find a publisher who would publish a dictionary actually classifying *here* as a preposition?[2] There is no reason to be particularly optimistic about that. Pullum (2009: 271) describes this situation in the following terms:

> The traditional categorizations given in the dictionaries for numerous items are simply in error. Some brave dictionary publisher must take the risk of being the first to abandon mistaken but well entrenched traditions, and of being out of step with all other dictionary publishers for a while as a result. That is not a small thing to ask: no publisher wants to have a dictionary written up in library magazines as too radical for a school librarian to recommend for purchase. But the problem is that in the area of English grammar the educated world has ceased to evolve, learn, or rethink; the whole subject has been frozen in time for the best part of 200 years.

So far, no dictionary publisher has taken this risk (although, as will be shown later, there are some rather positive developments in EFL lexicography).

---

[2] This is the approach taken by Huddleston and Pullum in the *Cambridge Grammar of the English Language* (2002). For a more detailed outline see Section 2.4.

Of course, classifying *here* as a preposition is a pretty silly thing to do when everyone knows it is an adverb. Not that anyone would really know what an adverb "is" or that the adverb had ever been the centre of the linguistic universe – but apparently even such a minor change in grammatical terminology has very little chance of being implemented in dictionaries or textbooks. Linguists who attempt to apply the descriptive apparatus of a particular framework are up against a massive bulwark of a firmly established tradition of traditional language teaching.³

The question is why this is so. Surely one reason is to be sought in the fact that it is difficult to pin down progress in a discipline in which there are so many different approaches – in part addressing different questions, in part addressing the same questions – which hardly ever result in a generally accepted solution. How can insights be applied to language teaching of a discipline that has devoted considerable attention to, say, the problem of how to analyse the relation between *They loaded the wagon with hay* and *They loaded hay onto the wagon* for at least four decades⁴ without solving the problem? Of course, how to deal with this alternation may seem a relatively marginal problem with respect to school teaching (although, of course, the underlying theoretical issues are not) but there is no unanimous agreement on such fundamental questions such as how many and which word classes are most appropriately postulated for a language such as English either (and very likely there never can be because any such classification is determined by its purpose up to a point). So even if textbook authors and dictionary makers were willing to incorporate the latest insights of linguistics, it would be almost impossible to achieve consensus amongst linguists of different schools what these insights actually are.

Of course, by no means all linguistic research is directly relevant to school teaching, neither are all theoretical approaches. Chomsky (1973: 234) states this quite clearly when he says:

> I am, frankly, rather sceptical about the significance, for the teaching of languages, of such insights and understanding as have been attained in linguistics and psychology.

Considering that Chomsky's theories have as a central element assumptions about L1 acquisition, this scepticism may seem rather surprising, although perhaps

---

3 I am not referring to teaching methodology here.
4 Of course, the discussion of this alternation has contributed to the development of new ideas in syntactic theory. For a discussion of examples of this kind (involving verbs such as *smear*, *paint* or *load*) see, for instance, Fillmore (1968: 48), who refers to Hall (1965), Palmer (1976: 137), Fillmore (1977: 22–23), Levin (1993: 2, 50–51), Boas (2003a), Goldberg (2006: 41–43) or Herbst (2010).

justified if what he had in mind is a direct application of the tree diagrams of that phase of transformational grammar.[5]

On the whole, however, I would argue that linguistics has a substantial contribution to make to the teaching of foreign languages (and also to L1-instruction, which, however, will not be discussed in this article).[6] It concerns two main issues, namely[7]
- identifying **what we teach**, i.e. identifying the items presented in dictionaries, grammars and other teaching materials,
- indicating **how we teach** it, i.e. how linguistic items are presented in dictionaries, grammars and textbooks and which **terminology** is to be used.

And, in fact, considerable progress has been made in both respects. Both the advent of corpus linguistics, which meant that "the analysis of language has developed out of all recognition" (Sinclair 1991: 1), and research done in the fields of pragmatics emphasizing the communicative function of language no doubt have had considerable influence on foreign language pedagogy, teaching materials and curricula.[8] Nevertheless, this has not gone far enough yet – in particular perhaps with regard to grammatical terminology, which will be discussed in the next section.

To come back to the football manager analogy: maybe if we choose the right kind of manager in the form of the right theory, linguists can convince the fans that linguistics has a contribution to make. At present, an increasing number of linguists seem to find the framework of what has been labelled Construction Grammar, and/or, in a wider sense, cognitive linguistics, very attractive. It is thus worth investigating whether and to what extent the insights of Construction Grammar can fruitfully be applied to the teaching of foreign languages. This is a question that will be pursued in Sections 3 and 4.

---

[5] Of course, attempts have been made to apply generative transformational grammar to language teaching; see e.g. Hüllen (1973: 103–130) and Zimmermann (1977: 25–29).
[6] See also Tyler (2012: 222–223).
[7] Boers, De Rycker and De Knop (2010: 4–5) make very much the same point with respect to Cognitive Linguistics (CL): "... ways in which CL insights can inform teachers, materials writers and course designers in their decisions about *what* to teach, i.e. the 'selection' of L2 targets for classroom treatment, and about *how* to teach these, i.e. the methodological choices involved in realising those targets most efficiently".
[8] Corpus linguistics has also resulted in the inclusion of information about the frequency of particular constructions in dictionaries such as the *Longman Dictionary of Contemporary English* or grammars such as Mindt (2000) or Biber et al. (1999) and the analysis of teaching materials (Mindt 2005). See also Mukherjee (2009: 161–182) and Leech (2011).

2 How not to describe or teach grammar

2.1 The state of grammar teaching

In this section, I would like to give a few examples supporting Pullum's (2009: 255) view that "English grammar as presented to schoolchildren, university students, and the general public is in a state resembling what biology might be like if teachers had paid no attention at all to *On the Origin of Species* (1859) or anything that followed". However, two things must be understood: firstly, given the large diversity that no doubt exists in the worldwide teaching of English as a foreign language (and my limited experience of it), the following remarks must not be seen as a general description of the "state of the art" in foreign language teaching as such, but merely as examples of what I consider inadequate descriptions. Secondly, it is obvious that teaching must involve simplification in some respects – one would certainly not expect a physics textbook for 14 year olds to give a comprehensive account of the present views of nuclear physicists on the structure of the atom, for instance. But that is not the point because, as will be shown, the problem is not so much simplification but unnecessary complication: history teachers would presumably not consider it a justified pedagogical simplification to talk about horse-drawn mail coaches, which were used as a means of transport in 18th and 19th century Europe, as high-speed trains because they have the same function and the concept of high-speed train is familiar to the students. But if anyone did, they would both miss the point and make things more complicated. In foreign language teaching, this sort of thing seems to be perfectly normal.

As far as grammatical terminology is concerned, the description of present-day English employed in some teaching materials suffers from two main weaknesses:
- an (often unreflected) use of terms that have been taken over from grammars of Latin and the grammatical tradition based on the teaching of Latin,
- an equally unreflected confusion of the levels of form, function and meaning (see also Pullum 2009).

2.2 Tense

A first case in point concerns the term 'tense'. While the two major standard reference grammars of English, the *Comprehensive Grammar of the English Language* by Quirk et al. (CGEL 1985) and the *Cambridge Grammar of the English Language*, edited by Huddleston and Pullum (CamG 2002), differ in their treatment of the *present perfect* and *past perfect* (as present/past tense plus perfec-

tive aspect in CGEL and as secondary tenses in CamG), they are agreed in their view that it would not be appropriate to apply the term future tense to English.⁹ Several reasons support such a view, namely
- that – unlike in Latin – there is no inflectional form to mark a future tense in English,
- that there is a large variety of ways of referring to future time in English such as constructions with the modal *will* or *going to*.

Nevertheless, *Englische Grammatik heute* (EGH; Ungerer et al. 1999) or *Collins Cobuild English Grammar* (CEG; Sinclair 1990) make a distinction between a future tense and a modal verb *will*, giving examples such as

(1) a. We will stay here. <CEG 1990: 4.41 p 233>
    b. ... my car's broken down. – I'll give you a lift in mine. <EGH 1999: 182>

(2) a. I'll drop by some time. <CEG 1990: 5.60 p 256>
    b. Just a moment. I'll write that down before I forget. <EGH: 1999: 142>

Just in case this is not clear: the examples under (2) illustrate the future tense use, those under (1) are given as examples of the modal verb. Linguistically, the point to make here is that quite obviously there is a gradient from uses of *will* in which future time reference is the most prominent (or only) meaning element and others where intention or prediction may be regarded as stronger, but any prediction refers to the future just as any reference to future events contains an element of uncertainty. Thus it seems an unnecessary and unhelpful complication of the linguistic facts to treat these as two different phenomena and to classify them into different grammatical categories. The main reason for postulating a future tense in English is to be sought in a teaching tradition based on Latin, for which six inflectionally different tense forms can indeed be identified.

Nevertheless, what is often referred to as "*will*-future" and "*going to*-future" are subsumed under the heading of tense in textbooks widely used at German schools such as *Green Line* and *English G*.¹⁰ Apparently, *Green Line* takes *will* + verb as a tense as being different from a modal verb *will*:

---

9 See also Mindt (2000). Radden and Dirven (2007: 225) speak of "the future tense forms *will* and *shall*". For a discussion of the future tense problem see Comrie (1985: 43–48) and Hilpert (2008: 4–8).
10 Cf. *English G 5 Bayern* (2007: 125) and *Green Line New Bayern 5* (2007: 114–117).

> Do not use **will** or **would** in if-clauses unless they are modal auxiliaries. (*Green Line New 6 Bayern*, 2008: 117)

(By the way: if the *will* of the "*will*-future" is not a modal auxiliary, why does it not take an –s in the third person singular, one might ask.)[11]

2.3 Distinguishing between gerunds and participles

A similar point can be made with respect to the distinction between *gerund* and *participle* in present-day English. Academic grammars such as CGEL (1985) and CamG (2002) refute making such a distinction, which is another typical relic of Latin grammar. In Latin, such a distinction is perfectly justified because it signifies a morphological distinction (*laudans* versus *laudandī*), which does not exist in English. It exists, however, in the English (to be) taught at German schools. Thus the curriculum for English at Bavarian *Gymnasien*[12] explicitly lists the use of "important gerund- and ... infinitive-forms" ("wichtige Gerund- und ... Infinitivformen") as a teaching aim for the 4th year of English. This may explain why an otherwise very laudable grammar book such as *A Grammar of Present-Day English* (Ungerer et al. 1984: 190) contains the following rule:

> Gerund constructions can only function as adverbials when they have a preposition in front of them.

This rule is anything but helpful to the learner. If learners know that *gerund* is a term for *-ing*-forms of verbs such as *returning*, they will come to the conclusion that (3a) is an acceptable sentence of English, whereas (3b) is not, which, however, is not the case:

(3) a. On returning from Prague, Mozart had completed his last instrumental piece ... <BNC: CEW 1021>
    b. Returning to the kitchen, Robyn turns down the thermostat of the central heating ... <BNC: ANY 726>

---

[11] Cf. also Langacker (2008a: 301): "Tense is normally said to indicate an event's location in time relative to the time of speaking, while modals pertain to its likelihood of occurring. Yet the distinction is anything but sharp, English being a parade example. After all, to indicate future time, English uses the modal *will*".
[12] http://www.isb-gym8-lehrplan.de/contentserv/3.1.neu/g8.de/index.php?StoryID=26275 (accessed 19 July 2014).

Look at the following five sentences used in a German schoolbook (intended for the 6th year of English at Gymnasium):

(4) a. On leaving the plane, I switched on my mobile.
   b. Instead of helping us to clean up after the party, Tom and Lisa just went home.
   c. My father has nothing against me studying art.
   d. The boy standing near the counter has stolen two CDs.
   e. I dropped my keys on the road while getting out of the car.
   <all examples taken from: *Green Line New 6 Bayern* 2008: 123>

These examples are to represent five different cases (not immediately obvious to a linguist even within Bavaria), namely (in abridged form) (*Green Line New 6* 2008: 123):

(4') a. gerund construction (after *on, before, after, for*) corresponding to a subordinate clause (*on leaving* = *When I left*).
   b. gerund construction (after *instead of, by, without, apart from, as well as, what about?, it's worth* and *it's no use*) where "there is no corresponding subordinate clause"
   c. "*-ing* form with a subject of its own". "In these constructions it is not clear whether the *–ing* form is a gerund or a participle".
   d. "Participles used to shorten relative clauses"
   e. "Participle constructions used as adverbials"

Apart from the fact that the distinction between gerund and participle does not really contribute to the understanding of these constructions (how many students will be able to appreciate the explanation given for c?), the accompanying text contains rather pointless information. According to standard models of grammatical analysis, all of the constructions containing a participle (or "gerund") listed under (4) with the exception of (4d) function as adverbials. Whether the difference between (4a–c), which represent prepositional phrases (a term not used in this textbook), and (4e), which can be analysed as a clause because it contains a conjunction, is relevant in this context may be a matter of debate.

2.4 Prepositions, conjunctions and adverbs

The examples under (4) link up with the next problem to be discussed: the system of word classes used. Here, even CGEL follows the model of established word class distinctions and assigns *since* different word class labels in sentences such as the ones under (5), namely conjunction (5a), preposition (5b) and adverb (5c):

(5) a. The old man has lived in that house ever *since* I can remember. <BNC: GW3 2225>
   b. ... he had eaten nothing *since* breakfast ... <BNC: GW3 1510>
   c. Nobody's seen him *since*. <BNC: GW3 161>

This case presents a good example of how one classificatory decision affects the whole architecture of the grammar: in a CGEL (1985: 2.26) type of analysis, prepositional phrases are characterized as non-headed because the preposition cannot stand for the phrase on its own. This argument is very similar to that made with respect to the gerund above: the logic behind this is that since prepositions cannot occur without a complement, *since* in (5c) cannot be analysed as a preposition because it does.

The alternative is to account for the different uses illustrated above in terms of valency properties of the word *since*, which means that it can be described as belonging to one word class, for which the term preposition (CamG 2002) or particle (Herbst and Schüller 2008) can be used.[13] The parallel to verb valency is more than obvious:

(6) a. I can *remember* he had a beard. <BNC: KCF 2807>
   b. I am trying to *remember* the exact circumstances. <BNC: GWB 902>
   c. Yes, I *remember*. <BNC: HWP 1045>

Most linguists would describe *remember* as a verb, so why should the same type of difference be taken as a criterion for assigning words such as *since* to different word classes? This all the more so since a classification in terms of three classes does not describe their syntactic properties in sufficient detail anyway. Thus it is pointed out in CGEL (1985: 9.2) that *-ing*-clauses can occur with both prepositions and conjunctions so that *since* in (7) could be classified either as a conjunction or a preposition (or both as a conjunction and a preposition):

(7) Wycliffe had scarcely spoken *since* leaving the hall ... <BNC: GW3 2367>

---

[13] For a more detailed discussion see CamG (2002: esp. 955–956 and 1011–1014) and Herbst and Schüller (2008: 61–68). For a similar use of the term preposition see also Aarts (2011).

On the other hand, not all conjunctions take V-*ing* clause complements:

(8) a. I began to wonder *whether* I'd made a mistake over the arrangement. <BNC: GW3 1863>
    b. *I began to wonder *whether* having made a mistake.

A further reason for using a valency approach towards the description of *since* is that the "adverb" use of CGEL is only possible in contexts where the point in time which is spelt out in the "preposition" and "conjunction" uses is known. Within valency theory, this is described as a contextually optional valency slot, providing a further parallel between particles and verbs.[14]

There are thus a number of reasons for not dealing with these linguistic facts in English in terms of the traditional word classes conjunction, preposition and adverb but to establish a particular class of function words with item-specific properties. From a teaching point of view, such an account seems commendable for practical reasons as well. A (relatively informal) survey carried out by Faulhaber, Herbst, and Uhrig (2013) with 75 students in their second semester of studying English at the University of Erlangen-Nürnberg showed, for instance, that 80 per cent were not able to interpret the word class label *prep* in a made-up dictionary entry for the novel preposition *tilc* to classify as ungrammatical a sentence such as

(9) We have been friends *tilc* we went to school together.

That many learners of English do not feel particularly confident about word classes such as conjunction or preposition may also be a reason for a learner's dictionary such as the *Longman Dictionary of Contemporary English* (LDOCE) to change their format of coverage for words such as *since*: while the first edition of LDOCE (1978) gives three main entries for *since* ("**since**¹ ... *adv*", "**since**² ... *prep*" and "**since**³ ... *conj*"), LDOCE6 (2014) only has one entry: "**since** ... *prep, conjunction, adv*".

2.5 Mixing up form and function

One of the greatest problems of describing language – not only in pedagogical materials – is the consistent distinction between form and function. In German

---

[14] Contextually optional valency slots can be compared to null instantiations in FrameNet; see Fillmore (2007: 146–148).

schoolbooks of English, one finds hair-raising examples of incorrect and confusing assignments of grammatical terms. In *Green Line*, students are confronted with the following chart (translation in brackets added by me):[15]

Das *gerund* als Subjekt des Satzes (The *gerund* as subject of the clause)				
Subjekt (Subject)	–	Verb (Verb)	Subjektergänzung (Subject complement)	–
Swimming	–	has always been	my favorite sport.	*Schwimmen* ...
Playing	basketball	can be	fun, too.	*Basketballspielen* ...
Skiing	in the USA	is	fantastic.	*Skifahren* ....

Figure 1: The gerund as subject (*Green Line New Bayern 4* 2006: 117)

Leaving aside the term *gerund*, this chart is highly misleading in that it is not the "gerunds" (*playing, skiing*) that function as the subjects of the respective clauses, but a subordinate clause headed by *playing* and *skiing*. *Basketball* and *in the USA* do not seem to have any grammatical status at all, whereas *fun, too* is presented as a single constituent. It has to be emphasized that this is an extract from one of the most widely used textbooks in Germany. This kind of explanation hardly adds to the understanding of English grammar nor does it provide any incentive to study grammar more closely.

What is to be criticized is that the formal units that have different functions in the clause are not identified. Failure to introduce the phrase and the functions of phrase constituents as a level of description results in rather squiggly kinds of description, in which the idea of "shortening" plays a central role. *Green Line New 5 Bayern* (2007: 122–123) contains rules such as the following (my English translation in brackets):[16]

– "Anstelle von Relativsätzen, in denen das Relativpronomen Subjekt ist, kann man verkürzende Partizipialkonstruktionen verwenden." (Instead of relative clauses with a relative pronoun as their subject, you can use shortening participle constructions. TH)

---

[15] For a more detailed discussion see Herbst (2013).
[16] Note that *English G 5 Bayern* (2007: 126) also contains a section "Participles that are used as adjectives", but the main headline reads "Participles that modify nouns" and the explanation provided is: "Participles can be used to modify a noun – like adjectives".

- "Partizipialkonstruktionen können auch adverbiale Nebensätze verkürzen."
  (Participle constructions can also shorten adverbial clauses. TH)
- "**Present** und **past participles** können als Adjektive verwendet werden."
  (*Present* and *past participles* can be used as adjectives. TH)

In each of these cases a functional description within the noun phrase is avoided and an explanation in the form of referring to another formal category with the same function is provided. If one considers not only attributive and predicative use as characteristics of adjectives, then this kind of rule is far too general because it does not prevent forms such as **the beautifully singing male voice choir.*

2.6 Summary

If these examples are not completely atypical, we must conclude that something is rotten with the state of language teaching – at least in some areas. The teaching of grammar seems to be rather unsystematic and to focus on a few selected problems, where some features happen to be mentioned (such as that *gerunds* can occur as subjects of clauses), whereas others are not (such as that *to-infinitive* clauses can also function as subjects). It is relatively simple to list the demands that would have to be made of an appropriate and useful description of the grammar of English, namely to introduce unambiguous terminology for the formal, functional and semantic levels of description.[17]

It is difficult to assess whether the overall approach of Construction Grammar would be instrumental in putting things right (see Section 5).

3 Construction Grammar

3.1 The attraction of Construction Grammar

Cynics might say that linguistic fashions come and go and no doubt the usage-based approach and Construction Grammar in particular have become relatively fashionable in the last twenty years or so. But maybe there is more to it than that:

---

[17] This does not contradict the basic credo of many usage-based approaches, described by Ellis and Larsen-Freeman (2009: 93) as: "Cognitive linguistics, corpus linguistics, and psycholinguistics are alike in their realizations that we cannot separate grammar from lexis, form from function, form from meaning, meaning from context, nor structure from usage".

- Firstly, Construction Grammar is not a unified theory but it exists in a number of varieties, some of which have a relatively low degree of formalization, which may add to its attraction for applied purposes (Boas 2013: 249).
- Secondly, usage-based approaches are (amongst other things) theories of language learning[18] (Tomasello 2003: 6; Lieven 2014).
- Thirdly, and most importantly in my view, Construction Grammar provides a cognitive framework to accommodate the insights of other approaches, in particular of corpus linguistics and foreign language linguistics. Many issues that are central in the field of foreign language learning such as valency and collocation are also at the centre of the Construction Grammar approach, and this is why one may have reason to believe that Construction Grammar has more to offer to language teaching than theories for which these issues belong to the periphery.[19]

With respect to foreign language learning and teaching, three key aspects of the usage-based approach can be identified:
- that it takes the view that languages are learnt (Goldberg 2006; Behrens 2009b: 284),
- that it is based on the insights "that speakers know tens or even hundreds of thousands of words, and just as many, if not more, prefabricated expressions which these words fit into, expressions such as *bright daylight, pick and choose, interested in, disposed to*, and so on" and that "the brain's capacity is impressively large" (Bybee 2010: 17), and
- that Construction Grammar "takes speakers' knowledge of language to consist of a network of learned pairings of form and function, or *constructions*" (Goldberg 2005: 17).

As is well known, the term construction can be used to cover linguistic items of varying size and varying degrees of abstraction and schematicity, ranging from morphemes to very abstract constructions such as Goldberg's (2006) argument structure constructions. The significance of this use of the term construction is to be seen in the assumption that all meaningful units of (a) language are basically acquired and stored in the same way.[20]

---

[18] Cf. Behrens (2009a) for Construction Grammar and language acquisition.
[19] Compare also Ellis (2008: 3).
[20] See also Croft (2005: 275): "This fully generalized notion of construction allows for a uniform representation of grammatical knowledge, subsuming what in other syntactic theories is divided into syntactic rules, idioms, morphology, syntactic categories and the lexicon".

Nevertheless, the term construction remains vague up to a point. While Goldberg (1995: 13) regards unpredictability as a necessary criterion for construction status, Goldberg (2006: 5) uses the term construction in a wider sense:

> Any linguistic pattern is recognized as a construction as long as some aspect of its form or function is not strictly predictable from its component parts or from other constructions recognized to exist. In addition, patterns are stored as constructions even if they are fully predictable as long as they occur with sufficient frequency.

Apart from the fact that "sufficient frequency" is probably relatively difficult to pin down, such a concept of constructions must also allow for differences between individual speakers, which it does.[21]

3.2 "Constructions all the way down"

Goldberg (2006: 18) argues that "it's constructions all the way down" and Fillmore (2014), in one of his last papers, has exemplified how stretches of text can be analysed in terms of a large number of constructions.[22] If we take collocations as constructions (Bybee 2010: 28) or describe the valency or complementation properties of verbs, adjectives, nouns and particles in terms of valency constructions (Herbst 2014a, 2014b), it is certainly the case that it is constructions everywhere.[23]

Learners of English must acquire item-specific knowledge such as it is *do one's homework* and not **make one's homework* as in the German *Hausaufgaben machen*, that French *prendre une décision* can be *make a decision* or, less frequently, *take a decision* in English (Gilquin 2007: 282), and that it is *wait for someone* and not *wait on someone* (in this sense) whereas in German you get *auf jemanden warten*.[24] Similarly, they must learn that (10) cannot be analysed

---

[21] For experimental evidence supporting such a view see Snider and Arnon (2012).

[22] For arguments in favour of accounting for linguistic knowledge in terms of constructions see also Stefanowitsch (2011).

[23] This does not necessarily mean, though, that all linguistic phenomena can be described in terms of constructions. It would seem difficult to apply the term to cases such as the allomorphs of {D} or {S} in English or the German *Fugen-s*, which is an apparently meaningless element in word formations, as is shown by the coexistence of the terms "Feuerwehranfahrtzone" and "Feuerwehranfahrtszone" on two road signs in the same street in Erlangen.

[24] Valency and collocation also touch upon the problem of restricting generalizations to the cases to which they actually apply. Similarly, from encountering *strong winds*, *strong sense of X*, *strong support*, *strong feeling* etc. learners might arrive at the generalization that *strong* can be used to express 'intensity'; but they will also have to learn that with *rain*, *rainfall* or *drinking*

in terms of a traditional conjunction followed by a finite clause, since *God knows* functions as a kind of premodifier for *when*, which is the complement of *since*:

(10) This is the first time I've been down here *since* God knows when.
 <BNC: GWB 1543>

Whereas this *God_knows*-construction (Herbst 2015) can be classified as an idiom in traditional phraseology, the status of the following construction is more difficult to determine. In English, it is quite common to refer to a group of a small number of people as in (11):

(11) a. *The three of them* ... would set the ball rolling. <BNC: HWP 495>
 b. *The two of you* were alone? <BNC: GWB 750>

This construction is difficult to capture lexicographically – would you expect to find it under *two, three, four* or under *we, us, you, they* or *them*? Similarly, it is not necessarily what you would expect a grammar to deal with. As such, the construction is relatively straightforward to describe as:

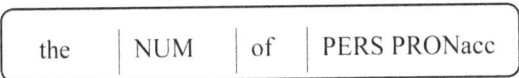

Figure 2: The *the_NUM_of_PERSPRONacc*-construction

The_NUM_of_PERSPRONacc represents the prototype of a construction: it is partly schematic and is located somewhere in between lexis and grammar, or in the centre of the lexicogrammatical continuum.

It deserves to be treated as a construction because it is frequently used and because it has a meaning of its own, namely 'a group of people (or animals) consisting of the number n'.

---

the adjective *heavy* is used for expressing more or less the same meaning. Similarly, any generalization as to the dative alternation on the basis of sentences such as *He wanted to see it and I showed it to him.* <BNC: HWP 2550> and *I understand that Matthew showed you those books.* <BNC: GWB 2730> should not take a learner to produce (*) *There was nobody who would explain him all those phenomena.* <ICLE: POSI 2001>. For the problem of generalizations and item-specificity with respect to argument structure constructions, see Boas (2003b), Faulhaber (2011), Goldberg (2006, 2011), or Herbst (2011b, 2014a, 2014b). This element of limited generalizability concerns many other areas of language learning as well, of course: learners of English will have to learn that *oe* is pronounced /əʊ/ as in *goes*, but not in the case of *does*, or that the past tense is formed by a {D}-suffix, but not with verbs such as *be, run* or *see*.

This latter aspect becomes particularly noticeable when you contrast English with other languages: in German, for example, one finds a similar construction:

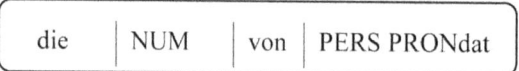

Figure 3: The German *die_NUM_von_PERSPRONdat*-construction

However, in German the number mentioned must be smaller than the group so that the construction has a partitive function (in the sense of *those three of you*):

English: *the_NUM_of_PERSPRONacc* | NUM ≡ PRON
German: *die_NUM_von_PERSPRONdat* | NUM < PRON

What is interesting (and plausible) is that this construction seems only to be used commonly with relatively low numbers, as Figure 4 shows.[25]

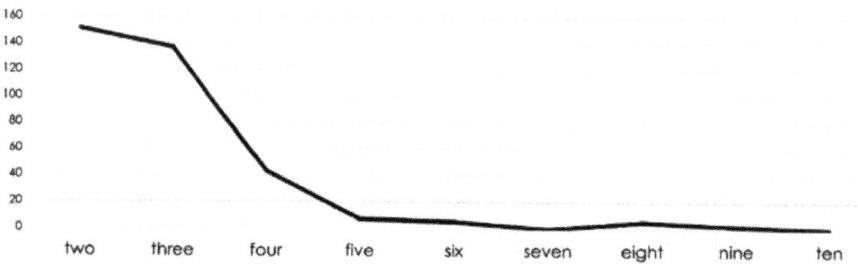

Figure 4: Occurrences of *the NUM of us* in the BNC

4 Pedagogical corpus-based Construction Grammar

4.1 Not only Construction Grammar

It was claimed at the beginning of this chapter that linguistics could make a contribution to the learning and teaching of foreign languages and it was shown that (at least in some areas of teaching in some parts of the world such as

---

[25] The table shows only figures spelt out in letters in the texts. There are a few instances in the BNC where figures are used: *3 of us* (1), *4 of us* (3; two of which refer to a band), *12 of us* (2). Otherwise, a search for *the _CDN of us* produced *nineteen, forty, forty-eight,* and *100,000*, all of which were followed by *who* as were 2 cases of *three* and 1 of *nine*.

Germany) there is definitely room for improvement. The question is whether the application of Construction Grammar can provide this improvement.

On the one hand, there is certainly reason to believe that this is indeed the case. Construction Grammar no doubt addresses many questions that are central to the teaching and learning of (foreign) languages including those that were considered peripheral by many working within a generative framework of the Chomskyan kind. Whether all of language can – or should – be accounted for in terms of constructions remains to be seen.

Usage-based approaches in general emphasize that languages are learnt and that this learning requires an immense amount of storage as well as the emergence of generalized knowledge, which is highly relevant to foreign language teaching. As pointed out above, the question is to what extent the different conditions under which foreign language learning usually takes place (Ellis 2003: 72–74) mean that the insights gained about L1 acquisition can be directly applied to foreign language teaching.[26] The relatively small amount of input presumably makes it much more difficult to arrive at generalizations. At the same time, certain generalizations may be easy to arrive at for learners on the basis of little input if they have generalizations of a similar nature in their L1. Thus, for German learners of English the fact that articles precede nouns in the NP can be arrived at relatively quickly. The same may be true of the meaning of the ditransitive construction (*She gives him a book*) or the caused motion construction (*He drove the car onto the ferry*), for instance. In fact, there is evidence to show that foreign learners also make use of constructions, as Gries and Wulff (2005: 190–191) argue:[27]

> Although foreign language learners have much less input in the foreign language than native speakers have in their native language, they are still able to arrive at generalizations that lend themselves to construction-based explanations.

---

26 For differences between L1 acquisition and L2 acquisition, see Ellis (2013: 366), who argues that second language acquisition "involves processes of construction and *re*construction". See also Beckner et al. (2009: 9–12). For foreign language learning see Boers, De Rycker, and De Knop (2010: 4). For the role of instruction in foreign language learning see Ellis (2002: 174). Compare also MacWhinney (1997: 278).
27 Note that testing verb-specific constructional preferences Gries and Wulff (2005: 191–192) also found: "The German subjects not only exhibit the same preferences of verbs to occur in one out of two semantically similar argument structure constructions as do native speakers of English ..., they also do *not* exhibit the preferences one might expect from the verbs' translational equivalents in German". Cf. also Verspoor and Behrens (2011: 30–31). For the use of chunks by foreign learners see De Cock (2000).

With respect to the English causative construction Gilquin (2010: 272–276) has made a practical proposal concerning the teaching of the caused-motion construction on the basis of learner language and a collostructional analysis. This kind of combination of corpus linguistics and a constructionist approach seems rather promising.[28]

On the other hand, a certain element of caution may also be in order. Firstly, Construction Grammar is by no means the only strand of linguistic research that has an important contribution to make: corpus linguistics is another obvious candidate since designing a dictionary or teaching materials without making use of corpora or of work based on corpora is inconceivable today.[29]

Secondly, not all Construction Grammar approaches are terminologically as stringent as one would like them to be. Simply renaming the future tense as future tense construction will not do the trick. Nevertheless, the term construction could indeed be usefully applied to language teaching, namely as a relatively neutral and non-committal cover term. Obviously, there is little to be gained in teaching by explicitly naming everything a construction that (some forms of) Construction Grammar call a construction (which in some forms of Construction Grammar is almost anything anyway): so language students are not likely to find it easier to remember words such as *goal* or collocations such as *lay the table, score a goal* when they are labelled constructions. However, the term construction may come in useful when it comes to correctly identifying larger units. If, for instance, the rules criticized in Section 2 made use of the term 'construction', this could be regarded as an improvement.

Instead of saying that "gerunds" or participles can occur as subjects or objects in English (which is true of some examples, but misleadingly simplistic in others), a term such as *V-ing*-construction (which implies that the construction consists of more elements than the verb in the *-ing*-form) could be used. Such rules could take the form of [A] in a textbook accompanying the lesson where *V-ing*-constructions are introduced or, more generally, of [B]:

---

28 It would be interesting to find out whether learners benefit from explicit explanations in terms of cognitive linguistics. For example, Radden and Dirven (2007: 68) do not only state that plural count nouns and mass nouns take the same range of determiners but offer an explanation in terms of motivation with respect to "bounded things" and "unbounded things". For the application of insights of cognitive linguistics in vocabulary teaching see Verspoor and Tyler (2009). See also De Knop and Dirven (2008) and Niemeier and Reif (2008). For a construction-based approach to the teaching of syntactic patterns and experimental evidence see also Tyler (2012: 183–213).

29 This concerns in particular the insights connected to Sinclair's (1991: 110) idiom principle. See also e.g. the contributions in Aijmer (2009). Cf. also Herbst (2011a).

[A] **V-ing-constructions** can have the following functions in the clause:
- subject   *Driving through London* costs city tax.
             Walking can be fun.
- object   They enjoy *going to Cornwall*.
- adverbial *Being on holiday*, he didn't want to be disturbed.

[B] Subjects can be   subject   predicate
- noun constructions   *Mousehole*   is a village in Cornwall.
                            Old fishing villages   are quite picturesque.
- V-ing-constructions   *Seeing Stonehenge*   is quite an experience.
- to-infinitive-   *To continue*   is to jeopardize future
  constructions   promotion. <BNC: BOH 1326>

etc.

Terms such as *noun construction* or *V-ing*-construction entail that it is larger units and not just the nouns or verbs that have a particular syntactic function without using terms such as *phrase, clause* or *head*. Similarly, in [C], there is no need to specify (and commit oneself to saying) whether *after, before* or *on* should be analysed as conjunctions, prepositions etc. (information which presumably would not be appreciated by the learners anyway):

[C] If you want to say why or when something happened, you can use a **V-ing-construction**:

Living in London, she could go to the theatre quite often.
Being a keen mathematician, she enjoys doing calculations.

If you want to say more precisely when something happened, you can use a particle such as **after, before, on + V-ing-construction**:

After taking her degree in medicine, she became a doctor in Scotland.
You should spend a few days in Wales *before going to Ireland*.
On seeing a red light, the train driver stopped immediately.

Furthermore, unnecessary and controversial terms such as "future tense" (for *will go*) or "conditional" (for *would go*)[30] can be avoided by talking about *will*-constructions or *would*-constructions in pedagogical grammars. Linguistically, this has the advantage of doing justice to the fact that there is no clear

---
30 Compare *Green Line 2* (2015: 197): "Im **if-Satz** verwendest du das **simple past** und im *Hauptsatz* **would(n't)/could(n't) + Grundform des Verbs** (= conditional)", where the term *conditional* is used but not central to the understanding of the rule.

dividing line between grammar and lexis and that we are dealing in such cases with constructions that are partially schematic and partially lexically specified. Pedagogically, such a policy has the advantage that it is easy to understand and simple to remember. The corresponding rules could thus take a form such as the following:[31]

[D] If you want to say that something happens in the future, you can use
   ▷ the **will-construction** if something is likely to happen or planned
   I'll definitely *go to the theatre* when I'm in Stratford.

   ▷ the ***going to*-construction** if you have evidence that something is going to happen
   It is *going to rain* soon.

Similarly, awkward form-function mix-ups such as that of "adjectives used as nouns" can easily be avoided by identifying a *the*_ADJ construction:

[E] If you want to refer to a group of people, you can use the ***the* adjective-construction:**
   Some people think *the rich* should pay more tax.

Of course, all of these rules could also be phrased differently, avoiding the term construction. In some cases, no general label will be needed at all ("if *the* is followed only by an adjective, you refer to a group of people"), in others terms such as phrase (or group) and clause might be preferable to the term construction. Maybe thinking about how Construction Grammar can be applied to (foreign) language teaching can be a reason for a radical (and open) discussion of the question how much (and which) terminology is helpful for language teaching purposes.

4.2 Towards Pedagogical Construction Grammar

4.2.1 Seven principles for Pedagogical Construction Grammar

What is particularly annoying about the state of some (and I would like to emphasize this *some*) textbooks and pedagogical grammars is that they could

---

[31] For a constructionist account of futurity in English see Bergs (2010), who, however, argues in favour of two independent *will* constructions, which are "maybe somehow related through family relations" (Bergs 2010: 228).

be improved considerably with relatively little effort. The following principles for designing foreign language textbooks and pedagogical grammars – which do not claim originality in any way and which are not exclusively related to the usage-based framework – might even suffice:[32]

Principle 1: The basic principle of Pedagogical Construction Grammar

If "it's constructions all the way down" (Goldberg 2006: 18) and language learning consists of the learning of constructions, then language teaching should consist of the teaching of constructions.

This implies that in the design of curricula and teaching materials insights gained in the context of L1 and L2 acquisition can be exploited concerning, for instance, the role of frequency of exposure and of pathbreaking verbs (Ellis 2006; Ellis and Larsen-Freeman 2009).

Whether a Construction Grammar-based approach to foreign language teaching must necessarily give up the distinction between a vocabulary part and a grammar part in textbooks may be debatable. There is a lot to be said for a separate vocabulary section for the sake of actually learning and revising new words, but it must be clear that this "vocabulary section" also contains a lot of grammatical information, namely all the (in the sense of the most important) item-specific properties of the vocabulary items introduced. Principles 3 to 5 specifically concern the vocabulary part of a textbook, all other principles equally apply to the grammar part and the vocabulary part.[33]

Principle 2: The principle of presenting constructions as form-meaning pairings

Constructions should be introduced as form-meaning pairings and not indirectly.

Since constructions are form-meaning pairings, they should be presented as such.[34] In the case of new vocabulary items, this is obvious anyway, but in the

---

[32] Obviously, the seven principles identified above do not constitute a complete list of the requirements to be made of textbooks in foreign language teaching. Furthermore, it goes without saying that the design of pedagogical materials to a large extent depends on the target group, the aims of the course, to what extent a grammar or a textbook can be explicitly or implicitly contrastive, and many other factors.
[33] An overall guiding principle can be seen in what Behrens (2011: 382) says about constructionist accounts of first language acquisition: "Kinder erwerben nicht die Wörter mit ihren Subkategorisierungseigenschaften, die dann bestimmen, an welchen syntaktischen Strukturen ein Wort partizipieren kann, sondern sie erwerben das Lexikon durch und in den Konstruktionen, in denen sie auftauchen." ("Children do not acquire words with their subcategorization properties, which then determine in which syntactic structures a word can occur, but they acquire the lexicon through and in the constructions in which the words occur." TH)
[34] See also Tyler (2012: 183) and Langacker (2008b: 15).

case of constructions such as the *the_ADJ*-construction or the *V-ing*-construction traditional grammars often, as was shown above, introduce the form of a construction and explain its use rather indirectly as being equivalent or as shortening another construction without actually stating the communicative impact of the construction as such. In view of the communicative function of language and the view of constructions as form-meaning pairings, it would appear far more rewarding to relate the form of a construction to its meaning, as was done in rules C, D and E proposed above.

Principle 3: The principle of one sense at a time

Lexical constructions should be presented in textbooks as units of lexical form and a single sense.

It may be a matter of debate whether different senses of a vocabulary item should be introduced at the same time. If language learning means building up a network of constructions, then one could argue that introducing several senses of polysemous words at the same time makes sense up to a point – also because the learners might encounter the other sense in a different context. Nevertheless, simply providing two different translation equivalents for a word such as *bat* and separating them by a comma without providing at least one example for the other sense as in (12a) does not seem ideal, whereas (12b) might be a possibility:

(12) a. bat [illustrations of a table tennis bat and a racket]   Schläger (Tischtennis-, Baseball-); Fledermaus <Green Line New Bayern 2 (2005: 141)>

     b. bat *Another good swing, and the ball jumps off his bat again.* <COCA: 2007 NEWS>   Tischtennisschläger; Baseballschläger

       bat *Bats do not fly in the same direction for long.* <BNC: GU8 1078>   Fledermaus

Principle 4: The principle of indicating chunks

In the vocabulary sections of textbooks, important collocations and phrases should be listed explicitly.

This holds both for chunks that are highly frequent but semantically transparent and for those where the co-occurrence of two words is unpredictable.

Thus if a textbook introduces the word *homework*, then the collocation *do one's homework* should also be listed (and be distinguished from mere examples), at least if the textbook is directed towards learners of English with German as their L1 since in German it is *Hausaufgaben machen*:[35]

(13) | homework | *Have you got a lot of homework?* | Hausaufgaben
 | do one's homework | *When are you going to do your homework?* | Hausaufgaben machen

The same applies to collocations such as *heavy smoker*:

(14) | smoker | *Are there many smokers around here?* | Raucher
 | heavy smoker | *My grandfather was a heavy smoker.* | starker Raucher

Principle 5: The principle of showing valency constructions

The most important (and most frequent) valency constructions should always be listed explicitly in the vocabulary sections of textbooks.

For most target groups, this is most appropriately done in the form of pattern illustrations (Herbst and Klotz 2003) as is common practice in the most recent editions of learners' dictionaries such as the *Oxford Advanced Learner's Dictionary* or the *Longman Dictionary of Contemporary English*:[36]

---

[35] For the use of collocations by learners of English see e.g. Gilquin (2007), Granger (1998), Howarth (1998), Herbst (1996) and Nesselhauf (2005). With respect to the idiom principle (Sinclair 1991: 110) and the "normal ways of saying things" (Langacker 2008a: 28) it is important that the frequency of constructions should play a role in teaching as well.

[36] Of course, many textbooks do precisely that. *Línea verde* 2 (2007: 133–135) lists verbs in the form of mini valency patterns, for instance: "separarse de algo/alguien – sich von etw./jdm. trennen", "enamorarse de alguien – sich in jdn. verlieben" etc. and gives examples in Spanish with a German translation. See also *English G 2000 Band 2 Bayern* (2004: 158, 160, 168–169), where one finds "(to) **be called** – heißen, genannt werden", "to **fly a kite** – einen Drachen steigen lassen", "(to) **discuss** sth – etwas besprechen, über etwas diskutieren", "(to) **send (to)** – schicken, senden an" etc.

(15) avoid sb/sth   *He has avoided her recently.*   jemanden/etwas vermeiden

  avoid doing sth   *She avoided talking about herself.*   vermeiden, etwas zu tun

Principle 6: The principle of moderate and meaningful use of grammatical terminology

The use of grammatical terminology should be restricted to a useful minimum, i.e. to cases in which the use of terminology contributes to language learning. In particular, the terminology used should be employed consistently, be appropriate for the language in question and not be based on the teaching traditions of another language.

This is probably a slightly controversial point. What is meant is that if the standard academic reference grammars agree that, say, distinguishing between a gerund and a participle does not make sense in present-day English, the term "gerund" should not be used in the description of English simply because (some!) students may know it from Latin. Similarly, the fact that other languages have a category future tense does not mean that a description of English should make use of the term. Some people (e.g. Schröder 2005) would argue that the use of inappropriate terminology can be justified on the grounds that it is "familiar" to the students and that they would be wondering what the future tense in English was, but this seems rather misconceived: what learners are looking for is a way of expressing futurity. Indeed, one could argue that it is part of the process of learning a foreign language that one should come to understand that different languages use different means to express similar meanings – in other words, we could hardly imagine a teaching grammar of English treating *him* in *She gave him a book* as a dative and *him* in *She saw him* as an accusative on the grounds that the first *him* corresponds to a dative and the second to an accusative in German. If it is thought advisable to refer to semantically equivalent constructions in other languages, then this should be done explicitly.

Principle 7: The principle of authenticity

Teaching materials should be based on the analysis of corpora or on reference works based on corpus analysis and the frequency of constructions should be reflected in the design of teaching materials.

At the beginning of the 21st-century, this is obvious (for languages for which such corpora are available).

4.2.2 Reinventing the wheel

None of this is particularly new. The importance of collocation for the teaching of foreign languages has been recognized for a very long time (Cowie 1981, 1992; Granger 1998; Hausmann 1984) and Hausmann's programmatic title "Wortschatzlernen ist Kollokationslernen" could now be generalized into "Language learning is construction learning". Similarly, the linguistic analysis of valency phenomena has often been closely connected with issues of foreign language learning – both in the British tradition of analysing verb patterns and the German tradition of valency research. Special collocation dictionaries and special valency dictionaries have been developed, also, if not primarily, addressing foreign learners' needs in the respective languages.[37] General learners' dictionaries of English show many features that are perfectly compatible with a Construction Grammar based approach to foreign language learning – the coverage of multi-word units in a dictionary such as the *Longman Dictionary of Contemporary English* (^{6}2014) being a case in point. Obviously, there will always be room for improvement: we shall see to what extent the possibilities of the electronic medium will result in reference works which have a greater variety of search mechanisms overcoming the purely alphabetical structure of most print dictionaries (which is very important for actually finding item-based constructions in the dictionary because God knows where to find *God knows* or *of course*) or which enable users to switch more easily between information that traditionally was found in a dictionary and information that was traditionally found in a grammar book. It can certainly be said that many developments in English (and not only English) learner lexicography over the last decades have been very encouraging, and so are prospects for the future.

It is rather deplorable that this cannot be said in the same way of the way that vocabulary and grammar are presented in some textbooks and other teaching materials. Whether this is due to the fact that fewer people buy grammar books than (used to) buy dictionaries or to the might of a long-standing teaching tradition or to a lack of a model of language that seems suitable to be applied to grammar teaching is difficult to say. The fact that Construction Grammar has its focus on aspects of language which also happen to be central problems of

---

[37] See, for example, the valency dictionaries by Helbig and Schenkel (1969), Schumacher et al.'s *VALBU* (2004), Herbst et al.'s *VDE* (2004), the pattern grammar approach by Francis, Hunston, and Manning (1996), the *Oxford Collocations Dictionary* (2002) and the *Macmillan Collocations Dictionary* (2010) as well as the two volume *Oxford Dictionary of Current Idiomatic English* (1975, 1983).

foreign language teaching (which is exactly why foreign language teaching is also useful to linguistic theory) certainly makes it a suitable candidate.

Nevertheless, there is no need to re-invent the wheel of foreign language teaching,[38] but consistently drawing upon the basic ideas of Construction Grammar (and radically throwing some inappropriate terminology and classifications overboard) may make it run more smoothly.

References

Aarts, Bas. 2011. *Oxford Modern English grammar.* Oxford: Oxford University Press.
Aijmer, Karin (ed.). 2009. *Corpora and language teaching.* Amsterdam & Philadelphia: Benjamins.
Beckner, Clay, Richard Blythe, Joan Bybee, Morton H. Christiansen, William Croft, Nick C. Ellis, John Holland, Jinyun Ke, Diane Larsen-Freeman & Tom Schoenemann [The Five Graces Group]. 2009. Language is a complex adaptive system: Position paper. *Language Learning* 59 Suppl. 1. 1–26.
Behrens, Heike. 2009a. Konstruktionen im Spracherwerb. *Zeitschrift für Germanistische Linguistik* 37. 427–444.
Behrens, Heike. 2009b. Usage-based and emergentist approaches to language acquisition. *Linguistics* 47(2). 383–411.
Behrens, Heike. 2011. Grammatik und Lexikon im Spracherwerb: Konstruktionsprozesse. In Stefan Engelberg, Anke Holler & Kristel Proost (eds.), *Sprachliches Wissen zwischen Lexikon und Grammatik,* 375–396. Berlin & Boston: de Gruyter.
Bergs, Alexander. 2010. Expressions of futurity in contemporary English: A Construction Grammar perspective. *English Language and Linguistics* 14(2). 217–238.
Biber, Douglas, Susan Conrad, Geoffrey Leech, Stig Johansson & Edward Finegan. 1999. *Longman grammar of spoken and written English.* London et al.: Longman.
Boas, Hans C. 2003a. A lexical-constructional account of the locative alternation. In Lesley Carmichael, Chia-Hui Huang & Vida Samiian (eds.), Proceedings of the thirtieth Western conference on linguistics, WELCO 2001, vol. 13, 27–42. Fresno, CA: Department of Linguistics, California State University. http://sites.la.utexas.edu/hcb/files/2011/02/Boas2003a_Locative_Alternation.pdf.
Boas, Hans C. 2003b. *A constructional approach to resultatives.* Stanford: CSLI Publications.
Boas, Hans C. 2013. Cognitive Construction Grammar. In Thomas Hoffmann & Graeme Trousdale (eds.), *The Oxford handbook of construction grammar,* 233–252. Oxford: Oxford University Press.
Boers, Frank, Antoon De Rycker & Sabine De Knop. 2010. Fostering language teaching efficiency through cognitive linguistics: Introduction. In Sabine De Knop, Frank Boers & Antoon De Rycker (eds.), *Fostering language teaching efficiency through cognitive linguistics,* 1–26. Berlin & New York: Mouton de Gruyter.
Bybee, Joan. 2010. *Language, usage and cognition.* Cambridge: Cambridge University Press.

---

38 See Ellis (2006: 113–114) for a discussion of the relative importance of approaches such as behaviourism and theories of first language transfer. See also Gilquin (2008: 25), who concludes that "transfer is still something of a mystery to linguists".

Chomsky, Noam. 1973. The utility of linguistic theory to the language teacher. In J. P. B. Allen and S. Pit Corder (eds.), *The Edinburgh course in applied linguistics. Volume 1. Readings for applied linguistics*, 234–240. London: Oxford University Press.

Comrie, Bernard. 1985. *Tense*. Cambridge: Cambridge University Press.

Cowie, Anthony P. 1981. The treatment of collocations and idioms in learners' dictionaries. *Applied Linguistics* 2. 223–235.

Cowie, Anthony P. 1992. Multiword lexical units and communicative language teaching. In Pierre J. L. Arnaud & Henri Béjoint (eds.), *Vocabulary and applied linguistics*, 1–12. London: Macmillan.

Croft, William. 2005. Lexical and typological arguments for Radical Construction Grammar. In Jan-Ola Östman & Mirjam Fried (eds.), *Construction grammars: Cognitive grounding and theoretical extensions*, 273–314. Amsterdam & Philadelphia: Benjamins.

De Cock, Sylvie. 2000. Repetitive phrasal chunkiness and advanced EFL speech and writing. In Christian Mair & Marianne Hundt (eds.), *Corpus linguistics and linguistic theory*, 51–68. Amsterdam & Atlanta: Rodopi.

De Knop, Sabine & René Dirven. 2008. Motion and location events in German, French, and English: A typological, contrastive and pedagogical approach. In Sabine De Knop & Teun De Rycker (eds.), *Cognitive approaches to pedagogical grammar. A volume in honour of René Dirven*, 295–324. Berlin & New York: Mouton de Gruyter.

Ellis, Nick. 2002. Frequency effects in language processing: A review with implications for theories of implicit and explicit language acquisition. *Studies in Second Language Acquisition* 24(2). 143–188.

Ellis, Nick. 2003. Constructions, chunking, and connectionism: The emergence of second language structure. In Catherine J. Doughty & Michael H. Long (eds.), *The handbook of second language acquisition*, 63–103. Malden, Oxford & Carlton: Blackwell.

Ellis, Nick. 2006. Cognitive perspectives on SLA: The Associative-Cognitive Creed. *AILA Review* 19. 100–121.

Ellis, Nick. 2008. Phraseology: The periphery and the heart of language. In Fanny Meunier & Sylviane Granger (eds.), *Phraseology in foreign language learning and teaching*, 1–13. Amsterdam & Philadelphia: Benjamins.

Ellis, Nick. 2013. Second language acquisition. In Thomas Hoffmann & Graeme Trousdale (eds.), *The Oxford handbook of construction grammar*, 365–378. Oxford: Oxford University Press.

Ellis, Nick, with Diane Larsen-Freeman. 2009. Constructing a second language: Analyses and computational simulations of the emergence of linguistic constructions from usage. *Language Learning* 59, Suppl. 1. 90–125.

Faulhaber, Susen. 2011. *Verb valency patterns: A challenge for semantics-based accounts*. Berlin & New York: de Gruyter Mouton.

Faulhaber, Susen, Thomas Herbst & Peter Uhrig. 2013. Funktionswortklassen im Englischen. Linguistische und lexikografische Perspektiven. In Eva Breindl & Annette Klosa (eds.), *Funktionswörter/buch/forschung*, 59–110. Hildesheim: Olms.

Fillmore, Charles. 1968. The case for case. In Emmon Bach & Robert T. Harms (eds.), *Universals in linguistic theory*, 1–88. New York: Holt, Rinehart and Winston.

Fillmore, Charles. 1977. The case for case reopened. In Klaus Heger & János S. Petöfi (eds.), *Kasustheorie, Klassifikation, semantische Interpretation*, 3–26. Hamburg: Buske.

Fillmore, Charles. 2007. Valency issues in FrameNet. In Thomas Herbst & Katrin Götz-Votteler (eds.), *Valency: Theoretical, descriptive and cognitive issues*, 129–160. Berlin & New York: Mouton de Gruyter.

Fillmore, Charles. 2014. Frames, constructions and FrameNet. In Thomas Herbst, Hans-Jörg Schmid & Susen Faulhaber (eds.), *Constructions, collocations, patterns*, 113–157. Berlin & Boston: de Gruyter Mouton.

Francis, Gill, Susan Hunston & Elizabeth Manning. 1996. *Collins Cobuild grammar patterns. 1: Verbs*. London: HarperCollins.

Gilquin, Gaëtanelle. 2007. To err is not all: What corpus and elicitation can reveal about the use of collocations by learners. *Zeitschrift für Anglistik und Amerikanistik* 55(3). 273–291.

Gilquin, Gaëtanelle. 2008. Combining contrastive and interlanguage analysis to apprehend transfer: Detection, explanation, evaluation. In Gaëtanelle Gilquin, Szilvia Papp & María Belén Díez-Bedmar, *Linking up contrastive and learner corpus research*, 3–33. Amsterdam & New York: Rodopi.

Gilquin, Gaëtanelle. 2010. *Corpus, cognition and causative constructions*. Amsterdam & Philadelphia: Benjamins.

Goldberg, Adele E. 1995. *Constructions: A construction grammar approach to argument structure*. Chicago: Chicago University Press.

Goldberg, Adele E. 2005. Argument realization: The role of constructions, lexical semantics and discourse factors. In Jan-Ola Östman & Mirjam Fried (eds.), *Construction grammars: Cognitive grounding and theoretical extensions*, 17–43. Amsterdam & Philadelphia: Benjamins.

Goldberg, Adele E. 2006. *Constructions at work*. Oxford & New York: Oxford University Press.

Goldberg, Adele E. 2011. Meaning arises from words, texts and phrasal constructions. In *Argument structure: Valency and/or constructions?* Thomas Herbst & Anatol Stefanowitsch (eds.) [Special issue] *Zeitschrift für Anglistik und Amerikanistik* 59(4), 317–329. Würzburg: Königshausen and Neumann.

Granger, Sylviane. 1998. Prefabricated patterns in advanced EFL writing: Collocations and formulae. In A. P. Cowie (ed.), *Phraseology: Theory, analysis, and applications*, 145–160. Oxford: Clarendon Press.

Gries, Stefan Th. & Stefanie Wulff. 2005. Do foreign learners have constructions? Evidence from priming, sorting, and corpora. *Annual Review of Cognitive Linguistics* 3. 182–200.

Hall [Partee], Barbara. 1965. *Subject and object in English*. Unpublished dissertation. M.I.T. (quoted in Fillmore 1968)

Hausmann, Franz-Josef. 1984. Wortschatzlernen ist Kollokationslernen. *Praxis des neusprachlichen Unterrichts* 31. 395–406.

Herbst, Thomas. 1996. What are collocations: *Sandy beaches* or *false teeth*? *English Studies* 77(4). 379–393.

Herbst, Thomas. 2010. Valency constructions and clause constructions or how, if at all, *valency grammarians might sneeze the foam off the cappuccino*. In Hans-Jörg Schmid & Susanne Handl (eds.), *Cognitive foundations of linguistic usage patterns: Empirical studies*, 225–255. Berlin & New York: de Gruyter Mouton.

Herbst, Thomas. 2011a. Choosing *sandy beaches*: Collocations, probabemes and the idiom principle. In Thomas Herbst, Susen Faulhaber & Peter Uhrig (eds.), *The phraseological view of language: A tribute to John Sinclair*, 27–57. Berlin & New York: de Gruyter Mouton.

Herbst, Thomas. 2011b. The status of generalizations: Valency and argument structure constructions. In Thomas Herbst & Anatol Stefanowitsch (eds.), *Argument structure: Valency and/or constructions?* [Special issue] *Zeitschrift für Anglistik und Amerikanistik* 59(4): 347–367. Würzburg: Königshausen and Neumann.

Herbst, Thomas. 2013. Von Fledermäusen, die auch Schläger sind, und von Gerundien, die es besser nicht gäbe. In Christoph Bürgel & Dirk Siepmann (eds.), *Sprachwissenschaft – Fremdsprachendidaktik. Neue Impulse*, 57–66. Hohengehren: Schneider.

Herbst, Thomas. 2014a. The valency approach to argument structure constructions. In Thomas Herbst, Hans-Jörg Schmid & Susen Faulhaber (eds.), *Constructions, collocations, patterns*, 159–207, Berlin & New York: de Gruyter Mouton.

Herbst, Thomas. 2014b. Idiosyncrasies and generalizations: argument structure, semantic roles and the valency realization principle. In Martin Hilpert & Susanne Flach (eds.), *Yearbook of the German Cognitive Linguistics Association, Jahrbuch der Deutschen Gesellschaft für Kognitive Linguistik*, Vol. II, 253–289. Berlin, München & Boston: de Gruyter Mouton.

Herbst, Thomas. 2015. Why construction grammar catches the worm and corpus data can drive you crazy: Accounting for idiomatic and non-idiomatic idiomaticity. *Journal of Social Sciences* 11(3). 91–110.

Herbst, Thomas & Michael Klotz. 2003. *Lexikografie*. Paderborn: Schöningh.

Herbst, Thomas & Susen Schüller [now Faulhaber]. 2008. *Introduction to syntactic analysis: A valency approach*. Tübingen: Narr.

Hilpert, Martin. 2008. *Germanic future constructions: A usage-based approach to language change*. Amsterdam & Philadelphia: Benjamins.

Howarth, Peter. 1998. The phraseology of learners' academic writing. In A. P. Cowie (ed.), *Phraseology: theory, analysis, and applications*, 161–186. Oxford: Clarendon Press.

Hüllen, Werner. 1973. *Linguistik und Englischunterricht 1*. Heidelberg: Quelle und Meyer. (1st edition 1971)

Huddleston, Rodney & Geoffrey K. Pullum (eds.). 2002. *The Cambridge grammar of the English language*. Cambridge: Cambridge University Press.

Langacker, Ronald W. 2008a. *Cognitive grammar: A basic introduction*. Oxford: Oxford University Press.

Langacker, Ronald W. 2008b. The relevance of Cognitive Grammar for language pedagogy. In Sabine De Knop & Teun De Rycker (eds.), *Cognitive approaches to pedagogical grammar*, 7–35. Berlin: de Gruyter.

Leech, Geoffrey. 2011. Frequency, corpora and language learning. In Fanny Meunier, Sylvie De Cock, Gaëtanelle Gilquin & Magali Paquot (eds.), *A taste for corpora: In honour of Sylviane Granger*, 7–31. Amsterdam & Philadelphia: Benjamins.

Levin, Beth. 1993. *English verb classes and alternations: A preliminary investigation*. Chicago & London: The University of Chicago Press.

Lieven, Elena. 2014. First language learning from a usage-based approach. In Thomas Herbst, Hans-Jörg Schmid & Susen Faulhaber (eds.), *Constructions, collocations, patterns*, 1–24. Berlin & Boston: de Gruyter Mouton.

MacWhinney, Brian. 1997. Implicit and explicit processes: Commentary. *Studies in Second Language Acquisition* 19. 277–282.

Mindt, Dieter. 2000. *An Empirical grammar of the English verb system*. Berlin: Cornelsen.

Mindt, Dieter. 2005. Schulenglisch mangelhaft: Wie lange noch endlich? In Thomas Herbst (ed.), *Linguistische Dimensionen des Fremdsprachenunterrichts*, 430–452. Würzburg: Königshausen und Neumann.

Mukherjee, Joybrato. 2009. *Anglistische Korpuslinguistik: Eine Einführung*. Berlin: Schmidt.

Nesselhauf, Nadja. 2005. *Collocations in a learner corpus*. Amsterdam: John Benjamins.

Niemeier, Susanne & Monika Reif. 2008. Making progress simpler? Applying cognitive grammar to tense-aspect teaching in the German EFL-classroom. In Sabine De Knop & Teun De Rycker (eds.), *Cognitive approaches to pedagogical grammar. A volume in honour of René Dirven*, 325–355. Berlin & New York: Mouton de Gruyter.

Palmer, Frank. 1976. *Semantics*. Cambridge: Cambridge University Press.

Pullum, Geoffrey K. 2009. Lexical categorization in English dictionaries and traditional grammars. *Zeitschrift für Anglistik und Amerikanistik* 57(3). 255–273.

Quirk, Randolph, Sidney Greenbaum, Geoffrey Leech & Jan Svartvik. 1985. *A comprehensive grammar of the English language.* London & New York: Longman.

Radden, Günter & René Dirven. 2007. *Cognitive English grammar.* Amsterdam & Philadelphia: Benjamins.

Schröder, Konrad. 2005. Einige unmaßgebliche Gedanken zur grammatischen Terminologie und zum Grammatikunterricht des Schulfaches Englisch: A somewhat personal account. In Thomas Herbst (ed.), *Linguistische Dimensionen des Fremdsprachenunterrichts*, 1–9. Würzburg: Königshausen und Neumann.

Sinclair, John (ed.). 1990. *Collins Cobuild English grammar.* London & Glasgow: Collins.

Sinclair, John. 1991. *Corpus, concordance, collocation.* Oxford: Oxford University Press.

Snider, Neal & Inbal Arnon. 2012. A unified lexicon and grammar? Compositional and non-compositional phrases in the lexicon. In Dagmar Divjak & Stefan Th. Gries (eds.), *Frequency effects in language representation*, 127–163. Berlin & Boston: de Gruyter.

Stefanowitsch, Anatol. 2011. Keine Grammatik ohne Konstruktionen: Ein logisch-ökonomisches Argument für die Konstruktionsgrammatik. In Stefan Engelberg, Anke Holler & Kristel Proost (eds.), *Sprachliches Wissen zwischen Lexikon und Grammatik*, 71–112. Berlin & Boston: de Gruyter.

Tomasello, Michael. 2003. *Constructing a language.* Cambridge, Mass. & London: Harvard University Press.

Tyler, Andrea. 2012. *Cognitive linguistics and second language learning: Theoretical basics and experimental evidence.* New York & London: Routledge.

Ungerer, Friedrich, Gerhard E. H. Meier, Klaus Schäfer & Shirley B. Lechler. 1984. *A Grammar of present-day English.* Stuttgart: Klett.

Ungerer, Friedrich with Christian Mair, Neale Laker, Angela Ringel & Jörg Siebold, Shirley B. Lechler, Gerhard E.H. Meier & Klaus Schäfer. 1999. *Englische Grammatik heute.* Stuttgart, Düsseldorf & Leipzig: Klett.

Verspoor, Marjolijn & Heike Behrens. 2011. Dynamic Systems Theory and a usage-based approach to second language development. In Marjolijn H. Verspoor, Kees de Bot & Wander Lowie (eds.), *A dynamic approach to second language development: Methods and techniques*, 25–38, Amsterdam & Philadelphia: Benjamins.

Verspoor, Marjolijn & Andrea Tyler. 2009. Cognitive linguistics and second language learning. In William C. Ritchie & Tej K. Bhatia (eds.), *The new handbook of second language acquisition*, 159–177. Bingley: Emerald.

Zimmermann, Günther. 1977. *Grammatik im Fremdsprachenunterricht.* Frankfurt: Diesterweg.

Dictionaries

A valency dictionary of English. 2004. Thomas Herbst, David Heath, Ian Roe & Dieter Götz. Berlin & New York: Mouton de Gruyter. [VDE]

Longman dictionary of contemporary English. ^{6}2014. Harlow: Pearson Education Ltd. [LDOCE6]

Macmillan collocations dictionary. 2010. Michael Rundell (ed.). Oxford: Macmillan.

Oxford advanced learner's dictionary of current English. ^{9}2015. A. S. Hornby, edited by Margaret Deuter, Jennifer Bradbery & Joanna Turnbull. Oxford: Oxford University Press. [OALD9]

Oxford collocations dictionary for students of English. 2002. Jonathan Crowther, Sheila Dignen & Diana Lea (ed.). Oxford: Oxford University Press.
Oxford dictionary of current idiomatic English. Vol. 1: Verbs with prepositions and particles. 1975. Anthony P. Cowie & Ronald Mackin. London: Oxford University Press.
Oxford dictionary of current idiomatic English. Vol 2: Phrase, clause and sentence idioms. 1983. Anthony Paul Cowie, Ronald Mackin & Isabel R. McCaig. Oxford: Oxford University Press. [ODCIE2]
VALBU – Valenzwörterbuch deutscher Verben. 2004. Helmut Schumacher, Jacqueline Kubczak, Renate Schmidt & Vera de Ruiter. Tübingen: Narr.
Wörterbuch zur Valenz und Distribution deutscher Verben. ^{2}1973. Gerhard Helbig & Wolfgang Schenkel. Leipzig: Enzyklopädie. First edition 1969.

Textbooks

English G 2000 Gymnasium Bayern Band 2. 2004. Hellmut Schwarz (ed.). Berlin: Cornelsen.
English G Gymnasium Bayern Band 3. 2005. Hellmut Schwarz (ed.). Berlin: Cornelsen. (2005)
English G Gymnasium Bayern Band 5. 2007. Hellmut Schwarz (ed.). Berlin: Cornelsen.
Green Line 2. 2015. Marion Horner, Carolyn Jones, Jon Marks, Alison Wooder, Paul Dennis, Barbara Greive & Cornelia Kaminski, edited by Harald Weisshaupt. Stuttgart & Leipzig: Klett.
Learning English. Green Line New 2. Ausgabe für Bayern. 2004. Stephanie Ashford, Rosemary Hellyer-Jones, Marion Horner & Robert Parr. Stuttgart, Düsseldorf & Leipzig: Klett.
Learning English. Green Line New 4. Ausgabe für Bayern. 2006. Stephanie Ashford, Rosemary Hellyer-Jones & Marion Horner. Stuttgart & Leipzig: Klett.
Learning English. Green Line New 5. Ausgabe für Bayern. 2007. Stephanie Ashford, Rosemary Hellyer-Jones & Marion Horner, Stuttgart & Leipzig: Klett.
Learning English. Green Line New 6. Ausgabe für Bayern. 2008. Stephanie Ashford, Rosemary Hellyer-Jones and Marion Horner. Stuttgart and Leipzig: Klett.
Línea verde 2. 2007. Peter Bade, Margit Dietz, Mechthild Honer-Henkel, Christel Hörner-Steim, Josefa Jimeno Patrón, Maria Engracia López Sanchez, Javier Navorro Gonzáles, Christiane Peck, Pilar Pérez Cañizares, Matthias Ruiz Holst, Beate Stascheit, Ina Steggewentz & Maria Suárez Lasierra. Stuttgart & Leipzig: Klett.

Corpora

BNC *The British National Corpus.* Distributed by Oxford University Press Computing Services on behalf of the BNC Consortium. http://www.natcorp.ox.ac.uk/
COCA = Davies, M. 2008–. The Corpus of Contemporary American English: 450 million words, 1990–present. Available online at http://corpus.byu.edu/coca/.
ICLE *International Corpus of Learner English*, Version 2. 2009. Sylviane Granger, Estelle Dagneaux, Fanny Meunier & Magali Paquot (eds.) Louvain-la-Neuve: Presses universitaires de Louvain.

Sabine De Knop and Fabio Mollica
A construction-based analysis of German ditransitive phraseologisms for language pedagogy[1]

Abstract: Earlier studies in phraseology described phraseologisms as idiosyncratic, idiomatic expressions with a meaning non-predictable from their constituent parts (Chafe 1968; Fraser 1970; Weinreich 1969). Such a definition is unsatisfactory, especially in language pedagogy, as it implies that phraseologisms have to be learnt by heart. In our paper we advocate a construction-based approach enriched by valency aspects for a more adequate description of phraseologisms, and more specifically of German ditransitive phraseologisms, e.g. *Petra zeigt ihrem Bruder die Krallen* (lit. 'Petra shows her brother the claws' = 'Petra threatens her brother'). Our study shows that German ditransitive phraseologisms have the same abstract semantic and syntactic pattern as non-phraseological ditransitive constructions, but with some additional figurative aspects. Inspired by tests conducted by Bencini and Goldberg (2000), but also Baicchi (2013), Della Costanza and Mollica (2015), and Valenzuela Manzanares and Rojo López (2008) we present some further tests based on sorting tasks with Italian- and French-speaking learners of German. The tests reveal that learners sort ditransitive phraseologisms in the same way as prototypical ditransitive constructional argument structures and not so much according to the verb or their idiomatic meaning. This link can be exploited for the development of an adequate teaching methodology, based among others on the principle of "structural persistence" as defined by Konopka and Bock (2009). This principle describes the productivity and predictability of ditransitive phraseologisms in terms of a generalization of syntactic structures even with a variation of lexemes constituting these structures. From the results of the tests we can conclude that a construction-based teaching methodology which integrates the study of ditransitive phraseologisms within the larger frame of literal and idiomatic abstract constructions should be

---

[1] The article is the result of close collaboration between the two authors; however, for academic purposes only, Sabine De Knop is responsible for Sections 1, 2, 4, 4.2, 4.4 and 5, and Fabio Mollica for Sections 3, 4.1, 4.3 and 6. This research is associated with project FFI2013-43593-P (Spanish Ministry of Economy and Competitiveness). We thank the reviewers for their constructive comments on an earlier version of this paper.

enriched by valency properties typical of the German verbs (Herbst 2011; Stefanowitsch 2011) and by the recognition of associations grounded in metaphor and/or metonymy.

Keywords: phraseologisms; ditransitive; construction-based description; valency; French-speaking learners; Italian learners; German L2; foreign language teaching

1 Introduction

For a long time issues related to the domain of phraseology have attracted the interest of linguists. Earlier theoretical studies in this research field have described the units of phraseology, i.e. phraseologisms, as idiosyncratic, idiomatic expressions with a meaning non-predictable from their constituent parts (Chafe 1968; Fraser 1970; Weinreich 1969). Such a view is unsatisfactory as it implies that the meaning of phraseologisms is not motivated or that their motivation cannot be determined by speakers from what they already know. From a pedagogical perspective too, such a definition is more than frustrating as it implies that phraseologisms can only be learnt by heart. In some studies (see Gibbs 1995; Matlock and Heredia 2002) it has been shown that learners sometimes attempt to establish connections between the literal and non-literal meanings of phraseologisms. However, this approach is also problematic as it cannot be generalized.

Our study proposes another approach with a particular focus on motivation. It advocates a construction-based approach enriched by the "Valency Realisation Principle" (Herbst 2011: 359) for a more adequate description of phraseologisms and further for a more efficient and easier teaching and learning of phraseologisms. More specifically, our study deals with conventionalized German ditransitive phraseologisms, for instance:[2]

(1) *Isabella gab ihrem Verlobten einen Korb.*
     Lit. 'Isabella gave her fiancé a basket.'
     = 'Isabella turned her fiancé down.'

(2) *Der Verkäufer zeigte mir die kalte Schulter.*
     Lit. 'The salesman showed me the cold shoulder.'
     = 'The salesman ignored me/could not be bothered.'

---

[2] In order to facilitate the understanding of the German examples, we will offer for each example a literal translation and additionally the correct translation in the form of a paraphrase or a functional equivalent phraseologism (Dobrovol'skij 2011) as far as possible.

If we have a closer look at these German examples, we realize that they have the same ditransitive pattern as non-phraseological ditransitive constructions, but with some additional figurative aspects. However, they are conventionalized in the sense that the lexemes used to express the predicate and the direct object are fixed. Accordingly, one could not replace the direct object in the phraseologism by a word with a similar meaning and say e.g. (1') *Isabella gab ihrem Verlobten eine Tasche* (lit. 'Isabella gave her fiancé a bag') or (2') *Der Verkäufer zeigte mir das kalte Knie* (lit. 'The salesman showed me the cold knee'). Using surveys conducted among French- and Italian-speaking learners of German we were able to show that learners identify the same patterns in ditransitive phraseologisms as in ditransitive non-phraseological constructions. This connection can be exploited for the development of a more adequate teaching methodology based on generalizations in Goldberg's (1995, 2006) sense. Traditional foreign language teaching dealt with phraseologisms very randomly and considered them to be fixed expressions which had to be learned by heart. We will show that Construction Grammar (CxG) is an ideal model for the development of some regularities. Because German is a strong flectional language, it will be necessary to also consider verb valency (compare Herbst 2011 and Stefanowitsch 2011).

Before we go on, we would like to deal with a few terminological issues. Phraseologisms have been described in various ways (see among others Burger 2010; Donalies 2009; Fleischer 1997; Gries 2008 or Wulff 2012, to name just a few). They "can range from free combinations to restricted collocations, figurative idioms, and pure idioms" and constitute a "subset of phrases maximally conventionalized" (Wulff 2012: 292). Gries (2008) discusses a list of defining properties of phraseologisms. A major characteristic for a linguistic unit to count as a phraseologism is "semantic unity, but not non-compositional semantics" (Gries 2008: 6). The term "phraseologism" competes with a variety of different terms that can be found in the scientific literature to designate literal and non-literal fixed expressions. Alternative terms for 'phraseologism' include "phraseological unit", "idiom", "phraseme", and "idiomatic expression" (Donalies 2009: 30).[3] Following Fleischer (1997: 3), we will use the term "phraseologism" as a generic term for fixed word combinations (also as opposed to free combinations of ditransitive constructions) which also include idioms, i.e. non-literal word

---

[3] All these terms do not exactly cover the same phenomena, however. For the differences between the terms, see Donalies (2009) and Fleischer (1997).

combinations (see also Burger 2010: 37). Ditransitive phraseologisms can have different degrees of idiomaticity. For instance, the above example (1) is more idiomatic than example (2), as it cannot be easily understood because of the complete lack of transparency of the word *Korb* ('basket') in this context. We will deal in more detail with different degrees of idiomaticity in Section 3.1.

Our paper is structured as follows. Section 2 first describes non-phraseological ditransitive constructions in the framework of Goldberg's (1995, 2006) Construction Grammar. Such constructions express the idea of a transfer and are characterized by the "Correspondence Principle" (Goldberg 1995: 50), which means that there is a fusion between the argument roles specified by the construction and the participant roles required by the verb (Goldberg 1995: 51). Such non-fixed ditransitive constructions can be considered to be prototypical. We further show how morpho-syntactic cases contribute to the realization of this fusion in German. Section 3 deals with ditransitive phraseologisms which can be classified into two types according to the degree of fusion between the construction and the verb valency pattern: (i) either the verb valency matches the prototypical ditransitive construction pattern, e.g. with prototypical ditransitive verbs like *geben* ('to give') or *zeigen* ('to show') in example (1) or (2); (ii) or construction pattern and verb valency are different, e.g.

(3) *Ich huste dir was.*
     Lit. 'I cough to you sth.'
     = 'You can wait a long time, but I will not do it'/'I tell you my opinion in a direct and sometimes offensive way'

In this example the dative object is not part of the verb valency. Section 4 presents the empirical study conducted with French- and Italian-speaking learners of German. Inspired by the tests by Bencini and Goldberg (2000), but also the studies by Baicchi (2013), Della Costanza and Mollica (2015), and Valenzuela Manzanares and Rojo López (2008), we describe some further tests based on sorting and multiple choice tasks among the learners. These surveys aim at confirming our hypothesis that learners recognize a link between phraseological and non-phraseological ditransitives. Section 5 shows how this link can be exploited to foster the teaching and learning of ditransitive phraseologisms. Phraseological and non-phraseological ditransitive constructions differ from each other in the degree of figurativeness. That is why the concepts of metaphor and metonymy are further needed. Finally, Section 6 summarizes the results of the study.

2 Prototypical ditransitive constructions

2.1 Brief description

Constructions in Goldberg's (1995, 2006) sense are form-meaning pairs. The ditransitive construction[4] is realized with a verb, a subject and two objects: [V Subj Obj1 Obj2].[5] It is associated with the abstract meaning: 'X CAUSES Y TO RECEIVE Z' which includes an agent, a recipient and a patient, CAUSE-RECEIVE <agt rec pat> (Goldberg 1995: 49). At the semantic level, the central sense of the ditransitive construction is the idea of a transfer: "the central sense is argued to involve transfer between a volitional agent and a willing recipient" (Goldberg 1995: 141). Figure 1 shows Goldberg's representation of this construction.

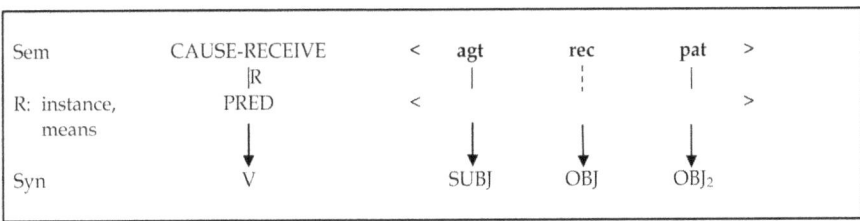

Figure 1: Ditransitive construction (Goldberg 1995: 142)

A prototypical illustration of this construction is:

(4) *Peter gibt Maria ein Buch.*
     'Peter gives Maria a book.'

in which *Peter* represents the agent [AGT], *Maria* the recipient [REC] and *ein Buch* the patient [PAT]. In the prototypical realization of the ditransitive construction, the meaning of the construction corresponds to the meaning of the verb, which means that there is a fusion between the argument roles specified by the construction and the participant roles required by the verb (Goldberg 1995: 51). The abstract construction specifies which argument roles in the construction are necessarily mapped onto the participant roles required by the verb (Goldberg 1995: 51).[6] This fusion is an illustration of what Goldberg calls

---

4 We describe this construction type very briefly and refer to Goldberg (1995) for further details.
5 In German the objects correspond respectively to the accusative object and the dative object (see Section 2.2 for further details).
6 Following Welke (2011: 185–190) we reject Goldberg's dichotomy between "argument roles" and "participant roles", as we assume that verbs can also be valency carriers which can select general argument roles or semantic roles (see Welke 2011: 190).

the "Correspondence Principle" (Goldberg 1995: 50–51). Additionally, it is the "Semantic Coherence Principle" which makes it possible to decide which argument roles can be mapped onto which participant roles, as a fusion is only possible with roles that are semantically compatible (Goldberg 1995: 50). For instance, the valency pattern of the verb *geben* ('give') is the prototypical realization of the ditransitive construction and of the Semantic Coherence and Correspondence Principles.[7] The central, prototypical construction can best be expressed with verbs of giving (in German: *geben*) which express a real transfer of an object to a recipient. But as Goldberg (1995: 32) emphasizes, "it is widely recognized that many ditransitive expressions do not strictly imply that the patient argument is successfully transferred to the potential recipient". This is for instance the case with the verbs *versprechen* ('to promise') or *backen* ('to bake'), which can be used in ditransitive constructions although they do not express a real transfer, e.g.

(5) *John verspricht Maria ewige Liebe.*
'John promises Maria eternal love.'

(6) *Seine Mutter backte ihm frische Brötchen.*
'His mother baked him fresh rolls.'

As a result the ditransitive construction as defined by Goldberg (1995) can be polysemous and can express various related meanings. For instance, example (6) expresses the intended, but not real transfer (Ekberg 2012: 170) as it cannot be guaranteed that the recipient indeed receives the freshly baked rolls (Goldberg 1995: 32). According to Ekberg (2012: 170–171) the meaning of the construction INTEND CAUSE-RECEIVE <agt rec pat> includes the possibility that the recipient never receives the rolls freshly prepared by the agent. The prototypical meaning of the ditransitive construction consists in a possessive relation caused by an agent between a recipient and a patient (Ekberg 2012: 6). However, the possessive relation between the patient and the recipient (or alternatively the beneficient or maleficient) does not necessarily have to take place. That is why verbs like *versprechen* ('to promise') or *backen* ('to bake'), which are not prototypically 'giving' verbs, are possible in the ditransitive construction.

---

[7] Goldberg's fusion concept has been criticized by a number of researchers (here we can refer among others to Boas 2003, 2013; Kay 2005; Nemoto 1998) who argue that "the types of abstract meaningful argument structure constructions are often too powerful and have the potential to over-generate unattested sentences" (Boas 2013: 238). For a detailed description of the arguments and possible solutions to overcome the problems, see Boas (2013: 238–239) and further Herbst (2011) who advocates the "Valency Realisation Principle" (see further Section 2.2).

2.2 Valency and case-marking in German

German is a strong flectional language (see Meibauer et al. 2002; Thieroff and Vogel 2011) in which the arguments are marked with morpho-syntactic cases, i.e. the nominative, the accusative, the dative, and the genitive. The ditransitive construction is realized with a subject in the nominative and further with the dative and the accusative object which respectively stand for the semantic roles recipient and patient. This is illustrated in the following example:

(7) *Peter*   *gibt*   *seiner Mutter*   *ein Stück Kuchen.*
     [AGT/SUB]   [REC/DAT OBJ]   [PAT/ACC OBJ]
     'Peter   gives   his mother   a piece of cake.'

In a few rare cases there is no correspondence between the morpho-syntactic realization and the verb semantics. This pertains to German verbs with two accusative objects that express different roles (the recipient and the patient, see Primus 2012: 46). Here we can mention the German verbs *(ab)fragen* ('to question'), *abhören* ('to listen to', 'to spy'), and *lehren* ('to teach'), as illustrated in (8) and (9).

(8) *Der Großvater*   *lehrte* *seinen Enkel*   *die deutsche Grammatik.*
                                    [REC/ACC]   [PAT/ACC]
    Lit. 'The grand-father taught   his grand-son   the German grammar.'

(9) *Der Lehrer*   *fragt regelmäßig die Schüler die Vokabel (ab).*
                                       [REC/ACC]   [PAT/ACC]
    Lit. 'The teacher asks regularly the pupils the vocabulary words (off).'

Although these verbs express a transfer, the recipient role is expressed with an accusative object and not – as could be expected from the semantics of the construction – with a dative object.[8] Consequently, not every semantically compatible verb can be fused with the ditransitive construction (compare Herbst 2011: 354 and Stefanowitsch 2011: 380). According to Herbst (2011), in order to define the idiosyncrasy of each lexeme, Goldberg's Principles of Correspondence and of Semantic Coherence must be enriched by the "Valency Realisation Principle". This principle does not simply define the formal properties of arguments but it further guarantees that the formal elements of an argument construction are

---

[8] For a description of the ditransitive construction and its prepositional variants in German, see Proost (2014).

realized if and only if they respect the valency properties of a verb (Herbst 2011: 355). This type of information is very relevant for foreign language teaching as it often diverges from one language to another. To come back to example (8), in French and Italian the verbs corresponding to German *lehren* ('to teach') are used in a ditransitive construction:

(8a) It. *Il nonno ha insegnato la grammatica tedesca al nipote.*
                              [PAT/DIR OBJ]   [REC/INDIR OBJ]

(8b) Fr. *Le grand-père a appris la grammaire allemande à son petit-fils.*
                                [PAT/DIR OBJ]   [REC/INDIR OBJ]

The Italian and French equivalents of the German verb *abfragen* (cf. example (9)) require a direct object for the recipient (It. *gli studenti*/Fr. *les étudiants*) and a prepositional object (It. *sui vocaboli*/Fr. *sur le vocabulaire*) for the path:

(9a) It. *L'insegnante interroga regolarmente gli studenti sui vocaboli.*
                                                  [REC/DIR OBJ] [PATH/PREP OBJ]

(9b) Fr. *L'enseignante interroge régulièrement les étudiants sur le vocabulaire.*
                                                  [REC/DIR OBJ] [PATH/PREP OBJ]

An adequate teaching methodology will have to deal with the valency properties of single lexemes in order to neutralize possible negative transfer phenomena which would lead, for instance, to a non-standard ditransitive use of the German verb *lehren*, as illustrated in the following example:[9]

(8c) ?*Der Großvater lehrte seinem Enkel die deutsche Grammatik*
                                    [REC/DAT]   [PAT/ACC]

The possible distance between the semantics of the construction and the morphosyntactic realization applies to ditransitive constructions, either in their non-fixed or in their phraseological use. In the next section, we will look at ditransitive phraseologisms, which constitute the central topic of our study.

---

[9] In a not so strict normative perspective, the use of the verb *lehren* with the dative case for the recipient is acceptable in today's German. See http://www.duden.de/rechtschreibung/lehren.

3 Ditransitive phraseologisms

In Section 1 we already proposed a few definitions of phraseologisms and we discussed some terminological issues. In the present section the characteristics of phraseological ditransitive constructions are defined and several types of ditransitive phraseologisms are described.

3.1 Degrees of idiomaticity

Ditransitive phraseologisms have the same syntactic structure and transfer semantics as prototypical non-fixed ditransitive constructions. However the direct objects are most of the time lexically fixed.[10] Here are some examples:

(10) *Peter zeigt seiner Schwester die Krallen.*
   Lit. 'Peter shows his sister the claws.'
   = 'Peter threatens his sister.'

(11) *Ihr schlechtes Verhalten hat ihm den Rest gegeben.*
   Lit. 'Her bad behaviour has given him the remainder.'
   = 'Her bad behaviour has been the final straw for him.'

(12) *Die Mutter verpasste ihrer Tochter einen Denkzettel.*
   Lit. 'The mother gave her daughter a think-card.'
   = 'The mother gave her daughter a warning/something to think about.'

(13) *Isabella gab ihrem Verlobten einen Korb.*
   Lit. 'Isabella gave her fiancé a basket.'
   = 'Isabella turned her fiancé down.'

(14) *Sie konnte ihm das Wasser nicht reichen.*
   Lit. 'She could not reach to him the water.'
   = 'She did not have his level/competence.'

(15) *Ich huste dir etwas.*
   Lit. 'I cough to you something.'
   = 'You can wait a long time, but I will not do it.'

---

10 By 'fixedness' we mean the impossibility to use another lexeme in this context.

As already pointed out, in their prototypical use ditransitive phraseologisms also express the idea of a transfer, but in a metaphorical or metonymical way. Ditransitive phraseologisms are characterized by different degrees of idiomaticity and can be defined on a continuum between fully idiomatic and partly idiomatic expressions. Depending on the degree of idiomaticity, learners of German are likely to recognize the intended transfer meaning or not. Example (10) for instance is fully transparent, the meaning of examples (11) and (12) is also quite transparent, but to a lesser degree than (10). The idea of a transfer also characterizes examples (13)–(15), but the expressions are completely idiomatic as none of the elements offers any hint about the overall meaning. Of course, a speaker's mother tongue (L1) plays a major role when it comes to understanding phraseologisms. If a foreign phraseologism has an equivalent expression in L1, it will be more easily understood, even if it is lexically complex. For instance example (10) has counterparts in French and Italian:

(10) a. Fr. *Pierre montre les griffes à sa sœur.*
 Lit. 'Peter shows the claws to his sister.'

 b. It. *Piero mostra gli artigli a sua sorella.*
 Lit. 'Peter shows the claws to his sister.'

3.2 Fusion between the construction and the verb valency

From a pedagogical point of view, it is not only the degree of idiomaticity which plays a major role in the understanding and learning process of ditransitive phraseologisms, but further the syntactic and semantic properties of the construction and its mapping on the verb valency. When used in ditransitive phraseologisms, verbs like *geben* ('to give'), *zeigen* ('to show'), or *verpassen* ('to give, to inflict') also have a ditransitive valency and semantics, which means that there is a fusion between the ditransitive abstract construction and the verb valency.

As we can see from the examples below, verbs with a ditransitive valency are, as can be expected, favorite verbs in ditransitive phraseologisms. Apart from the above examples (11) or (13), many similar examples can be found with *geben* ('to give'):

(16) *Der Arbeitgeber gab dem Mitarbeiter den Laufpass.*
 Lit. 'The employer gave the colleague the run passport.'
 = 'The employer kicked his colleague out.'

(17) *Die Stadt gab dem Bauunternehmen grünes Licht.*
Lit. 'The town gave the building company green light.'
= 'The town gave the building company its OK (to do sth).'

(18) *Gib ihm Saures!*
Lit. 'Give him something sour!'
= 'Give him beans/Scold him!'

(19) *Er gab seiner kleinen Schwester Zunder.*
Lit. 'He gave his small sister tinder.'
= 'He gave his small sister hell/He reprimanded his small sister severely.'

(20) *Mein Freund Max hat mir all den Jahren immer Pfeffer gegeben.*
Lit. 'My friend Max has given me all these years always pepper.'
= 'My friend Max put pressure on me to do something all these years.'

Many parallel examples of ditransitive phraseologisms can also be found with other prototypical ditransitive verbs like *zeigen* ('to show') (see also example (10) above):

(21) *Er zeigte mir die kalte Schulter.*
Lit. 'He showed me the cold shoulder.'
= 'He gave me the cold shoulder.'

(22) *Der LKW-Fahrer zeigte den anderen Autofahrern den Vogel.*
Lit. 'The lorry driver showed the other car drivers the bird.'
= 'The lorry driver flipped the other car drivers off.'

(23) *Er zeigte/bot seinem Chef die Stirn.*
Lit. 'He showed/offered his boss the forehead.'
= 'He confronted his boss/He stood up for himself.'

Prototypical ditransitive constructions can have a subordinate sentence as accusative object. This also applies to phraseological ditransitive constructions:

(24) *Er wollte in der Beziehung seiner Freundin zeigen, wer die Hosen anhat.*
Lit. 'He wanted in the relationship to show his girlfriend who is wearing the trousers.'
= 'In his relationship he wanted to show his girlfriend who the boss is.'

(25) *Ein guter Lehrer muss seinen Schülern auch mal zeigen, wo der Hammer hängt.*
Lit. 'A good teacher must also show his pupils where the hammer is hanging.'
= 'A good teacher must also show his pupils who the stronger one is.'

(26) *Und plötzlich zeigt er ihr, was eine Harke ist.*
Lit. 'And suddenly he shows her what a rake is.'
= 'And suddenly he gives her a piece of his mind.'

The examples (16)–(26) are characterized by "structural persistence" (Konopka and Bock 2009: 71). This principle "involves the tendency to generalize structures from one sentence to another even when the wording of the sentences differs" (Konopka and Bock 2009: 71). The structural account Konopka and Bock advocate predicts a "fundamental similarity in the structural processing carried out for lexicalized and nonlexicalized expressions, on the grounds that abstract syntactic procedures are not sensitive to variations in lexical compositionality" (Konopka and Bock 2009: 71). Structural persistence characterizes the structure of a specific construction, it increases substantially if the lexical items used in the constructions are identical (Konopka and Bock 2009: 71). This also applies to the kind of examples under study in this section: not only is there a replication of the ditransitive construction, but in the series of examples (16)–(26), it is the same ditransitive verb which is used, viz. *geben* or *zeigen*. Konopka and Bock tested the priming effects in expressions with phrasal verbs in three experiments (for a detailed description of the tests, see their article). They come to the conclusion that idiomaticity does not seem to disrupt normal persistence (Konopka and Bock 2009: 79). This is sustained by Mellado Blanco's (2015) study on "phraseme-constructions[11] and lexical idiom-variants", in which she shows that the possibility to build "variables" of one and the same structure reduces the idiomaticity of phraseologisms and reinforces the lexical specificity. The principle of structural persistence presents the advantage of minimizing the difference in processing and understanding of phraseological ditransitive constructions as they are based on the same pattern as literal ones, i.e. "lexically specific structural information should generalize across lexical items as easily as nonlexically specific structural information" (Konopka and Bock 2009: 72).

---

11 This term is used in Dobrovol'skij's (2011: 114) sense. It refers to phraseologisms that present one or more syntactic slots not lexically specified, and thus lexically open. In Fillmore, Kay, and O'Connor (1988: 505–506) these kinds of structures are called "formal idioms".

Applied to our examples, this minimization of the differences between literal and phraseological ditransitive constructions presents irrefutable advantages in teaching and learning methodology. If we assume that ditransitive phraseologisms with prototypical ditransitive verbs are processed in the same way as non-phraseological ditransitive constructions, we can expect the idiomatic meaning in the phraseological ditransitive constructions to be the result of the metaphorical or metonymical use of the accusative object. For instance, in example (16), repeated below, *Laufpass* is used in a metaphorical way to refer to the dismissal:

(16) Der Arbeitgeber gab dem Mitarbeiter den Laufpass.
Lit. 'The employer gave the colleague the run passport.'
= 'The employer kicked his colleague out.'

A metonymy motivates the use of *Vogel* in (22) or *Stirn* in (23):

(22) Der LKW-Fahrer zeigte den anderen Autofahrern den Vogel.
Lit. 'The lorry driver showed the other car drivers the bird.'
= 'The lorry driver flipped the other car drivers off.'

(23) Er zeigte/bot seinem Chef die Stirn.
Lit. 'He showed/offered his boss the forehead.'
= 'He confronted his boss/He stood up for himself.'

The bird in (22) or the forehead in (23) are metonymies for a specific behavior: the bird for craziness (in the past, people thought that insane persons had birds in their head, see Duden 1998: 768) and the forehead for a fronting reaction.

Examples (13) or (21) are more intricate as they combine a metonymy and a metaphor but with different degrees of idiomaticity:

(13) Isabella gab ihrem Verlobten einen Korb.
Lit. 'Isabella gave her fiancé a basket.'
= 'Isabella turned her fiancé down.'

(21) Er zeigte mir die kalte Schulter.
Lit. 'He showed me the cold shoulder.'
= 'He gave me the cold shoulder.'

Kalte Schulter in (21) is a metonymy for a negative, rejecting behavior. One offers one's shoulder to lean against it and to get some comfort. But the whole example is used metaphorically to express something like the lack of interest or the rejection. In (13) the basket is a metonymy for a premeditated action of getting rid of somebody, but the whole expression is used metaphorically to express a rejection, a non-acceptance. As we can see with these two examples, the degree of idiomaticity can vary a lot. Compared with the other examples, (13) is not transparent at all (not even for native speakers). It originally refers to a basket with a loose bottom, which was given as a present to rejected suitors – who then broke through the basket and thereby disappeared (Duden 1998: 409).

Following Fillmore, Kay, and O'Connor (1988: 504), a distinction between "decoding" vs. "encoding" idiom has to be made. Decoding idioms like example (13) cause the most difficulties in learning a foreign language (L2) since, unlike "encoding idioms", the L1 speaker or L2 learner cannot deduce the meaning from their knowledge of the language. In contrast, the following example:

(10) *Peter zeigt seiner Schwester die Krallen.*
      Lit. 'Peter shows his sister the claws.'
      = 'Peter threatens his sister.'

is an encoding idiom (Fillmore, Kay, and O'Connor 1988: 505), which implies that the learner can interpret it, even if s/he may not know that it is a conventional way of expression and further s/he would not necessarily be able to predict its usage. Accordingly, in spite of the same ditransitive construction, not every ditransitive phraseologism can be interpreted by learners in the same way, but still the idea of a (metaphorical/metonymical) transfer between the agent designated by the subject and the recipient expressed by the dative object can be recognized thanks to the principle of "structural persistence" and can be useful in the understanding process of such phraseologisms by learners.

3.3 Difference between construction and verb valency

As we have already explained in Section 2.2, in most ditransitive constructions – both the phraseological and the non-phraseological ones – the dative object expresses the recipient role. In most phraseologisms with a ditransitive structure the dative object is required by the verb valency; such phraseologisms correspond to 'grammatical idioms' (see Fillmore, Kay, and O'Connor 1988: 505). In some fewer cases the dative object is not foreseen in the argument structure of the verb. Here we have to distinguish two types of examples. The first class of examples includes constructions with the so-called 'free dative', e.g.

(27) Wir drücken dir die Daumen.
      Lit. 'We press you the thumbs.'
      = 'We keep our fingers crossed for you.'

The term 'free dative' is used in traditional German grammaticography to designate a nominal phrase in the dative which is not foreseen in the argument structure of the verb like other prototypical dative phrases. For instance, the verb *drücken* ('to press') in the above example (27) requires in principle two arguments, namely a subject and an object, as illustrated in e.g. *Wir drücken die Daumen*, lit. 'We press the thumbs'. The dative position (*dir*) in the above example (27) is not part of the basic valency[12] of the verb. When this verb is fused with the abstract ditransitive construction the verb valency gets three slots. The dative object *dir* is realized as a 'dativus commodi' (also called 'sympaticus') which always designates a human or animal being (most of the time a person), who is the benefactor of an action. This dative type appears with some verbs of production, destruction, change, transfer, or transportation (see Zifonun, Hoffmann, and Strecker 1997: 1340). In valency theory it is still controversial whether the dativus commodi belongs to the verb argument structure or not (see also Welke 2011: 202–213 and Mollica and Kuhn 2013). Construction Grammar offers the advantage of considering the dativus commodi and its antonymic variant, the dativus incommodi, as an argument of the ditransitive construction (see Goldberg 1995: 141–151 and Welke 2011: 202–213).

The second type of examples includes so-called "extra-grammatical idioms" (Fillmore, Kay, and O'Connor 1988: 505), in which the verb valency is not at all ditransitive and the use of a dative object would even be completely wrong in the literal usage, e.g.

(28) Ich huste dir etwas.
      Lit. 'I cough to you something.'
      = 'You can wait a long time, but I will not do it.'

(29) Der Nachbar hat den Kindern den Marsch geblasen.
      Lit. 'The neighbor has blown to the children the march.'
      = 'The neighbor has reprimanded the children.'

In these examples it is the phraseological construction which superimposes the ditransitive character upon the verb by the principle of coercion (see Goldberg

---

[12] See Welke (2011: 184) for the definition of 'basic valency' (in German, 'Grundvalenz').

1995: 159; Ziem and Lasch 2013: 115).[13] The valency of the verb *husten* in example (28) only requires one argument, i.e. a subject, as instantiated in e.g. *Max hustet*, 'Max coughs'. In the fusion process of the verb with the construction, an accusative and a dative object are possible as ad hoc arguments. *Husten* behaves like a verb of saying with a dative object encoding the recipient. In the same way, in example (29) the dative position is triggered by the ad hoc construction. From a pedagogical point of view, we expect most difficulties with this type of examples which are characterized by a distance between verb valency and ditransitive construction. In order to check the difficulties encountered by learners of German we designed a test that we will present in the following section.

4 Empirical study

The empirical study consists of three parts. Inspired by Bencini and Goldberg's (2000) experiment and by the studies by Baicchi (2013) and by Valenzuela Manzanares and Rojo López (2008), we designed a first part to investigate whether learners categorize ditransitive phraseologisms like prototypical ditransitive non-figurative constructions, or whether they sort the examples according to the verb valency or another criterion (Part 1 of the test). The aim was to exploit the possible constructional similarity between literal and non-literal ditransitive constructions to develop avenues for a better teaching methodology. Part 2 and 3 of the test were inspired by Della Costanza and Mollica (2015) and aimed at defining the learners' strategies for the understanding and the meaning processing of the ditransitive phraseologisms. Our aim was not to test our learners' knowledge of the phraseologisms and we even expected some of the ditransitive phraseologisms not to be known to them at all because of their specificity or low frequency. Instead, we wanted to see whether the context plays an active part in the disambiguation process (Part 3).

4.1 Participants

The participants consisted of two groups, i.e. a first group of 15 Belgian French-speaking master students in translation and interpretation studies at the high school Marie Haps in Brussels[14] and a second group of 15 Italian master students

---

[13] For a discussion of possible problems linked to the process of superimposition or fusion, see Boas (2003).
[14] We would like to thank our colleague Françoise Gallez for having conducted the tests with the students of the high school Marie Haps.

in language studies at the University of Milano. Both groups of students, whose level could be established with several tests done during their studies, had the B2-C1 level in the Common European Framework of Reference for Languages of the Council of Europe. The participants received the questionnaires in the classroom under the supervision of lecturers but without any additional information. They received the three parts of the test during the same session. They could not come back to the former part and make any changes once they had started the next part. We will describe the three parts in detail and discuss the results in the following sections.

4.2 Part 1

In Part 1 (see Appendix I), 25 mixed sentences were presented to the students; they consisted of 14 sentences with a ditransitive construction (including 11 phraseologisms) and 11 other sentences with mixed constructions. Either the sentences contained the same verb, but with a different argument structure, e.g. with the verb *geben* 'to give':

(30) *Die Kuh gibt Milch.*
 Lit. 'The cow gives milk.'
 = 'The cow produces milk.'

(13) *Isabella gab ihrem Verlobten einen Korb.*
 Lit. 'Isabella gave her fiancé a basket.'
 = 'Isabella turned her fiancé down.'

(31) *Die Müllers geben eine Party in ihrer neuen Villa.*
 'The Müllers give a party in their villa.'

Or the sentences contained different verbs, but were instantiations of the same constructions, e.g.

(10) *Peter zeigt seiner Schwester die Krallen.*
 Lit. 'Peter shows his sister the claws.'
 = 'Peter threatens his sister.'

(12) *Die Mutter verpasste ihrer Tochter einen Denkzettel.*
 Lit. 'The mother gave her daughter a think-card.'
 = 'The mother gave her daughter a warning/something to think about.'

(32) *Der Bauer versprach seiner Freundin goldene Berge.*
    Lit. 'The farmer promised his girlfriend golden mountains.'
    = 'The farmer promised his girlfriend the moon.'

The task consisted in classifying the 25 sentences according to their meaning and/or form with the aim to see whether they would notice a similarity in the construction or whether they would classify the examples according to the verb. The participants were asked to write down the sentences that they considered to be similar in one and the same box. They were also told that there is "no wrong answer".

This first part of the test led to interesting results. In the classification of the 25 sentences by the students of both groups we could recognize five different classes, i.e. according to the verb, as a ditransitive construction, as a (ditransitive) phraseologism, or as another non-ditransitive construction; a last class contained mixed examples where no classification principle could be determined. Interestingly, most learners recognized the different structures and did not mix them. For instance, they put the following examples (30) and (33) in one and the same category and (10) and (13) in another category:

(30) *Die Kuh gibt Milch.*
    Lit. 'The cow gives milk.'
    = 'The cow produces milk.'

(33) *Ich esse gerne Pasta.*
    'I like to eat pasta.'

(10) *Peter zeigt seiner Schwester die Krallen.*
    Lit. 'Peter shows his sister the claws.'
    = 'Peter threatens his sister.'

(13) *Isabella gab ihrem Verlobten einen Korb.*
    Lit. 'Isabella gave her fiancé a basket.'
    = 'Isabella turned her fiancé down.'

Another observation is that many ditransitive phraseologisms were classified in the same category, together with the prototypical, literal ditransitive constructions. As we are interested in the question of whether the examples were classified according to the ditransitive construction or according to the verb, we present in Table 1 the results for both categories and both test groups.

Table 1: Construction-based vs. verb-oriented classification of examples

	Italian learners	French-speaking learners
Ditr. Cx/Phraseol.	73%	69%
Verb-oriented	19%	38%

The results demonstrate that most learners intuitively classified the examples according to the ditransitive construction and less often according to the verb – in spite of the fact that some examples contained the same verb, e.g. *geben* or *zeigen*. Some learners classified the same example in several categories, which explains why we get more than 100 percent for the French-speaking group.

4.3 Part 2

Part 2 of the test contained 10 instantiations of common ditransitive phraseologisms (see Appendix II). The aim of this part of the test was to see whether the students knew the meaning of the phraseologisms or whether they tried to guess their meaning from the ditransitive structure. Learners were proposed four possible German paraphrases of the phraseologism and they had to select one of them in a multiple choice task. Additionally, the learners were asked to select whether they knew the meaning or if they guessed it. Here is one example of the task:

(34) *Isabella gab ihrem Verlobten einen Korb.*
 Bedeutet: (1) Isabella schenkte ihrem Verlobten einen Korb Obst.
  (2) Isabella erzählte ihrem Verlobten eine Lüge.
  (3) Isabella sagte ihrem Freund, dass sie ihn nicht heiraten würde.
  (4) Isabella erzählte ihrem Verlobten die Wahrheit.
 – Ich kenne die Bedeutung.
 – Ich kenne die Bedeutung nicht, habe sie erraten.
 (Lit. 'Isabella gave her fiancé a basket'
 Means: (1) Isabella gave her fiancé a basket with fruit as a present.
  (2) Isabella told her fiancé a lie.
  (3) Isabella told her friend that she would not marry him.
  (4) Isabella told her fiancé the truth.
 – I know the meaning
 – I don't know the meaning, I guessed it.)

A first observation is that even if the learners claimed not to know the ditransitive phraseologism, they guessed its meaning quite well, as attested by the results in Table 2 below. One could of course argue that this good score for the selection of the right answer depends on the quality of the paraphrases which can be either too informative or too distant from the correct answer so that they are irrelevant. However, in order to prevent such possible biases, we tried to keep the ditransitive structure in the paraphrase (see e.g. the paraphrases in example (34) and Appendix II), and we further tried not to deviate too much from the wording used in the example. Thus, in all the paraphrases of example (34), the subject and the dative object are the same (except for paraphrase (3) which has a different dative object, namely *ihrem Freund* 'her friend', but this is a synonym of *ihrem Verlobten*, 'her fiancé'). Table 2 summarizes the results for Part 2 of the test among Italian and French-speaking learners.

Table 2: Results of Part 2 of the test by Italian and French-speaking learners

	Italian learners		French-speaking learners	
	Correct answer	Know the phraseologism[15]	Correct answer	Know the phraseologism
10 sentences with 4 possible answers	37.4%	8.1%	70%	31.2%

The results suggest that the French-speaking students achieved much better results than the Italian students. In our search for an explanation we first thought that the Belgian students who grow up in a bilingual country with both French and Flemish (which corresponds to the Belgian Dutch language) are privileged as they probably know corresponding phraseologisms in Flemish. This language is, just like German, a Germanic language so that we can expect to find similar expressions in both languages. But when looking up the 10 phraseologisms of Part 2 and 3, it struck us that none of them has a corresponding equivalent form in Dutch. Only example *Er zeigte mir die kalte Schulter* has an approximate counterpart in Flemish, i.e. *de rug toekeren*, which means 'to turn the back'. A possible, still very tentative explanation for the difference in the results for both groups is the fact that the Belgian students have to learn phraseologisms at an early stage in the learning procedure, whereas in Italy the domain of phraseology tends to be ignored in the learning process (see Mollica 2015). Furthermore, Belgians are confronted with at least two different languages from early childhood, i.e. the Romance language French and the Germanic language

---

[15] This is the result for all correct and incorrect answers.

Flemish. This early bilingualism fosters the learning of further foreign languages, especially of a language which belongs to the same Germanic family, namely German.

A closer look at the results by both groups separately makes it possible to get a more fine-grained view and to conclude that the mother tongue of the test groups plays a major role in the understanding process. Let us start with the results of Part 2 by the Italian students, shown in Table 3.

Table 3: Results of Part 2 for Italian learners

	Idiom	Correct answer	Know the phraseologism
1[16]	*Peter zeigt seiner Schwester die Krallen.*	40%	7%
2	*Isabella gab ihrem Verlobten einen Korb.*	7%	7%
3	*Die Mutter verpasste ihrer Tochter einen Denkzettel.*	47%	0%
4	*Der Bauer versprach seiner Freundin goldene Berge.*	47%	33%
5	*Der Chef legte Anna Steine in den Weg.*	53%	13%
6	*Er zeigte mir die kalte Schulter.*	53%	0%
7	*Ich drücke dir die Daumen.*	47%	7%
8	*Sie kann ihm das Wasser nicht reichen.*	20%	7%
9	*Der LKW-Fahrer zeigte den anderen Autofahrern den Vogel.*	40%	0%
10	*Antonio gab seiner Freundin den Laufpass.*	20%	7%

It can first be observed that the Italian students hardly ever claim to know the phraseologisms of the test although these belong to common ways of expression in German – except for example (4) *Der Bauer versprach seiner Freundin goldene Berge* where 33% of the learners claim to know the expression. The best results for the multiple choice are achieved for examples which have equivalent expressions in Italian, cf. examples (5) *Der Chef legte Anna Steine in den Weg*, lit. 'The boss laid to Anna stones in the way' (= 'The boss put obstacles in Anna's way') and (6) *Er zeigte mir die kalte Schulter*, lit. 'He showed to me the cold shoulder' (= 'He gave me the cold shoulder'). The corresponding Italian expression for example (5) has a similar ditransitive structure, but it encodes a different image: *mettere i bastoni tra le ruote a qualcuno*, lit. 'to put somebody sticks into wheels'. In both German and Italian it is the same idea of an obstacle which is used. This can probably explain the better result (53%) for the understanding of this example. Example (6) triggers the same image in German and Italian with the metonymical use of 'shoulder' in *voltare le spalle a qualcuno*, lit. 'to turn somebody the shoulder'. Therefore it is amazing that only 53% of the Italian

---

[16] Some of the examples in the tables have already been mentioned before with a different number. In the following discussion we refer to the numbers of the examples in the tables.

students selected the correct answer. A possible explanation resides in the additional use of *kalt* 'cold' in the German phraseologism, which may have been perceived as a distractor by the students. But as suggested by one of the reviewers, it could also be due to the learners' avoidance of idioms that look too similar to those in their L1 (see Kellermann's (1977, 1978) hypothesis of 'non-transferability of idioms' with learners). Kellermann (1977) presented English translations of picturesque Dutch idioms to Dutch learners of English. "What happened was that students tended to reject these translations as not being good English, irrespective of whether these idioms existed in English or not" (Kellermann 1978: 61).

The relatively good scores (47%) for example (4) *Der Bauer versprach seiner Freundin goldene Berge*, lit. 'The farmer promised his girlfriend golden mountains' (= 'The farmer promised his girlfriend the moon') or (7) *Ich drücke dir die Daumen*, lit. 'I press you the thumbs' (= 'We keep our fingers crossed for you') are possibly also the result of the presence in Italian of similar expressions, namely *promettere a qualcuno mari e monti*, lit. 'to promise seas and mountains to someone', or *incrociare le dita per qualcuno*, lit. 'to cross the fingers for somebody'. In example (4), the German expression *goldene Berge* and the Italian *mari* and *monti* are used metaphorically to express something wonderful. Example (7) contains the expression of a somatism (Burger 2010: 47) for a non-verbal behavior (here fingers crossed). Somatisms are quite similar in our Western world, that is why phraseologisms with such expressions can be more easily understood by speakers of different speech communities. Example (2), on the other hand, does not have an Italian counterpart, which can explain that only 7% of the students selected the correct meaning.

Let us now look at the detailed results for the French-speaking learners (see Table 4).

Table 4: Results of Part 2 for Belgian French-speaking learners

	Idiom	Correct Answer	Know the phraseologism
1	*Peter zeigt seiner Schwester die Krallen.*	80%	20%
2	*Isabella gab ihrem Verlobten einen Korb.*	13%	13%
3	*Die Mutter verpasste ihrer Tochter einen Denkzettel.*	67%	20%
4	*Der Bauer versprach seiner Freundin goldene Berge.*	100%	60%
5	*Der Chef legte Anna Steine in den Weg.*	93%	60%
6	*Er zeigte mir die kalte Schulter.*	100%	33%
7	*Ich drücke dir die Daumen.*	80%	73%
8	*Sie kann ihm das Wasser nicht reichen.*	27%	13%
9	*Der LKW-Fahrer zeigte den anderen Autofahrern den Vogel.*	80%	13%
10	*Antonio gab seiner Freundin den Laufpass.*	60%	7%

All in all the results for the French-speaking learners are better than those for the Italian students. Possible explanations have been discussed above. Still, it is interesting to observe that the Belgian group has the same understanding difficulties with example (2) *Isabella gab ihrem Verlobten einen Korb*, lit. 'Isabella gave her fiancé a basket' (= 'Isabella turned her fiancé down)' or with example (8) *Sie kann ihm das Wasser nicht reichen*, lit. 'She cannot reach to him the water' (= 'She cannot have his level/competence'). However, both examples have to be distinguished in the understanding process. While in example (2) the lack of understanding is dependent on the opacity of the accusative object *Korb* 'basket', the understanding difficulties with (8) more likely depend on the whole expression – even if additionally the verb *reichen* ('reach') may not be known to learners. These idiomatic expressions can only be understood diachronically (compare Duden 1998: 409, 783). French being a Romance language like Italian, it is not surprising that it has corresponding phraseologisms very close to the Italian expressions we discussed above, e.g. *mettre des bâtons dans les roues à quelqu'un*, lit. 'to put somebody sticks into wheels' for example (5) or *tourner le dos à quelqu'un*, lit. 'to turn the back to somebody' for example (6), to name just a few.

4.4 Part 3

The same 10 examples tested in Part 2 were again used in Part 3. This time they were used in a clear context and we asked the learners to paraphrase the meaning of the phraseologisms. Here is an example of such a task:

(35) *Als Mario sie fragte, ob sie ihn heiraten wollte,*
<u>*gab Isabella ihm einen Korb*</u>, *weil sie ihn nicht*
mehr liebte.
Bedeutung:
....
....
....
....
....

(Lit. 'When Mario asked her if she wanted to marry him,
<u>Isabella gave him a basket </u>because she did not love
him anymore.'
Meaning: ....)

As the same examples were tested in Parts 2 and 3, Part 3 was a kind of double-check to see whether the learners had guessed more of the meaning of the phraseologisms in Part 2 than expected. With this third test part it was further possible to see whether the context played a major role for the disambiguation of the phraseologisms which might not have been understood in Parts 1 and 2. Table 5 provides a comparison of the results of Parts 2 and 3 for both groups.

Table 5: Comparison of correct answers in Parts 2 and 3 for Italian and French-speaking learners

	Italian learners	French-speaking learners
Correct answers Part 2	37.4%	70%
Correct answers Part 3	67.3%	74.5%

It is obvious that the Italian group makes real progress in the understanding of the phraseologisms thanks to the contextual embedding of the phraseologisms. Table 6 shows the detailed results for the Italian learners.

Table 6: Results of Parts 2 and 3 for Italian learners

	Idiom	Correct answer in Part 2	Correct answer in Part 3
1	Peter zeigt seiner Schwester die Krallen.	40%	33%
2	Isabella gab ihrem Verlobten einen Korb.	7%	60%
3	Die Mutter verpasste ihrer Tochter einen Denkzettel.	47%	47%
4	Der Bauer versprach seiner Freundin goldene Berge.	47%	87%
5	Der Chef legte Anna Steine in den Weg.	53%	80%
6	Er zeigte mir die kalte Schulter.	53%	93%
7	Ich drücke dir die Daumen.	47%	93%
8	Sie kann ihm das Wasser nicht reichen.	20%	67%
9	Der LKW-Fahrer zeigte den anderen Autofahrern den Vogel.	40%	33%
10	Antonio gab seiner Freundin den Laufpass.	20%	80%

As could be expected, the score has improved in the majority of the test items (7 out of 10). It is especially interesting to observe that better results are obtained even for the ditransitive phraseologisms which have no counterpart in Italian or which are very hard to understand because of their metaphorical and/or metonymical character, e.g. example (2) with a result of 60% in Part 3 as opposed to 7% in Part 2. A similar observation can be made for example (8) with 67% of right answers in Part 3 as opposed to only 20% in Part 2, or for example (10) with 80% of correct answers in Part 3 as against 20% in Part 2.

Because French-speaking students already achieved good results in Part 2 – which led us to expect that they already knew many phraseologisms – their progress in Part 3 is only minimal (improvement in 4 out of 10 test items). But still in the more fine-grained analysis we can observe a few interesting tendencies, see Table 7.

Table 7: Results of Parts 2 and 3 for Belgian French-speaking learners

	Idiom	Correct answer in Part 2	Correct answer in Part 3
1	Peter zeigt seiner Schwester die Krallen.	80%	6%
2	Isabella gab ihrem Verlobten einen Korb.	13%	73%
3	Die Mutter verpasste ihrer Tochter einen Denkzettel.	67%	67%
4	Der Bauer versprach seiner Freundin goldene Berge.	100%	93%
5	Der Chef legte Anna Steine in den Weg.	93%	87%
6	Er zeigte mir die kalte Schulter.	100%	100%
7	Ich drücke dir die Daumen.	80%	100%
8	Sie kann ihm das Wasser nicht reichen.	27%	46%
9	Der LKW-Fahrer zeigte den anderen Autofahrern den Vogel.	80%	80%
10	Antonio gab seiner Freundin den Laufpass.	60%	93%

As with Italian learners the opaque phraseologisms (2) and (8) are better understood by French-speaking learners when used in context: 73% in Part 3 as opposed to 13% for example (2) and 46% in Part 3 as against 27% in Part 2 for example (8). Surprisingly, example (1) got very bad results in context in Part 3 (only 6%), whereas 80% gave a correct answer in Part 2. A similar decreasing tendency was observed with Italian learners (only 33% in Part 3 as against 40% in Part 2). We can only explain the decreasing tendency by the fact that the context must have been misleading or by Kellermann's (1977, 1978) hypothesis of non-transferability of idioms among learners.

In the next section, we will see how the insights gained by the experiments and our observations can be exploited to develop an efficient teaching methodology.

5 Teaching methodology

As we have seen in the previous sections, ditransitive phraseologisms have the same argument structure and abstract meaning as prototypical ditransitive constructions. Our hypothesis is that if learners recognize the same pattern and meaning in ditransitive phraseologisms as in non-figurative ditransitive constructions, we can exploit this similarity for a more efficient learning and teaching of such phraseologisms. Our expectation about the intuitive categorization of ditransitive phraseologisms as ditransitive constructions has been confirmed in Part 1 of the test with both groups of learners. Most examples of ditransitive phraseologisms were classified by the participants as ditransitive constructions. This is a good starting point for a proper teaching methodology: teachers can first refer to the prototypical, non-phraseological ditransitive construction with the idea of transfer (concrete or abstract). Then, following the principle of structural persistence defined by Konopka and Bock (2009), the understanding process can be extended to cases of ditransitive phraseologisms, especially with verbs with a ditransitive valency, e.g. *geben/zeigen/versprechen*.

To distinguish ditransitive phraseologisms from non-phraseological ditransitive constructions, one will of course further need to talk about the figurative use of the accusative object or of the whole construction, as well as about the different degrees of idiomaticity (compare again examples (13) and (21) in Section 3.2). Both concepts of conceptual metaphor and metonymy (Lakoff and Johnson 1980) are needed to explain the idiomatic use of the ditransitive phraseologisms: "The conceptual mappings (i.e. the systematic correspondences between the source and target domains) help define the specific meaning of a given idiom" (Beréndi, Csábi, and Kövecses 2008: 73). It has been shown in the scientific literature (see Boers and Lindstromberg 2008: 33; Beréndi, Csábi, and Kövecses 2008: 81) that fixed expressions whose meaning can be explained with metaphors – and also by metonymy – are more transparent and easier to learn:

> Cognitive linguists [...] have shown that the imagery behind an idiom can easily be resuscitated either by enhancing people's awareness of the underlying CMs [conceptual metaphors] or by tracing the idiom back to its original, literal context (e.g. Gibbs 1994). (Boers and Lindstromberg 2008: 33)

Boers (2011: 229) describes how conceptual metaphor can be concretely exploited in foreign language teaching: "[T]he students may be asked to think of reasons for the existence of the given conceptual metaphors (i.e., their grounding in physical experience)". They may further be asked to give some associations related to the figurative units in the phraseologisms. Teachers have a wide range of instructional possibilities.

As we saw earlier, a further decisive element which facilitates the understanding of the phraseologisms' meaning has to do with the presence or not of a similar phraseologism in the learner's mother tongue. As we have seen, example (10) *Peter zeigt seiner Schwester die Krallen* (lit. 'Peter shows his sister the claws' = 'Peter threatens his sister') has parallels in Italian and French and is syntactically and semantico-pragmatically similar. In contrast, example (13) *Isabella gab ihrem Verlobten einen Korb* (lit. 'Isabella gave her fiancé a basket' = 'Isabella turned her fiancé down') does not have a one-to-one counterpart in French or Italian. Italian has the idiom *rispondere/dare (il due di) picche a qualcuno*, lit. 'to answer/give (two) spades to somebody', which has a similar meaning and syntactic structure, but a different image: *picca* 'spade' is one of the four symbols on playing cards. French has the idiomatic expression *envoyer promener quelqu'un*, lit. 'to send somebody stroll', also with a similar meaning, but with another syntactic form. Since different metaphorical and metonymical concepts are used in French and Italian on the one hand and in German on the other, it is understandable that Italian and French speakers will not associate the German example with the corresponding idiom in their mother tongue. That is why this German phraseologism remains opaque to most Italian or French-speaking learners.

6 Conclusions and perspectives

Because of their idiomatic status, phraseologisms do not have any priority in so-called 'DaF-Unterricht' ('Teaching of German as a foreign language'). German being a morphologically complex language, teachers often concentrate on grammar and less on phraseologisms. The Construction Grammar model offers a unified framework for the teaching of phraseological and non-phraseological ditransitive constructions. First, the definition of an abstract ditransitive construction, prototypically linked to (concrete or abstract) transfer semantics, is a way of instantiating the grammar-lexicon continuum (see also Stathi 2011: 151) rather than seeing the two linguistic domains as separate fields. As a result of this continuum, language units are learned in larger structures, i.e. as usage-based items. Such an approach fosters a more authentic way of teaching a foreign language.

Because of the postulate of an abstract ditransitive construction that can be realized either in a literal or in an idiomatic way, instantiations of ditransitive constructions should not be considered independently, but as linked to each other in a motivated way, i.e. by conceptual metaphor and/or metonymy. It is generally admitted in foreign language teaching (see Boers, De Rycker, and De Knop 2010) that motivation enhances learning and further memorization (Boers 2011: 231; Boers and Lindstromberg 2008: 33–36).

There is also a side effect to such a unified teaching methodology. Because of the morphological complexity of the German ditransitive construction with its different cases, learners often have difficulties when it comes to the selection of the accusative and/or the dative case. There are even additional difficulties depending on the nominal vs. pronominal realization of the accusative and dative object (see Mollica 2015). As learners usually show a great interest in idiomatic expressions, the learning and repetition of phraseological ditransitive constructions can help fix ditransitive structures with their morphological cases in their minds. To conclude, using the link with phraseological ditransitive constructions to explain and process ditransitive constructions offers the possibility of 'dedramatizing' and motivating the learning of such structures.

Because of the limited number of phraseologisms analyzed, the results of our study have to be taken with some reservations. Also, we have not tested on a larger scale yet whether the proposed teaching methodology indeed fosters the learning of ditransitive phraseologisms, but we are confident that future research projects will bring the necessary positive evidence.

References

Baicchi, Annalisa. 2013. The ontological status of constructions in the mind of Italian University learners of English: Psycholinguistic evidence from a sentence-sorting experiment. In Laura Di Michele (ed.), *Regenerating community, territory, voices*, 26–32. Napoli: Liguori.

Bencini, Giulia & Adele E. Goldberg. 2000. The contribution of argument structure constructions to sentence meaning. *Journal of Memory and Language* 43. 640–651.

Beréndi, Márta, Szilvia Csábi & Zoltán Kövecses. 2008. Using conceptual metaphors and metonymies in vocabulary teaching. In Frank Boers & Seth Lindstromberg (eds.), *Cognitive linguistic approaches to teaching vocabulary and phraseology*, 65–99. Berlin & New York: de Gruyter.

Boas, Hans. 2003. *A constructional approach to resultatives*. Stanford: CSLI Publications.

Boas, Hans. 2013. Cognitive Construction Grammar. In Thomas Hoffmann & Graeme Trousdale (eds.), *The Oxford handbook of construction grammar*, 233–254. Oxford: Oxford University Press.

Boers, Frank. 2011. Cognitive Semantic ways of teaching figurative phrases. *Annual Review of Cognitive Linguistics* 9(1). 227–261.

Boers, Frank, Antoon De Rycker & Sabine De Knop. (eds.). 2010. Fostering language teaching efficiency through cognitive linguistics: Introduction. In Sabine De Knop, Frank Boers & Antoon De Rycker (eds.), *Fostering language teaching efficiency through cognitive linguistics*, 1–26. Berlin & New York: Mouton de Gruyter.

Boers, Frank & Seth Lindstromberg. 2008. How cognitive linguistics can foster effective vocabulary teaching. In Frank Boers & Seth Lindstromberg (eds.), *Cognitive linguistic approaches to teaching vocabulary and phraseology*, 1–61. Berlin & New York: de Gruyter.

Burger, Harald. 2010 [1998]. *Phraseologie. Eine Einführung am Beispiel des Deutschen*, 4th edn. Berlin: Schmidt.
Chafe, Wallace. 1968. Idiomaticity as an anomaly in the Chomskyan paradigm. *Foundations of Language* 4. 109–127.
Della Costanza, Mario A. & Mollica, Fabio. 2015. 'Parli turco'/ 'me suena a chino/'Das kommt mir spanisch vor' – Nationalitätsbezeichnungen im Sprachvergleich: einige Überlegungen. In Eva Lavric & Wolfgang Pöckl (eds.), *Comparatio delectat II*, 287-305. Frankfurt am Main: Peter Lang.
Dobrovol'skij, Dmitrij. 2011. Phraseologie und Konstruktionsgrammatik. In Alexander Lasch & Alexander Ziem (eds.), *Konstruktionsgrammatik III. Aktuelle Fragen und Lösungsansätze*, 110–130. Tübingen: Stauffenburg.
Donalies, Elke. 2009. *Basiswissen Deutsche Phraseologie*. Tübingen: Francke.
Duden. 1998. *Redewendungen und sprichwörtliche Redensarten*. Mannheim: Dudenverlag.
Ekberg, Edith. 2012. *Aspekte des Dativs. Zur Relation zwischen der Dativ-DP und der Ereignisstruktur der Verben in ditransitiven Konstruktionen im Deutschen*. Lund: Media-Tryck.
Fillmore, Charles J., Paul Kay & Mary Catherine O'Connor. 1988. Regularity and idiomaticity in grammatical constructions: The case of 'let alone'. *Language* 64(3). 501–538.
Fleischer, Wolfgang. 1997. *Phraseologie der deutschen Gegenwartssprache*. Tübingen: Niemeyer.
Fraser, Bruce. 1970. Idioms within a transformational grammar. *Foundations of Language* 6. 22–42.
Gibbs, Raymond W. 1995. Idiomaticity and human cognition. In Martin Everaert, Erik-Jan van der Linden, André Schenk, Rob Schreuder & Robert Schreuder (eds.), *Idioms: Structural and psychological perspectives*, 97–116. Hillsdale, NJ: Lawrence Earlbaum Associates.
Goldberg, Adele E. 1995. *Constructions. A construction grammar approach to argument structure*. Chicago and London: The University of Chicago Press.
Goldberg, Adele E. 2006. *Constructions at work. The nature of generalization in language*. Oxford: Oxford University Press.
Gries, Stefan. 2008. Phraseology and linguistic theory: A brief survey. In Sylviane Granger & Fanny Meunier (eds.), *Phraseology: An interdisciplinary* perspective, 3–25. Amsterdam & Philadelphia: John Benjamins Publishing Company.
Herbst, Thomas. 2011. The status of generalizations. In Thomas Herbst & Anatol Stefanowitsch (eds.), *Argument structure – Valency and/or constructions? ZAA: Zeitschrift für Anglistik und Amerikanistik* LIX(4). 347–367.
Kay, Paul. 2005. Argument structure constructions and the argument-adjunct distinction. In Myriam Fried & Hans Boas (eds.), *Grammatical constructions. Back to the roots*, 71–100. Amsterdam & Philadelphia: John Benjamins.
Kellermann, Eric. 1977. Toward a characterization of the strategy of transfer in second language learning. *The Interlanguage Studies Bulletin* 2. 58–145.
Kellermann, Eric. 1978. Transfer and non-transfer: Where we are now. *Studies in Second Language Acquisition* 2. 37–57.
Konopka, Agnieszka E. & Kathryn Bock. 2009. Lexical or syntactic control of sentence formulation? Structural generalizations from idiom production. *Cognitive Psychology* 58. 68–101.
Lakoff, George & Mark Johnson. 1980. *Metaphors we live by*. Chicago: The University of Chicago Press.
Matlock, Teene & Roberto R. Heredia. 2002. Understanding phrasal verbs in monolinguals and bilinguals. In Roberto R. Heredia & Jeanette Altarriba (eds.), *Bilingual sentence processing*, 251–274. Amsterdam: Elsevier.

Meibauer, Jörg, Ulrike Demske, Jochen Geilfuß-Wolfgang, Jürgen Pafel, Karl Heinz Ramers, Monika Rothweiler & Markus Steinbach. 2002. *Einführung in die germanistische Linguistik.* Stuttgart: J.B. Metzler.

Mellado Blanco, Carmen. 2015. Phrasem-Konstruktionen und lexikalische Idiom-Varianten: der Fall der komparativen Phraseme des Deutschen. In Stefan Engelberg, Meike Meliss, Kristel Proost & Edeltraud Winkler (eds.), *Argumentstrukturen zwischen Valenz und Konstruktionen.* Tübingen: Narr.

Mollica, Fabio. 2015. Die Rolle der Kontrastivität in der Phraseodidaktik: eine kognitive und konstruktionsgrammatische Perspektive. In Claudio Di Meola & Daniela Puato (eds.), *Deutsch kontrastiv aus italienischer Sicht. Phraseologie, Temporalität und mehr,* 13–35. Frankfurt am Main: Peter Lang.

Mollica, Fabio & Julia Kuhn. 2013. Konstruktionen mit freiem Dativ in der Konstruktions- und Valenzgrammatik. In Sabine De Knop, Fabio Mollica & Julia Kuhn (eds.), *Konstruktionsgrammatik in den romanischen Sprachen,* 227–259. Frankfurt am Main: Peter Lang.

Nemoto, Noriko. 1998. On the polysemy of the ditransitive 'save': The role of frame semantics in Construction Grammar. *English Linguistics* 15. 219–242.

Primus, Beatrice. 2012. *Semantische Rollen.* Heidelberg: Universitätsverlag Winter.

Proost, Kristel. 2014. Ditransitive transfer constructions and their prepositional variants in German and Romanian: An empirical survey. In Ruxandra Cosma, Stefan Engelberg, Susan Schlotthauer & Gisela Zifonun (eds.), *Komplexe Argumentstrukturen. Kontrastive Untersuchungen zum Deutschen, Rumänischen und Englischen,* 19-84. Berlin & Boston: de Gruyter.

Stathi, Katerina. 2011. Idiome und Konstruktionsgrammatik: im Spannungsfeld zwischen Lexikon und Grammatik. In Alexander Lasch & Alexander Ziem (eds.), *Konstruktionsgrammatik III. Aktuelle Fragen und Lösungsansätze,* 149–163. Tübingen: Stauffenburg.

Stefanowitsch, Anatol. 2011. Argument structure: Item-based or distributed? In Thomas Herbst & Anatol Stefanowitsch (eds.), *Argument structure – Valency and/or constructions? ZAA: Zeitschrift für Anglistik und Amerikanistik* LIX(4). 369–386.

Thieroff, Rolf & Petra M. Vogel. 2011. *Flexion.* Heidelberg: Winter.

Valenzuela Manzanares, Javier & Ana María Rojo López. 2008. What can language learners tell us about constructions? In Sabine De Knop & Teun De Rycker (eds.), *Cognitive approaches to pedagogical grammar: A volume in honour of René Dirven,* 197–230. Berlin & New York: Mouton de Gruyter.

Weinreich, Uriel. 1969. Problems in the analysis of idioms. In Jaan Puhvel (ed.), *Substance and structure of language,* 23–81. Los Angeles: University of California Press.

Welke, Klaus. 2011. *Valenzgrammatik des Deutschen.* Eine Einführung. Berlin & New York: de Gruyter.

Wulff, Stephanie. 2012. Idiomaticity. In Peter Robinson (ed.), *The Routledge encyclopedia of second language acquisition,* 291–293. London: Routledge.

Ziem, Alexander & Alexander Lasch. 2013. *Konstruktionsgrammatik. Konzepte und Grundlagen gebrauchsbasierter Ansätze.* Berlin & Boston: de Gruyter.

Zifonun, Gisela, Ludger Hoffmann & Bruno Strecker (eds.). 1997. *Grammatik der deutschen Sprache.* Schriften des Instituts für deutsche Sprache. Berlin & New York: de Gruyter.

Appendix I

a) Datum: ....
b) Geburtsdatum (TAG/MONAT/JAHR): ....
c) Muttersprache: ....
d) Ich lerne Deutsch seit .... Jahren
e) Ich spreche noch folgende Fremdsprachen: ....

Part I

Sortieren Sie bitte folgende Sätze nach Ähnlichkeit in der Form und/oder der Bedeutung der Elemente im Satz! Schreiben Sie die Beispiele erneut auf und gruppieren Sie die ähnlichen Sätze untereinander. Verwenden Sie dafür die Kästchen auf den nächsten Seiten. Sie können so viele Gruppen bilden, wie Sie möchten (nicht alle Kästchen müssen besetzt werden; es gibt auch keine falsche Antwort)!

1. Ich musste dem Verlag 1000 Euro für die Publikation des Buches geben.
2. Ich drücke Dir die Daumen.
3. Peter zeigt seiner Schwester die Krallen.
4. Die Mutter verpasste ihrer Tochter einen Denkzettel.
5. Der Bauer versprach seiner Freundin goldene Berge.
6. Mein Chef hat mir keinen Urlaub gegeben.
7. Leider verpasste Maria ihren Zug.
8. Sie machte ihm schöne Augen.
9. Die Kuh gibt Milch.
10. Isabella gab ihrem Verlobten einen Korb.
11. Die junge Frau lacht viel.
12. Er zeigte mir die kalte Schulter.
13. Ich esse gerne Pasta.
14. Sie reichte ihm das Wasser nicht.
15. Maria bewundert ihren Professor.
16. Die Müllers geben eine Party in ihrer neuen Villa.
17. Die Jugendlichen zeigten dem Touristen den Weg.
18. Dem Lehrer platzte der Kragen.
19. Der LKW-Fahrer zeigte den anderen Autofahrern den Vogel.
20. Meine Eltern fliegen jeden Sommer in die Türkei.
21. Ich huste dir etwas.
22. Die Dienerin machte die Betten.
23. Er zeigte auf die vielen Menschen.
24. Meine neue Freundin kommt aus Schweden.
25. Antonio gab seiner Freundin den Laufpass.

Appendix II

Geburtsdatum (TAGTAG/MONATMONAT/JAHRJAHR) ....

Part II

Was bedeuten die folgenden Sätze? Kreuzen Sie bitte die richtige Antwort an.
1. *Peter zeigt seiner Schwester die Krallen.*
    Bedeutet: (1) Peter gibt seiner Schwester ein Zeichen seiner Liebe.
    (2) Peter spricht seiner Schwester eine Drohung aus.
    (3) Peter zeigt seiner Schwester seine blaugefärbten Nägel.
    (4) Peter bietet seiner Schwester seine Hilfe an.
    – Ich kenne die Bedeutung.
    – Ich kenne die Bedeutung nicht, habe sie erraten.
2. *Isabella gab ihrem Verlobten einen Korb.*
    Bedeutet: (1) Isabella schenkte ihrem Verlobten einen Korb Obst.
    (2) Isabella erzählte ihrem Verlobten eine Lüge.
    (3) Isabella sagte ihrem Freund, dass sie ihn nicht heiraten würde.
    (4) Isabella erzählte ihrem Verlobten die Wahrheit.
    – Ich kenne die Bedeutung.
    – Ich kenne die Bedeutung nicht, habe sie erraten.
3. *Die Mutter verpasste ihrer Tochter einen Denkzettel.*
    Bedeutet: (1) Die Mutter gab ihrer Tochter eine Einkaufsliste.
    (2) Die Mutter schenkte ihrer Tochter ein Spiel.
    (3) Die Mutter erteilte ihrer Tochter eine Lehre, damit sie ihren Fehler nicht noch einmal wiederholt.
    (4) Die Mutter half ihrer Tochter, die Hausaufgaben zu machen.
    – Ich kenne die Bedeutung.
    – Ich kenne die Bedeutung nicht, habe sie erraten.
4. *Der Bauer versprach seiner Freundin goldene Berge.*
    Bedeutet: (1) Der Bauer versprach seiner Freundin, große Berge zu besteigen.
    (2) Der Bauer versprach seiner Freundin großartige Dinge.
    (3) Der Bauer versprach seiner Freundin, eine Goldmine zu finden.
    (4) Der Bauer versprach seiner Freundin einen Goldring.
    – Ich kenne die Bedeutung.
    – Ich kenne die Bedeutung nicht, habe sie erraten.

5. *Jemandem Steine in den Weg legen*
   Bedeutet: (1) Jemandem Schwierigkeiten bereiten.
   (2) Für Jemand schöne Steine sammeln.
   (3) Jemandem das Leben einfach machen.
   (4) Jemandem Diamanten schenken.
   – Ich kenne die Bedeutung.
   – Ich kenne die Bedeutung nicht, habe sie erraten.

6. *Er zeigte mir die kalte Schulter.*
   Bedeutet: (1) Er zeigte mir seine Verletzung an der Schulter.
   (2) Er zeigte mir, wie man nicht zu sehr schwitzt.
   (3) Er zeigte mir, wie man die Schulter verbindet.
   (4) Er zeigte mir, dass es ihm egal ist.
   – Ich kenne die Bedeutung.
   – Ich kenne die Bedeutung nicht, habe sie erraten.

7. *Ich drücke Dir die Daumen.*
   Bedeutet: (1) Ich spreche dir eine Drohung aus.
   (2) Ich wünsche dir viel Glück.
   (3) Ich breche dir den Finger ab.
   (4) Ich bringe dir Unglück.
   – Ich kenne die Bedeutung.
   – Ich kenne die Bedeutung nicht, habe sie erraten.

8. *Sie kann ihm das Wasser nicht reichen.*
   Bedeutet: (1) Sie erreichte sein Niveau nicht.
   (2) Er hatte keinen Durst.
   (3) Sie war egoistisch ihm gegenüber.
   (4) Sie war unfreundlich ihm gegenüber.
   – Ich kenne die Bedeutung.
   – Ich kenne die Bedeutung nicht, habe sie erraten.

9. *Der LKW-Fahrer zeigte den anderen Autofahrern einen Vogel.*
   Bedeutet: (1) Der LKW-Fahrer zeigte auf seinen Mitfahrer, der wie ein Vogel sang.
   (2) Der LKW-Fahrer zeigte den anderen Autofahrern, dass ein Vogel im Graben lag.
   (3) Der LKW-Fahrer schenkte den anderen Autofahrern einen Vogel im Käfig.
   (4) Er zeigte den anderen Autofahrern, dass sie nicht richtig bei Verstand sind.
   – Ich kenne die Bedeutung.
   – Ich kenne die Bedeutung nicht, habe sie erraten.

10. *Antonio gab seiner Freundin den Laufpass.*
    Bedeutet: (1) Antonio verließ seine Freundin.
    　　　　　(2) Antonio heiratete seine Freundin.
    　　　　　(3) Antonio betrog seine Freundin.
    　　　　　(4) Antonios Freundin bekam einen neuen Ausweis.
    – Ich kenne die Bedeutung.
    – Ich kenne die Bedeutung nicht, habe sie erraten.

Appendix III

Geburtsdatum (TAGTAG/MONATMONAT/JAHRJAHR) ....

Part III

Was bedeuten folgende Sätze? Paraphrasieren Sie die unterstrichenen Satzteile bitte (auch in Ihrer Muttersprache):

1. *Wie lange will Peter sich die Frechheit dieses Mädchen noch gefallen lassen! Es wird Zeit, dass <u>er ihr mal die Krallen zeigt</u>.*
   Bedeutung:
   ....

2. *Als Mario sie fragte, ob sie ihn heiraten wollte, <u>gab Isabella ihm einen Korb</u>, weil sie ihn nicht mehr liebte.*
   Bedeutung:
   ....

3. *Mathias hat dem Englischlehrer erzählt, wer den Ball durch die Fensterscheibe geworfen hat: „Peter ist so ein Verräter! Aber <u>wir haben ihm einen Denkzettel verpasst</u>, solche Prügel hat er noch nie gekriegt."*
   Bedeutung:
   ....

4. *Oft <u>verspricht eine politische Partei ihren Wählern goldene Berge</u>, aber wenn sie dann die Regierung übernimmt, ist alles vergessen.*
   Bedeutung:
   ....

5. Als Anna Karriere machen wollte, <u>legte ihr unser Chef Steine in den Weg</u>, weil er sie nicht mochte.
   Bedeutung:
   ....

6. Mario behauptete immer, mein bester Freund zu sein. Aber als ich seine Hilfe brauchte, <u>hat er mir die kalte Schulter gezeigt</u>.
   Bedeutung:
   ....

7. Ich wünsche dir viel Glück bei deinem Examen und <u>drücke dir ganz fest die Daumen</u>.
   Bedeutung:
   ....

8. Anton ist sehr klug und hat im Ausland studiert, <u>seine Freundin kann ihm aber das Wasser nicht reichen</u>!
   Bedeutung:
   ....

9. Der LKW-Fahrer regte sich über das Verhalten der anderen Autofahrer und <u>zeigte ihnen einen Vogel</u>.
   Bedeutung:
   ....

10. Nachdem Maria herausgefunden hat, dass ihr Mann sie ständig betrügt, <u>hat sie ihm den Laufpass gegeben</u>.
    Bedeutung:
    ....

Min-Chang Sung and Hyun-Kwon Yang
Effects of construction-centered instruction on Korean students' learning of English transitive resultative constructions[1]

Abstract: The English transitive resultative construction (TRC) is considered one of the most difficult constructions for learners of English as a foreign language (EFL). The present study investigates the instructional effects of construction-centered teaching on the learning of the TRC by Korean EFL students. It also explores whether verb types (i.e., light and heavy verbs) influence the learning of the TRC and to what extent the teaching of the TRC influences the correct use of other basic constructions in English, e.g., the intransitive motion, the caused-motion, and the ditransitive constructions. Ninety-three Korean EFL students were divided into two groups and were provided with either construction-centered (CC) or form-centered (FC) instruction. CC-instruction focused on the constructional properties of the TRC, whereas FC-instruction emphasized its syntactic composition. Prior to instruction, participants were assigned a Korean-to-English and an English-to-Korean translation task. After instruction, the same types of tasks were given as a posttest. Results reveal, first, that CC-instruction was more effective than FC-instruction, though both helped participants learn the TRC. Second, the light verb (e.g., *make*) played a significant and constructive role in facilitating the learning of the TRC. Finally, instruction of the TRC positively affected the learning of other basic constructions in English.

Keywords: Construction Grammar; argument structure constructions; hierarchical network; transitive resultative construction; light verbs; effect of instruction; construction-centered vs. form-centered; Korean-speaking English learners

1 Introduction

Constructions are basic units of language that have been known to be acquired naturally through everyday communicative experience (Goldberg 1995, 2006).

---

[1] Acknowledgement: this chapter is based on a paper with the title "Effects of instruction on the learning of the English transitive resultative construction", presented at the *Constructionist Approaches to Language Pedagogy* conference, Université Saint-Louis, Brussels, Belgium, on November 8, 2013. We wish to thank the editors and anonymous reviewers for their valuable and constructive comments on several versions of the manuscript.

Nonetheless, they are reported not to be readily available to foreign language learners, even though a certain level of competence to use them is a prerequisite for successful communication (Hijazo-Gascón, Cadierno, and Ibarretxe-Antuñano this volume; Fredsgaard 2013; Kim, Choi, and Yang 2013; Lee 2012). Among the many types of constructions, the English transitive resultative construction (hereafter TRC), which is defined as the pairing of the form *Subj-V-Obj-RP*[2] and the meaning *X causes Y to become Z_{state}*, has been noted as particularly challenging for Korean EFL learners: they have been known to have trouble not only producing TRC sentences (Rah 2014), but also comprehending them (Lee and Kim 2011).

The present study explores effects of instruction on the learning of the transitive resultative construction by Korean EFL learners. The study also examines whether verb types (i.e., light and heavy verbs) influence the learning of the TRC and to what extent the teaching of TRCs influences the correct use of other basic constructions in English.[3] In order to address these questions, 93 Korean secondary school students were divided into two groups and provided with either construction-centered (CC) or form-centered (FC) instruction. Their knowledge of constructions was measured by two types of translation tasks in a pretest and a posttest.

The paper is organized as follows. Section 2 provides an overview of the constructionist approach to argument structure constructions in English with a focus on the TRC. It further presents previous findings on construction learning in first and second language acquisition studies. The next section describes the methods used in the present study, including information about the participants, the instruction design, and the tests. Section 4 reports the main results, and Section 5 discusses major findings of the present study. Finally, Section 6 summarizes the findings and concludes the study with some implications for foreign language teaching and learning.

2 Previous studies

2.1 Construction grammar and argument structure constructions

Construction Grammar contends that language is composed of a multitude of constructions, with varying levels of generality and complexity, ranging from

---

2 RP stands for resultative phrase.
3 "Basic" constructions, according to Goldberg (1995), represent event types that are basic to human experience. These constructions include the intransitive motion, the caused-motion, and the ditransitive constructions.

free or bound morpheme to sentence structure (Goldberg 1995, 2006). Goldberg (2006: 5) states that:

> Any linguistic pattern is recognized as a construction as long as some aspect of its form or function is not strictly predictable from its component parts or from other constructions recognized to exist. In addition, patterns are stored as constructions even if they are fully predictable as long as they occur with sufficient frequency.

One important type of construction is the argument structure construction, which specifies syntactic and semantic properties of sentences (Goldberg 1995, 2006). Table 1 shows some representative argument structure constructions in English, which are of particular importance to the present study.

Table 1: Some argument structure constructions in English

	Form/Example	Meaning	Construction Label
1.	Subj V Obl$_{path/loc}$ e.g. *The fly buzzed into the room.*	X moves Y$_{path/loc}$	Intransitive Motion
2.	Subj V Obj Obl$_{path/loc}$ e.g. *Pat sneezed the foam off the cappuccino.*	X causes Y to move Z$_{path/loc}$	Caused-Motion
3.	Subj V Obj Obj$_2$ e.g. *She faxed him a letter.*	X causes Y to receive Z	Ditransitive
4.	Subj V Obj RP e.g. *She kissed him unconscious.*	X causes Y to become Z$_{state}$	Transitive Resultative

(Adapted from Goldberg 2006: 73)

According to Goldberg (2003: 220), "the interpretation and form of sentence patterns of a language are not reliably determined by independent specifications of the main verb". For example, the verb *sneeze* does not entail a three-argument sense, and yet it may appear in such a sentence as *Pat sneezed the foam off the cappuccino*. To be more specific, the meaning and structure of this sentence are not fully determined by the verb *sneeze*, but by the construction, called the caused-motion construction, which specifies the overall form (i.e., Subj V Obj Obl$_{path/loc}$) and meaning (i.e., *X causes Y to move Z$_{path/loc}$*). In other words, "[i]t is the argument-structure constructions that provide the direct link between surface form and general aspects of the interpretation" (Goldberg 2003: 221). Table 1 provides some major constructions, with meanings such as: someone moving somewhere (intransitive motion), something causing something else to move (caused-motion), someone causing someone to receive something (ditransitive), and someone causing something to change state (transitive resultative).

Several interesting proposals concerning the interrelationship between argument structure constructions have been made (Boyd and Goldberg 2011; Cappelle 2006; Goldberg 2002, 2011; Gries 2003), and the hierarchical network proposed by Goldberg (1995, 2006) and Hoffmann and Trousdale (2013) is arguably the most influential.[4] According to this framework, a network connects a construction to others in a super- and sub-node fashion, reflecting important formal and functional relationships between constructions in a manner of inheritance: the dominating construction at a super-node transmits its formal and functional information to the dominated construction at a sub-node, unless the information in the upper construction is in conflict with that in the lower construction. Figure 1 presents the hierarchical network of representative argument structure constructions in English.

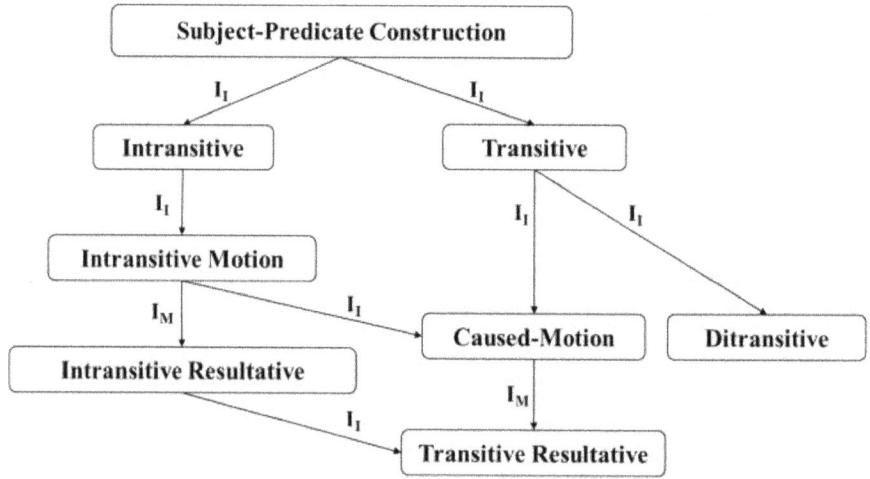

Figure 1: Hierarchical network of argument structure constructions (adapted from Goldberg 1995: 109)

In Figure 1, arrows indicate two types of inheritance links between constructions: I_I stands for *instance links* and I_M for *metaphorical extension links*.[5]

---

4 See Boyd and Goldberg (2011) and Goldberg (2011) for the notion of *statistical preemption* which tells how a construction is statistically preempted by another construction.
5 According to Goldberg (1995), there are two other types of inheritance links: *polysemy links* and *subpart links*. Polysemy links show how the prototypical meaning of a construction is associated with extended senses of the construction, and focus on the relationship among semantic variations within a particular construction. These links are not included in Figure 1, because they are not about relations between constructions. Also excluded are subpart links, because "an instance link always entails an inverse subpart link" (Goldberg 1995: 81).

Instance links are posited when "one construction is a more fully specified version of the other construction" (Goldberg 1995: 79). For example, the TRC, as more fully specified, is an instance of the intransitive resultative construction: the former has three argument roles (AGENT, PATIENT, and RESULT-GOAL), while the latter has two argument roles (THEME and RESULT-GOAL). On the other hand, *metaphorical extension links* are posited when "[t]he way the dominating construction's semantics is mapped to the dominated construction's semantics is specified by the metaphor" (Goldberg 1995: 81). For example, the TRC is a metaphorical extension of the caused-motion construction because the semantics of the latter is mapped to that of the former via a metaphor, namely "Change of State as Change of Location" (Goldberg 1995: 88).

One of the main research questions of the present study being on the role of the hierarchical network in construction learning, special attention is paid not only to TRCs, but also to intransitive motion constructions (IMCs), caused-motion constructions (CMCs), and ditransitive constructions (DCs), which have been reported as not readily accessible to many Korean EFL learners, unlike other basic constructions such as the intransitive resultative or the transitive construction (Lee and Kim 2011).

2.2 Transitive resultative construction

The TRC has a syntactic structure which consists of a subject, a verb, an object, and a resultative phrase, e.g., [*She*]-[*kissed*]-[*him*]-[*unconscious*]. This syntactic structure is associated with a constructional meaning, *X causes Y to become* Z_{state}. According to Goldberg and Jackendoff (2004), there are two types of TRCs: verbal and constructional resultatives. A verbal resultative has a 'light verb', such as *make*, as its main predicate, e.g., *Sally made me happy*, and a constructional resultative has a 'heavy verb', i.e., a verb whose semantic meaning is lexically heavy, as in *Willy hammered the metal flat*. Hereafter, the former is called LV-TRC, and the latter HV-TRC.

In addition to the difference in their type of main predicates, the LV- and the HV-TRC differ in the way they map the argument roles of the TRC onto the participant roles of the matrix verb (Figure 2).

The semantic structure of the TRC has three argument roles (AGENT, PATIENT, and RESULT-GOAL), which are to be mapped onto the participant roles specified by its main predicate (Goldberg 1995). In the LV-TRC, every argument role is linked to one and only one participant role, and the verb is interpreted as an *instance* of TRC events. In the HV-TRC, on the other hand, not every argument role is linked to a participant role. In particular, the argument role

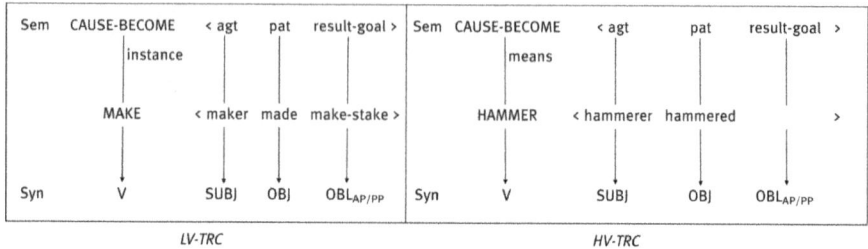

Figure 2: Form-meaning mapping in LV- and HV-TRC

RESULT-GOAL fails to map onto a participant role. According to Goldberg and Jackendoff (2004), the failure of this link calls for a special mechanism in which the two sub-events of the HV-TRC are associated with each other:

– HV-TRC Sentence : *Willy hammered the metal flat.*
– Constructional sub-event : *X causes Y to become Z_{state}*
　　　　　　　　　　　WILLY CAUSE [METAL BECOME FLAT]
– Verbal sub-event : *Means by which the constructional event takes place*
　　　　　　　　　　　WILLY HAMMER METAL
(Adapted from Goldberg and Jackendoff 2004: 538)

As shown above, the HV-TRC has two sub-events. One is the constructional sub-event, which outlines the overall semantics of a sentence (e.g., *X causes Y to become Z_{state}*), and the other is the verbal sub-event, specifying the MEANS to achieve the constructional sub-event. The two sub-events in the HV-TRC are associated with each other, and this results in the instrumental meaning – *Willy made the metal flat by hammering it.*

The main properties of English TRCs are reported to be shared by Korean TRCs (Hong 2002, 2011; Kim 1993; Kim and Maling 1997; Ko 2011; Lee and Lee 2003; Wechsler 1997; Wechsler and Noh 2001). The Korean resultative is a pairing of a meaning *X causes Y to become Z_{state}* and a form *Subj-Obj-RP-V*, with the resultative phrase marked by a suffixed particle *–key*, glossed as COMP (complementizer):

(1)　Sally-ka　　na-lul　　[haengpokha-key]　mandul-eoss-ta.
　　　Sally-NOM　me-ACC　happy-COMP　　　make-PST-DEC
　　　'Sally made me happy.'　(Adapted from Hong 2002: 9)

(2) Willy-ka   kumsok-ul   [napcakha-key]   twutulki-eoss-ta.
    Willy-NOM metal-ACC flat-COMP   hammer-PST-DEC
    'Willy hammered the metal flat.'
    (Adapted from Wechsler and Noh 2001: 393)

Korean TRCs have paraphrastic counterparts (Hong 2011). For instance, sentence (2) can be paraphrased as follows:

(3) Willy-ka   kumsok-ul twutulki-eoseo   [napcakha-key] mandul-eoss-ta.
    Willy-NOM metal-ACC hammer-CONNECTIVE flat-COMP   make-PST-DEC
    'Mary made the metal flat by hammering it.'

The paraphrastic relation between (2) and (3) is not different from the relation between English TRCs and their paraphrastic counterparts (e.g., the paraphrastic relation between *Willy hammered the metal flat* and *Willy made the metal flat by hammering it*).

2.3 Construction learning

Construction Grammar postulates that constructions emerge from usage just as abstract categories are induced from concrete exemplars (Casenhiser and Goldberg 2005; Collins and Ellis 2009; Ellis, O'Donnell, and Römer 2013; Goldberg, Casenhiser, and White 2007). This usage-based approach views language input as a critical factor in construction learning, and suggests that specific patterns in language input play facilitative roles in teaching and learning constructions (Boyd and Goldberg 2009; Bybee 2011; Casenhiser and Goldberg 2005; Chang and Maia 2001; Goldberg, Casenhiser, and Sethuraman 2004; Goldberg and Suttle 2010; Theakston et al. 2004; Tomasello 2003, 2006).

One such pattern was discovered by Goldberg, Casenhiser, and Sethuraman (2004). They explored the frequency and distribution of verbs over different argument structure constructions in a corpus of mothers-children speech, and found that a single prototypical verb occurs with high frequency in each of the constructions, both in the mothers' and the children's speech (e.g., *put* in the caused-motion construction). This led the researchers to conclude that construction learning in first language acquisition is predominantly guided by prototypical verbs of high frequency in the input. This proposal was confirmed by Casenhiser and Goldberg (2005), who found, through experiment, that skewed input, where "one verbal token accounts for the majority of utterances" (Casenhiser and Goldberg 2005: 503), was more effective than balanced input, where each verbal token occurs with similar frequencies, in helping native English speaking children to learn a novel argument structure construction. In the experiment, the participants in the skewed input group heard one novel verb (e.g., *moopo*) occur in half of the total eight sentences, with the other four novel verbs occurring once in each of the other four sentences (4-1-1-1-1). Those in the balanced input group heard each of the five verbs occur with roughly equal frequency (2-2-2-1-1). In the post-training test, which required the participants to listen to a sentence and match it with one of two film clips shown to them, the participants in the skewed input group performed significantly better than those in the balanced input group. This facilitative effect of skewed input in construction learning was also explored in second language acquisition contexts. Ellis and Ferreira-Junior (2009) investigated the distribution of verbs in three argument structure constructions – the IMC, CMC, and DC[6] – in the longitudinal data of seven English as a Second Language (ESL) learners' conversations with native English speakers. Observing that prototypical verbs for each construction (e.g., *go* for the IMC, *put* for the CMC, *give* for the DC) appeared most frequently both in native speakers' and ESL learners' utterances, the researchers suggested that these "path-breaking" verbs help ESL learners use and learn the argument structure constructions.

As the discussion surrounding effective input continues, many researchers have started to investigate construction learning in various instructional settings such as university-level English programs (Holme 2010, 2012; Rah 2014; Shin 2012), secondary school English classes (Jang 2014; Kim, H. 2013; Kim, R. 2012) and elementary school English classes (Hwang 2013). In his pilot study with university students, Holme (2010) devised a construction-based lesson where the students were instructed to focus on the forms and meanings of constructions in given texts and asked to produce the types of constructions they were taught. The participants showed notable improvement not only in the correct production of constructions, but also in "the accuracy with which they reproduced the text types where the constructions had been spotted" (Holme 2010: 130).

Shin (2012) and Rah (2014) devised construction-based instruction for university students learning English as a foreign language. Shin (2012) provided the participants with fourteen-week instruction on six different constructions – the transitive, the ditransitive, the caused-motion, the transitive resultative, the intransitive motion, and the intransitive resultative construction. Each class provided explicit instruction on the syntactic and semantic properties of a construction, as well as several writing activities such as dictation, picture description, and free writing. The participants were first instructed to use light verbs in the target construction and focus on the association between the form

---

[6] In Ellis and Ferreira-Junior (2009), *intransitive motion* is called "verb locative" (VL) and *caused-motion* is named "verb object locative" (VOL).

and the prototypical meaning of the construction. Other verbs were introduced later to teach the extended senses of the construction. For instance, light verbs such as *do*, *get*, and *take* were first introduced to teach the prototypical meaning of the transitive construction (i.e., *X acts on Y*), while other verbs such as *want*, *say*, and *know* were later presented to teach the extended senses of the construction. This transition of instructional focus from prototype to periphery verbs was found to be effective in teaching constructions: there was a significant improvement in the correct production of the target constructions in the participants' narrative writings.

Rah (2014) adopted the concept of construction network in developing instruction design to teach Korean university students argument structure constructions in English, and presented constructions in accordance with Goldberg's (1995, 2006) hierarchical networks. For instance, the IMC was instructed earlier than the CMC, because the formal and functional information of the former is inherited by the latter by the instance link (see Figure 1). The effects of instruction were measured by four types of tasks (i.e., Korean-to-English translation, picture description, video-clip description, and grammaticality judgment), and remarkable improvement was observed in the use of constructions among the students taught in the network frame.

Following the guiding spirit of the previous research, the present study examines effects of the two types of instruction – form-centered and construction-centered – on Korean EFL secondary school students' learning of the TRC, one of the most difficult argument structure constructions for Korean learners of English (Lee and Kim 2011; Rah 2014). It also explores whether and to what extent the EFL students' learning of the TRC is facilitated by the light verb, which has been shown to play a path-breaking role in first language (e.g., Goldberg, Casenhiser, and Sethuraman 2004) and second language acquisition (e.g., Ellis and Ferreira-Junior 2009). The study also focuses on the question whether the instruction of the TRC, which is shown to be related to other basic constructions in the hierarchical network (Goldberg 1995, 2006), has a significant influence on the students' learning of the related basic constructions. The research questions of the present study are threefold:
(1) Between construction-centered and form-centered instruction, which is more effective in teaching the TRC to Korean EFL students?
(2) Does the light verb facilitate Korean students' learning of the TRC?
(3) Does instruction of the TRC affect Korean students' learning of other basic constructions in English?[7]

---

[7] A similar question is suggested for future research in Goldberg (2003: 223): "Does learning one construction facilitate learning other related constructions?".

3 Method

3.1 Participants

A total of ninety-three Korean EFL learners from four different secondary school classes participated in the study. Two classes were chosen from the same high school, while the remaining two classes came from two different middle schools. The participants consisted of forty-four males and forty-nine females, with ages ranging from thirteen to sixteen (mean = 15.4). Their English proficiency was found to be rather low overall: in the pre-instruction narrative writings, they produced a very limited number of T-units[8] (mean = 4.29, SD = 4.92) with frequent errors in simple grammar and spelling. Measured by the American Council for the Teaching of Foreign Languages (ACTFL) proficiency guidelines (Swender, Conrad, and Vicars 2012), their proficiency was at the level of novice or novice-high.

The participants were divided into two instructional groups, i.e., form-centered (FC) and construction-centered (CC),[9] with one high school and one middle school class allotted to each (Table 2).

Table 2: Composition of instruction groups

	Form-centered Group	Construction-centered Group
Number	45 students	48 students
School	13 middle school students	17 middle school students
	32 high school students	31 high school students

3.2 Procedure

The experiment consisted of three sessions (i.e., a pretest, an instruction phase, and a posttest) and was conducted on four days over a week. The pre- and posttest were administered on the first and the last day, respectively, while instruction on the TRC was provided on the second and the third day. Details of the instruction lessons are provided in Section 3.3, and those of the tests are presented in Section 3.4.

---

[8] A T-unit is "one main clause with all subordinate clauses attached to it" (Hunt 1965: 20).
[9] Its primary goal being to compare the effects of the two types of instruction on the learning of the TRC, the present study has no control group.

3.3 Instruction

Two types of instruction were developed to teach the TRC: FC and CC instruction. They differed from each other in their understanding of the determining factor of the overall structure of sentences. The FC instruction considered sentences as structural units consisting of a verb and its subcategorizational argument(s), while the CC instruction regards the construction as playing a determining role in pairing the overall form and meaning of a sentence. This difference directly impacted the development of teaching activities for the two types of instruction. For instance, the FC instruction placed more focus on parsing tasks to draw the participants' attention to the syntactic composition of TRC sentences, while the CC instruction exploited not only parsing tasks, but also picture-related tasks to help students map the form and meaning of the TRC.

Both types of instruction consisted of two lessons, each lasting for approximately 25 minutes. In the first lesson, the instruction focused on the LV-TRC, and in the second lesson on the HV-TRC. Most of the sentences used in the lessons were adapted from Boas (2003), who presents verb-resultative combinations of high frequency from the British National Corpus.[10]

3.3.1 Lesson 1: Teaching the LV-TRC

The first lesson focused on the LV-TRC – a TRC sentence whose main predicate is lexically light or inherently resultative (i.e., *make*). In this lesson, which consisted of six activities,[11] the FC-group received form-focused instruction, which emphasized the structural composition of TRC sentences, focusing on subcategorizational properties of the verb *make*. The CC-group, on the other hand, was given construction-based instruction, which focused on the form-meaning pairing of the target construction. For instance, in introducing the sentence *Pooh made Piglet angry*, FC-instruction highlighted its syntactic composition (i.e., subject, verb, object, and complement), contrasting it with the syntactic composition of other sentences such as subject-verb-object or subject-verb-object$_1$-object$_2$. CC-instruction, on the other hand, focused on the constructional properties, drawing the learners' attention not only to the syntactic composition but also to the constructional meaning – the resultative aspects of "a change of state" experienced by *Piglet*.

---

[10] For instance, the verb *rub* frequently combines with a few resultative phrases such as *dry*, *warm*, or *smooth* (e.g., *Mothers tried to rub wet heads dry*).
[11] A full list of learning activities and their details are provided in Appendices 1 and 2.

3.3.2 Lesson 2: Teaching the HV-TRC

In the second lesson, both groups were first provided with a brief review of the LV-TRC, and then were taught the HV-TRC through six activities, including fill-in-the-blanks and scrambled sentences.

As described in Section 2.2, the HV-TRC relates two semantically separable sub-events: the constructional sub-event expresses the meaning *X causes Y to become Z_{state}* and the verbal sub-event refers to a MEANS to achieve the constructional event. In the CC instruction, the main focus was put on the latter semantic property. For instance, the students were provided with an LV-TRC sentence (e.g., *The man made the can flat*) and a picture describing it, and were taught that the main verb can be replaced by a heavy verb to indicate a specific means (e.g., *The man hammered the can flat*), with the overall meaning of the sentence maintained. The FC instruction, on the other hand, focused on the syntactic composition of TRC sentences (i.e., subject-verb-object-complement), showing that heavy verbs such as *throw*, *hammer*, and *wipe* can be used in the structure.

3.4 Tests

In the pretest and the posttest, the participants were asked to perform two different translation tasks, each lasting for ten minutes: a Korean-to-English translation (KET) task and an English-to-Korean translation (EKT) task. The KET task was designed to measure the learners' production of the TRC and other constructions in English, and the EKT task to assess their comprehension of the constructions.

The KET task presented the students with eighteen Korean sentences and asked them to translate the sentences into English. Each of the Korean sentences was about a scene which can best be described using an English TRC (transitive resultative construction), IMC (intransitive motion construction), CMC (caused-motion construction), or DC (ditransitive construction);[12] hereafter, Korean sentences which correspond to English TRCs, IMCs, CMCs, and DCs are called TRC-, IMC-, CMC-, and DC-equivalents respectively. As is shown in Table 3, among the eighteen Korean sentences, TRC-equivalents accounted for nine items, and

---

[12] The Korean sentences were adapted from studies on constructions in Korean (Hong 2002; Jeong 2005, 2006; Kim 1993; Kim and Maling 1997; Ko 2011; Lee and Lee 2003; Wechsler 1997; Wechsler and Noh 2001). The naturalness and appropriateness of the translations of these sentences into English was confirmed by a Korean/English bilingual speaker and advanced Korean learners of English.

the remaining nine items were evenly distributed over IMC-, CMC-, and DC-equivalents.

Table 3: Korean-to-English translation task

Input	Required Responses	Time	Number of Items [TRC-, IMC-, CMC-, DC-equiv.]
Korean Sentences	English Sentences	10 minutes	18[a] [9, 3, 3, 3]

[a] The items were sequenced in random order.

The nine TRC-equivalents in the KET task are further divided into three groups. The three TRC-equivalents in the first group have the Korean verb *mandulda*, which can be best translated into the English light verb *make*. On the other hand, those in the second group have Korean equivalents of *kick*, *rub*, and *wipe*, which were taught during instruction, and those in the third group have Korean equivalents of *paint*, *shake*, and *shoot*, which were not introduced in instruction.[13]

In the EKT task, the participants were given twenty-five English sentences[14] and asked to translate them into their mother tongue (i.e., Korean). Among the twenty-five sentences, TRCs accounted for ten sentences,[15] and the remaining fifteen sentences were five IMCs, five CMCs, and five DCs. The EKT and the KET tasks were carried out without interval, and the former was conducted after the latter so that the English input of the EKT task did not affect the students' performance in the KET task.

Table 4: English-to-Korean translation task

Input	Required Responses	Time	Number of Items [TRC, IMC, CMC, DC]
English Sentences	Korean Sentences	10 minutes	25[a] [10, 5, 5, 5]

[a] The items were sequenced in random order.

The pretest and the posttest consisted of the same types of tasks, but used different expressions. For example, in the pretest, the participants were asked

---

[13] These six heavy verbs – *kick*, *rub*, *wipe*, *paint*, *shake*, and *shoot* – have been known to combine with various adjective resultative phrases (Boas 2003).
[14] Of the twenty-five sentences, twenty were extracted from Lee and Kim (2011) and the other five were adapted from Boas (2003).
[15] The ten TRC sentences in the EKT task are not divided into subgroups.

to translate an English sentence *Muff painted the house green*, while in the posttest they were given a slightly different sentence *Muff painted the room white*.

3.5 Coding and analysis

The students' answers in the KET task were typed and examined to see whether or not they were the types of constructions expected in the task. In other words, it was determined whether or not the constructional meanings of the Korean sentences were translated into the corresponding construction forms in English. The students' answers in the EKT task were also typed and examined to see whether or not their translation of the English sentences reflected the core meanings of the constructions provided. To be more specific, the students' answers to a TRC item were considered to be correct if the constructional meaning *X causes Y to become Z* was expressed either by a Korean resultative construction or by its paraphrase.

In an effort to secure the reliability of the comparison between the groups, the students who met any of the following conditions were excluded from the analysis of each task: a) those who missed either the pretest or the posttest, b) those who responded to fewer than 30% of the task items, and c) those who were found to have imitated other participants' answers.[16] The number of each participant's correct responses was recalculated for each of the test sessions, the task types, the construction types and the verb types. The data were analyzed using a series of statistical devices such as a paired sample *t*-test, and the statistical analysis was conducted using the Statistical Packet for Social Sciences (SPSS 19 for Windows).

4 Results

4.1 Translation of the transitive resultative construction

This section presents the results from the KET and EKT tasks of the pre- and posttest, and investigates the effects of instruction on the learning of the TRC.

---

[16] In the KET task, nineteen students from the CC group and fourteen students from the FC group were excluded: the responses of the other students, twenty-nine from the former and thirty-one from the latter, were analyzed. In the EKT task, fifteen students from the CC group and sixteen students from the FC group were excluded: the responses of the other students, thirty-three from the former and twenty-nine from the latter, were analyzed.

Table 5 shows the means and standard deviations of the scores obtained in the pretest and the posttest.

Table 5: †Means and standard deviations of scores in the tests for the TRC

Group	Task	Pretest Mean	SD	Posttest Mean	SD	N
CC	KET	1.79[a]	2.11	4.14	3.10	29
	EKT	3.61[b]	1.60	5.36	1.95	33
FC	KET	0.55	1.18	2.58	2.67	31
	EKT	3.79	1.42	4.97	1.24	29

† The means and standard deviations are rounded to the nearest hundredth.
[a] The maximum score was 9.
[b] The maximum score was 10.

Before the instruction, the participants in both groups had very limited command of the TRC, but after the instruction, their performance in translating the construction showed notable improvement in both the KET and the EKT tasks.

Paired *t*-tests also revealed that there were statistically significant effects of instruction on learning the TRC in both groups (Table 6).

Table 6: Paired sample *t*-tests between pretest and posttest for the TRC

Group	Task	†Mean Increase (Posttest – Pretest)	T	df	Sign. (2-tailed)
CC	KET	2.35	4.70	28	.000***
	EKT	1.76	5.60	32	.000***
FC	KET	2.03	4.19	30	.000***
	EKT	1.17	5.27	28	.000***

† The mean increases and *t*-values are rounded to the nearest hundredth.
***$p < .001$

Table 6 shows the mean increases in the scores of the two groups in the two tasks. While both groups demonstrated remarkable improvements in their ability to translate the TRC, the CC group achieved more significant positive change: the increase in the mean scores of the CC group was 2.35 on the KET task and 1.76 on the EKT task, while the means of the FC group increased by 2.03 on the KET task and 1.17 on the EKT task.

4.2 Translation of the LV- and the HV-TRC

As described in Section 3.4, the nine TRC items in the KET task are classified into three groups according to the types of verbs that are expected in the students' responses: a) the light verb *make*, b) heavy verbs which were taught during instruction, and c) heavy verbs which were not introduced; the sentences in the first group are called LV-TRCs, and those in the other two groups instructed and uninstructed HV-TRCs respectively. This section examines the results from the KET task, and explores the effects of instruction on the production of the LV- and the HV-TRC.

Table 7 shows the means and standard deviations of the scores for the verb types of the TRC items in the KET task.

Table 7: †Means and standard deviations of scores for verb types in KET for the TRC

Group	Verb types	Pretest Mean	SD	Posttest Mean	SD	N
CC	Light	0.83[a]	1.14	1.69	1.31	29
	Instructed Heavy	0.41	0.57	1.28	1.10	
	Uninstructed Heavy	0.55	0.78	1.17	1.07	
FC	Light	0.32	0.70	1.39	1.26	31
	Instructed Heavy	0.10	0.40	0.55	0.96	
	Uninstructed Heavy	0.13	0.42	0.65	0.99	

† The means and standard deviations are rounded to the nearest hundredth.
[a] The maximum score was 3 for each of the verb type

The participants in both groups produced more LV-TRCs than HV-TRCs in the pretest as well as in the posttest. In addition, the increase in the mean scores was relatively higher in LV-TRCs than in HV-TRCs, while statistically significant increases were observed in every type of verbs (Table 8).

Table 8: Paired sample *t*-tests for verb types in KET for the TRC

Group	Verb types	†Mean Increase (Pretest – Posttest)	T	df	Sign. (2-tailed)
CC	Light	.86	4.01	28	***
	Instructed Heavy	.86	4.53	28	***
	Uninstructed Heavy	.62	2.92	28	**
FC	Light	1.07	4.20	30	***
	Instructed Heavy	.45	2.83	30	**
	Uninstructed Heavy	.52	2.71	30	*

† The mean increases and *t*-values are rounded to the nearest hundredth.
*$p < .05$, **$p < .01$, ***$p < .001$

The improvement in the translation of HV-TRCs was greater in the CC group than in the FC group. The respective mean score increase in the use of the instructed and uninstructed HV-TRC in the CC group was 0.86 ($t[28] = 4.53, p < .001$) and 0.62 ($t[28] = 2.92, p < .01$), while that in the FC group was 0.45 ($t[30] = 2.83, p < .01$) and 0.52 ($t[30] = 2.71, p < .05$). On the other hand, the improvement in the translation of LV-TRCs was greater in the FC group (mean increase = 1.07, $t[30] = 4.20$, $p < .001$) than in the CC group (mean increase = 0.86, $t[28] = 4.01, p < .001$).

4.3 Translation of other constructions

Both the KET and the EKT tasks were designed to measure the participants' performance on translating not only the TRC, but also the IMC, the CMC, and the DC (hereafter, non-TRCs). Table 9 presents the means and standard deviations of the scores for the non-TRCs in the two tasks, and Table 10 shows the results of paired t-tests for the non-TRCs.

Table 9: [†]Means and standard deviations of scores for non-TRCs

Task	Construction	Pretest		Posttest		N
		Mean	SD	Mean	SD	
KET	IMC	1.75[a]	1.07	1.97	0.80	60
	CMC	0.57	0.85	0.95	1.03	
	DC	0.20	0.58	0.38	0.74	
EKT	IMC	2.47[b]	1.28	2.79	1.32	62
	CMC	0.89	1.07	1.84	1.10	
	DC	0.97	0.99	1.65	1.31	

[†] The means and standard deviations are rounded to the nearest hundredth.
[a] The maximum score was 3.
[b] The maximum score was 5.

The participants' translation of the non-TRCs improved after the instruction of the TRC: the increase in the mean scores in the KET task was 0.22 for the IMC, 0.38 for the CMC, and 0.18 for the DC, and that in the EKT task was 0.32 for the IMC, 0.95 for the CMC, and 0.68 for the DC.

Most noteworthy is the significant improvement in the translation of the CMC (KET: mean increase = 0.38, $t(59) = 3.10, p < .01$; EKT: mean increase = 0.95, $t(61) = 7.16, p < .001$), which indicates that the instruction of the TRC most positively affected the translation of the CMC.

Table 10: Paired sample *t*-tests for non-TRCs

Task	Construction	†Mean Increase (Posttest – Pretest)	T	df	Sign. (2-tailed)
KET	IMC	.22	1.37	59	
	CMC	.38	3.10	59	**
	DC	.18	2.28	59	*
EKT	IMC	.32	1.91	61	
	CMC	.95	7.16	61	***
	DC	.68	4.02	61	***

† The mean increases and *t*-values are rounded to the nearest hundredth.
*$p < .05$, **$p < .01$, ***$p < .001$

5 Discussion

5.1 Instructional effects

The first research question concerns whether CC instruction is more effective than FC instruction in teaching the TRC to Korean EFL students. The analysis of the results in the pre- and posttest indicates that, while both instruction groups showed significant improvements in the KET and EKT task, the CC group outperformed the FC group in both translation tasks.

Given that translation tasks are assumed to be a reliable and valid measure of language proficiency (Buck 1992; Ito 2004; Kim 2008; Lococo 1976), the significant improvement in the KET and EKT tasks seems to indicate that instructional treatment does indeed facilitate the learning of the TRC for Korean EFL students. In particular, the more positive results observed in the CC group suggest that CC instruction is more effective than FC instruction in teaching the TRC to Korean EFL students.

An important pedagogical implication of this finding is that the TRC, which is one of the most difficult constructions to Korean EFL learners (Lee and Kim 2011; Rah 2014), is found to be teachable to secondary school students, whose English proficiency is at the level of novice or novice-high. Another meaningful implication is that the learning of TRC becomes more efficient especially when the construction is taught as a form-meaning pairing.

5.2 Effects of verb types

The second research question concerns whether the light verb facilitates Korean students' learning of the TRC. The analysis of the results in the KET task reveals that the participants produced more LV-TRCs than HV-TRCs in the pretest as well as in the posttest. In addition, the increase in the mean scores was relatively higher in LV-TRCs than in HV-TRCs (Table 8). The results may indicate that LV-TRCs are easier for participants to use and the instruction is more effective in teaching LV-TRCs than HV-TRCs.

Provided that both the LV- and the HV-TRC are identical in their syntactic structure *Subj-V-Obj-RP*, the poor performance and low improvement in using the HV-TRC may be attributed to the complex nature of its semantic structure. As was described in Section 2.2, the HV-TRC involves the association of two semantically distinct sub-events: the constructional sub-event (i.e., *X causes Y to become Z*) and the verbal sub-event (i.e., *means by which the constructional event takes place*). This rather complex property of the HV-TRC is in sharp contrast with the simple nature of the LV-TRC, which does not involve (the association of) sub-events, causing considerable difficulties in learning the construction.

Similar findings have been reported in previous research on construction learning (Casenhiser and Goldberg 2005; Ellis and Ferreira-Junior 2009; Goldberg 1999; Goldberg, Casenhiser, and Sethuraman 2004). With a special focus on the role of light verbs in the learning of argument structure constructions, these studies propose that light verbs are prototypical verbs with high frequency in the input and facilitate construction learning in the first and second language acquisition. The results of the present study confirm the facilitative role of light verbs in the foreign language learning context.

5.3 Network effects

The third research question concerns whether the instruction of the TRC affects Korean students' learning of other basic constructions in English. The analysis of the results in the pre- and posttest indicates that, while the participants' translation of non-TRCs improved after the instruction of the TRC, the most significant improvement was in the translation of the CMC (Table 10).

This facilitative effect of learning the TRC on using non-TRCs is attributable to the hierarchical networks among constructions (Figure 1). According to Goldberg (1995), the dominating construction in the networks is syntactically and semantically more basic than the dominated one. This hierarchical relationship between constructions is suggestive of the notion of *markedness* (Lakoff 1987: 60–61):

> In general, markedness is a term used by linguists to describe a kind of prototype effect – an asymmetry in a category, where one member or subcategory is taken to be somehow more basic than the other (or others).

Assuming that hierarchical relationships reflect markedness, the dominated construction (e.g., the TRC) is more marked than the dominating one (e.g., the CMC). Turning back to the effect of the TRC instruction on the learning of the non-TRCs, the improvements in the use of non-TRCs after the instruction of TRCs mean that, while the instruction of a more marked construction yields significantly positive effects on the learning of a less marked one, the effect would be strongest when there is a direct link between the two constructions, as is found between the TRC and the CMC.

6 Conclusion

The present study has shown that CC instruction offers Korean EFL students a substantial and meaningful advantage to learn TRCs in English. First and foremost, while both FC and CC instruction were found effective, the latter turned out to be more successful in teaching TRCs. In addition, while both LV- and HV-TRCs were teachable through instruction, the former were easier for the students to learn. Finally, while the instruction of the TRC positively affected the students' use of other basic constructions, the strongest effect was on the CMC, which is directly linked to and less marked than the TRC in the hierarchical network.

The findings have significant implications for foreign language teaching and learning. First, the discovery that CC instruction is more effective than FC instruction in teaching the TRC, which is known to be most difficult for Korean EFL learners, provides us with a firmer basis and better reason to introduce constructionist approaches into the practices of foreign language teaching.

Second, the facilitative role of light verbs bears considerable importance in foreign language teaching and learning. Despite their high frequencies and positive functions, light verbs are often overlooked in foreign language classes because of their idiomatic and polysemic properties. The facilitative role of light verbs in construction learning as observed in this study, however, calls for our close attention to light verbs when developing foreign language curriculum and instruction. For instance, when teaching a ditransitive construction, we are highly recommended to provide foreign language learners with authentic input where the prototypical light verb (e.g., *give*) appears frequently.

Finally, special attention needs to be given to the pedagogical significance of the hierarchical network of constructions in designing construction-centered instruction in foreign language teaching settings. Foreign language learners, when compared with second language acquirers, have excessively limited exposure to the target language, and often experience difficulty attaining desired levels of communicative competence. One way to cope with this problem, as suggested in Yang (2008, 2010), is to use the linguistic systems of the target language as an organizational base for foreign language teaching, and to provide foreign language learners with language instruction aimed at more efficient learning. The present study has shown that the instruction of a more marked construction positively affects the learning of a less marked construction which is not taught. This indicates that a systematic consideration of the positive role of a marked construction in construction teaching can provide a pedagogy that maximizes learning gains in foreign language teaching settings.

References

Boas, Hans. 2003. *A constructional approach to resultatives*. Stanford, CA: CSLI.
Boyd, Jeremy & Adele Goldberg. 2009. Input effects within a constructionist framework. *Modern Language Journal* 93(3). 418–429.
Boyd, Jeremy & Adele Goldberg. 2011. Learning what not to say: The role of statistical preemption and categorization in a-adjective production. *Language* 87(1). 55–83.
Buck, Gary. 1992. Translation as a language testing procedure: Does it work? *Language Testing* 9(2). 123–148.
Bybee, Joan. 2011. Usage-based theory and grammaticalization. In Heiko Narrog & Bernd Heine (eds.), *The Oxford handbook of grammaticalization*, 67–79. Oxford: Oxford University Press.
Cappelle, Bert. 2006. Particle placement and the case for "allostructions". *Constructions* SV1-7, 1–28.
Casenhiser, Devin & Adele Goldberg. 2005. Fast mapping between a phrasal form and meaning. *Developmental Science* 8(6). 500–508.
Chang, Nancy & Tiago Maia. 2001. Grounded learning of grammatical constructions. In *AAAI Spring Symposium on Learning Grounded Representations*. Stanford, CA.
Collins, Laura & Nick Ellis (eds.). 2009. Input and second language construction learning: Frequency, form, and function. [Special issue]. *The Modern Language Journal* 93(3). 329–470.
Ellis, Nick & Fernando Ferreira-Junior. 2009. Construction learning as a function of frequency, frequency distribution, and function. *The Modern Language Journal* 93(3). 370–385.
Ellis, Nick, Matthew Brook O'Donnell & Ute Römer. 2013. Usage-based language: Investigating the latent structures that underpin acquisition. *Language Learning* 63(s1). 25–51.

Fredsgaard, Heidi. 2013. A constructionist approach to the development of teaching materials for Danish politeness formulas. Paper presented at the *Constructionist Approaches to Language Pedagogy* conference, Université Saint-Louis, Brussels, 8–9 November.

Goldberg, Adele. 1995. *Constructions: A construction grammar approach to argument structure*. Chicago: The University of Chicago Press.

Goldberg, Adele. 1999. The emergence of the semantics of argument structure constructions. In Brian MacWhinney (ed.), *The emergence of language,* 197–212. Mahwah, NJ: Lawrence Erlbaum.

Goldberg, Adele. 2002. Surface generalizations: An alternative to alternations. *Cognitive Linguistics* 13(4). 327–356.

Goldberg, Adele. 2003. Constructions: A new theoretical approach to language. *Trends in Cognitive Sciences* 7(5). 219–224.

Goldberg, Adele. 2006. *Constructions at work: The nature of generalization in language*. New York, US: Oxford University Press.

Goldberg, Adele. 2011. Corpus evidence of the viability of statistical preemption. *Cognitive Linguistics* 22(1). 131–153.

Goldberg, Adele, Devin Casenhiser & Nitya Sethuraman. 2004. Learning argument structure generalizations. *Cognitive Linguistics* 15(3). 289–316.

Goldberg, Adele, Devin Casenhiser & Tiffani White. 2007. Constructions as categories of language. *New Ideas in Psychology* 25(2). 70–86.

Goldberg, Adele & Ray Jackendoff. 2004. The English resultative as a family of constructions. *Language* 80(3). 532–568.

Goldberg, Adele & Laura Suttle. 2010. Construction grammar. *Cognitive Science* 1(4). 468–477.

Gries, Stefan Thomas. 2003. *Multifactorial analysis in corpus linguistics: A study of particle placement*. New York: Bloomsbury Publishing.

Hoffmann, Thomas & Graeme Trousdale (eds.). 2013. *The Oxford handbook of construction grammar*. Oxford: Oxford University Press.

Holme, Randal. 2010. Construction grammars: Towards a pedagogical model. *AILA Review* 23(1). 115–133.

Holme, Randal. 2012. Cognitive linguistics and the second language classroom. *TESOL Quarterly* 46(1). 6–29.

Hong, Ki-Sun. 2002. Cognitive linguistic analysis of Korean causatives [in Korean]. *The Conference Proceeding of Discourse and Cognitive Linguistics Society.* 5–13.

Hong, Ki-Sun. 2011. English resultative construction and Korean "key" construction [in Korean]. *Korean Journal of Linguistics* 36(4). 1143–1169.

Hunt, Kellogg. 1965. *Grammatical structures written at three grade levels*. NCTE Research report No. 3. Champaign, IL, USA: NCTE.

Hwang, Hae Rim. 2013. *Phonetico-syntactic realization of pronouns in the English transitive construction*. Seoul, Korea: Seoul National University MA thesis.

Ito, Akihiro. 2004. Two types of translation tests: Their reliability and validity. *System* 32(3). 395–405.

Jang, Hwa-Young. 2014. *Effects of particle-focused instruction on the learning of verb-particle construction by Korean high school English learners*. Seoul, Korea: Seoul National University MA thesis.

Jeong, Ju-Ree. 2005. The constructional grammar approach to the meaning and frame of 'kada' verb in Korean language [in Korean]. *Korean Semantics* 17. 203–229.

Jeong, Ju-Ree. 2006. The structure and meaning of '-juda' construction [in Korean]. *Korean Semantics* 19. 181–207.

Kim, Hyo-Shin. 2008. *(The) criterion validity of translation as an EFL reading comprehension testing method*. Seoul, Korea: Seoul National University MA thesis.

Kim, Hyunwoo. 2013. *Instructional effects of construction grammar on learning English dative constructions by Korean high school learners*. Seoul, Korea: Seoul National University MA thesis.

Kim, Hyunwoo, Hyeyeon Choi & Hyun-Kwon Yang. 2013. Developmental patterns of Korean EFL learners' English argument structure constructions. *Procedia-Social and Behavioral Sciences* 97. 397–404.

Kim, Jong-Bok. 1993. Syntax and semantics of Korean resultative constructions. *Harvard Studies in Korean Linguistics* 5. 471–482.

Kim, Rakhun. 2012. *Effects of construction grammar-based instruction on the development of oral proficiency by Korean high school EFL students*. Seoul, Korea: Seoul National University MA thesis.

Kim, Soowon & Joan Maling. 1997. A cross-linguistics perspective on resultative formation. In Ralph C. Blight & Michelle J. Moosally (eds.), *Texas linguistic forum 38: The syntax and semantics of predication*, 189–204. Austin, TX: Department of Linguistics, University of Texas.

Ko, Heejeong. 2011. Predication and edge effects. *Natural Language & Linguistic Theory* 29(3). 725–778.

Lakoff, George. 1987. *Women, fire, and dangerous things: What categories reveal about the mind*. Chicago: Chicago University Press.

Lee, Ha Rim. 2012. *Korean middle school students' use of English verb-argument constructions and pause patterns in L2 speaking*. Seoul, Korea: Seoul National University MA thesis.

Lee, Jin-Hwa, & Hye Min Kim. 2011. The L2 developmental sequence of English constructions and underlying factors. *Korea Journal of English Language and Linguistics* 11(3). 577–600.

Lee, Junkyu & Chungmin Lee. 2003. Korean resultative constructions. *The Proceedings of the 9th International Conference on HPSG*. 169–186.

Lococo, Veronica Gongalez-Mena. 1976. A comparison of three methods for the collection of L2 data: Free composition, translation and picture description. *Working Papers on Bilingualism* 8. 59–86.

Rah, Yang On. 2014. *Effects of construction-grammar-based instruction on the sentence production ability of Korean college learners of English*. Seoul, Korea: Seoul National University Dissertation.

Shin, Gyu-Ho. 2012. On the effectiveness of argument structure constructions and basic verbs on adult Korean learners of English. Paper presented at the 7th International Conference on Construction Grammar, Seoul, Korea.

Swender, Elvira, Daniel Conrad & Robert Vicars. 2012. *ACTFL proficiency guidelines 2012*. Alexandria, VA: American Council for the Teaching of Foreign Languages. Retrieved from http://actflproficiencyguidelines2012.org/.

Theakston, Anna, Elena Lieven, Julian Pine & Caroline Rowland. 2004. Semantic generality, input frequency and the acquisition of syntax. *Journal of Child Language* 31. 61–99.

Tomasello, Michael. 2003. *Constructing a language*. Cambridge, Massachusetts: Harvard University Press.

Tomasello, Michael. 2006. Construction grammar for kids. *Constructions SV1-11/2006*.

Wechsler, Stephen. 1997. Resultative predicates and control. In Ralph C. Blight & Michelle J. Moosally (eds.), *Texas linguistic forum 38: The syntax and semantics of predication*, 307–321. Austin, TX: Department of Linguistics, University of Texas.

Wechsler, Stephen & Bokyung Noh. 2001. On resultative predicates and clauses: Parallels between Korean and English. *Language Sciences* 23(4). 391–423.

Yang, Hyun-Kwon. 2008. Educational grammar and English teaching [in Korean]. In Hyun-Kwon Yang & Young-kuk Jeong (eds.), *Understanding educational English grammar*, 11–34. Seoul, Korea: Hankook Press.

Yang, Hyun-Kwon. 2010. Linguistic systems of target language as organizational foundations of foreign language teaching [in Korean]. *Korean Language Education* 133. 63–81.

Appendix 1 Instruction Activities for Teaching LV-TRCs

No.	Form-Centered Instruction	Construction-Centered Instruction
1	**Introduction (Syntactic task)** Students classify three sentences (whose main predicate is *make*) into three types, SVO, SVOO, and SVOC.	**Introduction (Semantic task)** Students match three LV-TRC sentences with three pictures which describe their contents.
2	**Explicit instruction (True/False)** Students check whether each of four linguistic statements on syntactic composition is correct or incorrect, and correct incorrect statements.	**Parsing task** Students parse each of the three LV-TRC sentences, presented in the preceding activity, into four constituents – a subject, a verb, an object, and a resultative phrase.
3	**Parsing task** Students parse each of three SVOC sentences into four constituents – a subject, a verb, an object, and a complement.	**Explicit instruction (True/False)** Students check each of four linguistics statements on constructional properties or the verb *make*, and correct incorrect statements.
4	**Scrambled sentences** Students unscramble three scrambled sentences, and write three SVOC sentences.	**Scrambled sentences** Given three pictures about resultative scenes, students unscramble three scrambled sentences, and write three LV-TRC sentences about the pictures.
5	**Scrambled sentences in discourse** Students read three short texts, and unscramble the final scrambled sentence of each text.	**Scrambled sentences in discourse** Students read three short texts, and unscramble the final scrambled sentence of each text.
6	**Picture-based sentence writing** Students write SVOC sentences about seven pictures (e.g., *It makes hair dry*).	**Picture-based sentence writing** Students write LV-TRC sentences about seven pictures (e.g., *It makes hair dry*).

Appendix 2 Instruction Activities for Teaching HV-TRCs

No.	Form-Centered Instruction	Construction-Centered Instruction
1	**Explicit instruction** Students are instructed that various verbs other than *make* are used in SVOC sentences.	**Explicit instruction** Students are instructed that *make* does not imply specific means to achieve "change of state" while verbs such as *hit* do (as in *Pooh hit Piglet angry*).
2	**Parsing task** Students parse each of two SVOC sentences into four constituents – a subject, a verb, an object, and a complement.	**Verb replacement task** Given two pictures about the resultative scenes, students replace the verb *make* in two LV-TRC sentences with other verbs to express "specific means" meaning described in the pictures.
3	**Fill-in-blanks task** Given a list of verbs and four incomplete SVOC sentences, students write in a missing verb in each sentence (e.g., *The old lady watered the plants flat*).	**Fill-in-blanks task** Given a list of verbs and four incomplete HV-TRC sentences, students write in a missing verb in each sentence to express "specific means" meaning (e.g., *The old lady watered the plants flat*).
4	**Parsing task** Students parse each of the SVOC sentences, presented in the preceding activity, into four constituents – a subject, a verb, an object, and a complement.	**Parsing task** Students parse each of the HV-TRC sentences, presented in the preceding activity, into four constituents – a subject, a verb, an object, and a resultative phrase.
5	**Scrambled sentences in discourse** Students read four short texts, and unscramble the final scrambled sentence of each text.	**Scrambled sentences in discourse** Students read four short texts, and unscramble the final scrambled sentence of each text.
6	**Sentence writing in discourse** Students read three short texts, and write in a missing SVOC sentence in the middle of each text.	**Sentence composition task** Students read three short texts, and write in a HV-TRC sentence in the middle of each text.

Gaëtanelle Gilquin
Input-dependent L2 acquisition: Causative constructions in English as a foreign and second language

Abstract: Adopting a constructionist corpus-based approach, this chapter seeks to investigate the influence of acquisition context on the learning of constructions. It starts from a usage-based view of language acquisition to formulate the hypothesis of "input-dependent L2 acquisition", which predicts that learners of English as a second language, who get exposed to naturally-occurring language, should have a better command of constructions than learners of English as a foreign language, who rely almost exclusively on formal instruction. This hypothesis is tested for the causative construction, whose frequency, syntactic behaviour and phraseological preferences are compared in corpus data representing the two contexts of acquisition. The findings partly support the hypothesis, but also lead to a refinement of the usage-based model of L2 acquisition, suggesting that other factors than context should also be taken into account.

Keywords: acquisition context; foreign language learning; second language acquisition; EFL; ESL; causative construction; input-dependent L2 acquisition

1 Introduction

The existence of a causative construction, in English as well as other languages, has long been recognised, well before the advent of Construction Grammar (CxG), whose viability as a theoretical framework implies the very recognition of such "conventionalized pairings of form and function" (Goldberg 2006: 3). The term "causative construction" can be found in publications representing different theoretical orientations, ranging from Generative Semantics (Shibatani 1976) to Functional Grammar (Dik 1980: 53–89), through Natural Semantic Metalanguage (Wierzbicka 1998) and, of course, Cognitive Linguistics (e.g. King 1988; Kemmer and Verhagen 1994). Depending on the authors' understanding of the term, it can cover one or several types of constructions, among which lexical causative constructions (e.g. *John broke the window*), morphological causative constructions (e.g. *strengthen*, formed by adding an *–en* suffix to the noun *strength*) and syntactic causative constructions, which include periphrastic (or analytic) causative constructions (e.g. *He caused the bomb to explode*). For the present purposes, the term "causative construction" will be used to refer exclusively to English periphrastic causative constructions, which are constructions made up of a causative verb (like *cause* or *make*) controlling a non-finite complement clause, whose combination expresses the idea that a CAUSER acts upon a CAUSEE to bring about an EFFECT, as illustrated by the following example:

(1)   Michael (CAUSER) made Mary (CAUSEE) cry (EFFECT).

This chapter adopts a constructionist approach to investigate the use of periphrastic causative constructions with *cause, get, have* and *make* in corpora representing two non-native varieties of English, namely English as a foreign language and English as a second language. Relying on a usage-based view of language acquisition, it seeks to assess the possible influence of acquisition context on the use of the causative construction. It does so by considering three levels of analysis (corresponding to different degrees of abstraction of the construction) and by complementing the traditional techniques of corpus linguistics with the CxG-inspired method of collostructional analysis.

In the next section, the difference between English as a foreign language and English as a second language in terms of acquisition context is outlined, and the cognitive implications of this difference serve as a basis to formulate the hypothesis of "input-dependent L2 acquisition". Section 3 consists of the corpus analysis. After briefly describing the causative construction at the three levels of abstraction at which it is examined, as well as the corpora used and the method of data extraction applied, I present the results of the analysis of the frequency, syntactic usage and phraseological preferences of (some of) the causative constructions. These results make it possible, in Section 4, to refine the usage-based model linking input and output. Section 5 concludes the chapter.[1]

2 EFL and ESL: different acquisition contexts – and cognitive implications

The distinction between foreign and second languages is a well-known one. The two terms describe, respectively, "the learning of a nonnative language in the environment of one's native language" and "the learning of a nonnative language in the environment in which that language is spoken" (Gass and Selinker

---

[1] I am grateful to the audience at the *Constructionist Approaches to Language Pedagogy* (CALP) 2013 conference for discussion about some of the contents of this chapter, as well as two reviewers for their comments on an earlier draft.

2001: 5). In Second Language Acquisition (SLA) research, the latter situation has often referred to the experience of immigrant learners in "dominant L2 settings" (Siegel 2003: 181), as appears from the examples provided by Gass and Selinker (2001: 5) to illustrate the acquisition of a second (as opposed to foreign) language: "German speakers learning Japanese in Japan or Punjabi speakers learning English in the United Kingdom". However, next to these dominant or "majority language settings" (Ellis 2008: 291), one should also recognise "official language settings" (Ellis 2008: 291), environments in which the target language is a (semi-)official language which performs important functions in the media, administration, education, etc. Thus, in Madagascar French serves as an official language next to the local Malagasy language, and in Malaysia English is a semi-official language while Malaysian Malay is the official language. French in Madagascar and English in Malaysia are not native languages for a majority of the population, but because of their special status they are regularly used in people's everyday lives. Learning French in Madagascar or English in Malaysia thus involves learning a second language, just like learning French in France or English in Australia as an immigrant. In this chapter, I will use the term "second language", and more precisely "English as a second language" (ESL), to refer (only) to official language settings.[2] It corresponds to what has also been called "New Englishes", "institutionalised second-language varieties of English" or, in Kachru's (1985) model of the three concentric circles, "outer circle varieties of English". "English as a foreign language" (EFL), on the other hand, will be used in its usual sense, as a synonym of "learner English(es)" and "expanding circle varieties of English".

EFL and ESL are often presented as forming a continuum, rather than a dichotomy (see e.g. Broughton et al. 1980: 7; Nayar 1997). However, if we consider the poles of this continuum, that is, EFL and ESL in their most prototypical form, we can observe clear differences between these two varieties. The most important one, and the most relevant one for the present purposes, has to do with the acquisition context typical of EFL and ESL. For EFL, learning essentially takes place in an educational setting, i.e. in an institution like a school or a university, through (more or less) formal teaching of the target language. The main input comes from the language teacher, classmates and classroom materials, which can include textbooks, grammar books, dictionaries, articles, recordings of interviews and dialogues, etc. (most of this material is inauthentic, having been created specifically for learners, but some authentic material can be used

---

[2] For a constructionist approach to ESL in majority language settings, see e.g. Ellis and Ferreira-Junior (2009).

as well, especially at more advanced levels).[3] EFL learners can get exposed to the target language outside the classroom, for example through books, radio broadcasts, television shows or the internet, and the latter in particular has become widespread among learners,[4] but in the typical EFL situation, as pointed out by Broughton et al. (1980: 6), English "does not play an essential role in national or social life", and its use is limited to international communication. In the case of ESL, part of the input comes from language classes where learners receive formal instruction in the language, as in EFL contexts, but in addition the educational setting includes instruction **through** the target language, since the medium of instruction for subjects like history, geography or mathematics is often English, at least from a certain level of education onwards. More importantly, however, ESL learners also have the opportunity to acquire the target language in a natural setting, through a variety of situations (mostly institutional ones, since local languages are often preferred for more informal situations): by reading or listening to the media, or interacting with the administration, for instance, they get exposed to large amounts of authentic, naturally-occurring English in their daily lives. These differences in exposure between EFL and ESL are summarised in Table 1. The table also lists another difference that will be relevant in this study, namely the norm-dependent status of EFL and the norm-developing orientation of ESL: EFL standards rely on the norms of native English, whereas ESL may develop its own standards, which may be different from those of English as a native language (see Kachru 1985).

Table 1: Some differences between EFL and ESL

	EFL	ESL
Exposure in educational setting	Instruction in the target language	– Instruction in the target language – Instruction through the target language
Exposure in natural setting	Limited or non-existent, except for international communication	In a variety of situations, especially for institutional communication
Relation to the norm	Norm-dependent	Norm-developing

---

3 Note that in some EFL classrooms, a more communicative approach to language teaching is adopted, which shifts the focus away from formal instruction and towards more naturalistic input.
4 Most of the data included in the EFL corpus used here (see Section 3.2) have been collected before the internet revolution really began, though, which means that the influence of the internet on learners' degree of exposure to English should be limited.

The difference in acquisition context between EFL and ESL learners has important cognitive implications. In a constructionist, usage-based view of language acquisition, it is argued that constructions are learned from the available language input. In fact, this "input-driven inductive learning" (Goldberg 2006: 12) is one of the basic tenets of CxG and other usage-based models. It assumes that learners abstract over their cumulative experience with language (Bybee 2008: 218), in a process of "pattern-finding" (Tomasello 2009: 70) by which they generalise patterns from the concrete instances they get exposed to. While this theory has been described primarily in the context of first language (L1) acquisition (e.g. Lieven and Tomasello 2008), it is supposed to be true of second/foreign language (L2) acquisition as well (Eskildsen 2009). For the present purposes, based on the above view of input-dependent language acquisition, we can hypothesise the following: considering that (i) EFL learners learn English mainly in an instructional setting and receive relatively little exposure to the target language, and (ii) ESL learners, in addition, also acquire English in a natural setting and thus receive more exposure to the target language, it can be expected that ESL learners will have been exposed to more (authentic) instances of a given construction than EFL learners and will thus have better integrated its schema, resulting in a better, more native-like command of the construction. This "input-dependent L2 acquisition" hypothesis, which will be tested here for the causative construction, is assumed to apply to all aspects of the use of the construction. In the present analysis, its validity will be assessed by considering the frequency as well as syntactic and phraseological behaviour of the causative construction, relying on corpora and adopting a CxG-based approach.

3 The acquisition of the causative construction in an EFL and ESL context

3.1 The causative construction

As mentioned in Section 1, the construction under study in this chapter is the so-called periphrastic causative construction in English. Only a limited number of verbs can be used in this construction, and among these, I will focus on *cause*, *get*, *have* and *make*. Each of these verbs can be construed with certain non-finite complements, as shown in Table 2, which lists and exemplifies the patterns that can be found in standard native English.[5]

---

[5] All the corpus examples are reproduced as is and are followed by the name of the (sub)corpus from which they are taken: British National Corpus (BNC), NUS Corpus of Learner English (NUCLE), one of the components of the International Corpus of English – Hong Kong (ICE-HK),

Table 2: Causative constructions in English

Construction	Example
[X CAUSE Y $V_{to\text{-}inf}$]	Heating collapses the blue spectral peak, **causing** the violet luminescence to shift towards red. (BNC)
[X GET Y $V_{to\text{-}inf}$]	The therapist tried to **get** her to look at such situations from her parents' viewpoint. (BNC)
[X GET Y V_{pp}]	The use of this network will be required in order to **get** things done. (BNC)
[X GET Y V_{prp}]	In most countries a good deal more could be done to **get** people talking and thinking about proposed changes. (BNC)
[X HAVE Y V_{inf}]	The bulletin is not a wide ranging, objective, scientific review as De Melker would **have** us believe. (BNC)
[X HAVE Y V_{pp}]	Subsequently only the latter could pay to **have** complicated machinery repaired. (BNC)
[X HAVE Y V_{prp}]	After the day's work we **had** all the colony drilling for an hour or two in the yard, which formed a spacious square. (BNC)
[X MAKE Y V_{inf}]	It's difficult to avoid **making** his suicide sound too purposeful. (BNC)
[X BE made $V_{to\text{-}inf}$]	Even the famine area was **made** to pay one-half of the supplemental tax levied for famine relief. (BNC)
[X MAKE Y V_{pp}]	As trade picked up slowly towards the end of the year, genuine Nepmen started to **make** their presence felt. (BNC)

The complex structure of subordinate clauses, and non-finite subordinate clauses in particular, usually makes them quite difficult for non-native speakers. Parrott (2010: 427) points out that learners of English tend to use fewer non-finite clauses than native speakers. In the case of periphrastic causative constructions, there is the additional problem that each verb is limited to certain types of complements. *Cause* is only construed with a *to*-infinitive, but *get* and *have* can be followed by a present participle, a past participle or an infinitive (a *to*-infinitive with *get* and a bare infinitive with *have*). Causative *make* is noteworthy in that its complementation depends on the voice of the verb: in the active it takes a bare infinitive, whereas in the passive it takes a *to*-infinitive. It can also be used with a past participle, but this construction is quite restricted in use (see Gilquin 2010). The *Longman Dictionary of Common Errors* (Turton and Heaton 1996: 208–209) includes an entry for causative *make*, noting that it

---

Indian (ICE-IND), Jamaican (ICE-JAM), Kenyan (ICE-KEN), Nigerian (ICE-NIG), Philippine (ICE-PHI), Singaporean (ICE-SIN), Tanzanian (ICE-TAN) – or one of the components of the International Corpus of Learner English – Bulgarian (ICLE-BG), Chinese (ICLE-CH), Czech (ICLE-CZ), Dutch (ICLE-DU), Finnish (ICLE-FI), French (ICLE-FR), German (ICLE-GE), Italian (ICLE-IT), Japanese (ICLE-JP), Norwegian (ICLE-NO), Polish (ICLE-PL), Russian (ICLE-RU), Spanish (ICLE-SP), Swedish (ICLE-SW), Tswana (ICLE-TSW), Turkish (ICLE-TR).

should not be used with a present participle (*_The cold water made me shivering_) nor with a _to_-infinitive (*_What made you to decide to work in the theatre?_), except in the passive (_He was made to take the examination again_), which suggests that errors in the complementation of _make_ are common among learners. Next to syntactic difficulties, causative constructions can also pose phraseological problems to non-native speakers, who are not necessarily aware of the lexical associations between the constructions and certain (sets of) non-finite verbs (cf. Gilquin 2012). These and other characteristics of non-native speakers' use of causative constructions have been discussed in publications that focus on EFL (e.g. Liu and Shaw 2001) or ESL (e.g. Lee and Ziegeler 2006), but to my knowledge no attempt has been made so far to compare their use in these two varieties.

In CxG, constructions can be considered at several levels of abstraction. In what precedes, I have already referred to two different levels of analysis for periphrastic causative constructions: the higher level of **the** causative construction, which involves the use of a causative verb followed by a non-finite subordinate clause, and the lower level of the ten causative constructions listed in Table 2, which involve the use of a given causative verb with a specific type of non-finite complement. Given that different low-level causative constructions have been shown to present distinct features, and also lead to different errors or infelicities among non-native speakers (Gilquin 2010, 2012), it does not seem ideal to lump them together by considering the more abstract causative construction in our syntactic and phraseological analysis of non-native corpus data. On the other hand, adopting the level of analysis illustrated in Table 2 poses another problem, which has to do with the fact that non-native speakers may produce complementation patterns that differ from those found in standard native English, as appears from examples (2) to (4). In (2) _cause_ is used with a bare infinitive (instead of a _to_-infinitive); in (3) _make_ is followed by a present participle (instead of a bare infinitive); and in (4) the CAUSEE is missing (_It may cause_ **her** _to feel…_).

(2)   This problem **causes** us fail to recognize the opportunity to convert resources optimally so as to meet our objective, which is to meet desired needs of the public. (NUCLE)

(3)   This should **make** us thinking about it. (ICLE-IT)

(4)   It may **cause** to feel herself a murderer. (ICLE-TR)

In a study strictly based on the list of standard constructions, such patterns would be lost, despite their obvious interest from an SLA perspective. In this study, the lower level of analysis will therefore be combined with an intermediate level of analysis, which takes into account the nature of the causative verb, but also the voice of the causative verb and of the non-finite complement, as represented by [Caus.V$_{act/pas}$ Non-finiteV$_{act/pas}$]. For each causative verb, there are thus potentially four different patterns (or constructions), as shown for *make* in Table 3, which includes, for each pattern, a standard and a non-standard example. This intermediate level of analysis brings together the wide range of possible low-level constructions (see Table 4 for an example with *make*), but it also provides a useful *tertium comparationis* that will make it possible to compare like with like in the analysis, irrespective of the actual realisation at the low level and its degree of grammaticality.

Table 3: Causative constructions with *make* at intermediate level of abstraction (with standard and non-standard examples)

Causative verb	Non-finite verb	
	Active	Passive
Active	– *Guerrillas can **make** you think of Nostromo.* (BNC) – *They do this to **make** feel regretful.* (ICLE-TR)	– *they **made** their voices heard at the conference* (BNC) – *the factors which have **made** Kiswahili to be established as a National language* (ICE-TAN)
Passive	– *We are **made** to feel that the reversed meaning is wrong.* (BNC) – *women are still **made** feel guilty if they leave their children in day care* (ICLE-FI)	– *There is nothing secret that will not be **made** known.* (BNC) – *Matshego's fate to [be] **made** be known*[6]

Table 4: Comparison of intermediate- and low-level causative constructions with *make*

Intermediate-level constructions	Low-level constructions
[MAKE$_{act}$ V$_{act}$]	[X MAKE Y V$_{inf}$] [X MAKE Y V$_{to\text{-}inf}$] [X MAKE Y V$_{prp}$] [X MAKE V$_{inf}$] etc.
[MAKE$_{act}$ V$_{pas}$]	[X MAKE Y V$_{PP}$] [X MAKE Y be V$_{PP}$] [X MAKE Y to be V$_{PP}$] etc.
[MAKE$_{pas}$ V$_{act}$]	[X BE made V$_{to\text{-}inf}$] [X BE made V$_{inf}$] etc.
[MAKE$_{pas}$ V$_{pas}$]	[X BE made V$_{PP}$] [X BE made to be V$_{PP}$] etc.

---

6 Example taken from http://www.iol.co.za/sport/matshego-s-fate-to-made-be-known-1.591330#.Vb92ZUVXFRl; no non-standard example for this pattern was found in the corpora.

3.2 Corpora and data extraction

The corpus data come from the International Corpus of Learner English (ICLE) for EFL, and from the International Corpus of English (ICE) and the NUS Corpus of Learner English (NUCLE) for ESL. ICLEv2 (Granger et al. 2009) is made up of essays produced by EFL students from 16 mother-tongue backgrounds (Bulgarian, Chinese, Czech, Dutch, Finnish, French, German, Italian, Japanese, Norwegian, Polish, Russian, Spanish, Swedish, Tswana and Turkish). A selection was made on the basis of the learners' profiles: their native language had to be the main language they spoke at home and they had to live in a country where that language was dominant, e.g. Japan for Japanese-speaking students. This resulted in a corpus of 3,621,892 words. The ESL corpus sample was slightly less homogeneous, which was due to the difficulty of gathering a sufficiently large set of comparable data, likely to contain enough instances of causative constructions to allow for a reliable analysis. The non-professional writing sections (made up of student essays and examination scripts) of the Hong Kong, Indian, Jamaican, Kenyan, Nigerian, Philippine, Singaporean and Tanzanian components of ICE were included, together with the whole of NUCLE, which contains essays written by students at the National University of Singapore (see Dahlmeier et al. 2013). The ESL data amount to 1,435,187 words. However, it should be emphasised that about two thirds of them correspond to the NUCLE corpus, which make them more representative of the Singaporean variety than any other variety. On the other hand, the inclusion of NUCLE makes it possible to rely on a relatively large sample (though smaller than the EFL sample) that is comparable in genre to ICLE – novice academic writing – and whose data are produced by writers who have arguably reached the same level of cognitive development as the ICLE writers – students at a relatively advanced stage in their education. Finally, a five-million-word sample of the academic writing sections of the British National Corpus (BNC) was used as a reference corpus against which to compare the EFL and ESL data. This choice was mainly driven by practical reasons. Native corpora of student writing do exist (e.g. the Louvain Corpus of Native English Essays), but they tend to be very small in comparison with the EFL and ESL corpora used here (only a few hundred thousand words). Although not everybody may agree on the relevance of using a corpus of expert writing to compare with student writing, it may be argued that expert academic writing represents the ultimate target that non-native writers must aim to reach, and thus constitutes an appropriate yardstick for non-native writing. In addition, since the main goal here is to compare EFL and ESL, the native corpus should just be seen as a kind of neutral baseline that makes the comparison between EFL and ESL easier but is not central to the analysis itself.

Given that the causative construction is a relatively rare and rather complex syntactic structure, its retrieval from large corpora has to rely on (semi-)automatic methods involving part-of-speech (POS) tagging. Some of the above corpora were available in POS-tagged versions: ICLE, some ICE components (Hong Kong, Indian, Jamaican, Nigerian and Singaporean) and the BNC. The other corpora (NUCLE, as well as the Kenyan, Philippine and Tanzanian components of ICE) were POS-tagged by means of Wmatrix (Rayson 2009). Using WordSmith Tools (Scott 2004), I extracted from the non-native corpora all the forms of the verbs *cause*, *get*, *have* and *make* followed by a non-finite verb (infinitive, past or present participle) within one (or two) to five words.[7] The set of data resulting from this automatic search were manually disambiguated so as to keep only the instances of periphrastic causative constructions. A similar procedure had been applied to the native corpus within the frame of the analysis in Gilquin (2010), from which the native data are taken. Note that this method of extraction relies on the definition of the causative construction at the higher level of abstraction, as a causative verb followed by a non-finite subordinate verb, with no further specification as to the voice of the causative verb, the type of non-finite complement used, or the presence or position of a CAUSEE. In this way, the search strings used to extract (potential) causative constructions also allow for the retrieval of non-standard patterns at the lower level of abstraction, including unusual combinations of causative verbs and non-finite complements (5) and unusual formal structures (6).

(5) In the United State there are device that can also help to connect the elderly to the doctor without **having** them to go to the hospital everyday. (NUCLE)[8]

(6) It may **cause** to decrease the crime rate. (ICLE-TR)

In an Excel spreadsheet, each causative construction was then coded for a number of parameters, among which the subcorpus from which it was extracted, the lemma of the verb occurring in the non-finite verb slot, and of course informa-

---

7 For *get* and *have*, the search strings excluded the possibility of having a form of the verb directly followed by a past participle, as it would have extracted all the instances of *have* as a present perfect auxiliary (e.g. *have done*) and *get* as a passive auxiliary (e.g. *get killed*), which would have dramatically lowered the precision rate of the query and increased the amount of manual disambiguation work.

8 The combination of causative *have* and a *to*-infinitive is not totally impossible in native English. According to Butters and Stettler (1986: 184), however, it is "commonplace in the South and South Midland states [of America] but virtually unknown elsewhere".

tion about the construction, both at the intermediate level of analysis (active-passive pattern) and at the lower level of analysis (actual realisation). The spreadsheet served as a database from which the data for the different types of analysis below were taken. Note that, although the study is based on relatively large corpora, some of the constructions are so rare in (native and non-native) English that, for these, very few occurrences were retrieved, which means that certain parts of the analysis had to be performed on the most frequent constructions only. This should be seen as a limitation of the study, made inevitable by the frequency of the construction under investigation and by the limited availability of appropriate corpora.

3.3 Frequency of causative constructions

The first type of analysis carried out on the corpus data aims at establishing the frequency of causative constructions. At the higher level of analysis, that of the causative construction (with any of the four verbs under investigation and any type of non-finite complement), it appears that non-native writers, whether EFL or ESL, heavily overuse the construction in comparison with English as a Native Language (ENL), cf. Figure 1. The results range from about 150 occurrences per million words (pmw) in ENL, through some 350 occurrences pmw in ESL, to over 500 occurrences pmw in EFL, a difference that is statistically highly significant ($p < 0.0001$). Despite the syntactic complexity of the causative construction and learners' tendency to avoid non-finite subordinate clauses (Section 3.1), it thus seems as if non-native writers often rely on periphrastic constructions to express causation, although this tendency is stronger among EFL students than among ESL students, the latter being situated about half way between ENL and EFL. These results partly support a frequency-based interpretation of the hypothesis of input-dependent L2 acquisition (see Section 2), since ESL students appear to better approximate to the native frequency of the construction than EFL students, and thus presumably to have better integrated this aspect of the construction thanks to their increased input in English. On the other hand, overuse is not predicted by the hypothesis, since there is no particular reason to believe that non-native writers should produce more instances of a construction than they can get exposed to. If we assume that the language non-native students get exposed to contains a proportion of causative constructions that is similar to that found in the ENL corpus (see, however, Section 4), we would expect the following: (i) ESL students, who receive only part of their language input in English, do not get exposed to as many instances of the causative construction as a native speaker would, and therefore should produce it less often than in

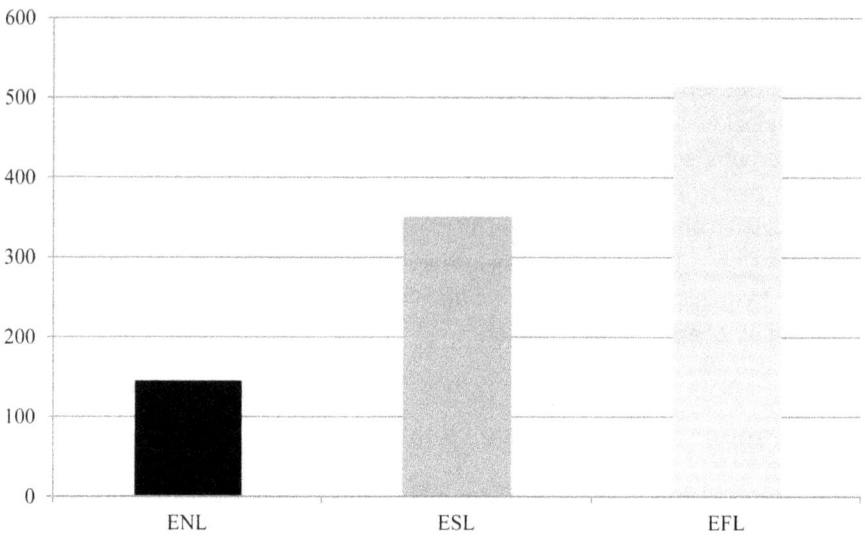

Figure 1: Relative frequency (pmw) of the causative construction in ENL, ESL and EFL (high level of abstraction)

ENL; (ii) EFL students, who have even less input in English than ESL students and hence fewer opportunities to get exposed to the causative construction, should produce it less often than ESL students. The frequency of the construction should thus be the lowest in EFL, followed by ESL, and then ENL with the highest frequency. The results obtained, however, are the exact opposite of what this usage-based view of language predicts. This might be explained by the competition between periphrastic constructions and synthetic verbs to express causation. As Slobin (1985: 14) points out, children tend to favour analytic over synthetic expressions. This tendency seems to apply to second language acquisition as well, as suggested by Giacalone Ramat (1995: 132) and Altenberg and Granger (2001: 184), who illustrate what they call learners' "analytic strategy" and "'decompositional' strategy", respectively. Following this preference, it might be that, compared to native students, non-native students overuse periphrastic (analytic) causative constructions as a way of compensating for their underuse of synthetic causative verbs, an assumption that should be tested through a study of synthetic causative verbs in native and non-native English. While such a study has to be left for future research, in what follows we will see whether the general overuse just observed applies to the different constructions that are covered by the high-level construct.

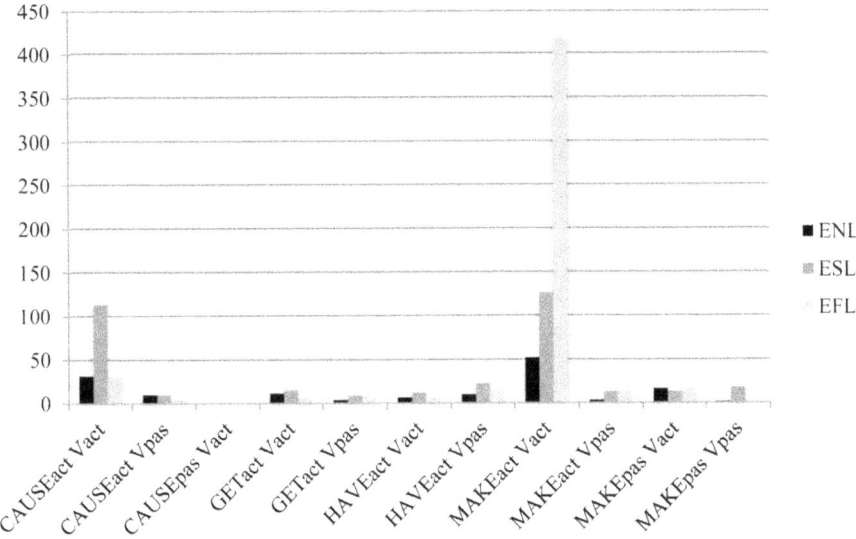

Figure 2: Relative frequency (pmw) of the active-passive causative constructions with *cause*, *get*, *have* and *make* in ENL, ESL and EFL (intermediate level of abstraction)

The results for the intermediate-level causative constructions, [Caus.$V_{act/pas}$ Non-finiteV$_{act/pas}$], show that most of the constructions are very uncommon in both the native and non-native corpora, with a relative frequency that is lower than 25 occurrences pmw (see Figure 2). The only constructions that display a higher frequency are [CAUSE$_{act}$ V$_{act}$] and [MAKE$_{act}$ V$_{act}$]. The former has a very similar frequency in ENL and EFL, but is overused by ESL students. The latter, on the other hand, is overused by both ESL and EFL students when compared to native speakers, but the overuse is much stronger among EFL students, who use this construction eight times as often as native speakers and three times as often as ESL students. These results partly confirm the hypothesis of input-dependent L2 acquisition, in that constructions that are rare in ENL (and hence, presumably, in non-native speakers' input) are rare in ESL and EFL, whereas constructions that are more frequent in ENL (over 30 occurrences pmw) are also more frequent in non-native English. In addition, for a number of constructions, like [MAKE$_{act}$ V$_{act}$], the frequency in ESL is closer to the native baseline than is the case in EFL. However, the relation between the frequencies of the constructions in EFL, ESL and ENL does not correspond to the expected gradation (see above). The only exception to this is [CAUSE$_{act}$ V$_{pas}$], which is least frequent in EFL, more frequent in ESL and most frequent in ENL, but the construction is very rare in the first place and only the difference between EFL and ESL/ENL is statistically significant. Among the constructions that are more frequent in non-native writing, we can notice a preference for the unmarked active voice, both on the causative verb and on the non-finite verb. The general overuse of (active) causative constructions with *make* could be explained by the fact that *make* is a high-frequency and general-purpose verb, which non-native speakers are bound to have heard before with different meanings and in different functions. Goldberg (2006: 77–79) also underlines the important role of general-purpose verbs in (first) language acquisition when it comes to generalising patterns from the input. The fact that ESL students also overuse [CAUSE$_{act}$ V$_{act}$], using it almost as often as [MAKE$_{act}$ V$_{act}$], might be related to the form of the verb, which directly evokes causation. Given that ESL students are often left to acquire English "spontaneously" in a natural setting, they are likely to instinctively associate this construction with causation and use *cause* as one of the default causative verbs, despite the fact that this verb is normally associated with more technical registers (Gilquin 2010: 230). [MAKE$_{act}$ V$_{act}$] and [CAUSE$_{act}$ V$_{act}$] are thus, each in their own way, particularly salient for ESL and EFL students, which results in a strong preference for (and, in effect, overuse of) these two constructions.

3.4 Syntactic analysis: the distribution and nature of patterns

In this section, we turn to the analysis of the lower-level constructions, that is, the actual realisations of the causative construction as they are produced by EFL and ESL students. Table 5 gives a broad overview of the distribution of these patterns, showing how many variants there are for each [Caus.V$_{act/pas}$ Non-finiteV$_{act/pas}$] construction in the three language varieties. What we notice is a slight tendency for the number of patterns to increase from ENL to ESL and from ESL to EFL. Consider the patterns for [CAUSE$_{act}$ V$_{act}$]: while ENL has just one, ESL has four, and EFL five. [MAKE$_{act}$ V$_{act}$] is realised by two patterns in ENL, four in ESL and as many as eight in EFL. The other constructions are less frequent, as we saw above, which results in a smaller number of variants, but the same increase is found with [CAUSE$_{act}$ V$_{pas}$], [GET$_{act}$ V$_{act}$] and [MAKE$_{pas}$ V$_{act}$] when moving from ESL to EFL. The other constructions have the same number of variants in the three varieties ([GET$_{act}$ V$_{pas}$], [HAVE$_{act}$ V$_{act}$] and [MAKE$_{pas}$ V$_{pas}$]) or present irregular patterns. Non-native students thus tend to show more structural variety in their use of the causative construction than native speakers, and EFL students more so than ESL students, which places ESL students in an in-between position, as was the case for the frequency of the causative construction (Section 3.3).

Table 5: Number of variants per [Caus.$V_{act/pas}$ Non-finite$V_{act/pas}$] construction in ENL, ESL and EFL

	ENL	ESL	EFL
[$CAUSE_{act}$ V_{act}]	1	4	5
[$CAUSE_{act}$ V_{pas}]	2	1	2
[$CAUSE_{pas}$ V_{act}]	1	–	–
[GET_{act} V_{act}]	2	2	3
[GET_{act} V_{pas}]	1	1	1
[$HAVE_{act}$ V_{act}]	3	3	3
[$HAVE_{act}$ V_{pas}]	2	2	1
[$MAKE_{act}$ V_{act}]	2	4	8
[$MAKE_{act}$ V_{pas}]	2	6	4
[$MAKE_{pas}$ V_{act}]	1	1	2
[$MAKE_{pas}$ V_{pas}]	1	1	1

This upward trend from ENL to EFL through ESL is clearly illustrated in Table 6, which lists and exemplifies the variants of [$MAKE_{act}$ V_{act}] in the three varieties. There are twice as many variants in ESL as in ENL, and twice as many in EFL as in ESL. Two patterns are common to the three varieties, viz. [X *MAKE* Y V_{inf}] and [X *MAKE* Y $V_{to\text{-}inf}$], and two further patterns are shared by ESL and EFL, viz. [X *MAKE* Y V_{prp}] and [X *MAKE* V_{inf}] (with no CAUSEE). The four remaining patterns ([X *MAKE* $V_{to\text{-}inf}$], [X *MAKE* V_{prp}], [X *MAKE* V_{inf} Y] and [X *MAKE of* Y $V_{to\text{-}inf}$]) are only found among EFL learners. It will be immediately obvious from the table that the patterns that are specific to non-native writing are incorrect according to the syntactic rules that govern the use of causative constructions.[9] These results suggest that EFL students display more variation than ESL students in their non-standard use of the construction.

In the rest of this section, which will be devoted to a more in-depth analysis of the patterns found in ESL and EFL, I will focus on causative constructions with *cause* and *make*, which turned out to be the most common causative verbs, and will leave aside constructions with *get* and *have*, which are too infrequent in the corpora to allow for reliable generalisations. Table 7 summarises the data that will be discussed in what follows. For each [Caus.$V_{act/pas}$ Non-finite$V_{act/pas}$] construction, it provides, in decreasing order of frequency, a list of the patterns found in the ENL, ESL and EFL corpora, together with the percentages these patterns represent in the language variety. The pattern in bold corresponds to

---

9 This, strictly speaking, is also the case of the [X *MAKE* Y $V_{to\text{-}inf}$] pattern that is found in ENL. However, this construction corresponds to only one occurrence in the five-million-word BNC sample (as opposed to 257 instances with a bare infinitive).

Table 6: Realisations of [MAKE$_{act}$ V$_{act}$] in ENL, ESL and EFL

ENL	ESL	EFL
[X MAKE Y V$_{inf}$] trying to **make** me <u>laugh</u>	[X MAKE Y V$_{inf}$] **made** them <u>assume</u> that...	[X MAKE Y V$_{inf}$] **make** all students <u>understand</u>
[X MAKE Y V$_{to-inf}$] **make** X-cells (...) <u>to behave</u> in a sustained manner	[X MAKE Y V$_{to-inf}$] can **make** our body <u>to become</u> healthier	[X MAKE Y V$_{to-inf}$] **made** me <u>to think</u> so
	[X MAKE Y V$_{prp}$] **made** our nation <u>continuing</u> to import	[X MAKE Y V$_{prp}$] **makes** people <u>trying</u> to find one
	[X MAKE V$_{inf}$] to **make** <u>ensure</u> the research continues	[X MAKE V$_{inf}$] to **make** <u>feel</u> regretful
		[X MAKE V$_{to-inf}$] try to **make** <u>to know</u> their position
		[X MAKE V$_{prp}$] **make** <u>interpreting</u> her
		[X MAKE V$_{inf}$ Y] what **makes** <u>arise</u> indignation
		[X MAKE of Y V$_{to-inf}$] have **made** of him <u>to be</u> apart

the most prototypical realisation of the [Caus.V$_{act/pas}$ Non-finiteV$_{act/pas}$] construction (that is, in actual fact, the most standard and usual pattern in native English).

The first observation is that the most prototypical pattern is always the most frequent one, for each [Caus.V$_{act/pas}$ Non-finiteV$_{act/pas}$] construction and in each language variety, which suggests that a majority of the causative constructions produced by non-native writers follow the rules of the English language. However, the proportion of these prototypical realisations varies quite a lot, ranging from 44% for [X MAKE Y V$_{pp}$] as a realisation of [MAKE$_{act}$ V$_{pas}$] in ESL to 100% for [X BE made V$_{pp}$] as a realisation of [MAKE$_{pas}$ V$_{pas}$] in ESL and EFL.

For the *cause* constructions, [CAUSE$_{act}$ V$_{act}$] and [CAUSE$_{act}$ V$_{pas}$],[10] there is a large predominance in ESL of the most prototypical pattern, that which is found

---

10 [CAUSE$_{pas}$ V$_{act}$] does not occur in the non-native data and occurs just once in the native data, while [CAUSE$_{pas}$ V$_{pas}$] is not found at all in the corpora.

Table 7: Realisations of *cause* and *make* causative constructions in ENL, ESL and EFL, with percentages

ENL		ESL		EFL	
[CAUSE$_{act}$ V$_{act}$] (e.g. *caused the alliance to break up*)					
[X *CAUSE* Y V$_{to\text{-}inf}$]	100%	[X *CAUSE* Y V$_{to\text{-}inf}$]	95%	[X *CAUSE* Y V$_{to\text{-}inf}$]	79%
		[X *CAUSE* Y V$_{prp}$]	3%	[X *CAUSE* Y V$_{prp}$]	10%
		[X *CAUSE* Y V$_{inf}$]	1%	[X *CAUSE* V$_{prp}$]	4%
		[X *CAUSE* Y *in* V$_{prp}$]	1%	[X *CAUSE* V$_{to\text{-}inf}$]	4%
				[X *CAUSE* V$_{to\text{-}inf}$ Y]	3%
[CAUSE$_{act}$ V$_{pas}$] (e.g. *caused toxic materials to be transported*)					
[X *CAUSE* Y *to be* V$_{pp}$]	98%	[X *CAUSE* Y *to be* V$_{pp}$]	100%	[X *CAUSE* Y *to be* V$_{pp}$]	73%
[X *CAUSE to be* V$_{pp}$ Y]	2%			[X *CAUSE to be* V$_{pp}$ Y]	27%
[MAKE$_{act}$ V$_{act}$] (e.g. *to make the system work*)					
[X *MAKE* Y V$_{inf}$]	99.6%	[X *MAKE* Y V$_{inf}$]	74%	[X *MAKE* Y V$_{inf}$]	85%
[X *MAKE* Y V$_{to\text{-}inf}$]	0.4%	[X *MAKE* Y V$_{to\text{-}inf}$]	23%	[X *MAKE* Y V$_{to\text{-}inf}$]	11%
		[X *MAKE* Y V$_{prp}$]	3%	[X *MAKE* Y V$_{prp}$]	3%
		[X *MAKE* V$_{inf}$]	<1%	[X *MAKE* V$_{inf}$ Y]	<1%
				[X *MAKE* V$_{inf}$]	<1%
				[X *MAKE* V$_{to\text{-}inf}$]	<1%
				[X *MAKE* V$_{prp}$]	<1%
				[X *MAKE of* Y V$_{to\text{-}inf}$]	<1%
[MAKE$_{act}$ V$_{pas}$] (e.g. *to make their presence felt*)					
[X *MAKE* Y V$_{pp}$]	94%	[X *MAKE* Y V$_{pp}$]	44%	[X *MAKE* Y V$_{pp}$]	77%
[X *MAKE* V$_{pp}$ Y]	6%	[X *MAKE* V$_{pp}$ Y]	28%	[X *MAKE* Y *to be* V$_{pp}$]	15%
		[X *MAKE* Y *to be* V$_{pp}$]	11%	[X *MAKE* Y *be* V$_{pp}$]	6%
		[X *MAKE* Y *be* V$_{pp}$]	5%	[X *MAKE* V$_{pp}$ Y]	2%
		[X *MAKE* Y *being* V$_{pp}$]	5%		
		[X *MAKE* V$_{pp}$]	5%		
[MAKE$_{pas}$ V$_{act}$] (e.g. *was made to sell off its hotels*)					
[X *BE made* V$_{to\text{-}inf}$]	100%	[X *BE made* V$_{to\text{-}inf}$]	100%	[X *BE made* V$_{to\text{-}inf}$]	95%
				[X *BE made* V$_{inf}$]	5%
[MAKE$_{pas}$ V$_{pas}$] (e.g. *will not be made known*)					
[X *BE made* V$_{pp}$]	100%	[X *BE made* V$_{pp}$]	100%	[X *BE made* V$_{pp}$]	100%

in ENL most of the time (with 100% and 98% respectively). With an active non-finite verb [X *CAUSE* Y V$_{to\text{-}inf}$] represents a high proportion of 95% in ESL, e.g. (7), and with a passive non-finite verb [X *CAUSE* Y *to be* V$_{pp}$] appears to be the only available option, e.g. (8). This large predominance leaves very little room for other variants.

(7) This increase in demand **causes** labor to become expensive therefore wages of labor increase (ICE-PHI)

(8) Nonetheless, the generalization of certain simple surveillance technologies **causes** their existence to be found everywhere. (NUCLE)

By contrast, the most prototypical pattern in EFL represents less than 80% in each case, and faces competition from other patterns, like the use of a present participle clause, which accounts for 10% of the active construction, the lack of a CAUSEE, which represents 8% in the active (4% with a present participle and 4% with a *to*-infinitive), or the postposition of the object, which is found with a proportion of 3% in the active and 27% in the passive. These three patterns are exemplified in (9) to (11).

(9) The other problem is that credit card may **cause** students getting into debt. (ICLE-CH)

(10) This **caused** to accept the system of new legislative acts which regulate prevention of crime. (ICLE-RU)

(11) Power of the money **caused** to be exploited and to be suffered privation by making use of people by each other. (ICLE-TR)

All this results in what looks like a poorer (formal) knowledge of the *cause* constructions among EFL students as compared to ESL students, whose behaviour is very similar to that of native speakers. The hypothesis of input-dependent L2 acquisition formulated in Section 2 thus seems to be confirmed as far as syntactic analysis is concerned: the students with the higher degree of exposure to (naturally-occurring) language demonstrate a better command of the syntactic rules of causative constructions with *cause*.

However, the picture turns out to be quite different when one examines the realisations of the *make* causative constructions. As Table 7 shows, it is in EFL, not in ESL, that the prototypical realisation is the most widespread – at least when causative *make* is in the active voice. With an active non-finite verb [X *MAKE* Y V_{inf}] represents 85% in EFL (cf. 12), as against 74% in ESL (and 99.6% in ENL), whereas with a passive non-finite verb [X *MAKE* Y V_{pp}] represents 77% in EFL (cf. 13), to be compared with a very low 44% in ESL (and 94% in ENL).

(12) What we must aim at is to **make** them regard ecological behaviour as a status symbol. (ICLE-SW)

(13) For those who are risk-takers speaking does not pose any problems at all, as they simply make use of the scope of vocabulary they have acquired so far and try to **make** themselves understood. (ICLE-PL)

In addition, some interesting patterns emerge, like the [X *MAKE* Y V$_{to\text{-}inf}$] pattern, which is quite common in ESL (23%), but less so in EFL (11%), e.g.

(14) This knowledge is powerful enough to **make** non-living things to evolve. (ICE-PHI)

Another widespread phenomenon, which is proportionally equally frequent in ESL and EFL (21% each), is the presence of a *be* auxiliary when the non-finite verb is in the passive. This auxiliary can take the form of a *to*-infinitive (15), which is the preferred option in the EFL and ESL corpora, a bare infinitive (16) or (only in ESL) a present participle (17).

(15) They grew up underprivillaged and this **made** them to be highly affected by the HIV/AIDS epidemic. (ICLE-TSW)

(16) He has his psychological realism but with a humoristic touch, that **made** him be accepted in his period. (ICLE-SP)

(17) This make people to or dump dirtes in the road which **makes** every places being hold up with dirty. (ICE-NIG)

A last interesting pattern, found as a realisation of [*MAKE*$_{pas}$ V$_{act}$], is [X *BE made* V$_{inf}$], which however only occurs in EFL (with a proportion of 5%), e.g.

(18) Czech students majoring in languages, for example, are often **made** believe that grammar is the most important part of language because it is extremely stressed by their teachers, while other aspects of language are often neglected. (ICLE-CZ)

Finally, note that the results for [*MAKE*$_{pas}$ V$_{pas}$] show no variation at all in any of the varieties, which all use [X *BE made* V$_{pp}$] in 100% of the cases, cf.

(19) The grievances of the people should be brought to the notice of the government & the government's policies should be **made** known to the public. (ICE-IND)

All in all, the *make* patterns do not provide particularly supportive evidence for the hypothesis of input-dependent L2 acquisition, according to which ESL students, with their greater and richer exposure to English, should exhibit a more native-like behaviour than EFL students. If anything, EFL students seem to be more familiar with the prototypical realisations of the *make* constructions than their ESL counterparts.

There are at least three possible explanations for these unexpected results. The first one has to do with another difference between EFL and ESL that was mentioned in Section 2, namely the norm-dependent status of the former and the norm-developing status of the latter. As a norm-developing variety, ESL may have developed new features, including non-standard causative constructions, which students are exposed to and which they may reproduce. This explanation seems to be quite plausible in the case of [X MAKE Y $V_{to\text{-}inf}$], for example, since the analysis of ICE data representing ESL adult, expert academic writing[11] reveals a proportion of 10% of this pattern, which suggests that in (some) ESL countries it might have become an acceptable variant of the more standard [X MAKE Y V_{inf}]. However, the fact that ESL students use this pattern more often than expert writers, in 23% of the occurrences of [$MAKE_{act}$ V_{act}], points to the existence of another explanation.

This second explanation, paradoxically, brings us back to the hypothesis of input-dependent L2 acquisition. While it is true that [X MAKE Y $V_{to\text{-}inf}$] does not follow the pattern of [$MAKE_{act}$ V_{act}], which is normally realised as [X MAKE Y V_{inf}], it follows another pattern, which is the more general pattern of non-finite complementation. As pointed out by Biber et al. (1999: 699), who base their analyses on the Longman Spoken and Written English Corpus, in non-finite complementation *to*-clauses are much more common than bare infinitive clauses, which only occur with a few controlling verbs, viz. causative *make* and *have*, *let*, *help* (which also occurs with *to*-infinitives) and some perception verbs (*feel*, *hear*, *see*, *watch*). ESL students producing the [X MAKE Y $V_{to\text{-}inf}$] construction may therefore be said to imitate the pattern of the *to*-infinitive clause, which they are more likely to have been exposed to than the pattern of the bare infinitive clause. This influence, if it exists, is less strong in EFL, where the [X MAKE Y $V_{to\text{-}inf}$] construction accounts for only 11% of the occurrences of [$MAKE_{act}$ V_{act}].[12]

---

[11] The sample was made up of the academic writing sections of the Hong Kong, Indian, Jamaican, Kenyan, Nigerian, Philippine, Singaporean and Tanzanian components of ICE.

[12] With [$MAKE_{act}$ V_{pas}], on the other hand, the proportion of the *to*-infinitive pattern [X MAKE Y to be V_{pp}] is slightly higher in EFL (15%) than in ESL (11%), but since the raw frequencies are very low (seven occurrences in EFL and one occurrence in ESL), no real generalisation can be made.

Note, incidentally, that the results for *cause* follow the same trend, with a higher proportion of *to*-clauses in ESL than in EFL. While in this case the *to*-clause corresponds to the standard pattern, it might still be that ESL students are guided by the non-finite complementation schema, rather than or in addition to the more specific schema of *cause*, when they produce a *cause* construction with a *to*-infinitive. This difference between the two varieties is consistent with what we know about their context of acquisition: ESL students, through their richer exposure, must have encountered more instances of the *to*-infinitive clause, and are thus in a better position to reproduce it. The situation is different for EFL students, who have received less input – and more formal instruction (see below). In fact, some of the patterns found in EFL writing are quite unexpected from a usage-based perspective. Consider [X BE made V_{inf}], which is the only non-standard variant found in the corpus data for [$MAKE_{pas}$ V_{act}] and which only occurs in EFL, with a proportion of 5%. Given the low frequency of bare infinitive clauses in English noted by Biber et al. (1999), it is somewhat surprising that students should have produced this pattern, especially when the standard realisation, [X BE made $V_{to\text{-}inf}$], follows the usual pattern of the *to*-infinitive clause and hence would have been a more natural choice. Other cases of unexpected patterns produced by EFL students can be observed with the verb *cause*. [$CAUSE_{act}$ V_{act}] is sometimes realised with a present participle in EFL: 10% of [X CAUSE Y V_{prp}], plus 4% of [X CAUSE V_{prp}], to be compared with 3% of [X CAUSE Y V_{prp}] in ESL. This does not correspond to the normal realisation of [$CAUSE_{act}$ V_{act}], which should be [X CAUSE Y $V_{to\text{-}inf}$], but it does not reflect the preferences of the more general pattern of subordinate clauses either, since, as noted by Biber et al. (1999: 754), "[o]verall, *that*-clauses and **to-clauses** are more than twice as common as *wh*-clauses and **ing-clauses**" (emphasis added). In other words, by producing [X CAUSE (Y) V_{prp}], EFL learners opt for a pattern that does not respect the syntactic rules governing the use of causative constructions with *cause*, nor the probabilistic rules of subordination in general (which would favour the *to*-infinitive clause). While doing so, they leave aside [X CAUSE Y $V_{to\text{-}inf}$], which would have obeyed both the syntactic rules of the causative construction with *cause* and the probabilistic rules of subordination. As a final example, we saw above that EFL learners sometimes use [$CAUSE_{act}$ V_{act}] with no CAUSEE (4% with a present participle and 4% with a *to*-infinitive), a pattern that is not found at all in ESL. A similar construction occurs with *make* in ESL, namely [X MAKE V_{inf}], but it is extremely rare, and outnumbered by the EFL variants, which can occur with a bare infinitive, but also with a *to*-infinitive and a present participle. These non-standard constructions in EFL, again, cannot be explained by reference to more general patterns of the English language, since in non-finite clauses different subjects must both be made explicit;

if a verb is followed by a non-finite complement with no noun phrase in-between, the two subjects are normally interpreted as being co-referential (compare *He wants to leave* vs *He wants **me** to leave*), while periphrastic causative constructions, almost by definition, imply two distinct entities.[13]

A third possible explanation for some of the results in Table 7 has to do with the role of teaching in ESL and EFL students' learning experience. As pointed out earlier, EFL students rely more heavily on formal instruction than ESL students. This could account for the former's generally better performance with *make*, which is considered as the most prototypical causative verb (Altenberg 2002) and is thus likely to have been taught as a prime example of a verb used in periphrastic causative constructions. *Make* may even serve as a pathbreaking verb in instruction, that is, a verb that is used to introduce the general characteristics of the construction, before the construction is extended to other verbs. Teachers are also likely to have put considerable emphasis on the fact that causative *make* is followed (in the active) by a bare infinitive – an exception to the rules of the English language (see above). In fact, it might be that EFL students have learned and absorbed this rule so well that sometimes they also use a bare infinitive in the passive, thus generalising from the active construction to the passive construction. *Cause*, by contrast, is less frequent in causative constructions, less useful for learners too since it is stylistically more restricted (cf. Section 3.3), and so teachers may not want to spend too much precious teaching time on this verb, hence EFL learners' poorer performance with *cause*.

The careful examination of the non-standard constructions found in the EFL and ESL corpus data thus reveals that when ESL students do not follow the patterns of the causative construction, they tend to rely on some other kind of pattern, which is related to the causative construction but on a higher level of abstraction, like the most common pattern of non-finite complementation. This is in contrast to EFL students, who do not seem to follow any common pattern of the English language, preferring instead patterns that are less frequent (e.g. present participle or bare infinitive clauses) or patterns that do not correspond to the semantic characteristics of the causative construction (e.g. subjectless non-finite clauses which imply co-referentiality between the subject of the main clause and the subject of the subclause, while periphrastic causative constructions typically involve a dissociation between the CAUSER and the CAUSEE). This, in a way, confirms the hypothesis of input-dependent L2 acquisition outlined in Section 2: ESL students being primarily dependent on natural input to acquire the target language, they can more easily extract patterns, although they

---

13 See, however, Gilquin (2007) on co-referential causative constructions, in which the CAUSER and the CAUSEE represent the same entity.

seem to do so not simply at the level of causative constructions, but also at a more abstract level. EFL students, on the other hand, when they fail to obey the rules learned in their educational setting, have less input to rely on and so tend to produce patterns that do not follow any probabilistic rules of the English language. Instruction may even have an aggravating effect here, as the rules taught, if not learned accurately, may create some confusion in the learners' minds (e.g. through overgeneralisation) and cause them to produce unusual patterns (cf. [X BE made V_{inf}]).

As a final note about the syntactic realisations of causative constructions, it must be underlined that there are also certain features which are shared by ESL and EFL, and which can probably be linked to general cognitive principles of L2 acquisition, i.e. principles that are valid in any process of acquisition of a non-native language, whatever the specific context of acquisition, such as simplification, analogy or redundancy (cf. Schneider 2012). This seems to be the case with [$MAKE_{act}$ V_{pas}], which in ESL and EFL (unlike ENL) regularly includes the verb *be*, cf. [X *MAKE* Y *to be* V_{pp}], [X *MAKE* Y *be* V_{pp}] and [X *MAKE* Y *being* V_{pp}], exemplified in (15) to (17) above. By inserting the passive auxiliary *be* where a native speaker would merely use a past participle, students make explicit the passive character of the non-finite verb, thus following a trend of explicitation which can be said to characterise non-native varieties (Gilquin 2015a).

3.5 Phraseological analysis: the association of causative construction and non-finite verb

Another aspect of causative constructions that is interesting to compare across non-native varieties is their phraseological behaviour. While it is often assumed that the causative verbs (and constructions) investigated in this chapter are roughly synonymous and more or less interchangeable, a corpus analysis reveals that they each have distinctive features, among which a unique phraseological profile, which leads to strong associations between a given construction and certain verbs (or semantic classes of verbs) in the non-finite verb slot (see Gilquin 2006). One may therefore wonder whether non-native speakers have somehow integrated these phraseological preferences (even if unconsciously) on the basis of the input they have received. If this is the case, we can expect, following the input-dependent L2 acquisition hypothesis, to find more native-like phraseological choices among ESL students than among EFL students.

In order to test this, a collostructional analysis was performed on the data, with the goal of measuring the strength of association between the causative constructions (intermediate level of abstraction) and the non-finite verbs within the constructions. More precisely, I carried out what could be referred to as a key-collostructional analysis, combining the objectives of a keyword analysis and a collostructional analysis to identify the collostructions that are more distinctive for one corpus over another (see Gilquin 2012 and 2015b for a similar application). It relies on the computation of the distinctive collexeme analysis (Gries and Stefanowitsch 2004), but instead of using the method in its usual way to compare the association of words with two constructions (e.g. [X MAKE Y V_{inf}] vs [X CAUSE Y $V_{to\text{-}inf}$]), it applies the technique to the comparison of the association of words with one construction in two corpora representing different language varieties (e.g. [X MAKE Y V_{inf}] in native vs non-native English). Like all phraseological analyses, it works best with a relatively large amount of data. This makes the application of the technique unsuitable for most of the causative constructions under study here. However, it provides quite promising results with the most frequent construction in the corpora, namely [$MAKE_{act}$ V_{act}], as will be shown below. Because the phraseological analysis is based on the study of one construction only, it is necessarily exploratory, but it should be seen as a preliminary investigation of the role played by input in the acquisition of the phraseological aspects of a construction.

After preparing a list of all the non-finite verbs (lemmas) occurring in the [$MAKE_{act}$ V_{act}] construction in ENL, ESL and EFL, two key-collostructional analyses were carried out by means of Coll.analysis 3.2 (Gries 2007): one comparing the construction in ENL and ESL, and another one comparing the construction in ENL and EFL. Based on the observed and expected frequencies of the verbs occupying the non-finite verb slot of [$MAKE_{act}$ V_{act}] in the two varieties, an index of distinctive collostruction strength is calculated (-log10(Fisher-Yates exact, one-tailed)). The higher the value, the more distinctive the so-called collexeme is for the specific variety. The statistically significant results (with $p < 0.05$) are presented in Table 8, where the collexemes are ordered according to their distinctiveness. The upper part of the table lists the verbs that emerge from the comparison of ENL and ESL as being distinctive for either ENL (left) or ESL (right), while the lower part provides the results for the comparison between ENL (left) and EFL (right). What is immediately striking is that the list is much longer in the case of the comparison between ENL and EFL, and also that the index of distinctive collostruction strength for the native collexemes tends to be higher. The presence of more – and more strongly distinctive – collexemes in the comparison between the ENL and the EFL corpora indicates that there are more differences between EFL and ENL than between ESL and ENL. This means that there is a tendency for the [$MAKE_{act}$ V_{act}] causative construction to be more

Table 8: Distinctive collexemes of [MAKE$_{act}$ V$_{act}$] in native vs non-native writing, with absolute frequency in native and non-native writing (N:N) and distinctive collostruction strength (Coll.strength)

	Native distinctive collexemes		Non-native distinctive collexemes	
	Verb (N:N)	Coll.strength	Verb (N:N)	Coll.strength
ENL vs ESL	seem (25:0)	6.0158	be (1:20)	6.8244
	appear (23:0)	5.5169	become (1:9)	2.6966
			have (0:5)	1.9311
			live (0:4)	1.5420
ENL vs EFL	seem (25:8)	14.6745	be (1:52)	2.6758
	appear (23:7)	13.7076	become (1:45)	2.2381
	refer (5:1)	3.4698	believe (1:44)	2.1764
	vanish (5:2)	2.9808	go round (0:25)	1.7264
	work (14:27)	2.9110	feel (21:191)	1.6672
	conform (3:0)	2.5112	lose (0:24)	1.6568
	ask (2:0)	1.6727	come (3:52)	1.5296
	fire (2:0)	1.6727	have (0:22)	1.5178
	jump (2:0)	1.6727	forget (0:20)	1.3790
	lie (2:0)	1.6727		
	submit (2:0)	1.6727		
	sound (3:2)	1.6105		
	look (10:27)	1.4680		

idiomatic (i.e. more native-like) in ESL than in EFL.[14] The input-dependent L2 acquisition hypothesis is thus confirmed: ESL students appear to have a better phraseological command of the construction than EFL students, which is presumably the result of a higher degree of exposure to authentic language in ESL settings as compared to EFL settings. In EFL settings, on the other hand, less exposure means fewer chances of integrating the phraseological preferences of causative constructions; as for formal instruction, it is unlikely to help EFL learners, as collocations in causative constructions are most often neglected in the curriculum (cf. Gilquin 2010: 267ff.). Interestingly, however, both EFL writing and ESL writing present distinctive collexemes that are semantically less specific than the native collexemes (compare, for example, the use of the copula *be* in the non-native corpora and the use of *seem*, *appear*, *sound* and *look* in the native corpus).[15] This suggests that, compared to native writers, neither EFL nor ESL students seem to have had enough – and sufficiently rich – exposure to the causative construction to make them aware of its full potential, phraseologically speaking. Therefore, they tend to fall back on high-frequency and general-

---

[14] This is supported by the calculation of the type-token ratio of the non-finite verb in the construction: with a result of 48.9%, ESL is very close to (in fact, slightly higher than) ENL (42.2%), whereas EFL is very different from (i.e. much lower than) both (19.9%).
[15] I thank a reviewer for pointing this out to me.

purpose verbs, which are common in the input they receive and thus part of their core vocabulary (see also Section 3.3), but which are not so characteristic of the causative construction.

Finally, as was the case with the syntactic features of causative constructions (Section 3.4), the key-collostructional analysis of [MAKE$_{act}$ V$_{act}$] reveals some phraseological similarities between ESL and EFL, which are arguably linked to general cognitive principles of L2 acquisition. A notable example of this is the redundancy (cited by Schneider (2012) as one of the processes typical of second language acquisition) of the verb *be*, which is the most distinctive collexeme for both ESL and EFL. In most of its occurrences, *be* is not necessary and would be left out in native English in favour of an adjectival causative construction. Instead of (20), for example, native speakers would probably prefer to say *make a patient more confident*, and a more natural alternative to (21) would be *to make us creative and imaginative*. This redundancy of the verb *be*, incidentally, can be related to the explicitation of the passive auxiliary *be* in [MAKE$_{act}$ V$_{pas}$], which was shown in Section 3.4 to characterise both ESL and EFL.

(20) These encouragements always **make** a patient to be more confident and brave, thus increasing their chances for survival in some cases. (NUCLE)

(21) Oh God only you can help us because You gave us talents, dreams, emotions everything to **make** us be creative and imaginative (ICLE-TSW)

As a last example of a shared feature, consider the verb *have*, which is significantly distinctive for both ESL and EFL. While its use is appropriate in a number of cases, in some sentences it is rather clumsy, cf. (22) and (23), where a more natural option would be to use a synthetic expression with the verb *give* (*To give people confidence...*, *It gives them a poor self-image...*). The analytic or 'decompositional' strategy typical of (first and second) language acquisition (see Section 3.3) leads non-native writers to use "semantic primitives as building blocks" (Altenberg and Granger 2001: 183), when native writers would probably opt for a more compact phrase.

(22) To **make** people to have a confidence of speaking English, we teachers should teach more understandable classes for students. (ICLE-JP)

(23) It **makes** them have a low concept of themselves since majority of the people are not like that. (ICE-KEN)

4 Revisiting the hypothesis of input-dependent L2 acquisition

The corpus-based analysis of causative constructions has shown that the hypothesis formulated at the beginning of this chapter, according to which ESL students should have a more native-like command of the construction, is only partly borne out by the data. In terms of frequency (at the higher and intermediate levels of abstraction) ESL students' behaviour is closer to that of native speakers than their EFL counterparts', and the number of different non-standard variants (types) they use at the lower level of abstraction is smaller than in EFL, as predicted by the hypothesis. However, both ESL and EFL students tend to overuse the causative construction (especially with the verb *make*), which one would not expect given the (more or less) restricted amount of input they receive and following a strict interpretation of the input-dependent L2 acquisition hypothesis. As for the distribution of the syntactic patterns actually produced by ESL and EFL students, it paints a mixed picture. With *cause*, ESL students seem to manage better than EFL students, as predicted by our hypothesis, but with *make* it is the EFL students who come closer to the native distribution. From a phraseological perspective, finally, although the results are preliminary, it looks as if, quantitatively, ESL students better approximate to the preferences displayed by native speakers in the non-finite verb slot than is the case for EFL students. Yet, semantically, both groups of students tend to overuse high-frequency and general-purpose verbs that contrast with the more specific verbs distinctive for native writing.

These findings prompt us to revisit and refine the usage-based prediction according to which more input should lead to better knowledge in second language acquisition. The first refinement is that not all aspects of a construction may benefit equally from enhanced exposure to language; for certain aspects, formal teaching might have more beneficial effects than natural(istic) input. In the case of causative constructions, phraseology seems to benefit more from exposure than syntax, since the constructions are generally more idiomatic but not necessarily more accurate in ESL than in EFL. Extrapolating from this, we may assume that not all constructions (in the broad sense of CxG) will be influenced in the same way by the degree of exposure. A high degree of exposure may very well be profitable to certain constructions, but not (or less so) to others.

The second refinement is that formal instruction should be included in the model, as one of the factors that can influence the acquisition of a construction, on a par with the amount of natural input. Usage-based views of language acquisition in general, and construction-based accounts in particular, have typically focused on child (i.e. first language) acquisition (e.g. Tomasello 2003), and it is from these descriptions of first language acquisition that the more recent models of second language acquisition have been derived (cf. Ellis's (2002: 168) remark that "[c]urrently, we must look to child language research for the development of construction-based theories of acquisition"). This probably explains why these models have often failed to properly recognise the role of formal instruction (and sometimes, even, the very distinction between first and second language acquisition). Yet, it is undeniable that teaching has a major impact on the process of language acquisition, not just through the input it provides to learners, but also (and perhaps more importantly) through an explicit focus on form. Admittedly, both input-based (implicit) acquisition and instruction-based (explicit) acquisition are supposed to lead to the same result (i.e. a good command of the rules of the language). However, in the former case the rules emerge gradually and spontaneously from learners' experience with language, whereas in the latter case the rules are "imposed" on learners, sometimes even before they have had the opportunity to encounter the construction by themselves. Input-based acquisition is thus mainly inductive, while instruction-based acquisition is essentially deductive.[16] It is therefore hardly surprising that, until they have reached the ultimate stage of acquisition (if one such thing exists), learners of the input-based system and learners of the instruction-based system may present differences in the state of their knowledge. In our analysis of causative constructions, we have seen the possible influence of instruction among EFL learners, positively, in their familiarity with the [X *MAKE* Y V_{inf}] construction, whose special complementation makes it a good candidate for teaching focus, and negatively, in the apparent extension of the "*make* + bare infinitive" rule to [*MAKE*$_{pas}$ V_{act}]. When EFL learners have no access to the rule (for example because they have forgotten it), their behaviour seems quite erratic, following no particular pattern. ESL students, on the other hand, when they cannot rely on an explicit rule, apply other, more general patterns, which they have internalised through their exposure to naturally-occurring language.

Another type of refinement of the model, which has not been explored in this analysis but whose implementation could perhaps explain some of the results obtained, has to do with the level of individuality at which one's experience with language is considered. Here, we have distinguished between a group of students who mainly learn the target language through instruction (EFL) and a group of students who, in addition, benefit from exposure to language in their natural environment (ESL). However, within these two groups, not all the populations will share exactly the same context of acquisition. As suggested in Section 2, EFL and ESL can be said to represent a cline rather than a dichotomy, which means that some EFL populations live in a more ESL-like context, while some ESL populations live in a more EFL-like context. The specifics of the acquisition context will necessarily have an effect on the constructions that a given

---

16 The distinction is not as clear-cut, however, since natural input may include formal corrective feedback, and instruction may involve inductive methods (e.g. data-driven learning).

population will have integrated. Besides the EFL-ESL distinction, it would therefore be desirable to further distinguish between the populations from different countries/areas and link their language production to the exact context in which they acquire the language. The ultimate level of individuality, of course, would be to consider individual speakers and try to establish their unique linguistic profile with a view to better predicting (or at least explaining) their language behaviour, an approach that would only be possible thanks to very detailed metadata about the authors of the different texts included in a corpus.

A final note is in order about the definition of the input received by EFL and ESL students. In this study, it has been assumed that their input approximately corresponds to the contents of the native corpus used here (a section of the BNC), so that, if they gradually build their knowledge of constructions on the basis of this input, the constructions they produce should be similar (in form, frequency, phraseological preferences, etc.) to the constructions found in the reference corpus. However, this may be a pretty bold assumption to make, and the BNC may not be representative of the language EFL and ESL students get exposed to. For one thing, the section used here represents only academic writing, but it is likely that students are also influenced by other registers they have access to (teacher talk, conversation, fiction, news, etc.), even when they have to produce academic writing as is the case in the non-native corpora selected. For another, native (British) English is not necessarily the language variety that they get (most) exposed to. Many teachers are not native speakers of the language they teach, and much of the communication taking place in ESL countries is between people who do not have English as a mother tongue. Also, some varieties of non-native English are less exonormative than others and may present emerging (non-standard) features that are judged to be acceptable in the community and thus are likely to be found in the learners' input. If learners get exposed to a form of English that is not native-like, we cannot expect them to produce native-like patterns, especially if we hold a usage-based view of language acquisition. In a refined model of input-dependent L2 acquisition, the representation of input (in a corpus-based approach, the reference corpus) should therefore be as closely matched with the actual input as possible. For EFL a representative corpus could include teacher talk and teaching materials (e.g. textbooks that students are likely to have worked with),[17] and for ESL it could include English produced by adult, expert writers/speakers of the same variety, as was done in passing in Section 3.4. A last caveat is that input does not necessarily become intake, so that even the best suited representation of

---

[17] Such corpora already exist, cf. CoNNECT and TeMa, two corpora developed at the Centre for English Corpus Linguistics, University of Louvain (http://www.uclouvain.be/en-cecl.html).

input may not correspond to what the learner has truly integrated and what will form the basis of his/her construction of a constructicon.

5 Conclusion and pedagogical implications

Using a corpus-based constructionist approach, this chapter tested the predictions of a usage-based hypothesis of input-dependent L2 acquisition against data representing EFL and ESL student writing. The frequency, syntactic patterns and phraseological preferences of periphrastic causative constructions were examined and compared to the students' (prototypical) context of acquisition. While the results did not unanimously support a simplistic application of the usage-based model, they made it possible to propose a refined model that distinguishes between different aspects of language (which may benefit differentially from exposure to language), takes formal instruction into account and tries to match (individual) learners' input as closely as possible. In this undertaking, the framework of CxG proved profitable on several accounts. On the one hand, it provided a *tertium comparationis* (cf. intermediate level of analysis) for the comparison of constructions in varieties that may have different usages, thus recognising the specificity of each variety, without imposing a native standard. On the other hand, CxG helped explain the presence of non-standard constructions, by analogy with more abstract constructions (in this case, the non-finite complement clause construction). The related method of collostructional analysis (or, more precisely, key-collostructional analysis) also made it possible to compare the idiomaticity of causative constructions in EFL and ESL, by measuring the degree of association between words and constructions in the two varieties.

The chapter also adds to our understanding of the relation between EFL and ESL, thus contributing to bridging the paradigm gap that has been shown to exist between second language acquisition research and research on institutionalised second-language varieties (see Sridhar and Sridhar 1986; Mukherjee and Hundt 2011). Besides some similarities between the two varieties, which may be linked to general cognitive principles of L2 acquisition like explicitation or redundancy, the analysis revealed interesting differences between EFL and ESL which provided insights into the way EFL and ESL students learn/acquire the language and how the context of acquisition may affect this process. One of the main findings was that ESL students, thanks to the natural input they get exposed to, seem to generalise at a higher level of abstraction than EFL students. By contrast, the explicit instruction that EFL students receive arguably focuses attention on more concrete, low-level constructions.

The results of this study have important pedagogical implications. The above observation that EFL and ESL students tend to make different generalisations suggests that a single type of acquisition is not sufficient: since it is necessary to acquire constructions at different levels of abstraction, one should seek to present language learners with a balanced combination of natural(istic) input and explicit instruction, compensating for whatever the context of acquisition has to offer inherently. Teachers should also be prepared to adapt to their students' specific difficulties by providing solutions to overcome them. In the case of causative constructions, it would thus be useful to introduce students to the different constructions available to express causation (including more synthetic expressions), and the type of contexts they most typically occur in (e.g. technical contexts for causative constructions with *cause*), so that they stop overusing active patterns with *make*. Not only should they extend the expression of causation to more diverse constructions, but they should also extend the constructions they produce to a wider range of non-finite verbs, especially the more specific verbs that are distinctively associated with a given construction. This could be done by providing students with pedagogical resources that display a rich diversity of (ideally authentic or semi-authentic) texts including different types of causative constructions, and having the students identify the constructions and describe their syntactic, semantic and/or lexical features. Since inductive learning tends to be time-consuming and time is of the essence in the classroom, certain results of the (native) corpus analysis could also be presented to the students, for example a list of the various patterns acceptable with a particular causative verb, in decreasing order of frequency, or a list of the most distinctive collexemes of a construction. Such results should be accompanied by exercises allowing the students to put the newly acquired knowledge into practice. Thus, to practise the different types of patterns found with a particular causative verb, the students could be asked to produce a sentence for each acceptable pattern or to match the beginning and end of sentences illustrating these patterns. As for the list of distinctive collexemes, it could come with an exercise where the students are required to fill in the non-finite verb slot of a construction with one of several given verbs or to replace a generic verb (e.g. *be*) by a more specific verb (e.g. *sound* or *look*). Data from the non-native corpora could also be used, for example by asking the students to correct non-standard patterns extracted from the corpora, although one should make sure that exposure to such constructions is limited so that they should not get stored in the students' constructicon. Through such activities, students should gradually reinforce the schematic representations of the causative constructions (at different levels of abstraction) but also flesh them out, with information about their frequency of occurrence, the registers they typically occur in, the verbs they tend to be associated with, etc. Since, according to CxG, learning a language is learning its constructions, there is no doubt that this should contribute to the improvement of students' proficiency and the development of their (written and spoken) fluency.

References

Altenberg, Bengt. 2002. Causative constructions in English and Swedish: A corpus-based contrastive study. In Bengt Altenberg & Sylviane Granger (eds.), *Lexis in contrast. Corpus-based approaches*, 97–116. Amsterdam & Philadelphia: John Benjamins.
Altenberg, Bengt & Sylviane Granger. 2001. The grammatical and lexical patterning of MAKE in native and non-native student writing. *Applied Linguistics* 22(2). 173–194.
Biber, Douglas, Stig Johansson, Geoffrey Leech, Susan Conrad & Edward Finegan. 1999. *Longman grammar of spoken and written English*. Harlow: Pearson Education.
Broughton, Geoffrey, Christopher Brumfit, Roger Flavell, Peter Hill & Anita Pincas. 1980. *Teaching English as a foreign language. Second edition*. London & New York: Routledge.
Butters, Ronald R. & Kristin Stettler. 1986. Existential and causative HAVE...TO. *American Speech: A Quarterly of Linguistic Usage* 61(2). 184–190.
Bybee, Joan. 2008. Usage-based grammar and second language acquisition. In Peter Robinson & Nick C. Ellis (eds.), *Handbook of cognitive linguistics and second language acquisition*, 216–236. London: Routledge.
Dahlmeier, Daniel, Hwee Tou Ng & Siew Mei Wu. 2013. Building a large annotated corpus of learner English: The NUS Corpus of Learner English. *Proceedings of the eighth workshop on innovative use of NLP for building educational applications*, 22–31, Atlanta, Georgia, June 13 2013. Association for Computational Linguistics.
Dik, Simon C. 1980. *Studies in functional grammar*. London: Academic Press.
Ellis, Nick C. 2002. Frequency effects in language processing. A review with implications for theories of implicit and explicit language acquisition. *Studies in Second Language Acquisition* 24(2). 143–188.
Ellis, Nick C. & Fernando Ferreira-Junior. 2009. Construction learning as a function of frequency, frequency distribution, and function. *The Modern Language Journal* 93(3). 370–385.
Ellis, Rod. 2008. *The study of second language acquisition. Second edition*. Oxford: Oxford University Press.
Eskildsen, Søren W. 2009. Constructing another language – Usage-based linguistics in second language acquisition. *Applied Linguistics* 30(3). 335–357.
Gass, Susan & Larry Selinker. 2001. *Second language acquisition. An introductory course*. Mahwah: Lawrence Erlbaum.
Giacalone Ramat, Anna. 1995. Iconicity in grammaticalization processes. In Raffaele Simone (ed.), *Iconicity in language*, 119–139. Amsterdam & Philadelphia: John Benjamins.
Gilquin, Gaëtanelle. 2006. The verb slot in causative constructions. Finding the best fit. *Constructions* Special Volume 1. Available at http://www.constructions-journal.com.
Gilquin, Gaëtanelle. 2007. Causing oneself to do something: The psychodynamics of causative constructions. In Eloina Miyares Bermúdez & Leonel Ruiz Miyares (eds.), *Linguistics in the twenty first century*, 37–46. Cambridge: Cambridge Scholars Press.

Gilquin, Gaëtanelle. 2010. *Corpus, cognition and causative constructions*. Amsterdam & Philadelphia: John Benjamins.

Gilquin, Gaëtanelle. 2012. Lexical infelicity in English causative constructions. Comparing native and learner collostructions. In Jaakko Leino & Ruprecht von Waldenfels (eds.), *Analytical causatives. From 'give' and 'come' to 'let' and 'make'*, 41–63. München: Lincom Europa.

Gilquin, Gaëtanelle. 2015a. At the interface of contact linguistics and second language acquisition research: New Englishes and Learner Englishes compared. *English World-Wide* 36(1). 91–124.

Gilquin, Gaëtanelle. 2015b. The use of phrasal verbs by French-speaking EFL learners. A constructional and collostructional corpus-based approach. *Corpus Linguistics and Linguistic Theory* 11(1). 51–88.

Goldberg, Adele E. 2006. *Constructions at work. The nature of generalization in language*. Oxford: Oxford University Press.

Granger, Sylviane, Estelle Dagneaux, Fanny Meunier & Magali Paquot. 2009. *International Corpus of Learner English, version 2 (handbook + CD-ROM)*. Louvain-la-Neuve: Presses universitaires de Louvain.

Gries, Stefan Th. 2007. Coll.analysis 3.2. A program for R for Windows 2.x.

Gries, Stefan Th. & Anatol Stefanowitsch. 2004. Extending collostructional analysis. A corpus-based perspective on 'alternations'. *International Journal of Corpus Linguistics* 9(1). 97–129.

Kachru, Braj B. 1985. Standards, codification and sociolinguistic realism: The English language in the outer circle. In Randolph Quirk & Henry G. Widdowson (eds.), *English in the world: Teaching and learning the language and literatures*, 11–30. Cambridge: Cambridge University Press.

Kemmer, Suzanne & Arie Verhagen. 1994. The grammar of causatives and the conceptual structure of events. *Cognitive Linguistics* 5(2). 115–156.

King, R. T. 1988. Spatial metaphor in German causative constructions. In B. Rudzka-Ostyn (ed.), *Topics in cognitive linguistics*, 555–585. Amsterdam & Philadelphia: John Benjamins.

Lee, Sarah & Debra Ziegeler. 2006. Analysing a semantic corpus study across English dialects: Searching for paradigmatic parallels. In Andrew Wilson, Dawn Archer & Paul Rayson (eds.), *Corpus linguistics around the world*, 121–139. Amsterdam & New York: Rodopi.

Lieven, Elena & Michael Tomasello. 2008. Children's first language acquisition from a usage-based perspective. In Peter Robinson & Nick C. Ellis (eds.), *Handbook of cognitive linguistics and second language acquisition*, 168–196. London: Routledge.

Liu, Eric T. K. & Philip M. Shaw. 2001. Investigating learner vocabulary: A possible approach to looking at EFL/ESL learners' qualitative knowledge of the word. *International Review of Applied Linguistics in Language Teaching* 39(3). 171–194.

Mukherjee, Joybrato & Marianne Hundt (eds.). 2011. *Exploring second-language varieties of English and learner Englishes: Bridging a paradigm gap*. Amsterdam & Philadelphia: John Benjamins.

Nayar, P. Bhaskaran. 1997. ESL/EFL dichotomy today: Language politics or pragmatics? *TESOL Quarterly* 31. 9–37.

Parrott, M. 2010. *Grammar for English language teachers. With exercises and a key. Second edition*. Cambridge: Cambridge University Press.

Rayson, Paul. 2009. Wmatrix: A web-based corpus processing environment. Computing Department, Lancaster University. http://ucrel.lancs.ac.uk/wmatrix/.

Schneider, Edgar W. 2012. Exploring the interface between World Englishes and Second Language Acquisition – and implications for English as a Lingua Franca. *Journal of English as a Lingua Franca* 1(1). 57–91.

Scott, Mike. 2004. WordSmith Tools version 4. Oxford: Oxford University Press.

Shibatani, Masayoshi. 1976. The grammar of causative constructions: A conspectus. In Masayoshi Shibatani (ed.), *The grammar of causative constructions* (Syntax and Semantics 6), 1–40. New York, San Francisco & London: Academic Press.

Siegel, Jeff. 2003. Social context. In Catherine J. Doughty & Michael H. Long (eds.), *The handbook of second language acquisition*, 178–223. Oxford: Blackwell Publishing.

Slobin, Dan Isaac. 1985. *The crosslinguistic study of language acquisition, vol. 1: The data*. Hillsdale, NJ: Lawrence Erlbaum Associates.

Sridhar, Kamal K. & S. N. Sridhar. 1986. Bridging the paradigm gap: Second language acquisition theory and indigenized varieties of English. *World Englishes* 5(1). 3–14.

Tomasello, Michael. 2003. *Constructing a language: A usage-based theory of language acquisition*. Cambridge, MA: Harvard University Press.

Tomasello, Michael. 2009. The usage-based theory of language acquisition. In Edith L. Bavin (ed.), *The Cambridge handbook of child language*, 69–87. Cambridge: Cambridge University Press.

Turton, Nigel D. & J. B. Heaton. 1996. *Longman dictionary of common errors. Second edition*. London: Longman.

Wierzbicka, Anna. 1998. The semantics of English causative constructions in a universal-typological perspective. In Michael Tomasello (ed.), *The new psychology of language. Cognitive and functional approaches to language structure*, 113–153. Mahwah, New Jersey & London: Lawrence Erlbaum Associates Publishers.

III Crosslinguistic applications of constructionist approaches

Francisco José Ruiz de Mendoza Ibáñez and
María del Pilar Agustín Llach
Cognitive Pedagogical Grammar and meaning construction in L2[1]

Abstract: In recent years scholars involved in advanced L2 training have postulated that fine-grained cross-linguistic L1–L2 analysis is necessary to teach L2 rules proficiently (cf. Dirven 2001; De Knop and De Rycker 2008). This kind of analysis may reveal areas of divergence between L1 and L2 that pose special difficulties to many L2 learners. Once these areas have been identified, it is possible to devise a Cognitive Pedagogical Grammar for explicit instruction purposes. In previous work on the requirements of a Cognitive Pedagogical Grammar (cf. Ruiz de Mendoza 2008) it is argued that this kind of teaching instrument needs to go beyond detailed cross-linguistic descriptive adequacy (i.e. the systematic identification of areas of similarity and contrast) into explanatory adequacy, i.e. motivating linguistic structure on the basis of high-level generalizations that take the form of usage-based rules and principles. It is the pedagogical grammarian's task to produce "user-friendly" versions of such generalizations together with ample usage-based illustration of the way they apply in L1 and L2, so that contrasts can be adequately conveyed to L2 students. Ruiz de Mendoza (2008) and Ruiz de Mendoza and Agustín (2013) discuss specific English and Spanish constructions (understood as form-meaning pairings; cf. Goldberg 1995, 2006) along these lines. In the present chapter we take a more ambitious stance and identify broad areas of contrastive analysis through the application of relevant cognitive modeling principles (cf. Ruiz de Mendoza and Galera 2014). We study the way cognitive modeling takes place in English and Spanish and suggest ways of exploiting the resulting explanations in the L2 explicit-instruction class. We deal with the way in which to construct hyperbole, irony, and other cases of non-descriptive use of language in English and Spanish for effective advanced communication. We also explore and illustrate possible pathways for pedagogical training depending on the kind of meaning construction task that we are dealing with.

---

[1] The research on which this chapter is based has been financed by the Spanish Ministry of Economy and Competitiveness, grant no. FFI2013-43593-P. The authors would like to express their gratitude to the referees of the present contribution and to the editors of the volume for their constructive criticism on a previous draft. Any remaining weakness is our sole responsibility. This contribution is dedicated to Professor Günter Radden (Hamburg University) on the occasion of his 80th birthday.

Keywords: Cognitive Pedagogical Grammar; constructional families; contrastive analysis; inferences; meaning construction; second/foreign language teaching

1 Introduction

Second/foreign language (L2) pedagogy has a long tradition of taking into account developments in theoretical linguistics, although theorists have often valued the role of combining both theoretical postulates and experience (see Stern 1990). Cognitive Linguistics (CL) is by no means an exception (cf. Boers and Lindstromberg 2006; Holme 2009). There is an increasing body of empirical research that explores the advantages of CL postulates to boost performance by language learners in a number of areas, such as the use of prepositions (Boers and Demecheleer 1998), vocabulary retention (Boers 2000), vocabulary acquisition (Deconinck, Boers, and Eyckmans 2010), developing L2 constructions (Valenzuela and Rojo 2008; Holme 2010), and metaphorical competence (MacArthur 2010). These encouraging experimental results have opened the way for a number of language teaching proposals, which, although still largely programmatic (cf. the collections of papers in, for example, De Knop and De Rycker 2008 or Littlemore and Juchem-Grundmann 2010), await systematization into a fully-fledged CL-oriented language teaching syllabus.

Within this context of applied research needs, the present chapter lays the groundwork for greater systematization of theoretical postulates and empirical findings. In our view, a highly reliable way to accomplish such a huge task is provided by an extension of the basic principles of so-called *Pedagogical Grammar* (PG) into *Cognitive Pedagogical Grammar* (CPG). Although not necessarily contrastive (Achard 2008), a PG can profitably take the form of a teaching method based on the broad-ranging contrastive grammatical analysis of the first language (L1) and the L2 (cf. Dirven 2001). This approach can help researchers to identify potential areas of difficulty for L2 learners and shed light on them. L2 rules can then be formulated in "user-friendly" terms accessible to L2 learners (cf. Odlin 1994). The focus of attention in this kind of pedagogical venture is on how grammar can be made more learnable. PG has been sustained by a number of cognitive linguists – following initial insights in Dirven (2001) – as a natural pathway for the application of CL principles to second/foreign language teaching (see, for example, De Knop and De Rycker 2008). The reason for this is not difficult to understand. Cognitive linguists reject the existence of Universal Grammar principles *à la* Chomsky, i.e. the assumption that humans are endowed, from birth, with abstract grammatical principles that set limits on the attainable languages, a process that takes place through exposure to specific languages at the earliest stages of growth of each individual on the basis of a highly limited input of data (cf. Chomsky 2007). The CL position on language acquisition is a usage-based one (Tomasello 2003), according to which language structure emerges from language use both at word and grammatical level on the basis of generalizations that reconstruct the abstract constructions of languages (see also Diessel 2004; Goldberg 2006). Before such generalizations are made, children have been noted to learn delimited sets of relatively fixed phrases that suggest an item-based approach rather than the parameterization of high-level innate principles (see Diessel and Tomasello 2000, 2001). In this view, language structure and language use generalizations are not dissociated from the constraints imposed on human thought processes by the nature of the human body. Linguistic categorization is dependent on conceptual processes that are shaped by the brain's neural structure, which is, in turn, shaped by bodily processes including our motor skills and perceptual mechanisms. A classic example of this assertion is provided by Talmy's (2000) study of 'fictive motion', where a motion event is predicated of a stationary entity that is not capable of physical movement, as in *The highway runs along steep valleys*. Visual scanning of a longitudinal object allows the mind to simulate motion (cf. Matlock 2004), which becomes the licensing factor for the use of *run* in this sentence. There is increasing evidence that first language learning is based on the human ability to make generalizations based on usage-based embodied processes rather than on "pre-wired" natural routes. That is, first language learning seems to be largely based on the observation of how others relate their linguistic output to meaningful situations. Ideally, L2 learning should proceed along the same lines and in fact it has been noted that task-based learning based on situations has a positive impact on learners' fluency and accuracy, initially, and ultimately on complexity (Ellis 2003: 342; see also Housen and Kuiken 2009). The difference with L1 learning is that, except for bilingual language development, L2 learners already master an L1 system, i.e. their linguistic categories correspond to L1 conceptualization and meaning realization patterns. This fact calls for L2 pedagogical strategies based on making students aware of the differences between L1 and L2 usage-based form-meaning patterns, which is precisely the foundation of a PG approach.

Of course, there are many factors to be taken into account in tailoring an adequate L2 syllabus, among them individual learner differences arising from gender, social background, and learning styles. However, PG proposals within CL have naturally focused their attention on what CL can best offer to a PG syllabus, which is the possibility of tracing linguistic structure to embodied thinking. This has resulted in a number of specific (often cross-linguistic) case studies on the possible pedagogical exploitation of the CL approach to a still limited range of phenomena such as phrasal verbs, idioms, the construal of motion, tense and aspect, metaphor and metonymy, and some constructions like middles, reflexives, and caused motion (see, for example, the studies in Pütz, Niemeier, and Dirven 2001, De Knop and De Rycker 2008, De Knop, Boers, and De Rycker 2010). The next logical step is to create a model of CPG, i.e. one that is capable of putting to the test of successful L2 pedagogy insights from the various "strands" of CL (Dirven 2005; Dirven and Ruiz de Mendoza 2010). As we mentioned above, this has to be a long-term systematic venture. We propose the following work rationale:

(i) Select two languages for contrastive work.
(ii) Select a small number of broad-ranging areas of linguistic enquiry for the two languages.
(iii) Carry out the contrastive study on the basis of the analytical tools supplied by previous CL work in the selected areas (this may require reexamining extant theoretical proposals).
(iv) Draw relevant cross-linguistic generalizations highlighting similarities and differences across the two languages for any given phenomenon.
(v) On the basis of (iv), identify potential areas of difficulty for L2 learners.[2]
(vi) For the areas identified in (v), derive pedagogical implications.
(vii) The implications in (vi) should finally lead to a teaching strategy that will result in a usage-based teaching program.

In what follows, we will offer the reader an example of how this rationale may turn into a teaching proposal. For reasons of space, we will work under the assumption that the reader is acquainted with the essentials of CL and we will constrain our proposal to advanced Spanish students of English as an L2, especially those seeking to attain the B2 (vantage or upper intermediate) and C1 (operational proficiency) levels within the Common European Framework of Reference for Languages (Council of Europe 2001). Finally, we have chosen two broad (and distinct) areas of linguistic enquiry, namely language-based inferential activity (e.g. figurative uses of language, implicated meaning, illocution) and construction-based meaning composition (in the sense given to the term "construction" by Goldberg 1995, 2006, as an entrenched form-meaning association at whatever level of formal and functional complexity). The reason for this

---

[2] Not all L1–L2 discrepancies necessarily involve special difficulties for all learners and in the same way or to the same extent. Complementary empirical analysis with real subjects may also be necessary at this stage. We conceive of a PG as a network of motivated descriptions of L2 principles, which are open to gradability in terms of real difficulty and L2 learning needs as ascertained through various empirical techniques.

is to make our proposal as comprehensive as possible, although space limitations will obviously take away from the degree of delicacy of the analysis. However, we are confident that all our claims are backed up by a significant amount of data.

2 Figurative language

We start with the understanding of figurative language in terms of cognitive modeling. The notion of 'cognitive model', or rather "idealized" cognitive model, derives from Lakoff's (1987) observation that conceptualization is more than just making reference to world objects (whether concrete or abstract) plus their properties and relations, which were captured by Fillmore's (1985) Frame Semantics. The Frame-Semantic approach is only part of a more complex picture that includes (i) topological (or spatial) categories, also called "image schemas" (Johnson 1987), (ii) the understanding of some categories in terms of others, a phenomenon called "metaphor", and (iii) the use of a category to make it stand for a related one, a phenomenon called "metonymy". In the following subsections we will first discuss some developments of Lakoff's insights into metaphor and metonymy (cf. Lakoff and Johnson 1980, 1999). Then, we will explore how cognitive modeling takes place in the case of a small selection of other cases of figurative language use (or figures of thought). We thus expand on the work carried out within Cognitive Semantics over the last three decades (see Ruiz de Mendoza 2014, and Ruiz de Mendoza and Galera 2014 for details).

2.1 Metaphor and metonymy

Metaphor and metonymy are constructed on the basis of frames and image schemas:

(1) *He's been dogging me all day.*

(2) *He's in trouble.*

(3) *The guitar has been drinking heavily.*

(4) *He drank the whole bottle.*

Example (1) makes use of frame knowledge about dog's behavior (the so-called metaphoric 'source') to reason about a person's persistent way of following the speaker (the metaphoric 'target'), which resembles a dog trailing an animal in hunting. In example (2) the image-schematic notion of 'container' (i.e. a bounded region in three-dimensional space) is used to talk about a person's condition. The reason behind this use of language lies in our common experience of associating states with locations (for example, darkness inside a cave, protected from the rain in a shelter, or cool in the shade of a tree). In example (3) there is a metonymy whereby we think of the musician from the perspective of the instrument that he plays, which is a matter of frame structure. Finally, example (4) is based on the container-contents relationship, which is image-schematic. The bottle perspective, as against the contents perspective, highlights the impact of the action on the speaker. The metonymy suggests that the action of drinking was carried out in a way that was probably unnecessarily exhaustive.

Metonymic thinking is involved in producing inferences on the basis of situational cognitive models or scenarios:

(5) John: Does your tooth still hurt?
Fred: I finally called my dentist

Calling the dentist is just one element of the 'going to the dentist' scenario, just as getting one's tooth fixed. In the context provided by John's question, calling the dentist is a metonymic source domain that affords access to the relevant elements of this scenario, which becomes the metonymic target domain containing the idea that John went to the dentist and had his tooth fixed. This simple explanation provides the cognitive grounding for the traditional account of pragmatic implicature (cf. Ruiz de Mendoza and Galera 2014: 152–154).

Finally, metonymy may also be involved in higher-level thinking with implications for grammar. There are many possible examples of this (cf. Ruiz de Mendoza and Pérez 2001). Let us take the following three:

(6) *They began the beer.*

(7) *We can guarantee your safety.*

(8) *There is a lot of Spain in South America.*

Examples (6)–(8) exploit high-level cognitive models metonymically: in (6) *beer* (an object) stands for any beer-related action (drinking, bottling, selling, etc.); in (7) *we can guarantee* (expressing potentiality) stands for *we actually guarantee* (expressing factuality); in (8) Spain stands for Spanish values and culture, i.e. the object stands for its properties.

2.2 Other cases of figurative thought: hyperbole, irony, and paradox

As we noted above, metaphor and metonymy work on the basis of frames and image schemas. There are other so-called figures of thought that have been the object of discussion, not only in linguistics but also in such disciplines as traditional rhetoric, literary theory, and the philosophy of language. Giving a complete picture of the various approaches to the other figures of thought is beyond the scope of this chapter (see the overview in Ruiz de Mendoza 2014 and Ruiz de Mendoza and Galera 2014). What is of interest for us is to relate at least the best known of these figures to metaphor and metonymy. We can do this easily if we think of them as involving cognitive operations as well. For the sake of brevity we will focus our attention on hyperbole, irony, and paradox.

Hyperbole involves exaggeration. For example, in *I can smell pizza from a mile away* the expression *a mile away* denotes 'a very long distance'. However, it connotes the speaker's reassurance about his fondness of pizza, which is evidenced by his ability to detect the smell of pizza from very far away. Hyperbole is often constructed on the basis of metaphor (*I'm dying of shame*) and simile (*She's as old as the hills*). In Ruiz de Mendoza (2014) it is argued that hyperbole involves, like metaphor, a mapping between conceptual domains. The source domain contains an impossible or virtually impossible state of affairs constructed on the basis of a 'strengthening' cognitive operation. By means of this operation, the hearer gets a magnified version of the real state of affairs that the speaker is actually referring to in the target domain. As a consequence of this, the addressee's attention is shifted from the denotational to the connotational aspects of the message. Table 1 below applies this idea to the example *I can smell pizza from a mile away*.

Table 1: Mapping of hyperbolic conceptual structure in *I can smell pizza from a mile away*

Source	Target
Imaginary scenario in which the speaker is so fond of pizza that he can detect its smell from a mile away	Real-world scenario in which the speaker is so fond of pizza that he can detect its smell from a more-than-average distance
Extreme speaker's feelings of self-assurance about his fondness of pizza within the imaginary scenario	Strong speaker's feelings of self-assurance about his fondness of pizza within the real-world scenario

Irony is also based on a mapping of conceptual structure whose source domain contains both the speaker's actual thoughts on a given state of affairs and an echo of a previously expressed or entertained thoughts on the same state of affairs, whether the previous thoughts were the speaker's or someone else's (including the hearer). The target domain contains the thoughts echoed in the source. In the source the actual and the echoed thoughts clash. The explanation of irony on the basis of the notion of echo comes from Relevance Theory (cf. Wilson and Sperber 2012). For relevance theorists, irony results from echoing a thought while expressing a mocking, critical, or skeptical attitude to such a thought. The speaker's attitude can be recognized by means of both paralinguistic and linguistic marking: gestures, tone of voice, and attitudinal interjections like *yeah, right, oh, yeah*, or *so*, as exemplified in (9).

(9) a. *Yeah, right, Mary is a great cook.*

b. *Oh, yeah, Mary is a great cook.*

c. *So, Mary's a great cook.*

But such marking is not strictly necessary since the speaker's attitude can be recognized if the clash between the speaker's actual thought and the echoed thought is evident. The examples in (9) call for a context where the speaker is skeptical of Mary's talent as a cook, in opposition to what someone else (for example, the hearer) believes. Table 2 captures the cognitive operations involved in (9).

Table 2: Mapping of conceptual structure in the derivation of ironic effects for *Mary is a great cook*

Source		Target
Speaker		Speaker
Hearer		Hearer
Mary		Mary
Speaker's belief in Mary's lack of talent as a cook		Mary's observable lack of talent as a cook
DOMAIN-INTERNAL CONTRAST ↕		
Speaker's echo of hearer's claim that Mary has a great talent as a cook	ECHO ↔	Hearer's claim that Mary has great talent as a cook

Finally, we have paradox. We can treat paradox in relation to oxymoron. A paradox is an apparently contradictory statement presenting two incompatible states of affairs as being true. A good example of this is the assertion *Sometimes you have to do harm to do good* in the context of medical practice. Doing harm and doing good are apparently opposite but they can be reconciled through *reframing*, i.e. by finding a background context that makes them mutually compatible. The context of life-saving painful medical procedures could be such a frame in the present case. Oxymoron is very similar to paradox, but it works by putting together two incongruous terms. An easy example is the combination *a student teacher*. On the face of it, a person cannot be a student and a teacher at the same time. But there is no contradiction in the context of supervised teaching for students pursuing to qualify for a degree in education. Table 3 maps out the meaning construction process in paradox, which is applicable to oxymoron too.

Table 3: Mapping of conceptual structure in the paradox *You have to do harm to do good*

Source	Reframed source	Target
A does harm to B	A does harm to B in order to prevent further harm from taking place, i.e. as a way of ultimately doing good to B	A makes the decision of using a painful medical procedure on B in order to save B's life
DOMAIN-INTERNAL CONTRAST		
A does good to B		

3 Pathways for meaning construction: constructional vs. inferred meaning

Our second step takes us into the contrast between meaning obtained inferentially and meaning derived from (conventionalized) form-meaning pairings or constructions. Meaning construction through language is a complex cognitive process that basically follows two pathways that often interact: (lexico-)constructional coding and language-based inferencing. Constructional coding makes reference to stable (i.e. cognitively entrenched) meaning (or function)-form associations. CL has studied constructional behavior for quite some time now. Seminal studies are found in Lakoff's (1987) well-known case study of *there* constructions, Kay and Fillmore's (1999) in-depth description of the *What's X Doing Y?* configuration, and Goldberg's (1995) discussion of the conceptual grounding of some central argument-structure constructions in English, among them the ditransitive (*Pat gave Mary a book*), dative (*Pat gave a book to Mary*), resultative (*The blacksmith hammered the metal black*), caused-motion (*The child kicked the ball into the net*), and *way* (*He elbowed his way through the crowd*) constructions.

Let us now consider the nature of the construction exemplified by (10). This is not an argument-structure construction, but an example of what Ruiz de Mendoza (2013) has called an *implicational* construction, i.e. one that conventionalizes a meaning implication that was originally derived inferentially:

(10)   *Who's been messing with my laptop?*

We can think of sentence (10) not as a mere information question, but either as a combination of a question and a complaint where the complaint element is more prominent or, if the speaker knows who is to blame, as a way for the speaker to obtain an admission of guilt and an apology. The *Wh*-pattern illustrated in (10) has a strong preference for the present perfect continuous and the use of any textual or contextual indicator that the action affects the speaker (e.g. the first person possessive *my* or the negative connotations of *mess with* 'use carelessly'). Changes in this pattern can affect the nature of the resulting meaning implications. For example, compare (11a) and (11b).

(11)   a.   *Who's been collecting stamps from the 1920's?*

   b.   *Who collects stamps from the 1920's?*

The question in (11a) is a strange one. It could make sense in a context in which the speaker has a right to feel bothered by someone collecting stamps from the 1920's (imagine that the speaker erroneously believed that he had a unique collection). By contrast, (11b) is simply an information question that lacks the emotional overtones found in example (11a).

Constructions code meaning to the extent that their formal part affords unmistakable access to it. But, as is well known, not all meaning is constructional. Take again example (10), which generally conveys a complaint grounded in the idea that the situation described in the question affects the speaker in a negative way. But we can have other readings. The same sentence could be a request to make amends for breaking a rule or a warning that the hearer should never touch the speaker's laptop again. These values are not intrinsic to the construction, but can be deduced in connection with contextual variables by following general principles of inference. These principles work on the basis of metonymic access to stereotyped scenarios. Again, we have situation-based thinking. A possible reasoning schema for (10) to be regarded as a call for redress is the following:

(a) Social rule (implicit background knowledge): People know that they are not supposed to use other people's property without asking for permission. If they do so, appropriate redress may be necessary if the owner gives evidence that he is troubled.
(b) Meaning directly derived from the linguistic expression: The hearer has been using the speaker's laptop without asking for permission, which has bothered the speaker.
(c) Implication: The hearer should apologize or otherwise make amends to the speaker in any other appropriate manner.

In simpler terms, the schema takes this condition-consequence form: (a) if A grieves B, A should make amends to B; (b) A has grieved B, so (c) A should make amends to B. Note that both (b) and (c) are part of (a). The inferential schema is metonymic: mentioning its condition part calls for the activation of its consequence part, which is the implicated meaning (see Ruiz de Mendoza and Galera (2014: 153) for detailed discussion of schemas of this kind).

Constructions form families. The caused-motion construction (*She pushed me into the kitchen*) and the resultative construction (*The child licked the bowl clean*), which we have briefly introduced above, are built on the basis of transitive patterns (*She pushed me*; *The child licked the bowl*) denoting what we can call *effectual* actions, i.e. actions whose impact on an object results in a change of location or a change of state. Transitive patterns denoting non-effectual actions like climbing, reading, and holding cannot give rise to caused-motion and resultative constructions. Understanding the proximity between the caused-motion and the resultative constructions is important in order to understand related constructional developments (cf. Goldberg and Jackendoff 2004; Peña 2009). For example, consider:

(12) a. *The child pushed the clay into a mold* [caused-motion]
    b. *The child rolled the clay flat* [canonical resultative or adjectival phrase resultative]
    c. *The child molded the clay into a ball* [resultative based on figurative caused motion or prepositional phrase resultative]
    d. *The child made his way into the yard* [*way* construction]
    e. *The child found his way into the community* [figurative use of motion in the *way* construction]

All these sentences feature effectual actions that have a result. Example (12a) expresses result in terms of a caused change of location and (12b) as a caused change of state. In (12c) the expression of result is based on a figurative use of the caused-motion pattern. In (12d) there are two linked results in a row: an opening of the way (the initial result) and getting into the yard (the final result). Finally, (12e) exemplifies a version of the *way* construction that uses figurative motion, like (12c), in order to express a result. The use of caused-motion configurations with a resultative value is motivated by the frequent association between states and locations, which we mentioned above in relation to example (2). This frequent association, which also underlies the metaphorical treatment of changes of state as if they were changes of location (e.g. *Your students are going from bad to worse*), licenses the creation of the constructional variants of the canonical resultative construction and of the *way* construction, as mentioned above.

The constructions exemplified in (12a)–(12e) above originate in motivated changes of some element of the basic resultative pattern: $NP_{AG} + VP_{EFF} + AP_{RES}$.[3] A second way of creating related resultative configurations is through the combination of constructions:

(13) a. *The door slammed close* [inchoative + AP resultative]

b. *The vase broke into a thousand pieces* [inchoative + PP resultative]

(14) a. *John drank himself hoarse* [fake reflexive + AP resultative]

b. *John drank himself to sleep* [fake reflexive + PP resultative]

In examples (13a) and (13b) the resultative pattern arises from the inchoative construction. This can happen because, as we noted above, in inchoative constructions, the semantic object, which has been raised to syntactic subject position, has properties that make a change of state possible. In (14a) and (14b) a naturally intransitive pattern is transitivized by complementing it syntactically with an object reflexive, which is co-referential with the subject. However, this kind of reflexive is not a real semantic object of the action of the verb *drink*. The reflexive is possible only if construed as the object of the causal pattern provided by the resultative construction (in the examples, *John caused himself to be hoarse* or *sleepy by drinking*). Since the reflexive is a requirement of the resultative construction, but not of the verb, this explains why it cannot be omitted: *John drank *hoarse/*to sleep*. The resultative element is obligatory for the same reason: **John drank himself.*

---

[3] Following the standard notation, in this chapter NP stands for Noun Phrase, VP for Verb Phrase, AP for Adjectival Phrase, and PP for Prepositional Phrase. In turn, subscript AG stands for 'agent', EFF for 'effectual' (understood as having a perceivable impact on an object), and RES for 'result'.

Finally, a construction can be patterned on another construction with which it shares relevant semantic and syntactic structure. This third way of producing new constructional patterns within a family is exemplified by the 'manipulative' construction:

(15) a. *I want you in my office first thing in the morning.*

b. *We want it finished before 10 am.*

The manipulative construction, which makes use of secondary predications (i.e. predications that hold for the object) like resultative patterns, involves compulsion on the object, i.e. a causal element, like all resultatives. However, unlike resultatives and the related caused-motion configuration, the manipulative construction makes use of verbs conveying a speaker's need or desire (*need, want*) rather than verbs indicating caused changes of state or location. In English, secondary predications are used to ascribe a property to the object of a verb, whether the object is directly affected by the verbal action, which is the case of resultatives, or not, as in *I find this book useful* (Gonzálvez 2009: 666). The connection between the object and the ascribed property is tighter in secondary predications than in other constructional formulations of the same property ascription, as can be seen from the use of the same adjective in *I find that this book is useful*. A tighter connection is used to signal greater speaker's involvement in the ascription of the property, which is but a matter of syntax-meaning iconicity of the kind discussed by Givón (1995). Since manipulative constructions require a high degree of speaker's involvement in getting something done, they are reasonable candidates to make use of secondary predication. In addition, since they contain a compulsion ingredient, the best secondary-predication pattern to mold them is the transitive resultative, which contains a comparable causal ingredient.

4 Cross-linguistic generalizations

This section addresses major contrastive tendencies between English and Spanish, with a view to deriving pedagogical implications where Spanish is L1 and English L2. Following up on our previous discussion of meaning construction, we will make generalizations on the nature of (i) figurative language, (ii) argument-structure constructions, (iii) conventionalized inferences, and (iv) non-conventionalized inferences. Reasons of space will only allow us to touch briefly on the main generalizations, drawn on the basis of necessarily limited evidence.

This is a natural limitation of the present study, which is intended to be illustrative of a research program within the context of Pedagogical Grammar. A less programmatic, large-scale study is of course needed for future developments.

4.1 Generalizations on figurative language

Spanish shares with English the principles of cognitive modeling. That is, metaphor, metonymy, hyperbole, irony, etc. work in the two languages on the basis of the same kind of cognitive activity with comparable meaning effects. Compare the following examples:

(16) a. *The White House has not addressed the issue.*

b. *La Casa Blanca no ha abordado la cuestión.*

(17) a. *My neighbor is a pig.*

b. *Mi vecino es un cerdo.*

(18) a. *Her skin is as soft as silk.*

b. *Su piel están suave como la seda.*

(19) a. *This suitcase weighs a ton.*

b. *Esta maleta pesa una tonelada.*

(20) a. *John will always lie.*

b. *Juan siempre miente.*

(21) a. *Yeah, right she's an angel.*

b. *Si, claro. Es un ángel.*

(22) a. *Sometimes, you have to do harm to do good.*

b. *A veces hay que hacer daño para hacer un bien.*

In (16) we have metonymy, in (17) metaphor, in (18) simile, in (19) hyperbole, in (20) an extreme case formulation, in (21) irony, and in (22) paradox. The (b) examples are direct translations into Spanish of the (a) examples, i.e. the target sentence preserves the meaning implications of the source sentence in every case. Where there are differences, they can arise from realization conventions of the same conceptual patterns or from cross-linguistic discrepancies in the selection of the relevant features to be mapped. Let us first think of realization conventions in connection to metonymy. English metonymies often have straightforward equivalents in Spanish (cf. *Spain has won the world cup/España ha ganado la copa del mundo, He has broken the window/Ha roto la ventana, Tie your shoes/Átate los zapatos*). This holds true of situational metonymies underlying implicature. In the following exchange in English and in its Spanish counterpart, 'being a great shot' affords metonymic access to the idea that the hunt was successful within the context of a hunting scenario:

(23) a. *A: Did they have a successful hunt? B: Jim is a great shot.*

 b. *A: ¿Tuvieron una buena caza? B: Jim es un gran tirador.*

Exact equivalence is also the case with some high-level metonymies, like POTENTIALITY FOR ACTUALITY. In (24) *I can guarantee/promise* stands for 'I actually guarantee/promise':

(24) a. *I can guarantee/promise that you will have your money back.*

 b. *Puedo garantizarle/prometerle que se le devolverá su dinero.*

But there are conventional realizations for which English and Spanish have different syntactic strategies. A well-known case is the use of metonymy instead of a definite description in well-defined script-based contexts. Two examples are provided by the metonymy ORDER FOR CUSTOMER, in the context of a restaurant, and DISEASE FOR PATIENT, in the context of a hospital:

(25) a. *The French omelet wants his check.*

 b. **La tortilla francesa quiere la cuenta.*

(26) a. *The gallbladder needs another painkiller.*

 b. **La vesícula quiere otro calmante.*

The metonymic solution is not possible in Spanish, which has opted for a construction that grammatically nominalizes a *de*-PP by eliding the noun identifying the target referent (e.g. the customer, the patient) while preserving, as a sign of the implicit existence of such a noun, the definite article modifying it. The *de*-PP is an obligatory element pointing to the nature of the noun (the kind of order for the customer and the type of surgery for the patient):

(27) El   [cliente]   de la   tortilla   francesa
     DEF-ART   [customer]   of DEF-ART   omelet   French

(28) El   [paciente]   de la   [operación]   de   vesícula
     DEF-ART   [patient]   of DEF-ART   [operation]   of   gallbladder

Sometimes, differences arise from the selection of properties in cross-domain mappings. The metaphor PEOPLE ARE ANIMALS, which is active both in English and Spanish, provides some illustration. For example, *She is catty* 'malicious' cannot be translated literally into Spanish as *Ella es una gata*, which refers to a (generally young) woman who dresses and behaves in ways specifically intended to attract men sexually. Differences in property selection and in linguistic realization can combine, making it more difficult to set up cross-linguistic equivalences: *He's been dogging me all day* 'tracking me non-stop' could be rendered in Spanish as *Me ha estado siguiendo como un perro*, lit. 'He has been following me like a dog', where the metaphor is replaced by a simile. But this rendering suggests a different scenario where people are followed by those that seek to obtain some benefit.

4.2 Generalizations on constructions

Constructional behavior can vary across languages when formal realization changes for similar underlying meaning. A family of English constructions most of whose members have no straightforward formal equivalent in Spanish is the resultative. Following Ruiz de Mendoza and Luzondo (2014), we shall distinguish the following members of this constructional family:

(29) a. *The blacksmith hammered the metal flat* (transitive resultative).

 b. *The wind blew the leaf off the windowsill* (caused motion).

 c. *The blacksmith hammered hot iron into a knife* (figurative caused motion).

 d. *The audience laughed the actor out of the theater* (self-instigated motion).

 e. *She drank herself silly* (fake reflexive resultative).

 f. *The cup broke into a thousand pieces* (intransitive resultative).

 g. *I want you in my office now* (subjective-manipulative).

Examples (29a–e) have no constructional equivalent in Spanish, which conveys similar meaning by means of causative verbs or causative periphrastic forms containing a resultative ingredient. For example, *hammer flat* (29a) can be rendered as *aplanar* 'flatten' or *dejar plano* (lit. 'leave flat', i.e. 'cause to become flat'); *blow off* (29b) needs a causative: *hacer volar* 'cause to fly'; *hammer something into something else* (29c) requires the use of the verb *hacer* in the sense of 'making' (i.e. causing something to exist) followed by a complement expressing the result of the creative action (*hacer un cuchillo* 'make a knife'); *laugh someone out* (29d) can be expressed in Spanish by means of a causative verb (*sacar* 'take out'), or a causative periphrastic form (*hacer salir* 'cause to leave'), combined with a manner of action complement (*a carcajadas* 'with laughter'); finally, *drink oneself silly/into a stupor*, etc. (29e) requires a construction with the periphrastic *hasta quedarse + adj.* ('until becoming') or any verbal predicate denoting a telic activity (e.g. *quedarse tonto/atontarse* 'become silly'). Examples (29'a–e) give us reasonable Spanish equivalents of (29a–e):

(29') a. *El herrero aplanó el metal a martillazos* (lit. 'The blacksmith flattened the metal by [dint of] hammering [on it]').

  b. *El viento hizo volar la hoja desde el alféizar de la ventana* (lit. 'The wind made the leaf fly from the windowsill').

  c. *El herrero hizo un cuchillo aplanando hierro candente a martillazos* (lit. 'The blacksmith made a knife by flattening hot iron by [dint of] hammering [on it]').

  d. *El público sacó/hizo salir al actor del teatro a carcajadas* (lit. 'The audience caused the actor to leave the theater by laughing [at him]').

  e. *Bebió hasta quedarse tonta/atontarse* (lit. 'She drank until he turned silly').

Interestingly enough, (29f–g) do have direct constructional equivalents in Spanish:

(29') f. *La taza se rompió en mil pedazos.*

  g. *Le quiero en mi oficina ahora.*

In the case of (29f) and (29'f) the only difference between English and Spanish is the starting point for the resultative pattern. As we saw in our comments on examples (13a–b) above, some resultatives are built on the basis of an inchoative pattern. This is so because the inchoative construction has an intrinsic telic component that can be made explicit for reasons of specificity, thereby yielding an intransitive resultative construction. Compare, in this respect, *The cup broke*, where the result is generic (i.e. the cup 'became broken'), and *The cup broke into pieces*, where the result is specific. In Spanish the resultative pattern is built on the basis of a reflex passive with *se*. This construction, like the English inchoative, has the function of presenting a caused event as if it had happened by itself (see Ruiz de Mendoza and Peña 2008). The difference boils down to two different syntactic pathways: Spanish uses a pseudo-reflexive pronoun that is co-referential with the syntactic subject, while conceptually it remains the object (i.e. the pretense strategy consists in construing the cup as breaking itself); English, on the other hand, makes the semantic object into a syntactic subject.

A very interesting case is provided by the subjective-manipulative construction, which we briefly introduced above. This construction, which can be illustrated by (29g) for English and (29'g) for Spanish, has been studied in detail in Gonzálvez (2009), for both languages, in the context of other constructions based on secondary predications, including those not involving a change of state but the subjective ascription of a property to the syntactic object of an evaluative verb (e.g. *I consider you a good friend*/Sp. *Te considero un buen amigo*). Secondary predications with verbs involving subjective evaluation (*pensar* 'think', *creer* 'believe', *considerar* 'consider', etc.) are common in Spanish, as in English. The subjective-manipulative construction is midway between causative resultatives expressing a change of state or location and evaluative constructions: there is no actual change of state or location, but a strong wish or forceful desire that someone will bring it about. This may be one of the reasons why the subjective-manipulative construction is possible in Spanish: it only requires a straightforward transition from 'X think-V Y have attribute Z' (e.g. *She considers you a real expert*) to 'X want-V Y have attribute Z' (e.g. *She wants you to be a real expert*), which is grounded in the evaluative (i.e. non-factual) grounds that the two constructions share. The causative (i.e. transitive) resultative requires a different transition from 'X think-V Y have attribute Z' to 'X cause-V Y have attribute Z', i.e. from evaluative ascription to caused change of state, for which Spanish has chosen resultative formulations like those exemplified in (29'a–e) above, while English uses secondary predications. The common ground between the evaluative and the factual use of secondary predications, in the case of English, is the existence of an ascription of properties to the object of the verbal predicate, whether the property is or is not resultative in nature.

4.3 Generalizations on conventionalized inferences

Entrenched inferences, as we have seen in Section 3, are a source of new constructional meaning. This explains why *What's X Doing Y?* is usually not a question but an expression of speaker's concern about what X is doing. Since inferences are largely coincidental between English and Spanish, because of their shared patterns of cognitive modeling, conventionalized inferences are not expected to vary sharply provided that the two languages can make use of the same or at least highly similar formal realization conventions. This is the case of some implicational constructions, among them English *What's X Doing Y?*, whose Spanish equivalent is *¿Qué Está Haciendo/Hace X Y?*, and of illocutionary constructions such as *Can You X?*, together with its sister constructions (*Will You X?*, *Could You X?*, *Would You X?*, *Do You Think You Could X?*, etc.), all of which have exact equivalents in Spanish (*¿Puedes X?*, *¿Querrás X?*, *¿Podrías X?*, *¿Harías X?*, *¿Crees Que Podrías X?*). The following examples provide additional illustration of the use of other implicational and illocutionary constructions that are equivalent in Spanish and English:

(30) a. Who do you think you are to say that?

 b. *¿Quién te piensas que eres para decir eso?*

(31) a. Who's been sleeping in my bed?

 b. *¿Quién ha estado durmiendo en mi cama?*

(32) a. I wonder if you could visit her.

 b. *Me pregunto si podrías visitarla.*

(33) a. I would appreciate it if you could answer my question.

 b. *Estaría agradecido si respondiera a mi pregunta.*

Examples (30a–b) and (31a–b) are implicational constructions; (32a–b) and (33a–b) are illocutionary constructions. In (30a–b) the speaker is upset about the addressee's behavior. The origin of this (now conventionalized) meaning implication is to be found in the fact that constraints on behavior can only be overruled when there are compelling social prestige or power conditions. In a context in which the addressee is evidently not in any privileged position, asking him about it becomes rhetorical and acts as a pointer to the speaker's attitude toward the addressee's misconduct. In (31a–b) the speaker is troubled by the fact that someone has inappropriately used his bed to sleep. We have already addressed, in Section 3 above, the details of the reasoning process underlying meaning implications for this kind of construction. In essence, the speaker is not only asking about the identity of the misbehaver, but also expressing his dissatisfaction with the deed. (32a–b) has a directive value, based on the social convention that people are expected to do whatever they know will benefit others if they have the ability to do so. Originally, the *I wonder* part of the construction was, descriptively, a way of asking the addressee about this ability to do what one would normally expect of him, and, inferentially, it was a way of making the addressee aware of his responsibility to act if he can. The inferential value has now been built into the constructional interpretation. Finally, (33a–b) is a case of a directive speech act built on the basis of the expressive act of thanking. The rationale behind this communicative strategy is the following: a question demands an answer, so one is entitled to urge others to answer any question that has not been answered yet. But answering imposes an obligation on others; so, it should also be expected that if an answer is given, the speaker will thank the addressee for this. In the absence of an answer, expressing thankfulness in anticipation of it being produced implies the speaker's expectation that it will be supplied anyway. All these reasoning patterns are the same for English and Spanish speakers, since they share the same underlying sociocultural conventions.

4.4 Generalizations on non-conventionalized inferences

Like their conventionalized counterparts, non-conventionalized meaning inferences in English and Spanish are largely coincidental. For this reason, figures of thought pose virtually no equivalence challenges except when the figure requires a specific constructional use that varies across the two languages in question. For example, litotes in English exploit the negation of a (prefix-)negated adjective (*He is not unreasonable/unattractive*, etc.). This construction in Spanish is only possible when Spanish has the negated adjective (*His behavior was not irrational* is directly rendered as Sp. *Su conducta no fue irracional*) or a negative adjective such as *poor* or *bad* (e.g. *He is not precisely poor* finds an exact equivalent in Sp. *No es precisamente pobre*). Much the same holds for hyperbole, irony, paradox, and oxymoron, briefly discussed earlier in Section 2.2, to the extent that they require interpretation based on general inference-making principles rather than on constructional cues. Hyperbole, however, can have a constructional dimension when its expression relies on special linguistic devices such as frequentatives (*a thousand, a million*, etc.) (see Claridge (2011) for an exhaustive description of such devices).

However, metaphor, metonymy, and simile have lesser degrees of equivalence owing to the fact that they often make use of conventionalized formulations, as we have already discussed in Section 4.1. We have a comparable situation with metaphorical complexes. For example, *He got the idea across to her* translates rather poorly as *Le hizo llegar la idea a ella*. A better rendering would be *Le transmitió la idea* (lit. 'He conveyed the idea to her') or *Le ayudó a com-*

prender la idea (lit. 'He helped her understand the idea'), but the meaning implications are not exactly the same (i.e. in the English version, but not in Spanish, the idea is "explored" and controlled). Similarly, metaphor or simile-based hyperbole will work to the extent that the conventional formulation of the base metaphor/simile is shared by the two languages (e.g. *He is as old as the hills*, lit. 'Es tan viejo como las colinas', should be rendered as *Es tan viejo como Matusalén* 'He is as old as Methuselah').

Implicatures and inferred illocution pose no problem either provided that the underlying cultural models (which are situational) are coincidental between the two languages. For example, the sentence *She called a taxi* suggests that she took the taxi that she called to go somewhere, both in English and in its Spanish literal equivalent (*Llamó un taxi*). Both languages use the precondition of an action to stand for the action. In turn, *I'm thirsty* in English and its literal Spanish counterpart *Tengo sed* can easily be interpreted as a request to give the speaker something to drink, since, as we have noted before, the two languages share the cultural convention that we are expected to help other people when we see they are affected by a negative situation.

5 Pedagogical implications

Our discussion of cross-linguistic generalizations in the previous section allows us to derive two broad pedagogical implications for the teaching of English (L2) to native speakers of Spanish (L1):

> IMPLICATION 1: It is necessary to devise specific teaching strategies for figures of thought with a strongly conventionalized lexical or constructional grounding when such conventionalization has taken different paths for L1 and L2.
>
> IMPLICATION 2: Constructions are to be taught in connection to one another in terms of family-internal and family-external similarities. For example, the English caused-motion construction is best taught in relation to its sister resultative constructions, with which it shares much of its conceptual and formal structure.

These two implications are closely related. They arise from the observation that inferential mechanisms are largely shared by speakers of the two languages. What may vary is the lexical and constructional conventionalization pathways. In relation to Implication 1, Section 5.1 below gives an example of a teaching strategy for the conventional metaphorical amalgam that was briefly spelled out above. Implication 2 further acknowledges the existence of degrees of overlap between constructional families in L1 and L2, which, as we propose in

Section 5.2 below, can be exploited as part of a productive teaching strategy for L2 constructions without clear equivalents in L1.

5.1 Teaching *get an idea across*

The conceptual layout of the English expression *get an idea across*, which has no direct Spanish equivalent, was initially discussed in Section 4.4. We assume that the specific formal aspects of the expression do not involve much difficulty for advanced learners of English, who will be familiar with comparable causative expressions involving motion of an object from one side of a surface to another, as is the case in *They laid the bridge across the river, He sailed the ship across the sea, The pilot flew the plane across the Pacific*, etc. What may be more difficult is the complexity of the underlying conceptual configuration. We suggest a three-step procedure, consonant with the principles of Cognitive Pedagogical Grammar, to deal with such complexity in an amicable format. The procedure is described below.

Step 1: Teach the cognitive motivation behind the figurative expression worded in accessible terms. In a different context, Ruiz de Mendoza (2008: 124–125) provides the following user-friendly description of the conceptual make-up of *get across*, which we think covers the requirements of this first step:

> Sometimes we talk about ideas as if they could be seen, touched, and handled. They are like objects. They can also move or we can make them move. If an idea reaches me, I can handle it and create a picture in my mind of what it is like. That is why we say that ideas get across or that we get ideas across to someone, as if ideas could move (in contact with a surface) from where they are to where we are so we can deal with them.

Step 2: Illustrate the use of *get an idea across* on the basis of an ample selection of examples. Here are some examples, selected from Google searches, which flesh out the basic description given in Step 1:

(34) a. *The demonstrations and dynamic diagrams really get the ideas across effectively.*[4]

b. *We don't need to rely on my presentation skills to get the ideas across to the client.*[5]

---

4 http://www.reading.ac.uk/ssc/n/SADC%20DVD/Resources/CAST/CAST%20for%20Africa%20transcript_aug2.pdf. Accessed on November 7, 2014.
5 http://hotgloo.com/showcases/ixd. Accessed on November 7, 2014.

c. Do the pictures help get the ideas across?[6]

d. Quite often, parents and teachers rely on lectures and discussions to get the ideas across.[7]

e. He was a terrible lecturer, but he got the ideas across and I liked him.[8]

f. The fridge didn't work, and I couldn't get the idea across to the staff with limited English to come and fix it.[9]

g. Why can't I get the idea across?[10]

h. With some individual help, we managed to get the idea across to all of them.[11]

i. If you can't get the idea across in just a couple of sentences, you have some more work to do.[12]

Step 3: Specify usage constraints and their connection with the cognitive motivation in Step 1. For example, a simple corpus query in the Contemporary Corpus of American English (COCA) reveals that:

1) *Get an idea across* is often related to skills and efficacy; so the expression collocates well with inherent modality markers expressing ability like *manage to* and *be able to*.
2) The figurative destination of motion is often omitted when it represents any possible recipient, as in (34a), (34c), (34d), (34g), and (34i), or when the recipient is straightforwardly retrievable from context, as in (34e).

This three-step strategy is intended to help students to come to terms with some of the challenges involved in the (often complex) relationship between language and cognition, and with the meaning impact of such a relationship in L2 use.

---

[6] http://medicine.osu.edu/sitetool/sites/pdfs/ahecpublic/HL_Write_It_In_Plain_Language.pdf. Accessed on November 7, 2014.
[7] http://www.thesimpledollar.com/personal-finance-experiences-for-older-kids/. Accessed on November 7, 2014.
[8] Google Books Corpus, 2014.
[9] http://hotels.informer.com/china/guilin/guilin-vienna-hotel-252571. Accessed on November 7, 2014.
[10] Contemporary Corpus of American English (COCA, 1993).
[11] http://treasuredarts.wordpress.com/2013/09/02/zentangle-class-in-monroe-wa/. Accessed on November 7, 2014.
[12] http://blogs.wsj.com/accelerators/2013/07/12/dayna-grayson-say-the-most-in-the-fewest-words/. Accessed on November 7, 2014.

5.2 Teaching the English caused-motion construction

The English caused-motion construction, which belongs to the family of resultatives, has no direct equivalent in Spanish, which gives rise to a teaching problem that needs to be sorted out. We shall here refer to the English caused-motion construction as a "target construction", i.e. one that requires special attention in a teaching strategy that complies with the principles of Cognitive Pedagogical Grammar. We propose, again, a three-step strategy that is based on some of the generalizations discussed in Section 4.2.

Step 1: Find an L2 "source construction", i.e. one bearing family resemblance to the L2 target construction, which has a reasonable equivalent in the learners' L1. In the case of the English caused-motion construction, it could be the manipulative construction (*They wanted him out of the country/Le querían fuera del país*). This close L2 construction thus becomes an L2 source construction for comparison with the L2 target construction. Subsequently, the L2 source construction has to be studied in terms of its formal features, semantic structure, and actual use. As part of this step, it is necessary to make sure that the L2 learners master this L2 source construction.

Step 2: Use the L2 source construction to understand the L2 target construction. Once mastered, the L2 source construction can be used to understand formal and functional aspects of the L2 target construction. For the comparison between the subjective-manipulative and the caused-motion constructions, this kind of analysis reveals the following similarities:
- Formal: The two make use of secondary predications: NP(subj)+V+NP(obj)+PP(loc)
- Semantic: In both, someone causes someone else to change (location or state)
- Use: They both convey compulsion on the object; the two can be used either literally or figuratively:

(35) a. Manipulative (lit.): *I want you in my office.*

  b. Manipulative (fig.): *I want you out of my life.*

  b. Caused-motion (lit.): *She pushed me into her office.*

  c. Caused-motion (fig.): *She stared me into her office.*

The differences, which we have discussed in Section 4.2, are a matter of the evaluative and non-factual nature of the source construction versus the non-evaluative and factual nature of the target construction.

Step 3: Identify other L2 targets for the same L2 source construction and follow through steps 1 and 2 again. The new targets should be other members of the family of constructions to which the L2 source and target constructions belong. This step is necessary for learners to have a real grasp – and achieve full mastery – of the constructional idiosyncrasy of L2. In the present case, once the caused-motion construction has been learned and rehearsed sufficiently, the L2 instructor will find it easy to go into the AP and PP transitive resultatives, and from these further on into the rest of the constructions exemplified in (29) above.

This strategy, unlike the one described in Section 5.1, does not require full reorganization of the learners' assumptions about a domain of L2 conceptualization, but only the ability to apply an L1 form-meaning pattern, in a principled way, to areas of L2 that have no exact equivalent in L1 but with which the selected pattern is in a family resemblance relationship.

6 Pedagogical implementation

On the basis of the proposals in Section 5, the present section will provide readers with an outline of possible teaching materials that instructors can use to implement the pedagogical implications discussed in the previous section. The purpose here, as was hinted at in the introduction to the present chapter, is to be partially illustrative of what the final stage of a Cognitive Pedagogical Grammar could look like.

Learners at advanced levels of L2 proficiency need to be trained into understanding cognitive phenomena by applying a set of principled steps that will contribute to developing their autonomy. Following our previous discussion, the general program for construction learning includes five steps, as outlined below.

1. Contrastive analysis. Learners need to look into the target construction and find its equivalent in their L1. Cognitive motivation of the form-meaning link can be very helpful in implementing this step. A possible practical illustration of this stage can take the following form:

> Look at the following sentence: *They laughed Mary out of the room*. It contains an unusual use of the verb *to laugh*. The sentence means that somebody laughed so much that Mary had to leave the room, generally in a state of shame or embarrassment. Can you think of an equivalent sentence in Spanish/your L1? Try to think of the meaning of the sentence and not so much of its form. You can also think of a similar expression in Spanish, for example: *La quiero fuera/ I want her out; Lo quiero en mi equipo/ I want him in my team*. This will help you find a relationship between the English and the Spanish expression.

These are some possible solutions:
- Sacaron a María de la habitación a carcajadas [lit. 'They took Mary out of the room with a loud laugh']
- Se rieron hasta que María se fue de la habitación. [lit. 'They laughed until Mary left the room']
- De tanto que se rieron María tuvo que abandonar la habitación. [lit. 'They laughed so much that Mary had to leave the room']
- Se rieron tanto que lograron que María se fuera de la habitación. [lit. 'They laughed so much that they got Mary to leave the room']

Clearly, the original English sentence and the possible Spanish equivalents have different forms that express roughly the same idea by using different words and combinations of words. They represent different ways of visualizing the same event while emphasizing different aspects of it. Thus, the English version draws our attention to the way in which Mary is compelled to leave the room. By contrast, the Spanish versions give more emphasis to Mary actually leaving the room.

The next exercise will give students a better understanding of how the English expression works and why.

2. Explicit explanation. Learners are provided with explicit explanations about the constructions, their form, meaning, and underlying cognitive structure. This explicit instruction will contribute to enhancing learners' comprehension of the construction and, we hope, to helping them to derive their usage constraints. This will enable learners to use the constructions in other similar contexts.

In English, it is frequent to find sentences where the verb expresses the way in which the subject is made to perform an action. Prepositions and other complements help achieve this goal. In the example from the previous exercise, the verb *to laugh* is used to convey the way in which the subject Mary is forced to leave the room (helped by the prepositional phrase: *out of the room*). Additionally, these expressions convey the idea that the subject is forced to do something (in the current example, leave the room). In short, common English expressions like these focus on two main ideas: first, somebody being forced to do something and, second, the way in which this is made to happen and the result that follows. We can see that the use of these expressions involves a different way of looking at the events or phenomena, that is, we do not so much look at the result of the action, but at what someone does to come up with such a result.

Note: This type of expression has another variant that can be called 'fake reflexive' because it formally looks like a reflexive sentence, but the meaning it conveys is slightly different. For example, in the sentence *He shouted himself hoarse* the action expressed by the verb does not have the subject as a recipient, but rather the subject is involuntarily forced into something, expressed by the adjective *hoarse* in this case. Again, we have the idea of force plus involuntariness in this case.

3. Exemplification and guided reflection. Students need to be provided with further examples illustrating the target construction. This can be a useful and

effective way to expose learners to repeated input and help them in the task of abstracting and generalizing. Furthermore, they can be guided in the manipulation of the examples to aid them in that process of abstraction.

> Other examples of similar expressions appear below. Look at them and see if you can find the working pattern explained above.
> - John kicked Peter out of the room.
> - They kicked Peter out of the team.
> - My mother stared me out of the room.
> - They helped her out of a difficult situation.
> - She shouted her husband out of bed.
> - He was startled out of a deep sleep.
> - The parents kissed the baby into sleep.
> - The child molded clay into different shapes.
> - Men danced themselves into a frenzy.
> - He worked himself into a higher position in the company.
> - He drank himself into a heart attack.
> - He kicked/eased/let/started the horse into a gallop.

The sentences above express result through the combination of a preposition and a noun. The result can be a change of location, as in *John kicked Peter out of the room*. Here we have a situation where John compels Peter to leave the room by kicking him. Sometimes motion is not externally caused, as in *My mother stared me out of the room*. In this sentence, the speaker leaves the room on his own probably because he interprets that this is what his mother wants him to do.

The same kind of expression can be used to talk about changes of state. There is a reason why this is possible. Think of yourself in the shade of a tree in a hot summer day. If you step out of the shade you will feel hotter. If you step back into the shade, you will feel cooler. When you move from some places into others, the change of location can correlate with a change of state. Other situations where this happens are the following:

- Jumping into a swimming pool.
- Walking into a dark cave.
- Getting into a mountain shelter as a blizzard strikes.
- Walking into an air-conditioned room on a hot summer day.

Could you point out what changes of state you would expect for each of these situations? Now focus your attention on one of the sentences above: *They kicked Peter out of the team*. In this sentence the verb *kick* is not literal and there is no real motion "out of" a location. The idea is that Peter has been forced to leave the team. We use *out of* to express the loss of a property or a condition. By contrast, we use *into* to express the acquisition of a property or a condition. For example, in *The parents kissed the baby into sleep*, the kissing action has an emotional effect on the baby that helps him fall asleep. Could you point out which properties are lost or acquired in the rest of the examples above?

Now take the following sentences:

- The blacksmith hammered the metal flat.
- He drank himself insensible.
- The hunter shot the duck dead.
- The doors suddenly burst open.
- The blow knocked him silly.
- The dog ate the bowl clean.
- He ran his sneakers threadbare.
- The lion broke the cage open.

These sentences are also used to express a change of state. However, here the English language can express the resulting state by means of an adjective. When this is not possible, English speakers can make use of *into* or *out of"* and a noun:

- The blacksmith hammered the metal into different shapes.
- He drank himself into a stupor.
- A stroke shot him into a coma.
- The bus burst into flames.
- The blow knocked him out of his mind.
- The child ate the bowl out of cereal.
- He ran his car out of gas.
- He broke the door out of its frame.

4. Practice. Once learners have been exposed to the target construction and explicitly informed about its specificities, practice exercises are called for to automatize this knowledge and put it into use. We recommend a combined approach in which isolated practice is followed by contextualized or meaning-based exercises (e.g. Doughty and Williams 1998). Practicing the target construction explicitly and devoid of context will improve learners' understanding and fluency of use. By contrast, contextualized exercises will enhance students' ability to use the target construction in communicative settings.

a) Isolated practice. We propose comprehension exercises followed by exercises where students are required to produce new language.

Now, it is time for you to put to real use what you have learned in the previous exercises. Below you have a series of expressions in English of the type studied before. Can you find the Spanish equivalent?

- He was beaten into a coma.
- My former colleague sucked up to a pay increase.
- The coach trained the players into exhaustion.
- The news struck me speechless.
- The girl cut/chopped the meat small.
- The dog span itself dizzy.

Possible solutions:

- Le pegaron hasta dejarlo en coma.
- Mi colega se consiguió un aumento de sueldo haciendo la pelota.
- El entrenador dejó a los jugadores exhaustos del entrenamiento.
- Las noticias me dejaron muda.
- La chica cortó la carne en trozos pequeños.
- El perro dio vueltas hasta marearse.

It is your turn to use this expression now. Can you write original sentences with the verbs and complements given below?

- Train/slimness
- Beat/dead
- Walk dog/boredom
- Argue/agreement
- Shape/perfection

Possible solutions:

- He trained himself into slimness.
- They beat the snake dead.
- The boy walked the dog into boredom.
- The couple argued into an agreement.
- The sculptor shaped the state into perfection.

b) Contextualized practice. Automation of many aspects of the target constructions follows from isolated practice, but meaning-based exercises help learners to use them for communicative purposes.

We propose some situations where it would be appropriate to use the expression we have practiced above. Please read the description of the situations and summarize it with an expression of the type we have been studying.

Situation 1: The deputies of the European Commission are discussing a new law. They do not leave the room until an agreement has been reached.

Situation 2: A thirsty young boy is drinking water out of a bottle until it is empty.

Situation 3: A famous actor is standing on stage and the audience is clapping enthusiastically uninterruptedly until the actor leaves the stage.

Possible solutions:[13]

Situation 1: The deputies discussed the law into agreement.

Situation 2: The young boy drank the bottle empty.

Situation 3: The audience clapped the actor enthusiastically out of the stage.

---

[13] Note that this activity is intended to place the learner within a pre-defined situation. For this reason, the present progressive is used. However, the learner is asked to summarize the situation seen as already past. Other tenses are also possible and correct.

5. Self-assessment. Reflecting on one's own learning process is an essential component in the acquisition of an L2. Assessing one's own abilities to understand and use the new language is a necessary step towards the development of autonomy and a milestone of the life-long learning process.

> Now the time has come to reflect on what you have learned. Please read these questions carefully and answer them in writing.
>
> Questions for self-assessment:
> - What have I learned about these common expressions in English?
> - How can I explain it to other classmates or learners?
> - Can I understand and use in communicative situations the expressions I have learned?
> - What about similar expressions? And other contexts?

7 Conclusion

We have argued that Cognitive Pedagogical Grammar can become a central part of a productive L2 teaching syllabus. Its grounding in the principles of Cognitive Linguistics allows the designer of a teaching program to elaborate pedagogical implementations that go beyond the control of morphology and syntax into how L2 speakers actually work at the conceptual level. This is a must if the aim is to train L2 learners into a native-like competence. The aim is not only to endow learners with a working knowledge of how concepts combine and how such combinations relate to formal configurations, but also to help them to become immersed in the conceptual world of native speakers. With Cognitive Pedagogical Grammar accuracy is not to be sacrificed to fluency. Both are necessary and accuracy is not simply a matter of grammatical (i.e. formal) competence but it extends to meaning-making ability at all levels. In terms of practical communication a native speaker of English may tolerate a sentence like *He made me understand the idea*, but in terms of native-like competence a similarly accurate but more spontaneous sentence like *He got the idea across to me* is preferable.

With these goals in mind, we have laid out a work rationale for the construction of a Cognitive Pedagogical Grammar, based on formal and cognitively-oriented contrastive work between languages with a view to identifying areas where the L2 can be particularly challenging. We have shown how contrastive work allows analysts to draw relevant cross-linguistic generalizations that can be used to derive related pedagogical implications. Such implications are crucial for a usage-based pedagogical implementation of theoretical principles.

References

Achard, Michel. 2008. Teaching construal: Cognitive pedagogical grammar. In Peter Robinson & Nick C. Ellis (eds.), *Handbook of cognitive linguistics and second language acquisition*, 432–455. New York: Routledge.

Boers, Frank. 2000. Metaphor awareness and vocabulary retention. *Applied Linguistics* 21. 553–571.

Boers, Frank & Murielle Demecheleer. 1998. A cognitive semantic approach to teaching prepositions. *English Language Teaching Journal* 53. 197–204.

Boers, Frank & Seth Lindstromberg. 2006. Cognitive Linguistic approaches to second or foreign language instruction: Rationale, proposals and evaluation. In Gitte Kristiansen, Michel Achard, René Dirven & Francisco J. Ruiz de Mendoza Ibáñez (eds.), *Cognitive linguistics: Current applications and future perspectives*, 305–358. Berlin & New York: Mouton de Gruyter.

Chomsky, Noam. 2007. Approaching UG from below. In Uli Sauerland & Hans-Martin Gärtner (eds.), *Interfaces + recursion = language? Chomsky's minimalism and the view from syntax-semantics*, 1–30. Berlin & New York: Mouton de Gruyter.

Claridge, Claudia. 2011. *Hyperbole in English. A corpus-based study of exaggeration*. Cambridge: Cambridge University Press.

Council of Europe. 2001. *Common European framework of reference for languages: Learning, teaching, assessment*. Cambridge: Cambridge University Press.

Deconinck, Julie, Frank Boers & June Eyckmans. 2010. Helping learners engage with L2 words. The form–meaning fit. In Jeannette Littlemore & Constanze Juchem-Grundmann (eds.), *Applied cognitive linguistics in second language learning and teaching*. Special issue of *AILA Review* 23. 95–114.

De Knop, Sabine, Frank Boers & Antoon De Rycker (eds.). 2010. *Fostering Language Teaching efficiency through cognitive linguistics*. Berlin & New York: Mouton de Gruyter.

De Knop, Sabine & Teun De Rycker (eds.). 2008. *Cognitive approaches to pedagogical grammar: A volume in honour of René Dirven*. Berlin & New York: Mouton de Gruyter.

Diessel, Holger. 2004. *The acquisition of complex sentences*. Cambridge: Cambridge University Press.

Diessel, Holger & Michael Tomasello. 2000. The development of relative clauses in spontaneous child speech. *Cognitive Linguistics* 11. 131–151.

Diessel, Holger & Michael Tomasello. 2001. The acquisition of finite complement clauses in English: A corpus-based analysis. *Cognitive Linguistics* 12. 1–45.

Dirven, René. 2001. English phrasal verbs: Theory and didactic application. In Martin Pütz, Susanne Niemeier & René Dirven (eds.), *Applied cognitive linguistics II: Language pedagogy*, 3–27. Berlin & New York: Mouton de Gruyter.

Dirven, René. 2005. Major strands in Cognitive Linguistics. In Francisco Ruiz de Mendoza & Sandra Peña (eds.), *Cognitive linguistics. Internal dynamics and interdisciplinary interaction*, 17–68. Berlin & New York: Mouton de Gruyter.

Dirven, René & Francisco Ruiz de Mendoza. 2010. Looking back at 30 years of Cognitive Linguistics. In Elżbieta Tabakowska, Michał Choiński & Łukasz Wiraszka (eds.), *Cognitive linguistics in action. From theory to application and back*, 13–70. Berlin & New York: Mouton de Gruyter.

Doughty, Catherine & Jessica Williams. 1998. Pedagogical choices in focus on form. In Catherine Doughty & Jessica Williams (eds.), *Focus on form in classroom second language acquisition*, 197–261. Cambridge: Cambridge University Press.

Ellis, Rod. 2003. *Task-based language learning and teaching*. Oxford: Oxford University Press.

Fillmore, Charles J. 1985. Frames and the semantics of understanding. *Quaderni di Semantica* 6. 222–255.

Givón, Talmy. 1995. Isomorphisms in the grammatical code: Cognitive and biological considerations. In Raffaele Simone (ed.), *Iconicity in language*, 47–76. Amsterdam & Philadelphia: John Benjamins.

Goldberg, Adele. 1995. *Constructions: A construction grammar approach to argument structure*. Chicago: University of Chicago Press.

Goldberg, Adele. 2006. *Constructions at work*. Oxford: Oxford University Press.

Goldberg, Adele & Ray Jackendoff. 2004. The English resultative as a family of constructions. *Language* 80(3). 532–568.

Gonzálvez, Francisco. 2009. The family of object-related depictives in English and Spanish: Towards a usage-based constructionist analysis. *Language Sciences* 31. 663–723.

Holme, Randal. 2009. *Cognitive linguistics and language teaching*. UK: Palgrave Macmillan.

Holme, Randal. 2010. Construction grammars: Towards a pedagogical model. In Jeannette Littlemore & Constanze Juchem-Grundmann (eds.), *Applied cognitive linguistics in second language learning and teaching*. Special issue of *AILA Review* 23. 115–133.

Housen, Alex & Folkert Kuiken. 2009. Complexity, accuracy and fluency in Second Language Acquisition. *Applied Linguistics* 30(4). 461–473.

Johnson, Mark. 1987. *The body in the mind: The bodily basis of meaning, imagination, and reason*. Chicago: University of Chicago Press.

Kay, Paul & Charles J. Fillmore. 1999. Grammatical constructions and linguistic generalizations: The 'What's X doing Y?' construction. *Language* 75. 1–33.

Lakoff, George. 1987. *Women, fire, and dangerous things: What categories reveal about the mind*. Chicago: University of Chicago Press.

Lakoff, George & Mark Johnson. 1980. *Metaphors we live by*. Chicago: University of Chicago Press.

Lakoff, George & Mark Johnson. 1999. *Philosophy in the flesh*. New York: Basic Books.

Littlemore, Jeannette & Constanze Juchem-Grundmann (eds.). 2010. *Cognitive linguistics and second language learning and teaching*. Special issue of the *AILA Review*.

MacArthur, Fiona. 2010. Metaphorical competence in EFL: Where are we and where should we be going? A view from the language classroom. In Jeannette Littlemore and Constanze Juchem-Grundmann (eds.), *Applied Cognitive Linguistics in Second Language Learning and Teaching*. Special issue of *AILA Review*, 23. 155–173.

Matlock, Teenie. 2004. Fictive motion as cognitive simulation. *Memory and Cognition* 32(8). 1389–1400.

Odlin, Terence (ed.). 1994. *Perspectives on pedagogical grammar*. Cambridge: Cambridge University Press.

Peña, Sandra. 2009. Constraints on subsumption in the caused-motion construction. *Language Sciences* 31(6). 740–765.

Pütz, Martin, Susanne Niemeier & René Dirven (eds.). 2001. *Applied cognitive linguistics II: Language pedagogy*. Berlin & New York: Mouton de Gruyter.

Ruiz de Mendoza, Francisco. 2008. Cross-linguistic analysis, second language teaching and cognitive semantics: The case of Spanish diminutives and reflexive constructions. In

Sabine De Knop & Teun De Rycker (eds.), *Cognitive approaches to pedagogical grammar. A volume in honour of René Dirven*, 121–152. Berlin & New York: Mouton de Gruyter.

Ruiz de Mendoza, Francisco. 2013. Meaning construction, meaning interpretation, and formal expression in the Lexical Constructional Model. In Brian Nolan & Elke Diedrichsen (eds.), *Linking constructions into functional linguistics: The role of constructions in grammar*, 231–270. Amsterdam & Philadelphia: John Benjamins.

Ruiz de Mendoza, Francisco. 2014. Mapping concepts: Understanding figurative thought from a cognitive-linguistic perspective. *Spanish Journal of Applied Linguistics* 27(1). 187–207.

Ruiz de Mendoza, Francisco & Pilar Agustín. 2013. La construcción reduplicativa de base léxica en español: un estudio preliminar para estudiantes de español como L2. In Sabine De Knop, Fabio Mollica & Julia Kuhn (eds.), *Konstruktionsgrammatik in den romanischen Sprachen*, 205–225. Frankfurt am Main: Peter Lang.

Ruiz de Mendoza, Francisco & Alicia Galera. 2014. *Cognitive modeling. A linguistic perspective*. Amsterdam & Philadelphia: John Benjamins.

Ruiz de Mendoza, Francisco & Alba Luzondo. 2014. Figurative and non-figurative motion in the expression of result in English. *Language and Cognition* Available on CJO 2014 doi:10.1017/langcog.2014.41.

Ruiz de Mendoza, Francisco & Sandra Peña. 2008. Grammatical metonymy within the 'action' frame in English and Spanish. In María de los Ángeles Gómez González, J. Lachlan Mackenzie & Elsa M. González-Álvarez (eds.), *Current trends in contrastive linguistics: Functional and cognitive perspectives*, 251–280. Amsterdam & Philadelphia: John Benjamins.

Ruiz de Mendoza, Francisco & Lorena Pérez. 2001. Metonymy and the grammar: Motivation, constraints, and interaction. *Language and Communication* 21. 321–357.

Stern, H. H. 1990. Analysis and experience as variables in second language pedagogy. In Birgit Harley, Patrick Allen, Jim Cummins & Merrill Swain (eds.), *The development of second language proficiency*, 93–109. Cambridge: Cambridge University Press.

Talmy, Leonard. 2000. *Toward a cognitive semantics*. Vol. 1. Cambridge, Mass.: MIT Press.

Tomasello, Michael. 2003. *Constructing a language: A usage-based theory of language acquisition*. Cambridge, Mass.: Harvard University Press.

Valenzuela, Javier & Ana Rojo. 2008. What can foreign language learners tell us about constructions? In Sabine De Knop & Teun De Rycker (eds.), *Cognitive approaches to pedagogical grammar. A volume in honour of René Dirven*, 197–229. Berlin & New York: Mouton de Gruyter.

Wilson, Deirdre & Dan Sperber. 2012. Explaining irony. In Deirdre Wilson & Dan Sperber (eds.), *Meaning and relevance*, 123–145. Cambridge: Cambridge University Press.

Alberto Hijazo-Gascón, Teresa Cadierno and
Iraide Ibarretxe-Antuñano

Learning the placement caused motion construction in L2 Spanish*

Abstract: Placement events are one type of caused motion events where an Agent causes an object to move to a specific location in space. The cross-linguistic differences regarding the encoding of this sort of events make these placement caused motion constructions a challenge for second language learners. In this study, a comparison is drawn between the placement caused motion constructions in L1 Spanish and L2 Spanish by Danish speakers. The data show learners' difficulty to "re-think for speaking" due to the different degrees of specificity between the typical construction in Danish and Spanish, especially with regard to containment relationships, force dynamics and intentionality. Learners encountered learning difficulties when they had to adapt the semantic categories in their native language to those in the second language. Finally, some pedagogical activities are proposed to raise students' awareness of the prototypical construction in the second language and the use of the general placement verb and other more specific placement verbs.

Keywords: placement events; motion; crosslinguistic influence; Spanish; Danish

1 Introduction

Motion is a widely studied semantic domain in Cognitive Linguistics (Talmy 1991, 2000; Slobin 1996). According to Talmy (1985, 2000) several components define a caused motion event, namely the element changing position (Figure), the Agent that makes possible the change of position, the Path or trajectory of the Figure, and the Ground, which is the new place where the Figure is located. For example, in *Pedro puts an orange on the table*, *Pedro* is the Agent, *an orange* is the Figure, *on* is the Path and *the table* is the Ground. Languages differ with

---

* The present project has been financed by the Velux Foundation and by the Spanish Government (MovEs, FFI2013-45553-C3-1-P). We would like to thank Carola Pedersen for her help in the data collection, Thomas Nielsen for his help in data transcribing and coding, Isabel Casas and Toker Doganoglu for their help in the statistical analyses of the data, and Francisco Gonzálvez-García for his comments.

respect to the constructions that are used to describe placement events (Kopecka and Narasimhan 2012) and these cross-linguistic differences constitute a challenge in the acquisition of a second language. Learners need to be aware of the similarities and differences between the L1 and L2 constructions when encoding these events and they need to adapt to the rhetorical style of the language. In fact, the acquisition of these constructions implies what has been called learning to "think for speaking in a second language" (Cadierno 2004, 2008a) or learning to "re-think for speaking" (Robinson and Ellis 2008).

This paper discusses Danish and Spanish placement caused motion constructions with a special focus on the acquisition of Spanish as an L2 by Danish native speakers (NSs). These two languages differ in the semantic distinctions encoded in placement verbs as well as in the type of constructions that are characteristically used in the description of these events. Specifically, we examine the impact of these cross-linguistic differences on the acquisition of placement caused motion constructions in L2 Spanish and discuss some pedagogical implications of our findings.

2 The placement caused motion construction

In his typological framework, Talmy (1991, 2000) classifies the languages of the world according to whether they tend to encode the semantic component of Path within the main verb or in what he calls a satellite. In verb-framed languages, e.g. in Spanish *La niña sale de la casa* 'The girl exits the house', the whole trajectory of the movement, what Talmy calls the Path, is coded in the main verb of the event, *salir* 'exit'. By contrast, satellite-framed languages tend to encode the Path outside the verb, e.g. in a satellite, for example in English *The girl went out of the house*, where the Path is encoded in *out*.

Stemming from this typological classification, Slobin (1991, 1996, 2000) puts forward the "thinking for speaking" hypothesis. It claims that speakers are influenced by the linguistic elements provided by their languages during the verbalisation of experience. In other words, when speakers have to describe an event, they have to use the linguistic resources available in their language. Native speakers thus have their own rhetorical style, i.e. their characteristic ways to describe and encode a given situation. It is very important to distinguish between rhetorical style and grammaticality. Rhetorical style is not based on grammatical restrictions, but on speakers' preferred and habitual choice of linguistic structures. While most of the previous literature on thinking for speaking is based on spontaneous or voluntary motion events, recent studies collected in Kopecka and Narasimhan (2012) show that placement events, a subtype of caused motion events, are also relevant from this theoretical point of view.

Choi and Bowerman (1991) and Bowerman (1996a) are some of the first studies to focus on cross-linguistic differences with regard to placement events in English and Korean. Korean speakers distinguish between events in which the relation between the Figure and the Ground is tight-fit (verb *kkita*) and those in which it is loose-fit (verb *nehta*). For English speakers, on the other hand, this distinction is not obvious and they focus on other configurational characteristics such as the two- or three-dimensionality of the Ground, e.g. *put the book on the shelf* vs. *put the apple in the box* where the former depicts a support type of relation between the Figure and the Ground and the latter a containment type of relation between these two elements. Differences in the encoding of placement events are found in a wide variety of languages. In Kopecka and Narasimhan (2012) there are data from 19 languages. Using the same elicitation tools, they found out that the same placement events can be described with more or less detail depending on the linguistic resources each language has. The encoding of placement events has also been studied in child first language acquisition in several languages (e.g. Bowerman 1996b; Hickmann and Hendriks 2006; Hickmann 2007; Gullberg and Narasimham 2010; Narasimhan and Gullberg 2010; Slobin et al. 2011) and also in relation to speech and gesture (e.g. Gullberg 2009).

One of the first studies on the encoding of placement events in second language acquisition is Viberg's (1998) analysis of L2 Swedish placement events produced by speakers of Finnish, Spanish, and Polish. His study shows that learners either overgeneralised one of the possible Swedish placement verbs or used avoidance strategies. Evidence from cross-linguistic influence also arose in this study. Polish speakers, who have two placement verbs in their language (*kłaść* 'lay' and *stawiać* 'stand'), used the Swedish verbs *lägga* 'lay, put (horizontally)', *ställa* 'put (vertically)', and *sätta* 'place in a fixed position' more appropriately than Finnish and Spanish speakers, who have only one general placement verb, *panna* 'put' and *poner* 'put' respectively. Gullberg (2009) found similar results with English learners of L2 Dutch. English learners of L2 Dutch did not use posture verbs (e.g. *zetten* 'put (vertically)', *leggen* 'lay') as frequently as Dutch speakers usually do and struggled with the use of the specific posture verbs in their L2. English learners also used avoidance strategies, such as the use of general verbs and overgeneralisation of one of the posture verbs over the others.

In the present study we analyse descriptions of placement events produced by Danish speakers of L2 Spanish and compare them with data from functional

monolingual Danish and Spanish speakers including the analysis of verbs and particles. We use the cover term 'spatial particle' as a short-hand way to refer to particles, adverbs, and prepositions. More concretely, our research questions are:
- How similar or different are the placement caused motion constructions in L2 Spanish with respect to those in L1 Spanish?
- If differences are found, how do these affect the rhetorical style of L2 Spanish learners?
- What are the pedagogical implications of these results?

3 Methodology[1]

3.1 Informants

Three groups of participants took part in this study: ten native speakers of Spanish, all students at the University of Zaragoza (Spain) without previous knowledge of Danish; fourteen native speakers of Danish, all students at the University of Southern Denmark without previous knowledge of Spanish; and fourteen native speakers of Danish, first year Spanish undergrads also at the University of Southern Denmark. The learners had a B1-B2 proficiency level in Spanish according to the *Common European Framework of Reference for Languages*. Their level was tested through the use of the online test of the Cervantes Institute (http://ave.cervantes.es/prueba_nivel/default.htm), a governmental agency devoted to teaching and promoting the Spanish language and culture internationally. The first two groups can be considered functional monolingual, Spanish and Danish being their respective daily basis languages (Brown and Gullberg 2012). However, the Danish speakers also reported good knowledge of English and some other languages (e.g. German and Greek).

3.2 Data collection

Data were collected with the stimuli of the 'put' task, designed at the Max Planck Institute for Psycholinguistics (henceforth MPI) in Nijmegen, the Netherlands (Bowerman et al. 2004; Kopecka and Narashiman 2012). They consist of 61 short video clips in which a caused motion event is performed. Participants were

---

[1] The results presented here are part of a wider project that studies placement and removal events in Danish and Spanish in L2 acquisition. This paper only discusses placement events in L2 Spanish, and therefore, the methodology section will describe the data collection for this specific dataset.

asked to describe the action shown in the video. Videos, arranged in three different randomised orders, were designed taking into consideration different features that can lead to cross-linguistic variation, such as the nature and spatial configuration of the Figure and the Ground, the presence of an instrument (e.g. tongs), the manner in which the Figure is moved, and so on. Although our data were collected using the full video set (61), this study focuses only on the 'put' or placement subset (31) (names of these clips are written in small caps). Removal events are thus not considered in this paper.

3.3 Data analysis

Oral data were transcribed and coded based on the MPI guidelines for the 'put' task (Bowerman et al. 2004). Two types of analysis were carried out. First, the verb types and tokens were computed, as well as the type-token ratio for each group. The same was done for the particles. Second, a video-clip-by-verb matrix was created for each of the three groups where the frequency of each verb per scene was specified. The results were analysed using a hierarchical agglomerative cluster analysis, following previous studies in semantic categorisation (cf. Majid et al. 2007; Jessen 2013; Jessen and Cadierno 2013).

4 Results

In this section, we analyse what we call the 'typical placement caused motion construction' in each of the three groups of participants. We use the term 'construction' in the sense of Goldberg's (1995, 2006) Construction Grammar. That is, we investigate those pairings of form and meaning that our informants used more frequently and prototypically to describe a placement caused motion event. In terms of Construction Grammar, a caused motion event can be defined as follows (see Goldberg 1995: ch. 7; Goldberg, Casenhiser, and Sethuraman 2004):

(1) Form   Meaning   Construction label
     Subj V Obj Obl$_{path/loc}$ X causes Y to move Z$_{path/loc}$ Caused motion
     Pat sneezed the napkin off the table

Results show that both groups of Spanish speakers (Spanish NSs and Spanish L2 learners) provided very similar typical placement caused motion constructions as far as their general structure is concerned. However, these similarities are only superficial and disappear when we look at the internal components of these constructions. Spanish L1 and L2 speakers differed considerably with regard to verb usage (what verbs were used), semantic categorisation (what meanings were coded in verbs), and particle usage.

4.1 Typical placement caused motion construction in L1 Spanish, L1 Danish, and L2 Spanish

According to Talmy's (1985) lexicalisation framework, Spanish and Danish are typologically different languages with regard to the encoding of motion events. Spanish is a verb-framed language; therefore, Path information is usually codified in the main verb and Manner information in another linguistic element (e.g. *salir corriendo* 'exit running'). Danish, on the other hand, is a satellite-framed language; this means that Path is usually coded in a satellite outside the verb and Manner in the main verb (e.g. *løbe ud* 'run out') (see Cadierno 2004, 2010 for more details).

These different lexicalisation patterns also arise in placement caused motion constructions. In Spanish, our data show that the most frequent placement caused motion construction (174 tokens out of 270, 62.6%) is (NP) [subject] V NP [direct object] PP [where]² or, using Goldberg's template, Subj V Obj Obl$_{loc}$, as illustrated in (2):

(2) *Deja   la   taza   en   la   mesa*
    leaves.3SG ART   mug   LOC   ART   table
    'She leaves the mug on the table'

In (2), the subject is omitted (Spanish is a pro-drop language), the main verb is the caused motion verb *dejar* which means 'allow, let' in general but 'leave on a place' in this context, the direct object is the NP *la taza* 'the mug' and the location information (Goldberg's Obl$_{loc}$) is the PP *en la mesa* 'on the table'. Apart from the structure, there are a couple of interesting issues worth mentioning. One is the information about the force dynamics provided in the main verb. *Dejar* 'leave on a place' involves a soft and gentle type of placement, which is crucial for the scale of force dynamics and intentionality that some placement caused motion constructions exhibit in Spanish (see Section 4.3.3). The other one is the type of meaning encoded in the preposition *en* in (2). This preposition refers to a general location, that is, it expresses that the Figure occupies a certain place but it does not specify the type of spatial arrangement established

---

2 Non-compulsory elements are in brackets ( ) and functions in square brackets [ ].

between Figure and Ground. This spatial configuration is inferred by the speaker both from the semantic content of the two-dimensional Ground (*the table*) and his/her own world knowledge (mugs are usually placed on tables). If needed, speakers can also provide more information about the exact place where Figures are located. In (3), the fact that the marker is placed inside the tree hole comes from both the semantics of the verb, *meter* 'put in', and the spatial nominal adverb *dentro (de)* 'inside (of)'.

(3) Mete   el   rotulador dentro del   agujero del   árbol
    puts.3SG ART   marker   inside of.ART hole   of.ART tree
    'She puts the marker into the tree hole'

In the case of Danish, there are two types of constructions that appear more frequently: one with the structure NP [subject] V NP [direct object] PP [where] or, using Goldberg's template, Subj V Obj Obl$_{loc}$ (190 tokens out of 434, 43.8%), as illustrated in (4), and another more complex construction with the structure NP [subject] V NP [direct object] DIR PAR[3] [Path] PP [where] or, using Goldberg's template, Subj V Obj Obl$_{path}$ Obl$_{loc}$ (170 tokens out of 434, 39.2%), as illustrated in (5).

(4) En kvinde sætter   et   krus på et bord
    a   woman   puts.vertically   DET mug   on a   table
    'A woman puts a mug on a table'

(5) Manden   stiller   en   æske op på hylden
    the man puts.vertically   DET box   up on shelf.the
    'The man puts a box up on the shelf'

The Danish placement caused motion construction illustrated in (5) not only contains more elements to describe the spatial arrangement (Obl$_{path}$) than those in (2) and (3) but also different information. The main verb *stille* 'put vertically' specifies that the Figure is vertically situated with respect to the Ground. The directional particle *op* 'up' depicts the upward motion (Path) followed by the box from where it stands at the beginning of the clip until it reaches the final destination, the shelf, and the prepositional phrase *på hylden* 'on the shelf' describes the support relationship between the Figure (the box) and the Ground (the shelf).

---

[3] DIR PAR = directional particle.

Finally, the typical placement caused motion construction for L2 Spanish learners shows the structure (NP) [subject] V NP [direct object] PP [where] or, in Goldberg's template, Subj V Obj Obl$_{loc}$ (280 tokens out of 391, 71.6%), which is identical to the construction used by Spanish L1 NSs as illustrated in (6). Learners also occasionally include a spatial adverb to provide more specific details, like *dentro de* 'inside (of)' in (7):

(6) *Pone   la   taza   en   la   mesa*
    put.3SG   ART   mug   LOC   ART   table
    'S/he puts the mug on the table'

(7) *Pone   la   piedra   dentro   del   bol*
    put.3SG   ART   stone   inside   of.ART   bowl
    'S/he puts the stone in the bowl'

However, this type of construction is not the only one that L2 Spanish learners use. They also frequently employ a static construction, NP V-*estar* 'be (stative)' PP, that is not present in the L1 Spanish data. Examples (8) and (9) illustrate this pattern:

(8) *Una   persona   toma   la   copa   y   el   agua   está   en*
    a   person   take.3SG   ART   cup   and   ART water   is.3SG   LOC
    la   mesa
    ART   table
    'A person takes the cup and the water is on the table'

(9) *Una   mujer   tiene   un   libro   en   su   mano   y   hace*
    a   woman   has.3SG   a   book   LOC   her   hand   and   makes.3SG
    algo   y   después   no   tiene   el   libro   en   su
    something   and   afterwards   no   has.3SG   ART book   LOC her
    mano   y   el   libro   está   en   el   suelo
    hand   and   ART   book   is.3SG   LOC   ART   floor
    'A woman has a book in her hand and makes something and afterwards she does not have the book in her hand and the book is on the floor'

In these examples, learners seem to divide the caused motion event into two or more sub-events by means of different clauses. Whereas the first clause(s) tell(s) the location of the Figure before the caused motion event takes place, the next clause describes where and how the Figure ended up after the caused motion event occurs. It is interesting to notice that the same type of strategy is found in research on the L2 expression of spontaneous motion events involving boundary-crossing. Cadierno (2010) reports that whereas Danish NSs used the expression *Manden kravler over tæppet* 'The man crawls over the carpet' to describe a scene where a man is crawling over a carpet, Spanish learners of L2 Danish tended to use structures such as *Manden kravler til tæppet og så bevæger sig fra tæppet* 'the man crawls to the carpet and then moves (away) from the carpet'. Here, the motion event is sub-divided into two sub-events by means of two clauses: the first one for the motion towards the boundary and the second one for the motion away from the boundary. It can be argued that this type of 'divided structures' responds to a communicative strategy of avoidance. That is, learners seem to resort to this strategy when they cannot find the adequate linguistic means – usually the appropriate caused motion verb – to encode the meaning of the event.

In general, our data show that L2 speakers seem to have acquired the basic structure of the placement caused motion construction, provided that they count with the right vocabulary. L2 speakers are aware of which pairings of form and meaning are frequently used in Spanish (Subj V Obj Obl_{loc}) and how these differ from their native Danish construction (the use of the Obj_{path}). However, there are important differences between the learner and the Spanish native group with regard to: (i) verb usage, (ii) semantic categorisation, and (iii) particle usage. In other words, learners seem to have acquired the Spanish general constructional pattern (Subj V Obj Obl_{loc}), but they seem to have difficulties with the internal components that instantiate these abstract patterns. These will be discussed in the following sections.

4.2 Verb usage

The use of verbs in the three groups differs with respect to both the number of tokens and number of types (for a more detailed analysis, see Cadierno, Ibarretxe-Antuñano, and Hijazo-Gascón 2016). Table 1 shows the mean values for the verb tokens and verb types used by the three participant groups along with the type-token ratios. A Mann-Whitney U test conducted on the mean type-token ratios revealed no significant differences between the two native groups, i.e. L1 Spanish and L1 Danish ($p = 0.584$). By contrast, a significant difference was found between the L1 Spanish and L2 Spanish groups ($p = 0.000$): the mean type-token ratio of the L2 Spanish group was significantly smaller than that of the L1 Spanish group. This means that the L2 Spanish group used a more restricted repertoire of placement verbs in comparison to the L1 Spanish group.

Table 1: Verb tokens, types and type-token ratios in the three participant groups (mean values)

Speaker group	Tokens	Types	Type-token ratio
L1 Spanish	30.9	12.5	0.40
L1 Danish	31	12.86	0.41
L2 Spanish	28	6.71	0.25

Apart from similarities and differences in the number of types and tokens, it is also crucial to compare the types of verbs that each group used in order to see whether the semantic information contained in these verbs coincides or not. As shown in Figure 1, two verbs are predominantly used in L1 Spanish, *dejar* 'leave, put' and *meter* 'put in', followed by *poner* 'put'.

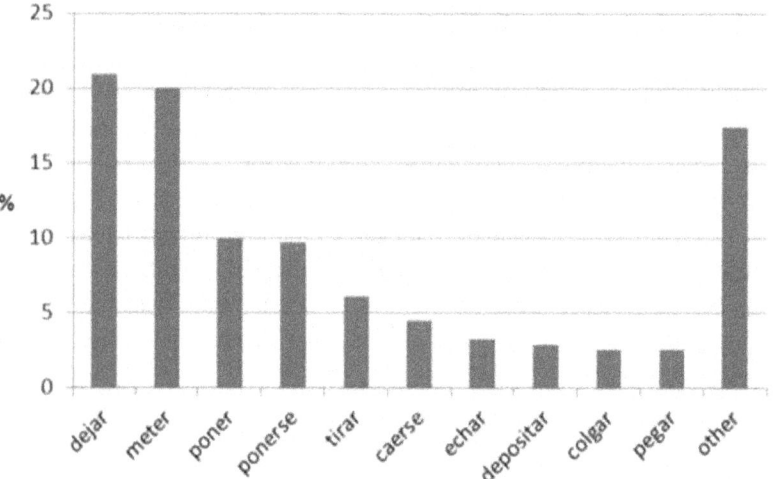

Figure 1: Verbs used in L1 Spanish[4]

In the case of L1 Danish in Figure 2, *lægge* 'lay' and *sætte* 'set' were the predominant verbs, followed by *putte* 'put, put in' and *tage* 'take'.

---

[4] The category 'other' includes verbs with much lower frequency such as *introducir* 'introduce', *posar* 'place carefully', and *derramarse* 'spill'.

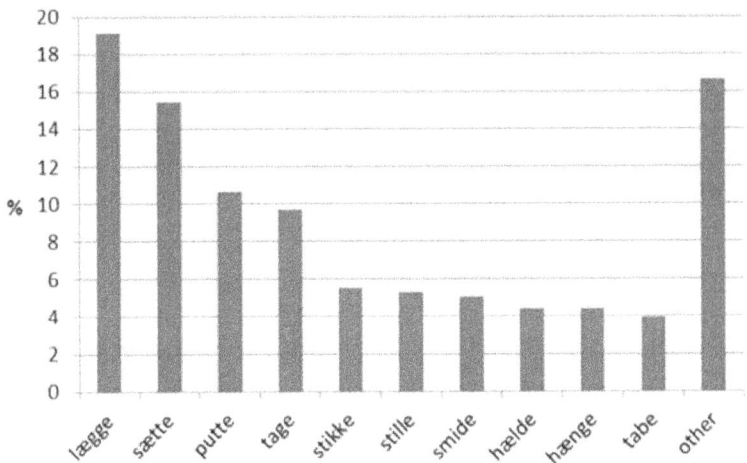

Figure 2: Verbs used in L1 Danish[5]

Finally, Figure 3 shows the verb choices in L2 Spanish. Here, a single verb clearly stands out in the learners' production, the verb *poner* 'put'. It is also worth pointing out that learners employed non-caused motion verbs such as *estar* 'be', *llevar* 'take', and *tener* 'have' to describe these clips. Learners also made up some neologisms resulting from calques and borrowings from Danish or English. The verb *placear*, an adaptation from Danish *placere* 'place' or English *place*, is an example; interestingly enough, *placear* occupies the third position in Figure 3.

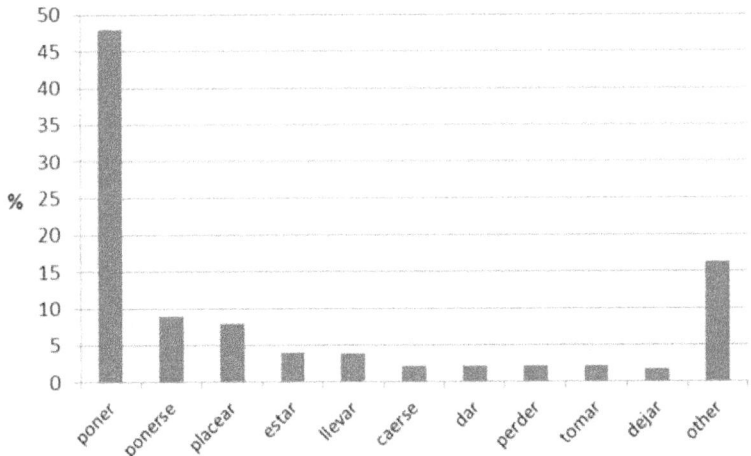

Figure 3: Verbs used in L2 Spanish[6]

---

[5] As in Figure 1, the category 'other' includes less frequent verbs such as *kaste* 'throw', *skubbe* 'push', and *falde* 'let fall'.

[6] The 'other' category includes verbs such as *hælde* 'pour', *smide* 'throw', and *putte* 'put, put in'.

The verb usage analysis points to crucial differences with respect to the semantic categories that each group discriminates or pays attention to. The following section focuses on these differences in more detail.

4.3 Differences in semantic categories

The verbs used by the three participant groups have different meanings because of the different semantic categories they encode. Spanish and Danish belong to different lexicalisation patterns and this is reflected in the results of our study. Based on the data elicited with our set of video stimuli, there is only one semantic category that coincides in the two languages, namely dressing events. Each language has just one verb for all these events: Spanish *ponerse* and Danish *tage (på)* 'put (on) clothes'. Spanish and Danish differ, however, with regard to three semantic categories: support, containment and force dynamics. The following sections provide basic details about these three groups (see Cadierno, Ibarretxe-Antuñano, and Hijazo-Gascón (2016) and Ibarretxe-Antuñano, Cadierno, and Hijazo-Gascón (in press) for detailed cluster analyses on these semantic categories).

4.3.1 Support

There is an important difference with regard to the semantic category of support. Danish necessarily includes information about the position of the Figure with respect to the Ground whereas Spanish lacks this type of information. Spanish speakers predominantly used just one verb *dejar* 'leave on a place' for support scenes such as PUT PLASTIC CUP ON A TABLE WITH MOUTH, PUT BOX UP ON SHELF, PUT ARMLOAD OF BOOKS ON TABLE, PUT CUP ON TABLE, PUT BOOK ON FLOOR, PUT BANANA ON TABLE WITH LONG TONGS (see Figure 4). Danish speakers, on the other hand, needed to choose between the verb *lægge*, which is used for horizontally placed objects or objects that lack a functional base (PUT BOOK ON FLOOR, PUT BANANA ON TABLE WITH LONG TONGS), and *sætte / stille* 'set' for vertically placed objects or objects that have a functional base (PUT PLASTIC CUP ON A TABLE WITH MOUTH, PUT CUP ON TABLE, PUT BOX UP ON SHELF, PUT ARMLOAD OF BOOKS ON TABLE) (Serra Borneto 1996; Coventry and Garrod 2004; Gullberg and Burenhult 2012).

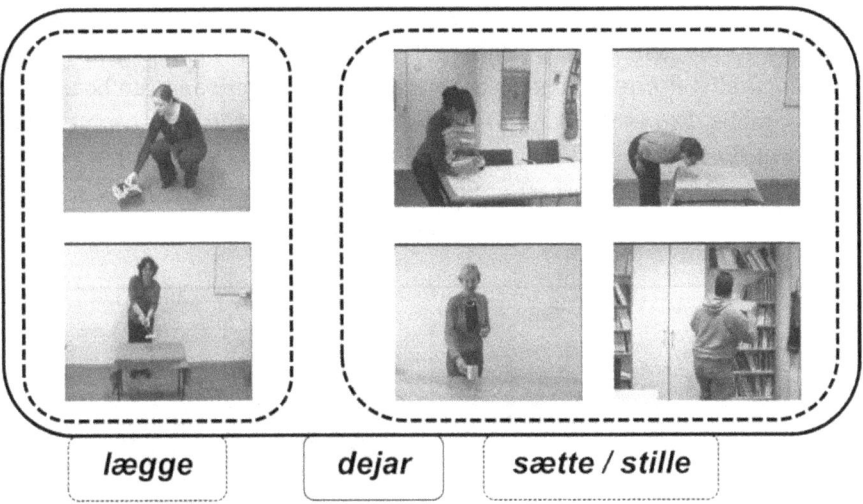

Figure 4: Semantic categories for support in Spanish (*dejar*) and Danish (*lægge* vs. *sætte/stille*) (adapted from Bowerman et al. 2004)

This means that in the case of the acquisition of L2 Spanish by native speakers of Danish, learners need to move from two semantic categories to one category. Our results show that L2 Spanish learners are able to do so; they reduce the number of categories and use the verb *poner* 'put'. However, their choice of verb, grammatically correct as it may be, does not correspond to the native speakers' preferred verb, *dejar* 'leave, put', which is not as general as *poner* 'put'.

4.3.2 Containment

Spanish native speakers described containment scenes with the verb *meter* 'put in' (see Figure 5). Danish speakers, on the other hand, used three different verbs: *lægge* 'lay' when Figures are placed horizontally (e.g. PUT STONE INTO POT OF WATER, PUT PEN IN HOLE IN TREE TRUNK); *stikke* 'put in, stick' when the (often pointed-shaped) Figure follows a trajectory along a path to penetrate (totally or partially) the container and the resulting relation between the placed object and the container is often one of tight-fit (e.g. PUT HEAD INTO BUCKET, PUT HAND INTO HOLE IN TREE); and *putte* 'put, put in' that does not seem to have a specific use (this verb is frequent in oral contexts in both tight-fit and loose-fit types of relations, e.g. PUT STUFF RAG INTO CAR EXHAUST PIPE, PUT CELERY BUNCH INTO RECORDER CASE, PUT STONE INTO POCKET, DROP APPLE INTO BAG). Therefore, for the semantic category of containment, Danish learners of Spanish should make a transition from three categories to one. Our learners did so but once again they resorted to the general verb *poner* 'put'. As in the previous case, this is not grammatically incorrect; *poner* is a general placement verb and can be used on all occasions. However, Spanish native speakers did not use this verb for containment types of events; they preferred the specificity in *meter* 'put in'. This also suggests that the learners of Spanish might not be aware of the semantic distinction between support and containment in Spanish.

Figure 5: Semantic categories for containment in Spanish (*meter*) and Danish (*lægge, stikke, putte*) (adapted from Bowerman et al. 2004)

4.3.3 Force dynamics and intentionality

Another example of the different semantic categorisation in Danish and Spanish comes from the conceptual elements of intentionality and force dynamics. These are two important features in Spanish placement events (Ibarretxe-Antuñano 2012). Intentionality refers to the degree of the Agent's involvement in the event and force dynamics to how the Agent and Figure interact with respect to the force (Talmy 1988). In the stimuli, there are three clips that illustrate different degrees of intentionality and force dynamics, namely DROP BOOK ACCIDENTALLY ON FLOOR, DROP BOOK DELIBERATELY ON FLOOR, and TOSS BOOK ON FLOOR (see Figure 6).

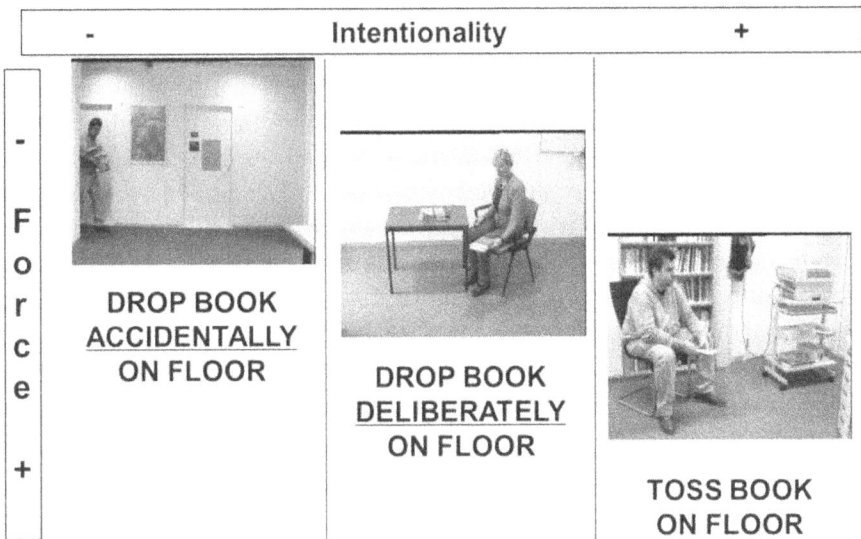

Figure 6: Degrees of intentionality and force dynamics in video clips (adapted from Bowerman et al. 2004)

The boundaries between the three events are quite clear in Spanish, and Spanish NSs coded the increase of force and intentionality by means of different constructions for these three clips: *caerse* 'fall'+ clitic for the first clip, *dejar caer* 'let fall' and *tirar* 'throw' for the second clip, and *tirar* 'throw', *lanzar* 'throw away', and *arrojar* 'throw away violently' for the third clip. These categories are quite different in Danish, and Danish NSs used different verbs: *tabe* 'drop, lose' and *spilde* 'spill' for dropping accidentally; *smide* 'throw', *tabe* 'drop, lose', *lade falde* 'let fall', *lægge* 'lay', *give* 'give', and *kaste* 'throw away violently' for dropping deliberately, and *smide* 'throw' and *kaste* 'throw away violently' for the last category, TOSS BOOK ON FLOOR. Therefore, in the second language acquisition process, Danish learners of L2 Spanish need to move from more verbs in Danish to fewer verbs in Spanish. The L2 Spanish learner group employed a total of nine different verbs. For the first scene – DROP BOOK ACCIDENTALLY ON FLOOR – the learners used *caerse* 'fall' + clitic (5 occurrences), *perder* 'lose' (2 occurrences), *estar* 'be (stative)' (1 occurrence), *llevar* 'take' (1 occurrence), and *tener* 'have' (1 occurrence). The descriptions for the video DROP BOOK DELIBERATELY ON FLOOR show the use of nine different verb types with very few tokens each: *caer* 'fall' (2), *estar* 'be (stative)' (2), *perder* 'lose' (2), *caerse* 'fall + clitic' (1), *dejar caer* 'let fall' (1), *lanzar* 'throw away' (1), *quitar* 'remove' (1), *tirar* 'throw' (1), and *tocar* 'touch' (1). Finally, for the video TOSS BOOK ON FLOOR the learners used the verbs *perder* 'lose' (2), *irse* 'go away' (1), *lanzar* 'throw away' (1), *quitar* 'remove'

(1), *saltar* 'jump' (1), *tener* 'have' (1), and *tirar* 'throw' (1). Thus, the verbs used by the learners in the description of the three scenes do not coincide entirely with the verbs used by the Spanish native speakers. Learners used eight verbs that were not employed by the Spanish NS group. There were five verbs used by both the NS and the learner groups; however, only two (*dejar caer* 'let fall' and *tirar* 'throw') cover the appropriate semantic categories, and just with one occurrence per verb in each scene. Other verbs (e.g. *lanzar* 'throw away' and *caerse* 'fall' + clitic) were used across categories. It seems that Spanish L2 learners do not make clear linguistic distinctions between intentional and accidental dropping, and between intentional dropping and throwing.

In addition, there is one case that can be considered an example of probable cross-linguistic influence in the form of semantic transfer as illustrated in the use of the verb *perder* 'lose':

(10) Un   hombre   pierde   un   libro   del   piso
     a   man   loses.3SG   a   book   from.ART   floor
     'A man drops a book on the floor'

The learner in (10) uses the verb *perder* 'lose' for the video clip DROP BOOK ACCIDENTALLY ON FLOOR. This verb in Spanish only means 'lose something' and cannot be used to describe such an event. The verb *tabe* in Danish, on the other hand, has two meanings: 'lose something' as in Spanish but also 'let fall an object'. Danish learners seem to have picked the wrong meaning of the Danish verb *tabe*, using the Spanish verb *perder* 'lose', instead of the appropriate one, *dejar caer* 'let fall'. As Jarvis and Pavlenko (2008: 75) explain, semantic transfer consists in the "use of an authentic target-language word with a meaning that reflects the influence from the semantic range of a corresponding word in another language", and this is exactly what happens in this case. It is crucial to bear in mind that semantic transfer is different from conceptual transfer. The former involves the mapping between words and concepts which determines how many concepts and which particular concepts words can express whereas the latter relates to the nature and structure of those concepts (Jarvis and Pavlenko 2008).

4.4 Spatial particle usage

As mentioned before, we use the cover term 'spatial particle' to refer to particles, adverbs, and prepositions. The linguistic elements under this general label have different morpho-syntactic features in Spanish and Danish (see Pavón Lucero

1999; Morimoto and Pavón Lucero 2003; Hansen and Heltoft 2011); however, in this paper, we are not interested in these formal features but in the role that these elements play within the placement caused motion construction and in their different usage for the description of spatial relations in Spanish and Danish as L1s and in Spanish as an L2.

As shown in Table 2, Spanish speakers used 55 tokens and only 2 types of particles (type-token ratio = 0.036). The particles used are the spatial nominal adverbs *dentro* 'inside' and *encima* 'on top of'. As previously pointed out, the use of these adverbs is not compulsory, but in some scenes the addition of the particle makes the description more natural, even if it repeats information already mentioned in other parts of the construction (see Ibarretxe-Antuñano 2012 for more details).

Table 2: Usage of particles in Spanish

Particles	Tokens
Dentro 'inside'	18
Encima 'on top of'	37

By contrast, Danish speakers used a wide range of particles very frequently – more concretely, 216 tokens and 12 types (type-token ratio = 0.056). The most frequent ones were *ned* 'down' and *ind* 'in' as can be seen in Table 3. This high frequency of use of particles is natural considering that the typical placement caused motion construction in Danish includes such particles in its structure (see Section 4.1.1).

Table 3: Usage of particles in Danish

Particles	Tokens
Bag 'behind'	1
Hen 'along'	1
Ind 'in'	14
Inde 'in-static'	1
Ned 'down'	113
Nede 'down-static'	1
Op 'up'	25
Oven 'above'	9
Over 'over, across'	4
På 'on'	38
Tilbage 'back'	3
Ud 'out'	6

Since there is an important cross-linguistic difference in the usage of particles in Danish and Spanish, we further examined whether this difference could have an impact on the expression of placement events in L2 Spanish. In this case our learners needed to move from a frequent category in their L1 placement caused motion construction to a more combinability-restricted and optional category in the second language. Results showed that learners used only 10 particle tokens but 4 types (type-token ratio = 0.4). In other words, L2 learners used fewer tokens than Spanish native speakers did, possibly because particles are difficult to use in a foreign language and/or because they noticed that particles are not needed in the Spanish construction. This explanation is in line with what Kellerman (1978, 1986) calls "psychotypology", that is, learners' perceived differences between the constructions in the L1 and L2. On the other hand, learners produced two particle types which were not in the native speakers' data: *abajo* 'down' and *arriba* 'up'.

Table 4: Usage of particles in L2 Spanish

Particles	Tokens
Dentro 'inside'	5
Abajo 'down'	1
Encima 'on top of'	2
Arriba 'up'	2

5 Discussion

Having presented the results of our speaker groups in the description of placement events, there are some issues worth mentioning before turning to some theoretical and pedagogical implications. First, it is important to bear in mind that even though the typical construction in native and learner Spanish is structurally the same, that is, both constructions have the same formal elements, the specific elements used to fill in each gap (main verb, prepositional phrase, and so on) are not the same. In fact, some features in the L2 constructions are not appropriate in the L1 (or at least not as frequently used by native speakers). For instance, the verb *poner* 'put' is overused in the learners' descriptions. This is probably due to a process of overgeneralisation. *Poner* is a general placement verb and it is not agrammatical in most of these descriptions; however, it is not the preferred choice for Spanish native speakers. Goldberg, Casenhiser, and Sethuraman (2004) argue that highly frequent verbs in specific constructions may facilitate the acquisition of a specific construction. In their corpus study of child production of caused motion constructions, Goldberg, Casenhiser, and Sethuraman (2004) found that the verb *put* in English was the most frequently used verb not only in the children's production but also in their parents' input. These authors consequently argued that "very frequent and early use of one verb in a pattern facilitates the learning of the meaning of that abstract pattern" and "the highly frequent verb serves as a readily available prototype with which other verbs may be associated" (2004: 303–304). What our data revealed is that L2 Spanish learners have actually acquired the abstract pattern and the general verb for placement caused motion construction but they still need to learn the specific and prototypical placement verbs used by native speakers for certain placement events. In other words, learners need to be aware that Spanish NSs prefer verbs such as *meter* 'put in' for containment placement events and *dejar* 'leave (on a place)' for placing things gently on a surface (see below) rather than the general placement verb *poner* 'put'. In fact, the need to learn the verbs that native speakers characteristically choose for a placement situation does not contradict Goldberg's proposal. Construction Grammar is a usage-based theory, and as such, what is important is precisely what speakers frequently use, i.e. *meter* and *dejar* instead of *poner*. It might be then just a question of reconsidering what the basic verbs for caused motion constructions are on each occasion and teach them to learners. In addition, learners used static constructions, for example, with the verb *estar* 'be (stative)'; these constructions describe the result of the placement event rather than the process. Both the overgeneralisation of the verb *poner* 'put, put in' and the use of static constructions can be considered instances of avoidance strategies on the part of the learners. These results are coherent with previous findings in L2 studies in other languages (Viberg 1998; Gullberg 2009).

With regard to semantic categorisation, L2 Spanish learners used *poner* 'put' for both support and containment relationships between the Figure and the Ground. As previously mentioned, this is not what Spanish NSs did. Instead they tended to use the verb *dejar* 'leave on a place' for support and the verb *meter* 'put in' for containment relations. In the case of force dynamics and intentionality, the results showed that L2 speakers used a larger number of verbs than the Spanish NSs and that the boundaries of their semantic categories did not always correspond to the L1 boundaries.

Finally, Spanish learners used spatial particles less often than the Spanish L1 group. As argued above, this might be due to learners' psychotypology (Kellerman 1978, 1986). In addition, when these particles were used, they were usually employed with the verb *poner* 'put' (e.g. *poner dentro* 'put inside'), whereas Spanish speakers combined them with different verbs (e.g. *meter dentro* 'put in', *tirar dentro* 'throw inside'). The use of the adverbs *arriba* 'up' and *abajo* 'down' by the L2 Spanish learner group was not target-like in these contexts.

Our main conclusion is that all the semantic criteria that we have discussed (support, containment, force dynamics and intentionality) are part of the rhetorical style of Spanish. The acquisition of all these features goes beyond the simple acquisition of the target-like construction. All these aspects should be taken into account both theoretically and pedagogically so that learners can achieve a re-thinking for speaking in their L2, and thus a more idiomatic discourse in the target language. Our Danish learners of L2 Spanish seem to have come to grips with the structure of the placement caused motion construction in the L2 but they do not sound idiomatic enough in the L2.

5.1 Theoretical implications

The theoretical implications of this study are mainly related to the notions of thinking for speaking (Slobin 1996) and cross-linguistic influence (Jarvis and Pavlenko 2008). The cross-linguistic differences between Spanish and Danish in semantic categorisation and rhetorical style create difficulties for learners in their process of adjusting to the thinking for speaking patterns of the foreign language (Cadierno 2008a; Robinson and Ellis 2008).

Some of the results cannot be explained as an outcome of cross-linguistic influence and are probably due to general aspects of the second language acquisition process and to the use of avoidance communicative strategies. This is probably the case, for example, for the overuse of *poner* 'put' to express both support and containment relations and the use of stative constructions in which the event is divided into two parts. However, there is evidence for possible cross-linguistic transfer caused by the differences between Spanish and Danish in the placement caused motion construction as well as in the different semantic categorisation of placement events. Examples of probable cross-linguistic influence include the verbs used to express different semantic categories (e.g. lack of target-like distinctions in marking intentionality and force dynamics), the use of the directional particles *abajo* 'down' and *arriba* 'up', and the use of *perder* 'lose' as an inappropriate verb for the placement caused motion construction. As mentioned above, the use of the verb *perder* 'lose' is based on one of the meanings of the Danish verb *tabe* 'lose, drop', and as such it can thus be considered an example of semantic transfer.

Overall these findings are coherent with previous studies on motion events and second language acquisition (Cadierno 2004; Cadierno and Ruiz 2006) which already pointed out difficulties in the change of rhetorical style in the second language, as well as with other studies on the L2 expression of placement events (Viberg 1998; Gullberg 2009).

5.2 Pedagogical implications

The first pedagogical implication that arises from these results is that L2 learners should be aware of the differences between grammatical correctness and rhetorical style. This is valid not only for Danish learners of Spanish but in general in the process of acquisition of a second language. Grammatical correctness concerns the grammatical rules of a language and determines what is grammatically correct or not. Conversely, rhetorical style refers to the type of expression typically used by native speakers. Some of the non-target-like linguistic elements produced by Danish learners in L2 Spanish are grammatically correct but they are not (often) used by Spanish native speakers. For example, the use of particles is frequent and quite ubiquitous in Danish but sparse and scarce in Spanish; therefore, if Danish learners of L2 Spanish use Spanish particles, they have to know when it is appropriate to use them and when it is not.

It is also important to bear in mind that the information provided in the placement caused motion construction, despite sharing one of the typical caused motion constructions (Subj V Obj Obl$_{loc}$), is not the same in the two languages. For instance, the information about the spatial configuration of Figures in support and containment events is different in Danish and Spanish, and this contrast can constitute a potential source of conceptual transfer. In Danish, the Figure position (horizontal or vertical) is of paramount importance for the choice of an appropriate lexical verb. Support is mostly expressed by *lægge* (horizontal support) and *sætte / stille* (vertical support), whereas Containment is coded by *sætte* (partial containment), *lægge* (full horizontal containment), *stikke* (full tight fight containment), and *putte* (full general containment). This is not the case in Spanish. The position of the Figure is irrelevant and verbs are not discriminated on the basis of this information. Thus, the verb *dejar* 'leave, put' is preferred in support relations, *poner* 'put' in partial containment, and *meter* 'put in' in cases of full containment. Therefore, once the basic construction is acquired, it would be necessary to focus on the different nuances that the L2 language pays attention to. In other words, following Goldberg, Casenhiser, and Sethuraman (2004) suggestions, the learner should be aware of the prototypical verb(s) use in the construction in general (e.g. *poner* in Spanish) and from there he/she should learn the use of other specific verbs associated with the construction. Whether this is the right path to follow with the placement caused motion construction is an open question for future research.

These cross-linguistic differences should be taken into account in second language pedagogy. One of the pedagogical approaches on second language teaching that can help us to do so is the *Focus on Form* approach (Long 1991; Long and Robinson 1998). This approach proposes the teaching of grammar within communicative activities. It is argued that the simple exposure to the language or the use in communicative contexts may not be enough to acquire certain aspects of the second language. Therefore, learners can benefit from some type of focus on form while they are engaged in communicative activities.

Miquel López and Ortega Olivares (2014) provide some sample activities that follow the basic principles of this approach. These activities include interpretation-oriented activities, including activities inspired by processing instruction (see VanPatten and Cadierno 1993a, 1993b; VanPatten 1996), and production-oriented activities. In line with Cadierno's (2008b) proposals for spontaneous motion events, some of these pedagogical options could be adapted to teach placement events in L2 Spanish. For example, the use of one-way picture tasks could be adapted to depict placement events instead of manner of motion verbs. One-way map direction tasks could also be changed to provide instructions using the picture of an untidy bedroom instead of a map (e.g. *Put the blue book on the shelf*). Another possibility would be to use two-way spot-the-difference-tasks in which students are given two similar pictures that only differ in terms of how objects are placed, e.g. pictures where the intentionality and the force dynamics differ across the pictures. On the basis of our results, another pedagogical option would be to use TPR (Total Physical Response). The teacher could verbalise various placement events and the learners would be asked to act out the spoken-aloud actions. Another activity could involve a sort of 'memory game' with two types of cards: some cards containing L2 sentences describing placement events and others containing pictures depicting those types of placement events. Students could play in pairs or in small groups. All cards would be placed face down and each student in turn would have to turn up two cards and take them away when they find the card with the picture (e.g. someone putting a cup on a table) and the corresponding card with the written form (e.g. *Deja la taza en la mesa* 'She leaves the cup on the table'). The winner is the player who ends up with more cards.

Some other activities could focus on the learners' production of the placement caused motion construction. A possible task could be to ask learners to write instructions for an imaginary game or sport, in which they should describe how to play (if they have to put an object inside a basket or a box, how many points they get to throw it away, what happens if they drop the ball, etc.). These are some examples of possible types of activities that can be developed and included in future pedagogically-oriented research.

6 Conclusions

In this paper we analysed the use of the placement caused motion construction in L1 Spanish and L1 Danish and compared these to the type of constructions produced by Danish learners of L2 Spanish. We focused on the differences and similarities between Danish and Spanish constructions and how these might affect and explain the Spanish learners' production.

The data showed learners' difficulty to "re-think for speaking", that is, learners encountered problems when they had to adapt the semantic categories in their native language to those in the second language. Our findings provide answers to our first and second research questions, namely, how different the placement caused motion constructions are in L1 and L2 Spanish, and how these differences affect the rhetorical style of L2 Spanish learners. We argue that the difference between the constructions lies mainly in the different degrees of specificity and focus on the various semantic distinctions. Learners seem to be unaware of some of the cross-linguistic differences between Danish and Spanish and some of the specificities of Spanish (in particular, containment relationships, force dynamics and intentionality).

Our third research question concerned the pedagogical implications of this approach. We argue that (i) raising awareness of the semantic typological differences between languages in the language classroom can be beneficial for the development of appropriate L2 thinking for speaking patterns; and (ii) going beyond grammar as such and taking into account the preferred rhetorical style of native speakers can be crucial for achieving a more target-like and idiomatic production in the second language. The need for grammatically correct sentences in L2 production is, of course, an important requirement, but if these grammatically correct sentences are infrequently used by native speakers or if they sound unnatural, the learner might have achieved a high level of grammatical accuracy but he/she may not have developed the level of idiomatic expressivity needed to achieve communicative competence in all its complexity.

The importance of usage and frequency is clear, especially from a usage-based perspective on second language acquisition. Future lines of pedagogical interventions should take into account corpus-based analyses to gain a deeper understanding of the types of lexical items ('construction islands' as named by Ellis and Ferreira-Junior 2009) that are more frequent in the L2 placement caused motion construction. The development of pedagogical materials along the lines suggested above should be accompanied by experimental intervention studies that would measure their degree of effectiveness. Finally, it would also be interesting to replicate the present study with learners from different proficiency levels or use longitudinal designs in order to examine the development of re-thinking for speaking with longer exposure to the L2 or with more specific instruction.

References

Bowerman, Melissa. 1996a. Learning how to structure space for language: A crosslinguistic perspective. In Paul Bloom, Mary A. Peterson, Lynn Nadel & Merrill F. Garrett (eds.), *Language and space*, 385–436. Cambridge, MA: The MIT Press.
Bowerman, Melissa. 1996b. The origins of children's spatial semantic categories: Cognitive vs. linguistic determinants. In John J. Gumperz & Stephen C. Levinson (eds.), *Rethinking linguistic relativity*, 145–176. Cambridge: Cambridge University Press.
Bowerman, Melissa, Marianne Gullberg, Asifa Majid & Bhuvana Narasimhan. 2004. Put project: The cross-linguistic encoding of placement events. In Asifa Majid (ed.), *Field manual 9. Max Planck Institute for Psycholinguistics. Language and Cognition Group*, 10–24. Nijmegen: Max Planck Institute for Psycholinguistics.
Brown, Amanda & Marianne Gullberg. 2012. Multicompetence and native speaker variation in clausal packaging in Japanese. *Second Language Research* 28(4). 415–442.
Cadierno, Teresa. 2004. Expressing motion events in a second language: A cognitive typological perspective. In Michel Achard & Susanne Niemeier (eds.), *Cognitive linguistics, second language acquisition, and foreign language teaching*, 13–49. Berlin & New York: Mouton de Gruyter.
Cadierno, Teresa. 2008a. Learning to talk about motion in a foreign language. In Peter Robinson & Nick C. Ellis (eds.), *Handbook of cognitive linguistics and second language acquisition*, 239–275. New York & London: Routledge.
Cadierno, Teresa. 2008b. Motion events in Danish and Spanish: A focus on form pedagogical approach. In Sabine De Knop & Teun De Rycker (eds.), *Cognitive approaches to pedagogical grammar*, 259–294. Berlin & New York: Mouton de Gruyter.
Cadierno, Teresa. 2010. Motion in Danish as a second language. Does the learner's L1 make a difference? In ZaoHong Han & Teresa Cadierno (eds.), *Linguistic relativity in second language acquisition: Thinking for speaking*, 1–33. Clevedon: Multilingual Matters.
Cadierno, Teresa & Lucas Ruiz. 2006. Motion events in Spanish L2 acquisition. *Annual Review of Cognitive Linguistics* 4. 183–216.
Cadierno, Teresa, Iraide Ibarretxe-Antuñano & Alberto Hijazo-Gascón. 2016. Semantic categorization of placement verbs in L1 and L2 Danish and Spanish. *Language Learning* 66(1). 191–223. DOI: 10.1111/lang.12153.
Coventry, Kenny R. & Simon C. Garrod. 2004. *Saying, seeing and acting. The psychological semantics of spatial prepositions*. Hove & New York: Psychology Press, Taylor and Francis.
Choi, Soonja & Melissa Bowerman. 1991. Learning to express motion events in English and Korean: The influence of language-specific lexicalization patterns. *Cognition* 41. 83–121.
Ellis, Nick & Fernando Ferreira-Junior. 2009. Constructions and their acquisition: Islands and the distinctiveness of their occupancy. *Annual Review of Cognitive Linguistics* 7. 187–220.
Goldberg, Adele. 1995. *Constructions: A construction grammar approach to argument structure*. Chicago: University of Chicago Press.
Goldberg, Adele. 2006. *Constructions at work: The nature of generalization in language*. Oxford: Oxford University Press.
Goldberg, Adele, Devin M. Casenhiser & Nitya Sethuraman. 2004. Learning argument structure generalizations. *Cognitive Linguistics* 15(3). 289–316.
Gullberg, Marianne. 2009. Reconstructing verb meaning in a second language: How English speakers of L2 Dutch talk and gesture about placement. *Annual Review of Cognitive Linguistics* 7. 222–245.

Gullberg, Marianne. 2011. Language-specific encoding of placement events in gestures. In Jürgen Bohnemeyer & Eric Pederson (eds.), *Event representation in language and cognition*, 166–188. Cambridge: Cambridge University Press.

Gullberg, Marianne & Bhuvana Narasimhan. 2010. What gestures reveal about how semantic distinctions develop in Dutch children's placement verbs. *Cognitive Linguistics* 21(2). 239–262.

Gullberg, Marianne & Niclas Burenhult. 2012. Probing the linguistic encoding of placement and removal events in Swedish. In Aneta Kopecka & Bhuvana Narasimhan (eds.), *Events of putting and taking: A crosslinguistic perspective*, 167–182. Amsterdam: John Benjamins.

Hansen, Erik & Lars Heltoft. 2011. *Grammatik over det danske sprog, vol. II. Syntaktiske og semantiske helheder*. Odense: Syddansk Universitetsforlag.

Hickmann, Maya. 2007. Static and dynamic location in French. Developmental and crosslinguistic perspectives. In Michel Aurnague, Maya Hickmann & Laure Vieu (eds.), *The categorization of spatial entities in language and cognition*, 205–231. Amsterdam: John Benjamins.

Hickmann, Maya and Henriette Hendriks. 2006. Static and dynamic location in French and in English. *First Language* 26(1). 103–135.

Ibarretxe-Antuñano, Iraide. 2012. Placement and removal events in Basque and Spanish. In Aneta Kopecka & Bhuvana Narasimhan (eds), *Events of putting and taking: A crosslinguistic perspective*, 123–144. Amsterdam: John Benjamins.

Ibarretxe-Antuñano, Iraide, Teresa Cadierno & Alberto Hijazo-Gascón. In press. The role of force dynamics and intentionality in the reconstruction of L2 verb meaning: A Danish-Spanish bidirectional study. *Review of Cognitive Linguistics*.

Jarvis, Scott & Aneta Pavlenko. 2008. *Crosslinguistic influence in language and cognition*. New York & London: Routledge.

Jessen, Moiken. 2013. Semantic categories in the domain of motion verbs by adult speakers of Danish, German, and Turkish. *Linguistik Online* 61. 57–78.

Jessen, Moiken & Teresa Cadierno. 2013. Variation in the categorization of motion in L2 Danish by German and Turkish native speakers. In Juliana Goschler & Anatol Stefanowitsch (eds.), *Variation and change in the encoding of motion events*, 133–159. Amsterdam: John Benjamins.

Kellerman, Eric. 1978. Transfer and non-transfer: Where are we now? *Studies in Second Language Acquisition* 2. 37–57.

Kellerman, Eric. 1986. An eye for an eye: Crosslinguistic constraints on the development of the L2 lexicon. In Eric Kellerman & Michael Sharwood-Smith (eds.), *Crosslinguistic influence in second language acquisition*, 35–47. Oxford: Pergamon.

Kopecka, Anetta & Bhuvana Narasimhan (eds.). 2012. *Events of putting and taking: A crosslinguistic perspective*. Amsterdam: John Benjamins.

Long, Michael H. 1991. Focus on form: A design feature in language teaching methodology. In Kees de Bot, Ralph B. Ginsberg & Claire Kramsch (eds.), *Foreign language research in cross-cultural perspective*, 39–52. Amsterdam: John Benjamins.

Long, Michael H, & Peter Robinson. 1998. Focus on form: Theory, research and practice. In Catherine Daughty & Jessica Williams (eds.), *Focus on form in classroom second language acquisition*, 15–41. Cambridge: Cambridge University Press.

Majid, Asifa, Marianne Gullberg, Miriam van Staden & Melissa Bowerman. 2007. How similar are semantic categories in closely related languages? A comparison of cutting and breaking in four Germanic languages. *Cognitive Linguistics* 12(2). 179–194.

Miquel López, Lourdes & Jenaro Ortega Olivares. 2014. Actividades orientadas al aprendizaje explícito de recursos gramaticales en niveles avanzados de E/LE. In Alejandro Castañeda, Zeina Alhmoud, Irene Alonso, Jordi Casellas, M. Dolores Chamorro, Lourdes Miquel & Jenaro Ortega (eds.), *Enseñanza de gramática avanzada de ELE. Criterios y recursos*, 89–178. Madrid: SGEL.

Morimoto, Yuko & María Victoria Pavón Lucero. 2003. Dos construcciones idiomáticas basadas en el esquema [nombre+adverbio]: Calle arriba y boca abajo. *Foro Hispánico* 23. 95–106.

Narasimhan, Bhuvana & Marianne Gullberg. 2010. The role of input frequency and semantic transparency in the acquisition of verb meaning: Evidence from placement verbs in Tamil and Dutch. *Journal of Child Language* 38. 504–32.

Pavón Lucero, María Victoria. 1999. Clases de partículas: Preposición, conjunción y adverbio. In Ignacio Bosque & Violeta Demonte (eds.), *Gramática descriptiva de la lengua española*, 564–555. Madrid: Espasa-Calpe.

Robinson, Peter & Nick C. Ellis. 2008. Conclusion: Cognitive linguistics, second language acquisition and L2 instruction – issues for research. In Peter Robinson & Nick C. Ellis (eds.), *Handbook of cognitive linguistics and second language acquisition*, 489–545. New York & London: Routledge.

Serra Borneto, Carlo. 1996. *Liegen* and *stehen* in German: A study in horizontality and verticality. In Eugene H. Casad (ed.), *Cognitive linguistics in the redwoods: The expansion of a new paradigm in linguistics*, 459–505. Berlin: Mouton de Gruyter.

Slobin, Dan I. 1991. Learning to think for speaking: Native language, cognition and rhetorical style. *Pragmatics* 1. 7–26.

Slobin, Dan I. 1996. From 'thought and language' to 'thinking for speaking'. In John Gumperz & Stephen C. Levinson (eds.), *Rethinking linguistic relativity*, 70–96. Cambridge: Cambridge University Press.

Slobin, Dan I. 2000. Verbalized events: A dynamic approach to linguistic relativity and determinism. In Susanne Niemeier & René Dirven (eds.), *Evidence for linguistic relativity*, 107–138. Amsterdam: John Benjamins.

Slobin, Dan I., Melissa Bowerman, Penelope Brown, Sonja Eissenbeiβ & Bhuvana Narasimhan. 2011. Putting things in places. In Jürgen Bohnemeyer & Eric Pederson (eds.), *Event representation in language and cognition*, 134–165. Cambridge: Cambridge University Press.

Talmy, Leonard. 1985. Lexicalization patterns: Semantic structure in lexical forms. In Timothy Shopen (ed.), *Language typology and syntactic description. Volume 3: Grammatical categories and the lexicon*, 36–149. Cambridge: Cambridge University Press.

Talmy, Leonard. 1988. Force dynamics in language and cognition. *Cognitive Science* 12. 49–100.

Talmy, Leonard. 1991. Path to realization: A typology of event conflation. *Proceedings of the Seventeenth Annual Meeting of the Berkeley Linguistics Society* 17. 480–520.

Talmy, Leonard. 2000. *Toward a cognitive semantics. Volume II: Typology and process in concept structuring*. Cambridge, MA: The MIT Press.

VanPatten, Bill. 1996. *Input processing and grammar instruction*. Norwood, NJ: Ablex.

VanPatten, Bill & Teresa Cadierno. 1993a. Input processing and second language acquisition: A Role for instruction. *The Modern Language Journal* 77(1). 45–57.

VanPatten, Bill & Teresa Cadierno. 1993b. Explicit instruction and input processing. *Studies in Second Language Acquisition* 15. 225–243.

Viberg, Åke. 1998. Crosslinguistic perspectives on lexical acquisition: The case of language-specific semantic differentiation. In Kirsten Haastrup & Åke Viberg (eds.), *Perspectives on lexical acquisition in a second language*, 175–208. Lund: Lund University Press.

Annalisa Baicchi
The role of syntax and semantics in constructional priming: Experimental evidence from Italian university learners of English through a sentence-elicitation task[1]

Abstract: The phenomenon of priming is a form of persistence that has been widely employed as a powerful research methodology suitable to probe into the mental representation of concepts. This chapter discusses a psycholinguistic priming experiment conducted in an L2 acquisition context. Prompted by previous studies with native speakers of English (Bock and Loebell 1990; Hare and Goldberg 1999), this empirical research aims to ascertain whether, and to what extent, constructional priming plays a part in the learning process of two groups of Italian university students of English, whose L2 proficiency corresponds to the B1 and B2 levels of the Common European Framework of Reference for Languages (CEFR, Council of Europe 2001). The experiment results suggest that syntax-semantics mapping occurs in the mind of Italian learners of English: they yielded constructional generalizations, an outcome that was largely unexpected since two of the syntactic patterns contained in the experiment, viz. the double-object and the fulfilling constructions, are not part of the Italian language construct-i-con, thus amounting to a higher level of complexity for the subjects.

Keywords: constructional priming; second language acquisition; syntactic variation; thematic roles; conceptual similarity

1 Priming: by way of introduction

Priming is a widely employed methodology in psycholinguistics to study many mental mechanisms. The origin of priming research[2] is commonly traced to the

---
[1] The research on which this paper is based has been financed by the Spanish Ministry of Economy and Competitiveness, grant no. FFI2013-43593-P. I would like to thank Adele Goldberg for the invaluable suggestions she offered me during the CALP conference. My deep gratitude goes to the two anonymous reviewers for their detailed comments, and to the editors of the volume, Sabine De Knop and Gaëtanelle Gilquin, for their substantial observations that helped me improve this chapter. All faults are my own responsibility.
[2] For an overview of the historical origins of priming research the reader is referred to Pickering and Ferreira (2008).

work of Donald Hebb (1949), the Canadian neuropsychologist who studied how concepts are represented in our mind. He discovered that internal mental representations remain electrically active even in the absence of external stimulation, a phenomenon that he labeled 'cell assemblies', for concept representation occurs with the interconnected participation of many neuronal cells. These loops of neural activity trigger a synaptic modification, known as the 'Hebb synapse', which stands for a form of persistence amounting to the physiological rule essential for any type of learning. The persistence, or residual activation, of a mental representation was around the same years acknowledged by Karl Lashley in his research on language production. Lashley found that the activation of an aggregate of word units takes place "prior to the internal or overt enunciation of the sentence" (1951: 119), a phenomenon for which he coined the term "priming of expressive units".

Priming effects, i.e. the non-conscious repetition of structures due to prior experience, are pervasive in language comprehension and production. In dialogue interlocutors are in turn speakers and hearers, shifting from production to comprehension, and, while doing so, they align structurally, that is, they repeat each other's choices at any level of the linguistic and textual organization of communication (Tannen 1987). Repetition fosters alignment of conceptual knowledge: interlocutors indeed capitalize on priming to promote shared knowledge of a communicative event so as to achieve conversational success (Pickering and Garrod 2004). As a form of persistence in the subjects' mind, repetition is a phenomenon widely applied in empirical research in psychology because it discloses focal features of many underlying mental mechanisms. When we repeat behavior, actions or language, we demonstrate an acquired ability, which qualifies repetition as an essential stage in the learning process. Furthermore, empirical evidence has shown that repetition of stimuli reduces haemodynamic response and, in turn, neural activity of experience-related cortical dynamics, a phenomenon that vouches for the brain's processing economy (Maccotta and Buckner 2004; Grill-Spector, Henson, and Martin 2006).

To go into some detail, in the 1960s Mehler and collaborators conducted the first psycholinguistic experiments on language repetition: they asked their subjects to process ambiguous sentences and to match pictures with corresponding sentences, and they could show that the subjects systematically produced syntactic patterns in language comprehension (Mehler and Carey 1968; Carey, Mehler, and Bever 1970; Meyer and Schvaneveldt 1971). The tendency to syntactic persistence both in language comprehension and language production was evidenced in a few studies on some linguistic phenomena such as paraphrastic reproduction of sentences (Kempen 1977), pronoun resolution (Sheldon 1974; Grober, Beardsley, and Caramazza 1978), and parallelism in coordination

(Frazier et al. 1984). Some further more systematic experiments were conducted in the 1980s (Schenkein 1980; Levelt and Kelter 1982; Weiner and Labov 1983) with the most influential one being carried out by Kathryn Bock (1986): she proved that language users tend to repeat the syntactic structures recently heard or read, a phenomenon that Bock, banking on Lashley (1951), labeled 'syntactic priming'. Bock asked her participants to repeat a prime sentence uttered by the experimenter and then to describe a picture semantically unrelated to the primed sentence. The primed sentences were a dative construction (either a prepositional dative or a double-object pattern) and a transitive construction (either active or passive). The results she obtained showed that the subjects tended to describe the picture using the syntactic structure primed by the experimenter: they were more likely to produce a prepositional dative description if a prepositional dative had been primed, or to produce a passive description if a passive construction had been primed. Bock ascribed these syntactic priming effects to mental processes entailing phrase structure constructions. Bock's pioneering work paved the way for syntactic priming experiments conducted on a series of phenomena, like, for example, syllabic properties (Sevald, Dell, and Cole 1995), referring expressions (Brennan and Clark 1996), choice of verbs (Branigan, Pickering, and Cleland 2000) and of locative phrases (Watson, Pickering, and Branigan 2004), noun-noun compounds (Gagné 2002; Estes 2003) and noun-phrase structures (Cleland and Pickering 2003), as well as speech rate, accent and phonetic realization (Pardo 2006). Since Bock's pioneering work, structural priming methodologies have been devised to ascertain whether syntactic knowledge is independent of lexical knowledge or interplays with it. In the last thirty years, priming protocols have been applied in language production (Schenkein 1980; Levelt and Kelter 1982; Weiner and Labov 1983; Bock 1986; Bock and Loebell 1990; Bock, Loebell, and Morey, 1992) and in language comprehension (Smyth 1994; Wisniewski and Love 1998; Carslon 2001; Gagné, Spalding, and Ji 2005), in diverse experimental tasks (Potter and Lombardi 1988; Pickering and Branigan 1998; Branigan, Pickering, and Cleland 2000), with subjects of different ages (Brooks and Tomasello 1999; Huttenlocher, Vasilyeva, and Shimpi 2004) and with impaired subjects (Hartsuiker and Kolk 1988; Ferreira et al. 2005), with different methodologies, including functional magnetic resonance imaging and eye-tracking (Altmann and Kamide 1998; Kaschak and Glenberg 2004; Noppeney and Price 2004; Scheepres and Crocker 2004; Arai, Van Gompel, and Scheepers 2007; Traxler 2008), or with different constructions (Hartsuiker, Kolk, and Hiuskamp 1999; Ferreira 2003). It is only in the last decade that priming protocols found an application with language learners (Liang 2002; Loebell and Bock 2003; Meijer and Fox Tree 2003; Hartsuiker, Pickering, and Veltkamp 2004; Sepassi and Kamyab 2005; Gries and

Wulff 2005; Desmet and Declercq 2006; Schoonbaert, Hartsuiker, and Pickering 2007; Valenzuela and Rojo 2008; Noora 2009; Baicchi 2011; Della Putta and Baicchi 2013).[3]

The number of psycholinguistic empirical studies on syntax representation during language processing is huge, and two main perspectives have originated on the issue: some researchers interpreted their experimental results as evidence for the independence of syntactic knowledge from lexis and also from other mental or cognitive faculties, such as perception or attention, while others endorsed the opposite view and contended that syntax is dependent on or interplays with other types of knowledge, such as lexical semantics and pragmatic meaning. Advocates of the lexically independent nature of syntactic knowledge have adopted the phrase structure methodology of linguistic analysis and have shown that, in verbalizing mental representations, speakers, being biased by the primed sentence uttered by the experimenter, choose among a range of phrase-structure patterns (Bock 1986; Bock and Loebell 1990; Bock, Loebell, and Morey 1992; Fox Tree and Meijer 1999; Ferreira 2003; Loebell and Bock 2003; Hartsuiker, Pickering, and Veltkamp 2004; Branigan et al. 2006). However, phrase-structure formalism is independent of lexis and can be applied to a number of semantically different verbs; this means that syntactic priming can occur even without lexical repetition and irrespective of differences in the thematic relations between prime and target (Pickering and Ferreira 2008: 14). With the aim of showing that lexical and semantic knowledge indeed play a role in structural priming, other researchers have conducted psycholinguistic experiments by applying diverse methodologies like dialogue, sentence completion, or corpus-based analysis, and they have been able to demonstrate that phrase-structure rules are not the only factor that enhances priming effects, but that these effects are also lexically boosted (Pickering and Branigan 1998; Hartsuiker, Kolk, and Huiskamp 1999; Branigan, Pickering, and Cleland 2000; Hartsuiker and Westenberg 2000; Cleland and Pickering 2003, 2006; Gries 2005; Chang, Bock, and Goldberg 2003; Chang, Dell, and Bock 2006). As an example, verb semantics can influence the subjects' choice of a specific syntactic construction: two synonymous verbs like *donate* and *present* drive the choice of two different patterns, whereby the verb *donate* admits the prepositional dative construction only (*He donated a spinning top to the child*), while the verb *present* accepts both the prepositional dative construction (*He presented a spinning top to the child*) and the fulfilling construction (*He presented the child with a spinning top*). Those studies show that syntactic knowledge is lexically and also themati-

---

[3] Detailed reviews of structural priming are found in Pickering and Ferreira (2008) and Tooley and Traxler (2010).

cally boosted, a finding that tunes in to a constructional perspective of language processing, that is, one according to which syntax cannot be separated from semantics.

To sum up, the question about the type of information (syntactic, semantic, or pragmatic) driving priming effects received replies that can be subsumed under two main approaches. On the one hand, proponents of the form-mapping approach view syntactic structure and concepts as two distinct elements and they ascribe to syntax the primary role in sentence production, or even an exclusive role, because parsing, they argue, unfolds uniquely on the basis of syntactic considerations. On the basis of datasets of spontaneous conversation, although very restricted in size (e.g. Garnham et al. 1982; Garrett 1988; Rayner, Garrod, and Perfetti 1992), they have demonstrated that separation between syntax and semantics was valid not only for speech errors but also for error-free production of utterances. On the other hand, proponents of the meaning-mapping approach demonstrate that structural distinctions occur as a by-product of conceptual elements because sentence production involves the interaction of multiple sources of information, not only structural, but also semantic and pragmatic (Osgood and Bock 1977; Clark and Clark 1977; Trueswell, Tanenhaus, and Garnsey 1994).

We believe that Construction Grammar modeling offers a way out of this debate since it introduces the revolutionary notion of construction as a carrier not only of syntactic information but also of semantic and pragmatic meaning. Construction Grammar postulates that the basic unit of grammar is the construction, a free-standing theoretical assembly of one form and one meaning or function. Constructions are assumed to be stored as symbolic units alongside lexical items. Phonological, morphological, syntactic and lexical information, representing the structural pole of the construction, combines with semantic, pragmatic and discursive properties, i.e. the functional pole. Construction Grammar rejects the separation between lexis and grammar because the borderline between the lexicon and syntactic rules is not clear-cut, as idioms clearly exemplify; it proposes a constructional continuum instead, which enables a description of the idiosyncratic behaviour of idiomatic expressions ranging from fixed strings to more flexible stretches of language. Circumscribing our research in the constructional framework, we now set out to discuss an experiment on the priming of dative alternation in an L2 context. Specifically, our research takes the Lexical Constructional Model (henceforth, LCM; Ruiz de Mendoza and Mairal 2008) as its theoretical framework of reference. The LCM is currently the only theoretical framework able to account for all levels of meaning description: it is able to provide full treatment of argument structure constructions at the level of core grammar as well as of implicature, illocution and discourse at the higher levels of its overall constructional architecture. The building blocks of the model are lexical templates, lower-level configurations (e.g. verbal predicates and their associated arguments) that are subsumed into constructional templates, i.e. higher-level argument structures, a process that is regulated by internal (e.g. Aktionsart operations) and external (e.g. iconicity, parsing) factors. Our empirical research aims to provide the LCM with further psychological validity by showing (i) that language users store constructional templates instantiated by lexical templates in their mind, and (ii) that, since argument structure constructions have ontological status (Goldberg 2006), they are psychologically real entities driving linguistic processing mechanisms both in L1 and L2 speakers, and consequently their introduction in language pedagogy is highly advisable.

This chapter attempts to provide further validation of the notion of construction through a sentence-elicitation experiment conducted with the participation of university learners of English. More specifically, it aims to show that sentence priming involves not only syntax, as argued by Bock and Loebell (1990), but also semantics, as demonstrated by Hare and Goldberg (1999). After reporting on these two studies conducted with native speakers (Sections 2.1 and 2.2), the chapter describes the experiment carried out with learners (Section 2.3) and discusses whether and how constructional priming occurs in an L2 context. The final section offers some concluding remarks and touches on the presence of constructional templates in the interlanguage of L2 learners and on the importance of frequent exposure to constructions in the language classroom.

2 Empirical studies

Before describing the sentence-elicitation experiment conducted with Italian university learners of English, we will report on the two empirical studies conducted with native speakers of English that have prompted the research question (Bock and Loebell 1990; Hare and Goldberg 1999).

2.1 Syntactic variation in Bock and Loebell (1990)

Bock and Loebell (1990) tested whether the variation in syntactic form that occurs in native speakers during language production hinged on the syntactic structure with no need to invoke changes in conceptual processing, or on both syntactic and semantic operations. With this goal in mind, they devised their experimental procedure with recourse to the priming protocol: they considered repetition of the same sentence frame a valuable and plausible strategy because it usually occurs in spontaneous speech, as a number of studies had evidenced (Weiner and Labov 1983; Tannen 1987; Clark 1996). Bock and Loebell (1990) hypothesized that (a) if variation in syntactic form depended on the syntactic structure of the primes, prepositional datives and prepositional locatives should be likewise reliable primes for prepositional datives; whereas, (b) if variation in syntactic form depended on the conceptual structure of the primes, prepositional datives should be more reliable primes than prepositional locatives for prepositional datives. The participants were asked to look at a drawing depicting a situation that was totally dissimilar to the uttered sentence, for instance a picture of a man reading a story to a child. Hence, if the experimenter had uttered a prepositional dative priming construction (*The teacher is giving a book to the student*), the participants would have been induced to produce a description of the picture event with the same syntactic structure, i.e. *The man is reading a story to a child*; instead, if the priming sentence had been a double-object construction (*The teacher is giving the student a book*), the expected elicited utterance would have been *The man is reading the child a story*. Even though these types of hypotheses are plausible since it is quite usual that speakers engaged in conversation repeat what they have heard, the reason why they perform repetition is still highly debated. Two options can be envisaged: repetition is induced either by similarity in syntactic structure (prepositional dative, double-object) or by similarity in conceptual content (semantic roles). In Bock and Loebell's view, sentences such as *The wealthy widow gave her Mercedes to the church* and *The wealthy widow drove her Mercedes to the church* should prime prepositional-phrase patterns like *The girl is handing a paintbrush to the boy*. If, instead, it were conceptual similarity that motivated repetition, the two events of 'giving a Mercedes to a church' or 'handing a paintbrush to a boy' could be described with a prepositional dative or with a double-object dative according to the thematic role that the subject considers dominant or focal. Given the fact that the focal element is cognitively more salient (Langacker 1987) and that, in compliance with the end-weight principle, it is encoded in final position in English, when the theme role (*Mercedes, paintbrush*) is focal, the double-object pattern should be favored, e.g. *The wealthy widow gave the church her Mercedes*; when the beneficiary role (*church, boy*) is focal, the prepositional dative should be preferred. In other words, if repetition were sensitive to variation in focus, the subjects would produce sentences by replicating the same focus as the one heard in the prime. In addition, the authors observe that the prime *The wealthy widow drove her Mercedes to the church* does not contain a beneficiary but a locative role; hence, it should not be a good prime for a sentence like *The librarian is handing a book to the student*, a better prime sentence being *The wealthy widow gave her Mercedes to the church*. However, the examples offered by Bock and Loebell (1990) do not shed light upon the type of similarity that motivates repetition, whether syntactic pattern or conceptual arrangement of the events. It must be noticed that, although the *to*-phrases in the prepositional locative and in the prepositional dative constructions express a locative and a beneficiary role respectively, both roles can be subsumed under the higher-level category of 'goal', since both roles are associated with verbs indicating a change of state: specifically, the locative expresses a change of location, while the beneficiary expresses a change of possession (Jackendoff 1972, 1983; Lakoff and Johnson 1980; Goldberg 1995). The fact that both prepositional constructions share the same semantic role of 'goal' lowers their apparent dissimilarity.

Materials

Thirty pictures of dative events were matched with thirty sets of priming sentences. The pictures represented actions that involved two human participants, namely an agent and a receiver of an action, and a non-human entity undergoing the action. Each priming sentence set consisted of triplets, that is, three sentences including a prepositional dative, a prepositional locative, plus a double-object construction that provided a control for the elicitation of prepositional constructions. A sample of the priming sentences is offered in Table 1. The prepositional dative and the double-object constructions were realized with dative verbs (*offer, sell, promise, loan*), whereas the prepositional locative construction was instantiated with motion verbs (*walk, push, move, pull*). The control structure, i.e. the double-object construction, was produced in such a way as to repeat exactly the same noun phrase arguments, but with a dative verb different from the one used in the prepositional dative construction: this made it possible to avoid a kind of similarity that could influence the participants' performance.

Table 1: Sample of the priming triplets in Bock and Loebell (1990)

Prepositional dative	*The hospital showed the bill to the patient by mistake.*
Prepositional locative	*The hospital returned the bill to the patient by mistake.*
Double-object	*The hospital sent the patient the bill by mistake.*
Prepositional dative	*IBM promised a bigger computer to the Sears store.*
Prepositional locative	*IBM moved a bigger computer to the Sears store.*
Double-object	*IBM offered the Sears store a bigger computer.*
Prepositional dative	*The wealthy widow gave an old Mercedes to the church.*
Prepositional locative	*The wealthy widow drove an old Mercedes to the church.*
Double-object	*The wealthy widow sold the church an old Mercedes.*

The experiment materials were enriched with additional pictures and additional sentences differing broadly in content and form, which served as fillers in the presentation lists to mask the structural relationship between the priming sentences and the event depicted in the picture.

Participants

The 96 participants who took part in the experiment were undergraduate students at Michigan State University; they were tested individually.

Procedure

In the performance of the priming technique, the experimenter uttered a sentence, such as *The librarian handed the book to the student*, which the participants had to repeat aloud; then, they had to watch a picture and they were asked to describe the event depicted in the picture without the use of pronouns. The conditions of presentation were designed in such a way as to divert the participants' attention from the real purpose of the experiment: the participants were informed that they were taking part in a memory test. They were also told that they should try to remember pictures and sentences in order to recognize them during the slide presentation; most of the fillers were actually repeated at some point during the presentation list; specifically, 45 pictures and 45 sentences were repeated twice, while the other 30 pictures and 30 sentences occurred only once. When the stimulus was repeated, the participants had to respond 'yes' or 'no'. The participants' extemporaneous picture descriptions were collected: they constituted the set of data that would reveal whether the responses were motivated by the similarities of the syntactic form or by the similarities of the conceptual arrangement.

Scoring

A total of 2,880 responses were produced, but almost one third of them, exactly 965, were discarded because they were encoded through syntactic structures different from those of the experiment. On the whole, the set of produced utterances was composed of 1,915 scorable, i.e. valid responses: in detail, 33.6% of utterances were produced as double-object constructions, 33.4% as prepositional locative, and 33% as prepositional dative.

Discussion of results

The percentages of the three prime conditions are represented in the histogram in Figure 1.

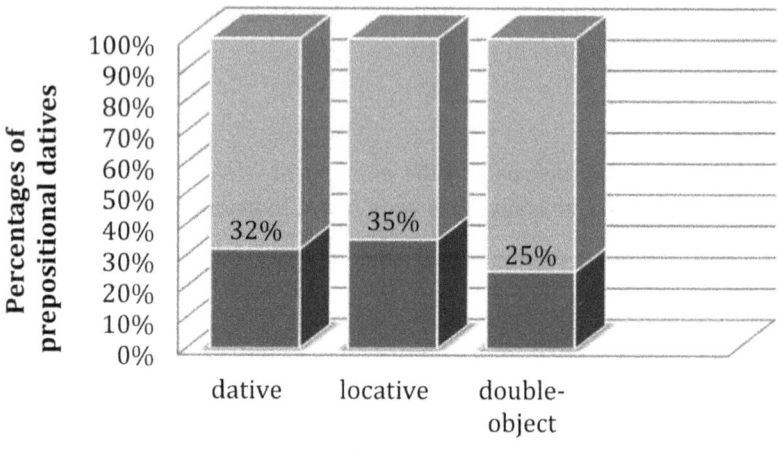

Figure 1: Percentages of prepositional datives in the three priming conditions

When the two prepositional constructions are compared to one another, little difference emerges in their production; but when they are compared with the double-object control, they both turn out to be widely employed by the participants.

Bock and Loebell (1990) interpreted their results as evidence of the fact that structural repetition does not depend on the semantic roles of the arguments; in other words, conceptual (dis)similarity had no role in the participants' experimental performance. According to the authors, conceptual similarity or dissimilarity appeared to be a neutral factor in structural repetition, since it remained approximately unchanged when the event roles were replaced.

When the thematic roles of the prime sentence contrasted with those involved in the picture, e.g. a prepositional locative in the prime and a prepositional beneficiary in the picture, the elicited sentence showed an increased use of the prime pattern. A comparison of the results revealed that when the dative and the locative constructions constituted the priming conditions, an increased use of the prepositional dative over the double-object form occurred; but when the two prepositional patterns were compared to one another, little difference could be observed. When the prime was a double-object pattern, the prepositional form decreased considerably, as shown in Table 2.

Table 2: Utterance forms yielded in the three priming conditions

Priming condition	Utterance form	
	Prepositional	Double-object
Prepositional dative	202	429
Prepositional locative	223	417
Double-object control	159	485

The subjects' performance, the authors finally stated, clearly evidenced the predisposition towards structural similarity in sentence production, which testified of the independence of syntactic configuration from conceptual meaning in sentence production.

2.2 Conceptual similarity in Hare and Goldberg (1999)

Hare and Goldberg (1999) decided to replicate Bock and Loebell's (1990) experiment in order to test whether sentence priming was entirely ascribable to syntax or whether semantics played a role.

Materials

The testing material consisted of ten pictures matched with ten sets of priming sentences. The sets of quadruplets were formed by a double-object construction, a prepositional dative construction, a third prime construction realized with verbs such as *credit sb with sth*, *supply sb with sth*, *provide sb with sth* ('verbs of fulfilling' in Levin 1993: 140), and an intransitive sentence that was meant to identify potential preferences for one of the two alternative constructions after a minimally related sentence type. A sample of Hare and Goldberg's (1999) 'example stimulus set' is offered in Table 3.

Table 3: Sample of the stimulus quadruplets in Hare and Goldberg (1999)

Prime type	Sentence
Double-object	*His editor offered Bob the hot story.*
Dative	*His editor promised the hot story to Bob.*
Provide-with	*His editor credited Bob with the hot story.*
Intransitive	*Sasha always dawdles over lunch.*
Target picture	*A man hands a woman a box of candy*

Verbs such as *present sb with sth* as in *Brown presented Jones with a plaque* correspond to verbs where "X gives something to Y that Y deserves, needs, or is worthy of" (Gropen et al. 1989). Following Levin (1993: 140), who classifies these verbs as 'verbs of fulfilling', we can label this pattern the 'fulfilling construction': it is characterised by the fact that it mingles aspects of the double-object and the prepositional dative constructions since it shares the syntactic structure of the prepositional dative (NP VP NP PP) and the semantic roles of the double-object construction (Agent, Recipient, Theme). Therefore the fulfilling construction lends itself well to testing whether semantic roles play a role in syntactic priming.

Experimental hypothesis

Hare and Goldberg (1999) hypothesized that the *provide-with* prime, i.e. the fulfilling construction, would prompt double-object responses due to semantic similarity between the two constructions. If this were empirically proved, the priming effect could be ascribed at least to both syntactic similarity and conceptual similarity, or even to conceptual similarity only.

Participants

A total of 48 subjects recruited from the Psychology and Cognitive Science Department of the University of Illinois participated in the experiment, but three of them were later excluded, so that the total number of participants lowered to 45.

Procedure

Hare and Goldberg (1999) retained the same protocol devised by Bock and Loebell (1990). However, although the procedure was basically the same, Hare and Goldberg (1999) claimed that it could prompt the production of transitive constructions: in order to avoid this, the experimenter cued the picture descriptions by uttering an NP-VP sentence fragment (e.g. *The man gave -*), which could be completed with either a double-object or a prepositional dative, but not with a transitive construction.

Scoring

Hare and Goldberg obtained 330 scorable responses, 126 of which were discarded because they consisted of syntactic structures different from the target constructions of their experiment. Thus, 204 responses formed their set of data, which equalled 62% of the total possible responses in the corpus.

Discussion of results

The set of data amounted to the following experimental percentages: 38% of the responses occurred in the prepositional dative, 32% in the double-object, and 30% in the fulfilling priming condition, as the histogram in Figure 2 summarizes.

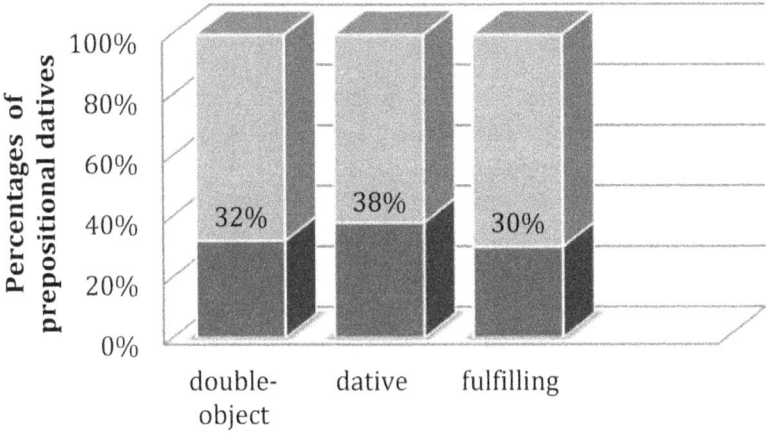

Figure 2: Percentages of prepositional datives in the three priming conditions

The results show that the semantic structure actually influenced the production of the target sentence, and, as Hare and Goldberg hypothesized, the mapping between syntax and semantics played a role in the priming effect.

Hare and Goldberg identified in the animacy order the peculiar semantic factor driving the priming effect; in fact, the post-verbal noun phrase, in both the double-object and the fulfilling constructions, is an animate object. This peculiarity contributes to rejecting Bock and Loebell's claim that the effect of animacy order is not connected with that of the mapping of semantic roles to syntactic positions. Three priming conditions offer clear exemplification of the way in which animacy stands out as a fundamental semantic factor in the phenomenon of priming: in one prime condition the syntactic structure and animacy conform to the double-object construction and in another prime condition they conform to the prepositional dative construction; in the third prime condition the structure and animacy align with two different constructions: the structure aligns with the prepositional dative, while animacy conforms to the double-object. Since the experiment gives evidence that the third prime condition conforms to the double-object, this suggests that semantic factors have a strong influence on the subjects' performance, thus evidencing that priming effects are clearly biased by the order of expressions of semantic roles. Hare and Goldberg show that syntactic priming is a conceptual, semantic phenomenon, and, at least, not only the outcome of syntactic features.

2.3 Constructional priming in Italian university learners of English

The empirical results obtained from native speakers of English in both studies described above represent the starting point as well as the basis for comparison of the two experiments conducted with Italian participants: they were Italian university learners of English whose language proficiency corresponded to two different levels of language proficiency according to the Common European Framework of Reference for Languages (CEFR, Council of Europe 2001), specifically a B1 group and a B2 group. The aim was twofold: on the one hand, we wanted to verify whether the syntactic priming of the dative alternation could occur also with foreign language learners, and, on the other, we intended to measure the differences between B1 and B2 learners in their performance of the sentence-elicitation experiment. If syntactic priming effects occurred in L2 learners, this would prove that their interlanguage contains argument structure constructions.

The two experiments reported above guided the investigation of priming effects in L2 learners for the more general ideas underlying the protocol design; however, we decided to use the materials that Hare and Goldberg (1999) devised because they represented an even harder challenge for Italian speakers since the Italian language does not contain the double-object nor the fulfilling pattern in its construct-i-con. Such university students were therefore faced with a more complex task and the results obtained may allow us to offer interesting observations on the role of syntax and semantics in constructional priming.

Participants

Two groups of Italian learners of English enrolled at the University of Pavia, namely a B1 group and a B2 group, volunteered to participate in the experiment. Each group was composed of sixteen learners, whose age mean amounted to 21 years old. In each group around 75% of the participants were female students. None of the thirty-two subjects had received any explicit teaching in Construction Grammar.

Materials

Ten pictures of dative events were matched with ten sets of priming sentences. The ten dative pictures represented actions involving two human participants, an agent and a receiver of the action, and a non-human entity undergoing the action. The pictures consisted of simple lines drawn in black on a white surface; five pictures presented the doer on the right and five pictures on the left so as to meet different hemisphere dominance. In order to prevent potential biases on the participants' performance, semantic and narrative connections between pictures were minimised. Each priming sentence set was composed of quadruplets from Hare and Goldberg's (1999) experiment (Table 4): three prime sentences (prepositional dative, double-object, and fulfilling) and an intransitive sentence that served as a filler. In total, the materials contained forty fillers.

Table 4: Sample of the stimulus set in the Italian experiment

Prime type	Sentence
Double-object	Her brother offered Jane a cake.
Dative	Her brother promised a cake to Jane.
Provide-with	Her brother supplied Jane with a cake.
Intransitive	Thomas always plods to school.
Target picture	A woman gives a man an umbrella

Procedure

The participants, who were tested individually, heard a priming sentence that they had to repeat aloud, with the distracting explanation that it would aid memory retainment. They were shown a picture on a slide and they had to describe the depicted event with no use of pronouns. Three practice items (two pictures and one sentence) were shown to ensure that the participants had clearly understood the task. The extemporaneous picture descriptions constituted the set of produced utterances, which allowed us to reveal whether (a) in the mind of the L2 learners the responses were triggered by the similarities of the syntactic form or by the similarities of the conceptual arrangement; and (b) whether significant differences existed across the two levels of language proficiency with respect to the double-object and the fulfilling constructions, which are absent from the Italian language construct-i-con.

Scoring

Out of 160 responses for each language proficiency level, some responses had to be discarded because they were produced through syntactic structures different from those included in the study object. More precisely, 71 responses in the performance of the B1 group were discarded; the 89 scorable responses amounted to 56% of the total responses and formed the set of data for the B1 level. As for the performance of the B2 group, 53 responses were discarded and 107 responses were scorable, which corresponded to 76% of the total responses and constituted the set of data for the B2 level (Table 5).

Table 5: Set of data at the two levels of language proficiency

	Language proficiency level	
	B1	B2
Scorable responses	89	107
Percentage	56%	76%

Discussion of results

The prepositional dative construction represents the prototypical Italian construction for the verbalization of the transfer schema; therefore, it was no surprise that it scored a high percentage (60%) in the performance of B1 level students. The double-object construction, which is absent from the Italian language, is usually explicitly taught; however, at the B1 language proficiency level, it scored 31% of the responses. The fulfilling pattern is not part of the Italian construct-i-con either, and only one occurrence emerged out of the 89 scorable responses (9%), a result that can be considered not significant.

The overall percentages of constructions produced by B1 level learners in the three priming conditions are summarized in the histogram in Figure 3.

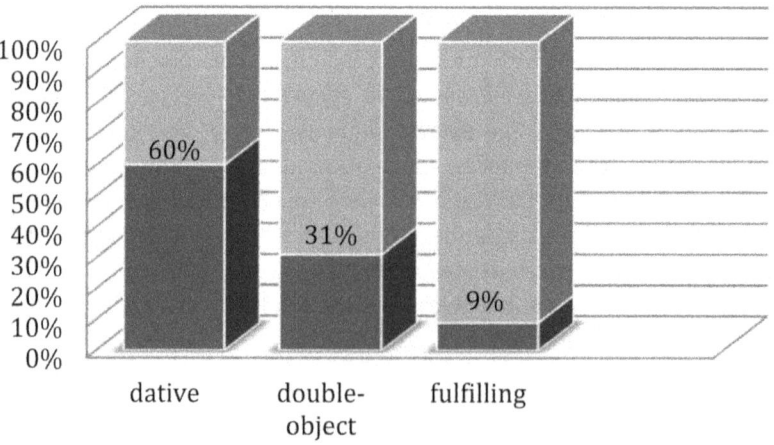

Figure 3: Percentages of constructions produced by B1 learners

If we combine the two constructions that are absent from the Italian construct-i-con, i.e. the double-object and the fulfilling, which must be learned in the acquisitional process, we see that they score 40%, while the prepositional dative construction, which scores 60% of the responses in the priming process, is still predominant.

An increase of the double-object construction (53%) is observable at the B2 level, whereas the prepositional dative construction lowers to 31%. The fulfilling construction has been primed just a little bit more (16%), but it still remains a relatively marked construction for Italian university learners of English at this proficiency level (Figure 4).

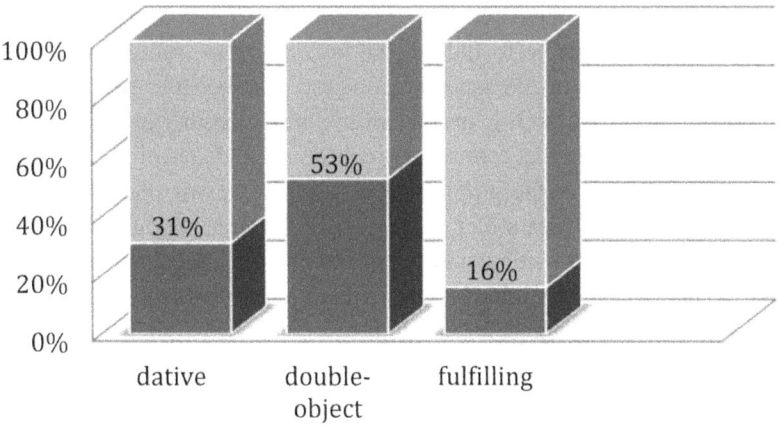

Figure 4: Percentages of constructions produced by B2 learners

If we add up the percentages of the double-object and the fulfilling constructions, we notice that they score 69% of the responses, that is, more than two thirds, while the percentage of the prepositional dative decreases to 31%.

A comparison of the results across the two levels of language proficiency allows for interesting observations (Table 6).

Table 6: Percentages at the two proficiency levels

Prepositional dative		Double-object		Fulfilling	
B1	60%	B1	31%	B1	9%
B2	31%	B2	53%	B2	16%

There is an increase of the double-object construction and a decrease by half of the prepositional dative construction, a result suggesting that the higher the proficiency level, the more the learners have recourse to English-specific constructions; still, the fulfilling construction is not easily primed at these two levels of foreign language proficiency. These percentages may indicate that B2 students' implicit learning of constructions has nevertheless improved through frequent exposure to and production of specific argument structure configurations.

The results shed interesting light on the factors that play an influential role in constructional priming. If we analyse a sentence such as *She provided the tourists with a roadmap*, we observe that the fulfilling construction coalesces the syntactic structure of the prepositional dative construction (NP-VP-NP-PP) with the order of semantic roles of the double-object construction (Agent-Recipient-Theme).

The performance of university Italian L2 learners of English fully met Hare and Goldberg's (1999) hypothesis. Indeed, the fulfilling prime prompted double-object responses because of the semantic similarity between the two constructions. Although further research is needed with a wider number of participants, these results obtained in the L2 context may contribute evidence of the influence that semantic roles have in the priming process, which means that conceptual similarity is more salient than structural similarity. The replication of Hare and Goldberg's experiment has demonstrated that the mapping between syntax and semantics occurs also in the mind of Italian learners of English, a result that was largely unexpected if one considers that two of the syntactic patterns contained in the experiment, viz. the double-object construction and the fulfilling construction, are not part of the Italian language construct-i-con, and therefore represent a higher level of complexity for the Italian participants. We can hypothesize that the Italian subjects produced the double-object construction and, although to a lesser extent, the fulfilling construction due to the markedness of these patterns, a type of structural markedness that foregrounds these constructions in the subjects' focus of attention. The conceptual representation of constructional configurations appears to occur not only in native speakers but also in L2 learners, and this leads us to think that argument structure patterns are present in their interlanguage.

The experimental aim was to test the occurrence of constructional priming in L2 learners. If we could ascertain that Italian university learners of English could be primed and that comparable effects could be obtained to those achieved in experiments conducted with native speakers of English, we would evidence that argument structure constructions are accessed when the learners are asked to perform a sentence-elicitation task, and that constructions are real entities also for foreign language speakers. By contrast, if our experiment could not prompt priming effects, we would have to conclude that constructional configurations are not present in their minds, and that their performance was dependent on other factors than formal structures. The results we obtained give us evidence that, as in Hare and Goldberg's experiment, constructional priming effects occur also in learners, and that it is conceptual similarity that learners have relied upon while performing the sentence-elicitation experiment. Such results are even more interesting when we consider the different construct-i-cons of the typologically unrelated language pair in our empirical research.

3 Concluding remarks

This chapter has described two sentence-elicitation experiments aimed at providing evidence for the ontological status of constructions in the mind of learners. As a matter of fact, not many studies have been devoted to the investigation of constructional priming in a second language context:[4] one such study is Loebell and Bock (2003), where the dative alternation was investigated through the elicitation of German and English dative constructions in a picture description task, but this was done with two languages belonging to the same typological family, two languages that basically share the same dative structure. Another study is Hartsuiker, Pickering, and Veltkamp (2004), in which Spanish-English bilinguals performed a passive sentence recall task, but the passive voice is structured alike in the two languages despite their belonging to two different typological families. Gries and Wulff (2005) replicated Bencini and Goldberg's (2000) experiment with two languages typologically belonging to the same family, English and German. In 2006 Desmet and Declercq investigated syntactic priming of relative clauses (nominal post-modification) in the English-Dutch language pair, again with the two languages sharing the same syntactic structure. In our experiment, results are obtained from speakers of a Romance language primed with constructions belonging to a Germanic language and that are absent from the Italian language: English includes the prepositional dative, the double-object and the fulfilling constructions, while Italian possesses the prepositional dative construction only; nonetheless, constructional priming effects occurred in the Italian learners. This appears to suggest that constructional templates are present in the interlanguage of L2 learners, which points to the need of devoting special attention to their teaching in the language classroom. L2 learning involves many instances of restructuring any time new inputs become part of the interlanguage and impose a re-shaping of what has been previously interiorized;

---

[4] Consider, however, some recent studies collected in a volume in the series *Language Learning & Language Teaching* edited by Trofimovich and McDonough (2011).

hence, since interlanguage is an open feedback-sensitive system that has to cyclically reorganize itself, frequent exposure to constructional templates should become a widespread pedagogical practice in exemplar-based approaches to language teaching. Priming is indeed something more than a transient activation phenomenon associated with language performance: it is a far-reaching form of implicit learning (Bock and Griffin 2000; Chang, Dell, and Bock 2006; Hartsuiker et al. 2008, inter alios) that strengthens mappings between linguistic structures and meanings, and enhances long-term learning effects. It should be implemented with explicit noticing (e.g. Schmidt 1990; Skehan 1998) of constructional configurations because, as Boers, De Rycker, and De Knop (2010: 8–9) put it, "learning cannot take place without a certain degree of consciousness on the part of the learner. Unless learners pay attention to a given element in the input, that element will not become a candidate for uptake in long-term memory". This calls for the necessity to draw learners' attention to detailed cross-linguistic L1–L2 analyses of constructions (De Knop and De Rycker 2008): a degree of constructional awareness and an explicit focus-on-form methodology boost the learning process and improve the proficiency level of the second or foreign language. Moreover, classroom instruction should encourage frequent usage of constructional templates, given the fact that repetition prompts memorization and automatization: the more frequently repetition occurs, the higher the degree of entrenchment and the stronger the automated activation (Langacker 1987: 59). Repetition of cognitive events results in mentally automated routines representing single gestalts that are memorized as symbolic pairings of form and meaning (Pawley and Syder 1983; Sinclair 1991; Ellis 1996; Goldberg 1999; Tomasello 2003; Ellis and Larsen-Freeman 2009). This happens because repetition produces bio-chemical mental traces that lead to entrenched behaviours. In the light of this, an explicit and frequent focus-on-form teaching methodology can help learners notice the different L2 constructional templates, and the development of such awareness can result in entrenched patterns and consequently in more native-like fluency and accuracy. Entrenchment of experiences has become a core notion in recent usage-based theories of grammar, and it should become a well-established practice in language teaching.

References

Altmann, Gerry & Yuki Kamide. 1998. Incremental interpretation at verbs: Restricting the domain of subsequent reference. *Cognition* 73. 247–264.
Arai, Manabu, Roger Van Gompel & Christoph Scheepers. 2007. Priming ditransitive structures in comprehension. *Cognitive Psychology* 54. 218–250.

Baicchi, Annalisa. 2011. Metaphoric motivation in grammatical structure. The case of the caused-motion construction from the perspective of the Lexical-Constructional Model. In Günter Radden & Klaus-Uwe Panther (eds.), *Motivation in grammar and the lexicon: Cognitive, communicative, perceptual and socio-cultural factors*, 140–170. Amsterdam & Philadelphia: John Benjamins.

Bencini, Giulia & Adele Eve Goldberg. 2000. The contribution of argument structure constructions to sentence meaning. *Journal of Memory and Language* 43. 640–651.

Bock, Kathryn. 1986. Syntactic persistence in language production. *Cognitive Psychology* 18. 355–387.

Bock, Kathryn & Zenzi Griffin. 2000. The persistence of structural priming: Transient activation or implicit learning? *Journal of Experimental Psychology: General* 129. 177–192.

Bock, Kathryn & Helga Loebell. 1990. Framing sentences. *Cognition* 35(1). 1–39.

Bock, Kathryn, Helga Loebell & Randal Morey. 1992. From conceptual roles to structural relations: Bridging the syntactic cleft. *Psychological Review* 99(1). 150–171.

Boers, Frank, Antoon De Rycker & Sabine De Knop. 2010. Fostering language teaching efficiency through cognitive linguistics: Introduction. De Knop, Sabine, Frank Boers & Antoon De Rycker (eds.), *Fostering language teaching efficiency through cognitive linguistics* 1–26. Berlin & New York: Mouton de Gruyter.

Branigan, Holly, Martin Pickering & Alexandra Cleland. 2000. Syntactic priming in written production: Evidence for rapid decay. *Psychonomic Bulletin and Review* 6. 535–540.

Branigan, Holly, Martin Pickering, Janet McLean & Andrew Stewart. 2006. The role of local and global syntactic structure in language production: Evidence from syntactic priming. *Language and Cognitive Processes* 21. 974–1010.

Brennan, Susan & Herbert Clark. 1996. Conceptual pacts and lexical choice in conversation. *Journal of Experimental Psychology: Learning, Memory and Cognition* 22. 1482–1493.

Brooks, Patricia & Michael Tomasello. 1999. Young children learn to produce passives with nonce verbs. *Developmental Psychology* 35. 29–44.

Carey, Peter, Jacques Mehler & Thomas Bever. 1970. Judging the veracity of ambiguous sentences. *Journal of Verbal Learning and Verbal Behavior* 9. 243–254.

Carlson, Katy 2001. The effects of parallelism and prosody in the processing of gapping structures. *Language and Speech* 44. 1–26.

Chang, Franklin, Kathryn Bock & Adele Eve Goldberg. 2003. Can thematic roles leave traces of their places? *Cognition* 90(1). 29–49.

Chang, Franklin, Gary Dell & Kathryn Bock. 2006. Becoming syntactic. *Psychological Review* 113. 234–272.

Clark, Herbert 1996. *Using language*. Cambridge: Cambridge University Press.

Clark, Herbert & Eve Clark. 1977. *Psychology and Language*. New York: Harcourt Brace Jovanovich.

Cleland, Alexandra & Martin Pickering. 2003. The use of lexical and syntactic information in language production: Evidence from the priming of noun-phrase structure. *Journal of Memory and Language* 49. 214–230.

Cleland, Alexandra & Martin Pickering. 2006. Do writing and speaking employ the same syntactic representations? *Journal of Memory and Language* 54. 185–198.

De Knop, Sabine & Teun De Rycker (eds.). 2008. *Cognitive approaches to pedagogical grammar*. Berlin & New York: Mouton de Gruyter.

Della Putta, Paolo & Annalisa Baicchi. 2013. Constructions at work in foreign language learners' mind. A comparison between two sentence-sorting experiments with English and Italian learners. Paper presented at the 31st AESLA Conference on *Communication, Cognition and Cybernetics*, Universidad de La Laguna, 19 April 2013.

Desmet, Timothy & Mieke Declercq. 2006. Cross-linguistic priming of syntactic hierarchical configuration information. *Journal of Memory and Language* 54. 610–632.

Ellis, Nick. 1996. Sequencing in SLA: Phonological memory, chunking, and point of order. *Studies in Second Language Acquisition* 18. 91–126.

Ellis, Nick & Diane Larsen-Freeman. 2009. *Language as a complex adaptive system*. Chichester: Blackwell.

Estes, Zachary. 2003. Attributive and relational processes in nominal combination. *Journal of Memory and Language* 48. 299–349.

Ferreira, Victor. 2003. The persistence of optional complementizer production: Why saying 'that' is not saying 'that' at all. *Journal of Memory and Language* 48. 379–398.

Ferreira, Victor, Kathryn Bock, Michael Wilson & Neal Cohen. 2005. Structural persistence in anterograde amnesia: Evidence from implicit learning. Paper presented at the 46th Annual Meeting of the Psychonomic Society. University of Toronto, Canada.

Fox Tree, Jean & Paul Meijer. 1999. Building syntactic structure in speaking. *Journal of Psycholinguistic Research* 28. 71–92.

Frazier, Lyn, Lori Taft, Tom Roeper, Charles Clifton, & Kate Ehrlich. 1984. Parallel structure: A source of facilitation in sentence comprehension. *Memory and Cognition* 12. 421–430.

Gagné, Christina. 2002. Lexical and relational influences on the processing of novel compounds. *Brain and Language* 81. 723–735.

Gagné, Christina, Thomas Spalding & Hongbo Ji. 2005. Re-examining evidence for the use of independent relational representations during conceptual combination. *Journal of Memory and Language* 53. 445–455.

Garnham, Alan, Richard Shillcock, Gordon Brown, Andrew Mill & Anne Cutler. 1982. Slips of the tongue in the London-Lund corpus of spontaneous conversation. In Anne Cutler (ed.), *Slips of the tongue and language production*, 251–263. Berlin & New York: Mouton de Gruyter.

Garrett, Merrill. 1988. Processes in language production. In Frederick Newmeyer (ed.), *Linguistics: The Cambridge survey* (vol. 3). Language: Psychological and biological aspects, 69–96. Cambridge: Cambridge University Press.

Goldberg, Adele Eve. 1995. *Constructions: A construction grammar approach to argument structure*. Chicago: University of Chicago Press.

Goldberg, Adele Eve. 1999. The emergence of argument structure semantics. In Brian MacWhinney (ed.), *The emergence of language*, 197–212. Hillsdale: Lawrence Erlbaum Publications.

Goldberg, Adele Eve. 2006. *Constructions at work. The nature of generalization in language*. Oxford: Oxford University Press.

Gries, Stefan Th. 2005. Syntactic priming: A corpus-based approach. *Journal of Psycholinguistic Research* 34. 365–399.

Gries, Stefan Th. & Stefanie Wulff. 2005. Do foreign language learners also have constructions? Evidence from priming, sorting, and corpora. *Annual Review of Cognitive Linguistics* 3. 182–200.

Grill-Spector, Kalanit, Richard Henson & Alex Martin. 2006. Repetition and the brain: Neural models of stimulus-specific effects. *Trends in Cognitive Science* 1. 14–23.

Grober, Ellen, William Beardsley & Alfonso Caramazza. 1978. A parallel function strategy in pronoun assignment. *Cognition* 6. 117–133.

Gropen, Jess, Steven Pinker, Michelle Hollander, Richard Goldberg & Ronald Wilson. 1989. The learnability and acquisition of the dative alternation in English. *Language* 65. 203–257.

Hare, Mary & Adele Eve Goldberg. 1999. Structural priming: Purely syntactic? In Martin Hahn & Scott Stones (eds.), *Proceedings of the 21st Annual Meeting of the Cognitive Science Society*, 208–211. London: Lawrence Erlbaum Associates.
Hartsuiker, Robert, Sarah Bernolet, Sofie Schoonbaert, Sara Speybroeck & Dieter Vanderelst. 2008. Syntactic priming persists while the lexical boost decays: Evidence from written and spoken dialogue. *Journal of Memory and Language* 58. 214–238.
Hartsuiker, Robert & Herman Kolk. 1988. Syntactic persistence in Dutch. *Language and Speech* 41. 143–184.
Hartsuiker, Robert, Herbert Kolk & Philippine Huiskamp. 1999. Priming word order in sentence production. *Quarterly Journal of Experimental Psychology* 52 A. 129–147.
Hartsuiker, Robert, Martin Pickering & Eline Veltkamp. 2004. Is syntax separate or shared between languages? Cross-linguistic syntactic priming in Spanish-English bilinguals. *Psychological Science* 15. 409–414.
Hartsuiker, Robert & Casper Westenberg. 2000. Syntactic persistence in written and spoken sentence production. *Cognition* 75(2). B27–B39.
Hebb, Donald. 1949. *The organization of behavior*. New York: Wiley.
Huttenlocher, Janellen, Marina Vasilyeva & Priya Shimpi. 2004. Syntactic priming in young children. *Journal of Memory and Language* 50. 182–195.
Jackendoff, Ray. 1972. *Semantic interpretation in generative grammar*. Cambridge, MA: Cambridge University Press.
Jackendoff, Ray. 1983. *Semantics and cognition*. Cambridge, MA: Cambridge University Press.
Kaschak, Michael & Arthur Glenberg. 2004. This construction needs learned. *Journal of Experimental Psychology: General* 133(3). 450–467.
Kempen, Gerard. 1977. Conceptualizing and formulating in sentence production. In Sheldon Rosenberg (ed.), *Sentence production: Developments in research and theory*, 259–274. Hillsdale, NJ: Erlbaum.
Lakoff, George & Mark Johnson. 1980. *Metaphors we live by*. Chicago: University of Chicago Press.
Langacker, Ronald. 1987. *Foundations of cognitive grammar. Vol. I: Theoretical prerequisites*. Stanford, CA: Stanford University Press.
Lashley, Karl. 1951. The problem of serial order in behaviour. In Lloyd Jeffress (ed.), *Cerebral mechanisms in behaviour*, 112–136. New York: Wiley.
Levelt, Willem & Stephanie Kelter. 1982. Surface form and memory in question answering. *Cognitive Psychology* 14. 78–106.
Levin, Beth. 1993. *English verb classes and alternations: A preliminary investigation*. Chicago: University of Chicago Press.
Liang, John. 2002. *How do Chinese EFL learners construct sentence meaning: Verb-centered or construction-based?* Guangdong University of Foreign Studies MA thesis.
Loebell, Helga & Kathryn Bock. 2003. Structural priming across languages. *Linguistics* 41. 791–794.
Maccotta, Luigi & Randy Buckner. 2004. Evidence for neural effects of repetition that directly correlate with behavioral priming. *Journal of Cognitive Neuroscience* 16(9). 1625–1632.
Mehler, Jacques & Peter Carey. 1968. The interaction of veracity and syntax in the processing of sentences. *Perception and Psychophysics* 3. 109–111.
Meijer, Paul & Jean Fox Tree. 2003. Building syntactic structures in speaking: A bilingual exploration. *Experimental Psychology* 50. 184–195.

Meyer, David & Roger Schvaneveldt. 1971. Facilitation in recognising pairs of words: Evidence of a dependence between retrieval operations. *Journal of Experimental Psychology* 90. 227–234.
Noora, Azam. 2009. Iranian undergraduate non-English majors' interpretation of English structures. GEMA 9(2). 89–100.
Noppeney, Uta & Cathy Price. 2004. An fMRI study of syntactic adaptation. *Journal of Cognitive Neuroscience* 16. 702–713.
Osgood, Charles & Kathryn Bock. 1977. Salience and sentencing: Some production principles. In Sheldon Rosenberg (ed.), *Sentence production: Developments in research and theory*, 89–140. Hillsdale, NJ: Erlbaum.
Pardo, Jennifer. 2006. On phonetic convergence during conversational interactions. *Journal of the Acoustical Society of America* 119(4). 2382–2393.
Pawley, Andrew & Francis Syder. 1983. Two puzzles for linguistic theory: nativelike selection and nativelike fluency. In Jack Richards & Richard Schmidt (eds.), *Language and communication*, 191–226. New York: Longman.
Pickering, Martin & Holly Branigan. 1998. Syntactic priming in language production. *Trends in Cognitive Science* 3. 136–141.
Pickering, Martin & Victor Ferreira. 2008. Structural priming: A critical review. *Psychology Bulletin* 134 (3). 427–459.
Pickering, Martin & Simon Garrod. 2004. Toward a mechanistic psychology of dialogue. *Behavioral and Brain Sciences* 27. 169–225.
Potter, Mary & Linda Lombardi. 1988. Syntactic priming in immediate recall of sentences. *Journal of Memory and Language* 38. 265–282.
Rayner, Keith, Simon Garrod & Charles Perfetti. 1992. Discourse influences during parsing are delayed. *Cognition* 45. 109–139.
Ruiz de Mendoza Ibáñez, Francisco José & Ricardo Mairal Usón. 2008. Levels of description and constraining factors in meaning construction: An introduction to the Lexical Constructional Model. *Folia Linguistica* 42(2). 355–400.
Scheepers, Christoph & Matthew Crocker. 2004. Constituent order priming from listening to comprehension: A visual world study. In Manuel Carreiras & Charles Clifton Jr. (eds.), *The online study of sentence comprehension: Eye-tracking, ERPs, and beyond*, 167–185. New York: Psychology Press.
Schenkein, Jim. 1980. A taxonomy for repeating action sequences in natural conversation. In B. Butterworth (ed.), *Language production*, 21–47. London, Academic Press.
Schmidt, Richard. 1990. The role of consciousness in second language learning. *Applied Linguistics* 11. 129–158.
Schoonbaert, Sofie, Robert Hartsuicker & Martin Pickering. 2007. The representation of lexical and syntactic information in bilinguals: Evidence from syntactic priming. *Journal of Memory and Language* 56. 153–171.
Sepassi, F. & Kamyab, P. 2005. Iranian university students preference for verb centered vs. construction cues to sentence structure. *The Asian EFL Journal* 7(5). Retrieved from http://www.asian-efl-journal.com/teaching articles (last accessed on 23 September 2012).
Sevald, Christine, Gary Dell & Jennifer Cole. 1995. Syllable structure in speech production: Are syllables chunks or schemas? *Journal of Memory and Language* 34. 807–820.
Sheldon, Amy. 1974. The role of parallel function in the acquisition of relative clauses in English. *Journal of Verbal Learning and Verbal Behavior* 13. 272–281.
Sinclair, John. 1991. *Corpus, concordance, collocation*. Oxford: Oxford University Press.

Skehan, Peter. 1998. *A cognitive approach to language learning*. Oxford: Oxford University Press.

Smyth, Ron. 1994. Grammatical determinants of ambiguous pronoun resolution. *Journal of Psycholinguistic Research* 23. 197–229.

Tannen, Deborah. 1987. Repetition in conversation: Towards a poetics of talk. *Language* 63. 574–605.

Tomasello, Michael. 2003. *Constructing a language: A usage-based theory of language acquisition*. Cambridge, MA: Harvard University Press.

Tooley, Kristen & Matthew Traxler. 2010. Syntactic priming effects in comprehension: A critical review. *Language and Linguistics Compass* 4. 925–937.

Traxler, Matthew. 2008. Lexically independent priming in online sentence comprehension. *Psychonomic Bulletin & Review* 15. 149–155.

Trofimovich, Pavel & Kim McDonough (eds.). 2011. *Applying priming methods to L2 learning, teaching and research: Insights from psycholinguistics*. Amsterdam & Philadelphia: John Benjamins.

Trueswell, John, Michael Tanenhaus & Susan Garnsey. 1994. Semantic influences on parsing: Use of thematic role information in syntactic disambiguation. *Journal of Memory and Language* 33. 285–318.

Valenzuela, Javier & Ana Rojo. 2008. On the existence of constructions in foreign language learners. In Rafael Monroy Casaa & Aquilino Sánchez (eds.), *25 años de Lingüística en España: Hitos y Retos*, 907–912. Murcia: Editum.

Watson, Matthew, Martin Pickering & Holly Branigan. 2004. Alignment of reference frames in dialogue. In K. Forbus, D. Gentner & T. Regier (eds.), *Proceedings of the 26th Annual Conference of the Cognitive Science Society*, 1434–1439. Mahwah, NJ: Erlbaum.

Weiner, Judith & William Labov. 1983. Constraints on the agentless passive. *Journal of Linguistics* 19. 29–58.

Wisniewski, Edward & Bradley Love. 1998. Relations versus properties in conceptual combination. *Journal of Memory and Language* 38. 177–202.

Paolo Della Putta
Do we also need to unlearn constructions? The case of constructional negative transfer from Spanish to Italian and its pedagogical implications

Abstract: In order to ascertain whether Spanish-speaking learners of Italian transfer two frequent Spanish partially-filled-in constructions to Italian, we carried out an experiment using a picture-based dialogue description task and immediate recalls. We divided our sample of informants into two groups: group A comprised 8 subjects with long-term exposure to Italian but almost no formal instruction, whereas group B was composed of 10 subjects with short-term exposure and three months of formal instruction in a university context. The Spanish constructions considered in this study are the planned future periphrasis [*ir a* + infinitive] ('go to' + infinitive), the iterative periphrasis [*volver a* + infinitive] ('return to' + infinitive) and their Italian literal equivalents. In Italian, overlapping syntactic templates (i.e. [*andare a* + infinitive] ('go to' + infinitive) and [*tornare a* + infinitive] ('return to' + infinitive)) are mainly limited to the expression of spatial-displacement meanings: iteration and planned future are usually expressed by affixation, lexical means and/or verbal morphology. The results of our study highlight that neither long-time exposure to Italian nor formal instruction (when not specifically directed to the issue tackled here) are sufficient to help Spanish-speaking learners unlearn the L1-based features used to construct iterative and planned future meanings. Therefore, drawing on a Cognitive Linguistics-inspired approach to language pedagogy, three kinds of pedagogical interventions aimed at discouraging this negative transfer phenomenon are described and discussed.

Keywords: Italian constructions; planned future construction; iterative construction; Spanish learners; exposure effect; instruction effect; unlearning process

1 Introduction

The need for a cognitive grounding for any pedagogical grammar has been addressed by scholars interested in applying the principles of Cognitive Linguistics (CL) to language pedagogy (De Rycker and De Knop 2009; Holme 2012; Ruiz de

Mendoza Ibáñez this volume). "Cognitive grounding" means, in broad terms, helping the learner recognize, understand and interiorize the cognitive mechanisms – such as conceptual metaphors, metonymies or figure-ground alignment – that rule the grammar of the target language. In recent years, various studies have proved that activities aimed at raising students' awareness of the non-arbitrariness of grammar are successful teaching interventions, particularly in those areas where the foreign language (L2) and the mother tongue (L1) diverge (see inter alia Holme 2010; Lysinger 2015; Tyler 2008; Tyler, Muller, and Ho 2011). A CL-principled pedagogical grammar indeed acknowledges a central role for contrastive analysis between L1 and L2, which is useful to predict those areas of the L2 in which teacher intervention is more needed (De Knop and Perrez 2014; Ruiz de Mendoza Ibáñez 2008, this volume).

Cognitive approaches to grammar teaching so far have largely been concerned with suggesting pedagogical activities that can help learners acquire *new* constructions, i.e. form-meaning pairings that must gradually be included in their interlanguage. However, up to now – to the best of our knowledge – one of the central issues of language acquisition and teaching, namely the transfer of constructions from L1 to L2, has hardly been considered. The effects of *transfer*, defined as "the influence of a person's knowledge of one language on that person's knowledge or use of another language" (Jarvis and Pavlenko 2008: 1) are stronger and longer-lasting when the L1 and the L2 are genetically and typologically related. In this case (which is the situation considered in this paper), the learners identify structures or properties common or apparently common to the two languages (Odlin 1989: 113–114; Ringbom 2007: chap. 4). The learning of the L2 will be facilitated by the resemblance of the two systems, especially in receptive tasks (Ringbom 2007: 11); however, learners will find it difficult to get rid of many transfer-generated errors, usually highly fossilized and impervious to pedagogical intervention. Therefore, teaching activity should help students learn new constructions but also unlearn L1-based form-meaning pairings, i.e. de-entrench L1 routines from learners' interlanguage.

This chapter is devoted to this rather neglected area, focusing on the transfer of two frequent partially-filled-in constructions (Goldberg 2003) from Spanish into Italian, viz. the planned future periphrasis (PFP) and the iterative periphrasis (IP). PFP is a tempo-aspectual periphrasis constructed in Spanish by a finite form of the verb *ir* ('go'), the preposition *a* ('to') and a meaning-bearing verb in the infinitive form. Its template is [*ir a* + infinitive] (1):

(1) Spanish
 ¿Qué vamos a hacer mañana?
 What go.1PL.AUX PREPOSITION do.INF tomorrow?
 'What are we going to do tomorrow?'

PFP is "associated to the values of immediacy, proximity to the act of speech, intentionality, or the speaker's conviction that the events situated in a future time will be performed" (Blas Arroyo 2008: 88). We use the label "planned future" to refer to this cluster of meanings (Aaron 2006).

IP is a tempo-aspectual periphrasis constructed by a finite form of the verb *volver* ('return'), the preposition *a* ('to') and a meaning-bearing verb in the infinitive form. Its template is [*volver a* + infinitive] (2):

(2) Spanish
Vuelvo   a   leer   el   libro
Return.1SG.AUX PREPOSITION   read.INF   the   book
'I read the book again'.

IP conveys the iterative and the restitutive aspect.[1]

According to constructionist approaches to grammar *à la* Goldberg, PFP and IP can be considered partially-filled-in constructions: one of their three configurational slots is variable (the infinitive verb) while the other two are lexically fixed in order to arrive at a grammatical construct (Brems 2011: 71). Partially-filled-in constructions are linguistic patterns (Goldberg 2003: 219) whose global meaning is constructed independently of the lexical meanings of their constituent content words, i.e. is not inferable by the simple semantic sum of their components.

These two constructions have only formal but not functional Italian counterparts. Italian displays perfectly overlapping syntactic templates which, unlike Spanish, construct rarer or not perfectly overlapping tempo-aspectual meanings. The formal Italian counterpart of PFP is [*andare a* + infinitive] (*andare* being the Italian for *ir*, 'go'). The formal Italian counterpart of IP is [*tornare a* + infinitive] (*tornare* being the Italian for *volver*, 'return'), which can be used to convey, besides physical displacement meanings, only the restitutive aspect and not the iterative one (Rosemeyer in press). In examples (3) and (4) only physical displacement meanings are expressed:

(3) Italian
Vado   a   lavorare   in   ufficio
Go.1SG.   PREPOSITION   work.INF   PREPOSITION   office
'I go to work in the office'

---

[1] In this work and elsewhere (Della Putta 2015), we distinguish the iterative and the restitutive aspect. With the latter we refer to the restoration of a previous state of affairs, whereas with the former we mean the repetition of an action. As Rosemeyer (in press) points out, Italian and Spanish IP differ strongly in respect to this point: the Italian IP can be used to convey restitutive meanings only, whereas the Spanish IP can be used to convey both iteration and restitution.

(4) Italian
Torno   a   far-mi   la   doccia
Return.1SG   PREPOSITION   do.INF-REFL.1SG   the   shower
'I go back to take a shower'

As we will see in detail in the following paragraphs, Spanish-speaking learners of Italian (SLI) face the difficulty of not relying on constructions of the type (3) and (4) to construct planned future and iterative meanings.

The aim of this chapter is twofold. First, we analyse whether input exposure and, albeit to a lesser extent, instruction can have an impact on the transfer of the Spanish PFP and IP. To verify this, we studied the possible negative transfer between two groups of SLI: group A consisted of virtually non-instructed but long-term input-exposed SLI, whereas group B was composed of instructed but short-term input-exposed SLI. The two groups completed a picture description and an immediate recall task in order to evaluate if either longer exposure to input or instruction can lead to a reduction of the negative transfer of these Spanish-based items.

Second, we briefly propose pedagogical interventions following the principles of a CL-based pedagogy that can be effectively brought into the classroom with the aim of discouraging the transfer of these structures.

2 Planned future and iteration in Spanish and Italian

Spanish and Italian are closely related languages in the Romance family, sharing a mutually intelligible phonetic system, a Latin-based lexical inventory, an inflective morphology, and similar syntax (Green 2009). For the aim of this study, we focus on the syntactic characteristics of these languages. The syntactic features of Spanish and Italian largely converge (Carrera Díaz 2007; Schmid 1994), thus giving the apparent image of two perfectly overlapping systems. Nevertheless, a few subtle differences do emerge and are those whose learning has proven to be more difficult. The presence of Spanish-based syntactic features in SLI's interlanguage has been detected by numerous studies even after long periods of formal education or input exposure (De Benedetti 2006; Ferrario 2013; Schmid 1994; Zurlo 2009).

We focus here on the transfer of PFP and IP in SLIs' interlanguage. Both PFP and IP can be used in Spanish with a literal meaning, thus expressing only spatial displacement, and in a periphrastic way, thus with tempo-aspectual meaning (García-Miguel 2005; Olbertz 1998):

(5) Spanish
Paco va   a   escribir   un libro sobre su teoría
Paco go.3SG PREPOSITION write.INF a   book about his theory

The literal meaning is: 'Paco goes to write a book about his theory';
The periphrastic meaning is: 'Paco is going to write a book about his theory'.

(6) Spanish
Volvió   a   duchar-se
returned.3SG PREPOSITION take a shower.INF-REFL.3SING

The literal meaning is: 'He returned to take a shower';
The periphrastic meaning is: 'He took a shower again'
(both examples from Olbertz 1998: 231).

The literal meaning is constructed by the simple semantic combination of the constituents, while the tempo-aspectual meaning is obtained by referring to the metaphorical mapping of time onto space (Lakoff and Johnson 1980) which transfers the meanings of the verbs *ir* ('go') and *volver* ('return') from a spatial to a temporal domain. Only in this second case can we speak about partially-filled-in constructions in a Goldbergian sense (Goldberg 2003) as only in this case do these patterns arrive at a global meaning that is not inferable from the simple semantic sum of their components.

Following Boas' (2010) ideas about the usefulness of a constructional contrastive analysis, we now examine how Italian expresses planned future and iterative meanings. Boas (2010) maintains that a study of how the same meanings are cross-linguistically mapped to different forms should begin by comparing pairs of languages whose constructional repertoire has already been carefully described. In this way we can identify and explain cross-linguistic constructional generalizations and, at the same time, keep a record of language-specific constructional properties.

As we have briefly seen in the introduction, PFP and IP have only non-tempo-aspectual counterparts in Italian (examples (3) and (4)). The iterative meaning constructed by IP in Spanish (7a) is commonly expressed in Italian by lexical means (7b) or by affixation, in the latter case by the use of the verbal affix *ri-* (7c):

(7) a. Spanish
¿Cuándo volvemos   a   vernos?
When   return.1PL.AUX PREPOSITION see.INF.REFLEXIVE.PRONOUN

b. Italian
   Quando ci   vediamo di nuovo?
   When we.REFLEXIVE.PRONOUN see.1Pl of new

c. Italian
   Quando ci   ri-vediamo?
   When we.REFLEXIVE.PRONOUN ITERATIVE.AFFIX.see.1PL
   All examples: "When are we going to see each other again?"

The planned future, constructed in Spanish by the PFP (8a), is mapped in Italian to the simple present (8b) or the simple future (8c) of the verb:

(8) a. Spanish
       ¿Qué   vamos   a   hacer   mañana?
       What go.3PL.AUX PREPOSITION do.INF tomorrow?

   b. Italian
       Che   facciamo   domani?
       What do.PRES.3PL tomorrow

   c. Italian
       Che   faremo   domani?
       What do.FUT.3PL tomorrow
       All examples: "What are we going to do tomorrow?"

It must be mentioned that in recent years some scholars have raised the question of whether the Italian [*andare a* + infinitive] ('go to' + infinitive, formally identical to the Spanish PFP as exemplified in the introduction) expresses a tempo-aspectual meaning similar to that constructed by the Spanish PFP. Bertinetto (1991) and Amenta and Strudsholm (2002) attest only statistically rare resultative periphrastic values for [*andare a* + infinitive]. According to Valentini (2007), [*andare a* + infinitive] displays unstable and less recurrent resultative and iterative values instantiated by some highly frequent transformative, continuative and resultative verbs. With frequent permanent and non-permanent stative verbs such as *essere* ('be') and *avere* ('have') no periphrastic meaning is attested, contrary to Spanish usage. Furthermore, the periphrastic value of [*andare a* + infinitive] is restricted to oral use or to less prestigious varieties of Italian and is not attested either in descriptive or in pedagogical grammar books because of its instability of use. Let us now examine how and why the Spanish PFP and IP are transferred by SLI to Italian.

3 Unlearning constructional transfer

According to the embodied semantic paradigm (Violi 2012), human beings conceptualize abstract domains such as time or aspect via conceptual metaphors, that is, by relying on concrete and bodily-experience based domains such as space. Odlin (2008) maintains that L1 figurative language is easily transferred into learners' interlanguage. The transferability of figurative language is facilitated by the fact that some metaphorical relations are widespread, if not universal: as it seems likely that every culture and every language map time onto space (Weger and Pratt 2008), it will be easy for learners to "assume certain constructions to be universal when in fact they involve language-specific meaning extension" (Odlin 2008: 325).

In the following examples we can see how SLI generate non-target sentences by transferring the Spanish PFP and IP to Italian:[2]

(9)   *Professore, che andiamo a studiare, oggi?*
      'Professor, what are we going to study today?'

(10) **Da domani vado a essere un bravo studente…*
      'Starting from tomorrow, I am going to be a good student'

(11) **Dobbiamo tornare a leggere il paragrafo, ora?*
      'Do we have to read the paragraph again now?'

In these examples, according to a detection-based approach to transfer[3] (Jarvis 2012), planned future meanings (examples (9) and (10)) and the iterative aspect (11) are constructed by erroneously using the non-constructional Italian counterparts of the Spanish PFP and IP. Instead of using target-like Italian means such as finite verbal morphology or affixation (see Section 2), SLI relied on the formal similarity of Spanish and Italian to construct planned future and iterative meanings, without being aware that Italian does not share the tempo-aspectual values of these syntactic patterns with Spanish.

Three factors can be put forward to account for such transfer phenomena. First we can refer to 'psychotypology' (Kellerman 1983), according to which transfer effects are stronger when the L1 and the L2 are thought by the learners

---

[2] These utterances were produced by SLI during real lessons where the author of this chapter was the instructor.
[3] The detection-based approach to transfer is defined by Jarvis (2012: 1) as "the detection of language-use patterns that are characteristic and distinctive of learners from specific L1 backgrounds".

to be typologically similar (Ringbom 2007). As shown by Bailini (2012) and Landone (2001) this often occurs with SLI.

Secondly, the 'transfer to somewhere' principle (Andersen 1983) states that a structure from the L1 is more easily transferred if the learners find or think they have found a "similar counterpart" (Jarvis and Pavlenko 2008: 174) in the L2. We put forward the idea that this is the case with SLI as they will surely find in the Italian input similar syntactic templates such as [*tornare a* + infinitive] ('return to' + infinitive) and [*andare a* + infinitive] ('go to' + infinitive). As soon as the meanings of Italian *tornare* and *andare* are equated with those of Spanish *volver* and *ir*, SLI will assume that they can rely on these syntactic templates also to express tense/aspectual meanings: the constructional negative transfer is triggered by the structural – but not functional – cross-linguistic resemblance between the two analytical constructions.

Finally, strong syntactic priming effects in bilinguals, L1 and L2 learners have been discovered by scholars aiming to better understand the nature of syntactic priming in language acquisition (see Flett, Branigan, and Pickering 2013 and Salamoura and Williams 2007 for a review of these studies). Gries and Wulff (2005) demonstrated that the mental representations of L1 and L2 speakers are primed not only by mere syntactic patterns but also by constructions, i.e. gestaltic form-meaning pairings bearing a meaning not inferable from the semantic combination of their components.

The difficulty for SLI is that they should not transfer the constructional values of the Spanish PFP and IP to Italian, which consequently means that they have to 'unlearn' the possibility of metaphorically shifting the meaning of the two finite verbs from a spatial domain to a temporal one. In order to arrive at target-like Italian constructions of planned future and iteration, SLI need to (1) be aware that the literal equivalents of the Spanish PFP and IP are ungrammatical in Italian; (2) de-entrench their presence from their interlanguage; 3) re-engage with the Italian input in order to find the correct grammatical means to construct planned future and iterative meanings.

Unlearning an L1 structure or property means coming to understand that this structure or property is not allowed in the L2 and, therefore, avoid its transfer. The 'unlearning problem' arises when the L2 input and its pedagogical manipulations are not sufficient to make the learner aware of the ungrammaticality of certain L1-based options in the target language (Yin and Kaiser 2011: 182). The target language can only provide 'positive evidence' of what is correct, but it fails to provide the 'negative evidence' needed to reveal the incorrectness of certain L1 properties transferred to the L2 (Gass and Mackey 2002). In such cases learners cannot generalize negative evidence from the input alone, i.e., in our case, the fact that two crosslinguistically analogous structures do not correspond to similar functions. It is therefore maintained by various scholars, working under both functional and generative paradigms (Gass and Mackey 2002; Lefebvre, White, and Jordan 2006), that the L1 influences learners' interlanguage more strongly and for longer in those domains where the input fails to provide robust evidence of what is ungrammatical in the target language.

Neither long-term input exposure nor formal instruction (unless focused on these transfer phenomena) can help students solve the unlearning problem, as confirmed by various studies (Inegaki 2001; Larrañaga et al. 2012; White 1991). In the study by Larrañaga et al. (2012) it is demonstrated that L1 English students of Spanish transfer English satellite configuration of particular motion events (boundary crossing) independently of their proficiency and length of exposure to the L2. Larrañaga and colleagues justify this persisting transfer-generated error in terms of a lack of positive and negative evidence in learners' exposure to L2 input: the expression of the manner of motion in Spanish is low salient and rare and it is never part of a syllabus designed for English-speaking students.

Similar considerations emerge from Inegaki's (2001) study. This was designed to test the hypothesis according to which L1 Japanese learners of English should be able to learn manner-of-motion verbs with goal prepositional phrases (PPs) in English from positive evidence, whereas L1 English learners of Japanese should be unable to learn that these constructions are impossible in Japanese because nothing in the input would tell them so. In English both manner-of-motion (such as *walk* or *run*) and directed motion verbs (such as *go* or *enter*) can occur with goal PPs, while in Japanese only directed motion verbs occur with goal PPs. The results of the study confirm the initial hypothesis: L1 Japanese learners of English experience less difficulty than their L1 English counterparts. The former can rely on the positive evidence provided by the input and thus 'add' a configuration to their L1 motion verbs argument structure, while the latter are shown to be unable to unlearn an L1-based argument structure (manner-of-motion verbs with PPs): this construction has proved to be constantly transferred to their interlanguage.

White's (1991) study focuses on English and French dative constructions. English allows for both prepositional and double-object datives (examples (12) and (13)), whereas in French, when the dative object is nominal, only prepositional datives are allowed[4] (examples (14) and (15)), sentence (15) being incorrect:

---

[4] If the dative is a pronoun, even French allows for a double-object construction, e.g. *Jean lui a donné le livre* ('John gave him the book').

(12) John gave the book to Mary

(13) John gave Mary the book

(14) French
Jean	a	donné	le	livre	à	Marie
Jean	have.3SG.AUX.	given	the	book	to.PREP	Marie

(15) French
*Jean	a	donné	Marie	le	livre
Jean	have.3SG.AUX	given	Marie	the	book

High-proficiency L1 English speakers of French considered (15) correct, ignoring the fact that French does not allow the double-object dative. The unlearning problem of double-object datives arises because nothing in the French input suggests that sentences such as (15) are not correct; the mere fact that learners do not find such structures in the input does not seem to be sufficient to avoid the transfer of such syntactic templates. French-speaking learners of English, on the other hand, use the English double-object dative as they can find positive evidence for it in the input they process.

Unlearning thus seems more troublesome than learning (Gabriele 2009; Schwartz 1998; Yin and Kaiser 2011) and in order to unlearn L1 features transferred to the L2, learners need explicit negative evidence provided by teacher interventions. We turn to this in the following sections.

4 Study

The transfer of the Spanish PFP and IP to Italian is reported in various non-experimental studies with different theoretical perspectives: sociolinguistic (Vietti 2005: 120–121), contrastive (Carrera Díaz 2007), pedagogical (De Benedetti 2006; Ferrario 2013; Morgana and Zaffaroni 2010; Zurlo 2009). The transfer of PFP is widely reported in all these studies, while the transfer of IP is attested to a lesser extent. The aim of these studies is descriptive and mainly based on the experience of Italian language teachers. Even though teachers' reports are a valid means to investigate cross-linguistic influence (Jarvis 2012: 11), we believe that more experimental evidence is needed to clearly state that these Spanish constructions are commonly part of SLI interlanguage.

The purpose of our study is therefore to answer the following research questions:
1) Do SLI receiving almost no explicit instruction but long-term input exposure (group A) and SLI receiving explicit L2 instruction (but without a specific focus on the constructions in question) over short-term input exposure (group B) both use the Italian counterparts of the Spanish PFP and IP – respectively [*andare a* + infinitive] ('go to' + infinitive) and [*tornare a* + infinitive] ('return to' + infinitive) – to express future planned and iterative meanings instead of relying on the target-like Italian linguistic means (affixation, lexicon or verbal morphology, see Section 2)?
2) Is there a (quantitative or qualitative) difference between group A and group B in the way these constructions are transferred?

If the transfer of these constructions is confirmed by our data and if no difference between the two groups is found, this will support the idea that neither long-term exposure to input nor not-focused instruction are sufficient to help SLI unlearn the recourse to these ungrammatical structures; this, then, would highlight the need for planned and targeted teaching intervention to help learners unlearn the use of these partially-filled-in constructions.

It has been pointed out to us that the main variable that distinguishes the two groups of SLI enrolled for this study is input exposure and not instruction for two main reasons: 1) as we will describe in the section below, some of the participants in group A have received a small amount of formal instruction and this of course weakens this distinctive feature of group A compared with group B; 2) group B has received formal instruction that was not directed explicitly at the issues addressed in this paper and therefore instruction should not be considered as a variable that clearly distinguishes between the two groups.

We agree that the strongest variable differentiating A from B is input exposure but we think it is also correct to consider, albeit as a less distinguishing variable, the fact that group B has received formal instruction in Italian. There are two reasons for our claim: 1) the instruction received by group B can at the very least be considered as a supplementary and better organized input received and processed by the learners during their stay in Italy (3 months) and during previous course(s) followed in their home country (Spain); 2) group B received instruction in both Spain and Italy. Even though the instruction provided in Italy was controlled in order not to give any explicit information or correction on the transfer of PFP and IP, the same cannot be firmly stated about the instruction received in Spain. The courses attended before our study were designed for beginner L1 speakers of Spanish and were probably of a comparative L1-L2 nature. Although it would be rare for such courses to deal with the transfer of PFP and IP (despite their comparative characteristics), we cannot be sure that in these courses no explicit correction or mention of this issue was made. We therefore reframe the two variables used to distinguish the two groups: the main variable is input exposure, which differs greatly between the two groups, but we feel it is necessary to at least mention instruction for the above reasons.

4.1 Participants

26 subjects took part in the study and fell into 3 groups. Group A was composed of 8 long-term exposed and almost non-instructed SLI; group B was composed of 10 short-term exposed instructed SLI. A third group, group C, comprised 8 monolingual Italian native speakers and was used as a control group. Details about the groups are provided in the following subsections.

4.1.1 Group A

Group A was composed of eight almost non-instructed SLI, aged 26 to 42 and living in Milan. By 'almost non-instructed' we mean: 1) that the amount of formal instruction for Italian declared by the subjects did not exceed three months and 2) that this instruction did not have a Spanish-Italian contrastive basis, i.e. it was designed for multilingual classes. Self-study cases were also considered: none of the eight subjects had taken online, one-to-one conversation lessons or had studied Italian with contrastive Spanish-Italian grammars or textbooks. The most important criterion followed to identify potential subjects for group A was the length of their stay in Italy, which had to be no less than three years, thus ensuring long-term exposure to Italian for all eight participants.

Proficiency level in Italian had to be comparable with that of participants from group B. In order to evaluate this, all eight subjects from group A took and passed the B1 level in the CILS (*Certificazione Italiano Lingua Straniera*) examination, one of the official proficiency certifications released by the University for Foreigners of Siena and recognized by the Italian Ministry of Education. The exam used to assess proficiency level in group A was that used for the June 2012 session, downloadable at: http://cils.unistrasi.it/89/197/Prove_Liv._B1.html (last accessed on 22/05/2014). The features of the eight subjects in group A are summarized in Table 1.

Table 1: Features of subjects in group A

Acronym	Age	Formal instruction	Period of stay in Italy
A1	26	3 hours per week for 3 months	3 years and 6 months
A2	35	Self-study with Italian grammar books	5 years and 2 months
A3	37	None	3 years and 8 months
A4	42	Self-study with grammar books after his arrival in Italy	Approximately 5 years with some long periods abroad
A5	40	Formal lessons at a local private school for two months; sporadic use of grammar books	7 years
A6	28	None	3 years and 8 months
A7	36	Some weeks of formal instruction on her arrival	5 years
A8	41	None	6 years and 3 months

4.1.2 Group B

Group B comprised ten instructed SLI, aged 20 to 26 and living in Bologna. All of them were Spanish university exchange students enrolled in a 60-hour course of Italian lasting three months. The entry level of these students was assessed via an entry test (both written and oral) and all were placed at the A2 level of the Common European Framework of Reference for Languages (CEFR). All participants had studied Italian formally in Spain. The class they were assigned to was taught by the author of the present chapter and was made up of sixteen SLI. The syllabus followed during the three-month course was aimed at: 1) improving performance of both receptive and productive tasks; 2) reviewing the most difficult features of Italian grammar studied in previous courses; 3) introducing new grammar elements to their interlanguage, such as simple future and conditional.

During the course in Italy no contrastive analysis between Italian and Spanish was performed as far as PFP and IP were concerned. At the end of the course, the students took the same CILS B1 proficiency test as the subjects in group A. The ten subjects who passed the exam were asked to voluntarily participate in the study. The features of the ten subjects in group B are summarized in Table 2.

Table 2: Features of subjects in group B

Acronym	Age	Formal instruction	Period of stay in Italy
B1	22	Around 50 hours in Spain and 60 hours in Italy	4 months
B2	20	One month (hours not specified) in Spain and 60 hours in Italy	3 and a half months
B3	26	60 hours in Spain and 60 hours in Italy	5 months
B4	23	40 hours in Spain and 60 hours in Italy	6 months
B5	22	Two months in Spain and 60 hours in Italy	4 months
B6	23	60 hours in Spain and 60 hours in Italy	5 and a half months
B7	24	Two months in Spain and 60 hours in Italy	4 months
B8	22	50 hours in Spain and 60 hours in Italy	4 months
B9	23	One month in Spain and 60 hours in Italy	5 months
B10	21	60 hours in two months in Spain and 60 hours in Italy	4 months

4.1.3 Group C

Group C was composed of eight Italian monolingual mother tongue subjects aged 29 to 38, all living in Milan. Subjects volunteered to participate in the study and were not aware of its aims. The eight subjects were selected mainly because their Italian could be classified as "standard Italian", i.e. a variety of Italian with no strong diatopic influence spoken commonly (but not exclusively) by highly-educated individuals living in northern industrial cities such as Milan and Turin (Dal Negro and Vietti 2006). All participants were graduates, but none had studied linguistics or related subjects.

4.2 Design of the study

The 26 subjects completed a picture-based task in which they were asked to complete the dialogues or the monologues of characters acting in planned future (pictures 1–4, Figure 1) or iterative contexts (pictures 5–8, Figure 2).

The task was performed orally: the subjects were sitting opposite the researcher who recorded their answers. The instructions were given in Italian according to the following formula: "Look at these pictures and complete the utterances with the words that sound best to you". We decided to use a strongly guided picture task in order to restrict as much as possible the linguistic options that could be used in the communicative contexts.

Figure 1: Planned future contexts[5]

After all the answers were given, the participants took an immediate recall test, which was delivered in Italian according to the following formula: "Can you tell me why you chose to complete this sentence with _____?". The aim was to try to understand the reason(s) that led the subjects to use particular linguistic items. It must be noted, however, that not all the subjects understood the question and some failed to answer.

4.3 Results of group C

For the stimuli used, we had assumed that in no case could the use of [*andare a* + infinitive] ('go to' + infinitive) and [*tornare a* + infinitive] to express planned

---

[5] Translation of Figure 1 (planned future contexts): Scene 1: "What .... tomorrow?" // "Shopping? Disco? Trip to the lake?". Scene 2: on the blackboard: "First day – Physics course" // "Good morning and welcome to the Physics course. Here is the programme: in this course .... the basis of Physics". Scene 3: "Good evening everybody! The first song that .... is 'Bitter Love'". Scene 4: written in the background: "Cooking school." // "First .... the spaghetti in the water."

Figure 2: Iterative contexts[6]

future and iteration be judged as grammatical in Italian. Nevertheless, as previously seen in Section 2, there are cases where the use of [*andare a* + infinitive] ('go to'+ infinitive) with similar constructional values to those of the Spanish PFP is recorded in oral and less prestigious varieties of Italian. Therefore, to better evaluate the performance of group A and B with respect to this issue, we first present the data from group C in order to see how many times Italian mother tongue speakers used such patterns to complete the eight utterances.

A qualitative analysis of the answers shows that pictures 4 and 8 were interpreted differently than expected by the author. In picture 4, three informants used the imperative form and one informant selected the modal verb *dovere* ('have to') because in this situation the role of the cook was judged as hierarchical

---

[6] Translation of Figure 2 (iterative contexts): Scene 5: Teacher: "Sara, your homework is not good." // Student: "Oh no! This afternoon ………. the homework". Scene 6: Girl: "Well, then… goodbye…". // Boy: "Goodbye… when……….?" // Girl: "Well, I don't know… Saturday or Sunday, maybe!". Scene 7: Nurse: "Oh no, I am so sorry!" // Patient: "Oh no, now I have to ………. the blood test?!" // Nurse: "Yes, but we will do everything very quickly". Scene 8: "Oh no, I have lost all my work! Now ………… everything!"

towards the woman, as emerged from the immediate recall task. The three imperative forms and the modal verb *dovere* were not included in the final scoring as the subjects did not interpret picture 4 as bearing a planned future meaning.

Picture 8 had been intended to elicit an iterative meaning but four informants out of eight interpreted it as a planned future meaning: "Here I used *rompo* ('I break') because the person is angry with his computer and he surely wants to break it",[7] one informant said; three other informants reported similar thoughts. We therefore decided to compute the different answers according to the subjects' interpretation: four of them were calculated as planned futures and four as iteratives.

Out of 32 answers about planned future meanings, one (2.7%) was given in picture 4 with [*andare a* + infinitive] ('go to' + infinitive). Iterative meanings were always constructed by resorting either to affixation (*ri-*) or to lexical means such as *di nuovo* or *ancora* ('again').

The subject who used [*andare a* + infinitive] ('go to' + infinitive) for picture 4 failed to explain his choice: "I said *andiamo a buttare* ('we go to throw') because the cook is doing an action that is also useful for the woman… he is teaching her, he is involving her in what he is doing". This explanation seems to account for the choice of a first person plural form rather than a singular one, but does not clearly state why the informant used the [*andare a* + infinitive] template in this case.

4.4 Results of group A

Turning now to the results of group A, it appears that in two cases subjects failed to answer, i.e. they were not able to fill the gaps in the captions. Similarly to the situation for group C, pictures 4 and 8 elicited unexpected answers: picture 4 elicited a directive modality four times and these were not included in the final scoring; picture 8 elicited a planned future five times and an iteration three times. The immediate recall task highlighted very similar reasons for these choices to those expressed by subjects in group C.

For pictures 1 and 2, four answers were not calculated because the subjects interpreted the characters' thoughts and utterances as expressions of doubt between different eligible options: the verbs *potere* and *volere* ('can' and 'want') were used. For picture 5, two answers were excluded because A6 and A8 did not recognize a possible iteration in the situation.

---

[7] Here and elsewhere in the chapter we report the subjects' motivations for their linguistic choices. The answers were given in Italian or, partially, in Spanish by subjects of group A and B. All the translations are our owns.

Out of 28 answers about planned future meanings, 17 were PFP-based, which corresponds to a percentage of 60.7%. The iterative meaning was constructed 13 times out of 22 by resorting to an IP-based pattern, making up 59% of the answers.

The immediate recall task only partially highlighted the reasons why subjects chose to use PFP and IP Italian counterparts. We report here some of the most significant answers which partially explained this point.

A2 reports for pictures 1 and 3: "well, I said *vado a fare* ['I go to do'] because he is thinking about tomorrow [...] here I said *vado a cantare* ['I go to sing'] because the concert has just begun".

A3's motivation for the use of lexical and IP-based means in pictures 5 and 6 respectively to construct iterative meanings shows that the two options are considered equivalent: "yes, well... *de nuevo* [Spanish for 'again'], *vuelvo a hacer algo* [Spanish for 'I return to do something'] ... they are the same situation, here the computer destroyed his work, here her homework... It is no good, says the professor, so... homework again!".

A5 reported as follows the reasons why she used a PFP-based option in picture 2 and a simple present in picture 3: "...because the teacher wants to work with the pupils... together... so he is working with them when he says *andiamo a leggere* ['we go to read']... here with the concert... I don't know, but... it is only the band who sings, they are not doing it together". A5's explanation reveals the fact that according to her the two forms can be used for two different situations, thus she sees both as being available in Italian.

For pictures 1 and 2, A7 reported: "here [no. 1] I said *andiamo a fare* ['we go to do'] because I think that he is talking to other people and because it is a moment for the future [*un momento por el futuro*, cited literally] whereas for this picture [no. 2]... well, I said *studieremo* ['we will study'] because there are many lessons to do in a course, over a long time". From A7's answer we can infer that she too believes that two different meanings correspond to the two choices.

A7's comment about picture 7 reveals that for her lexical and IP-based means might be equivalent: "here I said *tornare a fare* ['go back to do'] because, well... the tests are broken and the blood has fallen on the table [...] but maybe I can also say *fare ancora* ['do again'] or *fare una volta più le analisi* ['do the test one more time'], yes... maybe it is the same".

When A8 was asked about his choice for picture 3 (*vi vado a cantare*, 'I go to sing you'), he translated his answer into Spanish and overtly stated that, for him, Italian and Spanish overlap as far as PFP concerns: "*es como en Español, os voy a cantar...* [Spanish, 'it is like Spanish, I am going to sing you'], he sings for them and is starting in a few moments".

4.5 Results of group B

Picture 8 elicited both iterative (6) and planned future (2) interpretations. A total of 12 volitive and directive answers were not considered in the scoring procedure. Four missed answers were excluded from the final score. In picture 6, B2 interpreted the situation as a planned future and answered with *mi vai a chiamare* ('you are going to call me'). We computed this answer as a planned future meaning expressed by a PFP-based item.

The planned future meaning was constructed through PFP-based patterns 19 times out of 37, i.e. in 51.4% of the answers, while the iterative meaning was constructed through IP-based patterns 12 times out of 25, i.e. in 48% of the answers.

As for the results of the immediate recall task, we first mention B2's motivation for having answered with *canteremo* ['we will sing'], a simple future, in picture 3: "I do not really know why I said *canteremo* but this is something that is going to happen ['*qualcosa che va a capitare*', literal translation from Italian] in the future, so I used the future…". It is evident from this answer that B2 does not have clear control of his linguistic choices as he wrongly transfers the Spanish PFP to Italian while motivating his use of the simple future. We further asked B2 why he decided to use *andiamo a bagnare* ['we go to put in the water'] for picture 4 and why he used a simple future (*canteremo*) for picture 3. The answer stated that "here [picture 4] the difference is that they are cooking together, whereas in number 3 they are not singing together… and also, in number 4 they are doing it in that moment ['*lo stanno facendo in quel momento*', literal translation from Italian], which is not what is happening here [picture 3]". B2 perceives the Italian simple future and the Spanish PFP-based pattern as two alternative options.

B5's statement shows that, as far as the construction of the iterative meaning is concerned, the subject is not aware that an IP-based pattern is not grammatical in Italian as she compares it to the lexical means she used to express iteration: "I do not really get your question… Here [picture 8] he has to do everything again, the computer destroyed his work… number 5 is very similar, she has to do the homework again because it was wrong… that is why I used *ancora* ['again'] and *devo tornare a fare*… ['I have to go back to do']".

According to B7, *vado a fare* ['I go to do', a PFP-based pattern] can be equivalent to *faccio* ['I do', grammatical in Italian for planned future], as he states: "in this first picture I used *vado a fare* but I think I could use *faccio*… I was thinking about Spanish… It would be *voy a hacer* [Spanish, 'I go to do'], I would say that… but in Italian the future is more complicated…".

B9 explains his use of PFP-based patterns in pictures 1, 4 and 8 in this way: "these are cases where the action is planned for the future, as one can see from the pictures, that is why I chose to say, for example in number 8, *vado a rompere* ['I go to break'], etc.". In picture 3, B9 uses *canterò* ['I will sing'], which is grammatical in Italian for a planned future. In the immediate recall task, B9 expresses his doubts about the fact that the simple future can perhaps be substituted by either a PFP-based item or a present tense: "*Canterò* is a future, but now I cannot really say why I decided to use it… maybe I could also say *andiamo a cantare* or *canto*".

5 Comparison of the results and discussion

Results from group C further suggest that [*andare a* ('go to') + infinitive] and [*tornare a* ('return to') + infinitive] with periphrastic meanings expressing planned future and iteration are rare and basically ungrammatical in Italian as put forth by previous studies (see Section 2).

More specifically, for [*andare a* + infinitive], the picture task performed by group C supports the position that in Italian tempo-aspectual meanings cannot be mapped to this pattern. Nevertheless, we agree with Valentini (2007) that in some contexts this mapping exists, especially in oral and less prestigious varieties of Italian: as seen in Section 4.3, it was used in 2.7% of the occurrences in our sample. The difference between Valentini's study and ours is methodological in nature: Valentini analyzed excerpts of real language, totally uncontrolled by the speakers and part of longer discourse fragments, whereas our study allowed the speakers to better control their production, which was not part of a wider discursive context. Nevertheless, our aims are pedagogical in nature and, along with recent Italian grammars (see Maiden and Robustelli 2000: 290), which do not mention its existence, we would not consider [*andare a* + infinitive] with tempo-aspectual values as being part of an L2 Italian syllabus.

In order to answer the first research question, i.e. whether there is a difference between almost non-instructed long-term input exposure (group A) and instructed short-term input exposure (group B) as far as the transfer of the Spanish PFP and IP into Italian is concerned, we performed a Mann-Whitney U test to establish if the outcomes among the two groups show statistically significant difference. The scoring procedure for the test was operationalized as follows: 1) we considered correct all the answers that did not use PFP- or IP-based patterns to construct planned future or iterative meanings; 2) only planned future and iterative meanings were calculated; 3) we calculated the percentage of correct answers for each participant.

Table 3 summarizes the degree of accuracy in the two groups as far as planned future meanings are concerned. The results of the Mann-Whitney U test show that the better accuracy in group B does not have statistical significance (U = 35, p = .696), i.e. the two groups behaved similarly with regard to the transfer of PFP.

Table 3: Descriptive statistics on the accuracy of planned future meanings across groups

Group	Number of subjects	Mean	Standard Deviation
A	8	34.4%	24.5
B	10	41%	15.6

The descriptive statistics for the degree of accuracy across the two groups for iterative meanings is summarized in Table 4. Also for iterative meanings, the results of the Mann-Whitney U test show that better accuracy in group B does not have statistical significance (U = 26, p = .237). Just as for planned future meanings, the two groups behaved similarly.

Table 4: Descriptive statistics on the accuracy of iterative meanings across groups

Group	Number of subjects	Mean	Standard Deviation
A	8	35.4%	22.6
B	10	53.3%	18.9

Results from group C, if compared to group A and B, have statistical relevance both in the planned future and iterative conditions (p always <.05).

In conclusion, the quantitative analysis of the results of the picture task emphasises the fact that the recourse to PFP- and IP-based patterns to construct planned future and iterative meanings is equally common among both short-term and long-term input exposed learners. The analysis of the immediate recall task helps us better understand the causes of this transfer phenomenon. There are cases in which SLI think that meanings constructed through a PFP- or IP-based patterns are comparable to those constructed by grammatically correct means in Italian such as lexis, affixation or finite verbal morphology (see the statements by A6, A7, B5 and B9).

Other subjects (A2, A5, A7 and B2) stated that in Italian PFP- and IP-based structures are syntactic templates used to construct meanings that could not be expressed otherwise. In such cases, SLI feel these ungrammatical patterns are necessary to express certain tempo-aspectual values.

Our results confirm that SLI (both when instructed and non-instructed but long-term-input-exposed) seem unable to infer that the transfer of the Spanish PFP and IP into Italian is ungrammatical: no real quantitative differences between the two groups are to be found and the reasons for this transfer phenomenon seem to be very similar for both groups. A properly planned pedagogical intervention is therefore needed to give SLI the indispensable amount of negative evidence that might help them notice and automatize non-recourse to PFP- and IP-based patterns.

6 Pedagogical interventions

In this section, we propose some pedagogical activities aimed at helping SLI unlearn the recourse to PFP- and IP-based means to construct planned future and iterative meanings. In Della Putta (2015), similar suggestions are put forward and these are tested by concretely applying them to an SLI class. We will outline three different types of intervention:
1) transcodification activities (from images to language and vice versa), which aim at explaining the embodied nature of PFP and IP and making it cognitively accessible to learners;
2) interactive strategies aimed at helping students notice the ungrammaticality of PFP and IP transfer;
3) input-manipulation activities aimed at giving learners the positive evidence of what should be used in Italian to express planned future and iteration.

6.1 Transcodification activities

We propose a set of pedagogical interventions whose goal is to make SLI aware of the fact that in Spanish the constructional meanings of PFP and IP are instantiated by the embodied conceptual metaphor TIME IS SPACE. As proposed by Holme (2012), the embodied origins of linguistic phenomena can be experienced by learners through both 'actual embodied routines' and 'virtual embodied principles'.

Actual embodied routines are the physical enactment of the cognitive metaphors that construct meanings or grammar rules and have been proven useful in the teaching of e.g. English motion verbs and countable and uncountable lexicon (Holme 2012; Lindstromberg and Boers 2005). In our case, the teacher can first show students pairs of sentences such as:

(16) Spanish
Voy   a   estudiar   en   la   biblioteca
go.1SING   PREPOSITION study.INF PREPOSITION the   library
'I go/am going to study in the library'

(17) Spanish
Mañana   voy   a   estudiar   química
tomorrow go.1SING.AUX   PREPOSITION study.INF chemistry
'Tomorrow I am going to study chemistry'

The non-metaphorical meaning of (16) can be mimed by enacting a movement while reading or analysing the sentence, whereas the metaphorical meaning of (17) should be highlighted by not moving at all and attracting learners' attention to the presence of the temporal adverb *mañana* ('tomorrow').

After having presented Spanish sentence pairs such as these, the teacher can write Italian sentences that do not construct tempo-aspectual meanings such as:

(18) Italian
Vado   a   lavorare
go.1SING   PREPOSITION work.INF
'I go/am going to work'

(19) Italian
Fra   un   anno   vado   a   lavorare
PREPOSITION   one   year   go.1SING   PREPOSITION work.INF
a   Roma
PREPOSITION   Rome
'In one year I will go to work in Rome'

In both cases the instructor will mime a movement, attracting students' attention to the physical displacement value of the verbs and to their non-metaphorical behaviour, unlike in Spanish.

Another set of activities aimed at clarifying the cognitive mechanisms that rule students' L1 are virtual embodied principles, i.e. the use of drawings and/ or schemas to better cognize the cognitive principles essential to a language item. Csăbi (2004), Holme (2010), Tyler (2008) and Tyler, Mueller, and Ho (2011) have demonstrated the positive outcome of this kind of activity in learning English phrasal verbs, motion verbs and prepositions.

With SLI, the teacher can show students drawings such as those in Figure 3. S/he can draw students' attention to the fact that these Italian analytical structures serve to construct only physical meanings (as in pictures 3 and 4), while in Spanish they are used to also convey temporal meanings. Drawings of future temporal displacement similar to pictures 1 and 2 in Figure 3 can be given as practice, asking learners to translate or describe them in Italian without resorting to any PFP- or IP- based patterns.

Figure 3: Drawings to be shown to SLI[8]

6.2 Interactional moves

CL-inspired pedagogy emphasises the idea that learning should be participative, stressing the fact that both students and teachers are part of a constant dialogic

---

8 Translation of Figure 3: Scene 1 (from Spanish): "What are we going to do tomorrow?". Scene 2 (from Spanish): Boy: "When are we going to see each other again?" // Girl: "I will call you very soon". Scene 3 (from Italian): written on the two houses, respectively in foreground and background: "house" // "library" // Boy: "I go to study in the library". Scene 4: written on the two houses, respectively in foreground and background: "bar" // "office". Boy: "I go back to work in the office".

process where meanings and cognitive mechanisms are discovered "together" (Holme 2004: 226–227). We therefore consider a planned interactional strategy to be fruitful for our aims. Let us consider the interactional sequence below, quoted from two dialogues between the author and two SLI:

(20) S: *Per fare questo esercizio *devo tornare a leggere il paragrafo?*
      T: *Dove devi tornare, Alma?*
      [faking misunderstanding]
      S: *Come, dove... devo tornare? Il paragrafo...*
      [student's uptake: disorientation]
      T: *Devo rileggere il paragrafo?*
      [recast of student's utterance]
      S: *Sì, già, non tornare ma rileggere, leggere ancora...*
      [student's positive uptake]
      T: *Ok... Sì, devi rileggere il paragrafo, Alma.*
      S: *To do this exercise, do I have to go back and read this paragraph?
      T: Where do you have to go back to, Alma?
      S: How, where... where do I have to go back? The paragraph...
      T: Do I have to re-read the paragraph?
      S: Ah yes, not to go back to read but re-read, to read again...
      T: Ok... Yes, you have to read the paragraph again, Alma.'

By momentarily blocking a communicative event felt as natural and well-constructed by the learner, the teacher triggers the noticing, i.e. the attentive and conscious registration (Schmidt 1995) that the IP-based pattern used is incorrect. In cognitive terms the teacher does not enter the metaphorical field erroneously created by the learner but rejects the time-space mapping.

The second interactional move we suggest is meant to repair students' errors by giving them positive evidence of the structures that should be used. As Ellis (2010) points out, the effectiveness of recast, a less intrusive and non-metalinguistic corrective feedback technique, is strongly dependent on different variables such as the linguistic item to be corrected and learners' effective engagement with the corrections. Recasts have proven to be effective in real conversational events and are useful in drawing the students' attention to errors, especially when these arise in meaningful teacher-student interactions. We suggest that recasts are useful for our aims especially after having provided SLI with the negative evidence that the transfer of PFP and IP to Italian is incorrect. The communicative gap created by the teacher is the negative evidence that the input alone fails to give: after this first move, students are ready to be corrected and to receive teachers' positive evidence.

6.3 Input manipulation

Written input can be manipulated via input enhancement techniques (Wong 2005) such as input flood or visual input enhancement. Students can be given texts where planned future and iterative values occur very frequently, and where the recourse to non-PFP- and IP-based patterns is highlighted by textual manipulations. SLI's attention should therefore be overtly drawn to the linguistic means used by Italians to express such meanings, hopefully pushing them to draw cross-linguistic comparisons between Spanish and Italian. This can be exemplified by the following short text, which focuses on the iterative aspect:

Le strane abitudini del signor Rossi

Franco Rossi è un ingegnere che ha delle strane abitudini: fa sempre tutto due volte.

La mattina si alza, torna a letto e poi si __ri__alza ancora. Poi prepara il caffè per tutta la famiglia ma, subito dopo, lo __ri__prepara, un'altra volta! Poi va al lavoro, entra in ufficio, esce e __ri__entra ancora.

La sera, finalmente, torna a casa, saluta i figli, li __ri__saluta e poi bacia e __ri__bacia Anna, sua moglie.[9]

This text can be used with beginner SLI students: their attention should be drawn to the affix *ri-* and its iterative value. A simple comparison between the two languages can be made by asking students, once they have understood the meaning of *ri-*, how they would translate these verbs into Spanish, focusing on the fact that Spanish, contrary to Italian, makes use of IP.

7 Conclusions

In this study, an attempt was made to analyse and explain the transfer of partially-filled-in constructions from Spanish to Italian. We focused on PFP, for

---

9 Translation: "The strange habits of Mr. Rossi. Franco Rossi is an engineer who has strange habits: he makes everything twice. In the morning, he gets up, goes back to bed and then he gets up again. Then he prepares coffee for the entire family but, immediately after, he prepares it once more! Then he goes to work, enters his office, goes out and enters once again. In the evening, finally, he comes back home, greets his children, greets them once again and then kisses and kisses again Anna, his wife".

planned future meanings, and IP, constructing iterative values. The results of our study are in line with our hypothesis: the transfer of these two Spanish constructions is to be found equally in SLI with long and short input exposure. The motivation for this hypothesis lies in the failure of L2 input to provide the negative evidence needed to help SLI unlearn the recourse to L1 analytic structures to construct such meanings.

Although it comes from a small sample of informants, our data is indeed consistent with our hypothesis: neither instruction (although not focused on this phenomenon) nor input exposure are on their own sufficient, and teacher intervention is necessary to provide SLI with the negative evidence needed to align their interlanguage to native Italian in these domains.

In line with CL-inspired pedagogy, we suggested three kinds of teaching intervention that can be useful to this end: transcodification activities, interactional moves and input manipulation.

Our study focuses solely on Spanish and Italian, but we believe that similar constructional transfer phenomena can be detected within other closely-related language pairs. Studies on the acquisition of Italian by French speakers have also reported frequent transfer phenomena of the [*aller* + infinitive ('go' + infinitive)] construction, also expressing planned future meanings (Jamet 2009; Talé 2013). Furthermore, Dutch stative verbs such as *blijven* ('stay') and motion verbs such as *gaan* ('go') are grammaticalized by means of tempo-spatial metaphors into auxiliaries in aspectual periphrases such as (1) [*blijven* + infinitive] for the continuative aspect and (2) [*gaan* + object + infinitive] for the planned future (Lemmens 2002), something which does not happen in German, a closely-related language in the Germanic family. Similar constructional transfer issues might be found among Dutch-speaking learners of German, although we are not aware of work on this subject.

In conclusion, Littlemore (2011: 49–51) stresses the fact that L2 learners tend to avoid using the metaphorical meanings of words, preferring the use of their literal values, probably because learners fail to notice the metaphorical senses in the input or because "they lack the confidence to use them correctly" (Littlemore 2011: 94). We argue that, alongside the cases where the metaphorical values of certain L2 constructions have to be learned, there are other cases where recourse to L1 metaphors needs to be unlearned. Much attention has been allocated to the former case but less research and fewer pedagogical proposals have been devoted to the latter. Future directions of research could therefore focus on this, in order to evaluate if the claims made by the present paper are consistent with data from other language pairs.

References

Aaron, Jessi. 2006. Me voy a tener que ir yendo: A corpus-based study of the grammaticization of the *ir a* + infinitive construction in Spanish. In Nuria Sagarra & Jacqueline Toribio (eds.), *Selected proceedings of the 9th Hispanic linguistic symposium*, 263–272. Somerville: Cascadilla Proceedings Project.

Amenta, Luisa & Erling Strudsholm. 2002. Andare a + infinito in italiano. Parametri di variazione sincronici e diacronici. *Cuadernos de Filología Italiana* 9. 11–29.

Andersen, Roger. 1983. Transfer to somewhere. In Susan Gass & Larry Selinker (eds.), *Language transfer in language learning*, 177–201. Rowley: Newbury House.

Bailini, Sonia. 2012. La interlingua de lenguas afines: rasgos distintivos y perspectivas teóricas. *RSEI Revista de la sociedad española de italianistas* 16. 271–286.

Bertinetto, Pier Marco. 1991. Il verbo. In Luciano Renzi & Giampaolo Salvi (eds.), *Grande grammatica italiana di consultazione*, 13–162. Bologna: Il Mulino.

Blas Arroyo, José. 2008. The variable expression of future tense in Peninsular Spanish: The present (and the future) of inflectional forms in the Spanish of a bilingual region. *Language Variation and Change* 20. 85–126.

Boas, Hans. 2010. Comparing constructions across languages. In Hans Boas (ed.), *Contrastive studies in construction grammar*, 1–20. Amsterdam: John Benjamins.

Brems, Lieselotte. 2011. *The layering of size noun and type noun constructions in English*. Berlin & New York: Mouton de Gruyter.

Carrera Díaz, Manuel. 2007. Spagnolo e italiano: da una lingua all'altra. In Chiara Preite, Luciana Soliman & Sara Vecchiato (eds.), *Esempi di multilinguismo in Europa. Inglese lingua franca e italiano lingua straniera. La contrastività nella codificazione linguistica*, 249–260. Milan: Egea.

Csábi, Szilvia. 2004. A cognitive linguistic view of polysemy in English and its implications for teaching. In Michel Achard & Susanne Niemeier (eds.), *Cognitive linguistics: Second language acquisition and foreign language teaching*, 233–256. Berlin & New York: Mouton de Gruyter.

Dal Negro, Silvia & Alessandro Vietti. 2006. The interplay of dialect and the standard in anonymous street dialogues. Patterns of variation in northern Italy. *Language Variation and Change* 18. 179–192.

De Benedetti, Alessandro. 2006. Liscio come l'aceite. Errori di interferenza (e non) nell'apprendimento dell'italiano L2 in parlanti ispanofoni. In Franca Bosc, Carla Marello, Stefania Mosca (eds.), *Saperi per insegnare*, 205–217. Torino: Loescher.

De Knop, Sabine & Julien Perrez. 2014. Conceptual metaphors as a tool for the efficient teaching of Dutch and German posture verbs. *Review of Cognitive Linguistics* 12(1). 1–29.

De Rycker, Teun & Sabine De Knop. 2009. Integrating cognitive linguistics and foreign language teaching – historical background and new developments. *Journal of Modern Languages* 1. 29–46.

Della Putta, Paolo. 2015. Discouraging constructional negative transfer: Theoretical aspects and classroom activities for Spanish-speaking students of L2 Italian. In Kyoko Masuda, Carlee Arnett and Angela Labarca (eds.), *Cognitive linguistics and sociocultural theory. Applications for second and foreign language teaching*, 25–50. Berlin & New York: Mouton de Gruyter.

Ellis, Rod. 2010. A framework for investigating oral and written corrective feedback. *Studies in Second Language Acquisition* 32. 335–349.

Flett, Susanna, Holly Branigan & Martin Pickering. 2013. Are non-native structural preferences affected by native language preferences? *Bilingualism: Language and Cognition* 16(4). 751–760.

Ferrario, Gloria. 2013. L'italiano degli immigrati ispanofoni. L'influenza della lingua 1 nell'apprendimento di lingue affini. *Italiano LinguaDue* 5(1). 314–340.

Gabriele, Alison. 2009. Transfer and transition in the SLA of aspect: a bidirectional study of learners of English and Japanese. *Studies in Second Language Acquisition* 31. 371–402.

García-Miguel, José. 2005. Verbos aspectuales en Español. La interacción de significado verbal y sognificado aspectual. In María Rio-Torto, Olívia Figueiredo & Fátima Silva (eds.), *Estudos em homenagem ao Professor Doutor Mário Vilela*, 405–418. Porto: Facultades de Letras da Universidade de Porto.

Gass, Susan & Alison Mackey. 2002. Frequency effects and second language acquisition. *Studies in Second Language Acquisition* 24. 249–260.

Goldberg, Adele. 2003. Constructions: A new theoretical approach to language. *Trends in Cognitive Sciences* 7(5). 219–224.

Green, John. 2009. Romance languages. In Bernard Comrie (ed.), *The world's major languages*, 2nd edn., 164–170. London & New York: Routledge.

Gries, Stefan & Stefanie Wulff. 2005. Do foreign language learners also have constructions? Evidence from priming, sorting, and corpora. *Annual Review of Cognitive Linguistics* 3. 182–200.

Holme, Randal. 2004. *Mind, metaphors and language teaching*. Basingstoke: Palgrave.

Holme, Randal. 2010. Construction grammars. Towards a pedagogical model. *AILA Review* 23. 115–133.

Holme, Randal. 2012. Cognitive linguistics and the second language class. *TESOL Quarterly* 46(1). 6–29.

Inegaki, Shunji. 2001. Motion verbs with goal PPs in the L2 acquisition of English and Japanese. *Studies in Second Language Acquisition* 23. 153–170.

Jamet, Marie-Cristine. 2009. Contact entre langues apparentées: les transfert négatifs et positifs d'apprenants italophones en français. *Synergies Italie* 5. 49–59.

Jarvis, Scott. 2012. The detection-based approach: An overview. In Scott Jarvis & Scott Crosley (eds.), *Approaching language transfer through text classification*, 1–34. Bristol: Multilingual matters

Jarvis, Scott & Anita Pavlenko. 2008. *Crosslinguistic influence in language and cognition*. New York: Routledge.

Kellerman, Eric. 1983. Now you see it, now you don't. In Susan Gass & Larry Selinker (eds.), *Language transfer in language learning*, 112–134. Rowley: Newbury House.

Lakoff, George & Mark Johnson. 1980. *Metaphors we live by*. Chicago: University of Chicago Press.

Landone, Elena. 2001. Consciousness raising e la traduzione per unità lessicali. In Antonella Cancellier & Renata Londiero (eds.), *Italiano e spagnolo a contatto, Atti del XIX convegno dell'A.I.S.P I.*, 141–150. Padova: Unipress.

Larrañaga, Pilar, Jeanine Treffers-Daller, Francois Tidball & Mari Gil Ortega. 2012. L1 transfer in the acquisition of manner in Spanish by native speakers of English. *International Journal of Bilingualism* 16(1). 117–138.

Lefebvre, Claire, Lydia White & Christine Jordan. 2006. Introduction. In Claire Lefebvre, Lydia White & Christine Jordan (eds.), *L2 acquisition and creole genesis*, 1–14. Amsterdam & Philadelphia: John Benjamins.

Lemmens, Maarten. 2002. The semantic network of Dutch posture verbs. In John Newman (ed.), *The linguistics of sitting, standing and lying*, 103–139. Amsterdam & Philadelphia: John Benjamins.

Lindstromberg, Seth & Frank Boers. 2005. From movement to metaphor with manner-of-movement verbs. *Applied Linguistics* 26. 241–261.

Littlemore, Jeanette. 2011. *Applying Cognitive Linguistics to second language learning and teaching*. Basingstoke: Palgrave Macmillan.

Lysinger, Diana. 2015. The case for hidden meaning: An application of Cognitive Linguistics in the Russian classroom. In Kyoko Masuda, Carlee Arnett and Angela Labarca (eds.), *Cognitive linguistics and sociocultural theory. Applications for second and foreign language teaching*, 233–258. Berlin & New York: Mouton de Gruyter.

Maiden, Martin & Cecilia Robustelli. 2000. *A reference grammar of Modern Italian*. London: Arnold.

Morgana, Silvia & Anna Zaffaroni. 2010. L'insegnamento dell'italiano L2 a ispanofoni. Aspetti e proposte didattiche. In Maria Vittoria Calvi, Giovanna Mapelli & Milin Bonomi (eds.), *Lingua, identità e immigrazione*, 191–208. Milan: Franco Angeli.

Odlin, Terence. 1989. *Language transfer: Cross-linguistic influence in language learning*. Cambridge: Cambridge University Press.

Odlin, Terence. 2008. Conceptual transfer and meaning extension. In Peter Robinson & Nick Ellis (eds.), *Handbook of cognitive linguistics and second language acquisition*, 306–340. New York: Routledge.

Olbertz, Hella. 1998. *Verbal periphrases in a functional grammar of Spanish*. Berlin & New York: Mouton de Gruyter.

Ringbom, Håkan. 2007. *The importance of cross-linguistic similarity in foreign language learning: Comprehension, learning and production*. Clevedon: Multilingual Matters.

Rosemeyer, Malte. In press. The development of iterative verbal periphrases in Romance. To appear in *Linguistics*.

Ruiz de Mendoza Ibáñes, Francisco. 2008. Cross-linguistic analysis, second language teaching and cognitive semantics: The case of Spanish diminutives and reflexive constructions. In Sabine De Knop & Teun De Ryker (eds.), *Cognitive approaches to pedagogical grammar: A volume in honour or René Dirven*, 37–66. Berlin & New York: Mouton de Gruyter.

Salamoura, Angeliki & John Williams. 2007. Processing verb argument structure across languages: Evidence for shared representations in the bilingual lexicon. *Applied Psycholinguistics* 28, 627–660.

Schmid, Stephan. 1994. *L'italiano degli spagnoli*. Milan: Franco Angeli.

Schmidt, Richard. 1995. Consciousness and foreign language learning: A tutorial on the role of attention and awareness in learning. In Richard Schmidt (ed.), *Attention and awareness in foreign language learning*, 1–63. Honolulu: University of Hawai'i.

Schwartz, Bonnie Dale. 1998. The second language instinct. *Lingua* 106. 133–160

Talé, Gilles Kuitche. 2013. Variazione diatopica del francese e didattica dell'italiano L2: i transfer negativi degli apprendenti camerunensi nell'italiano. *Italiano LinguaDue* 2. 79–95.

Tyler, Andrea. 2008. Cognitive linguistics and second language instruction. In Peter Robinson & Nick Ellis (eds.), *Handbook of cognitive linguistics and second language acquisition*, 456–488. New York: Routledge.

Tyler, Andrea, Charles Mueller & Vu Ho. 2011. Applying cognitive linguistics to learning the semantics of English *to*, *for* and *at* : An experimental investigation. *VIAL* 8. 181–205.

Valentini, Ada. 2007. La perifrasi andare a + infinito nell'italiano contemporaneo. *Studi Italiani di Linguistica Teorica e Applicata* XXXVI(2). 215–234.

Vietti, Alessandro. 2005. *Come gli immigrati cambiano l'italiano*. Milano: Franco Angeli.

Violi, Patrizia. 2012. How our bodies become us: Embodiment, semiosis and intersubjectivity. *Journal of Cognitive Semiotics* IV(1). 57–75.

Weger, Ullrich & Jay Pratt. 2008. Time flies like an arrow: Space-time compatibility effects suggest a mental timeline. *Psychonomic Bullettin & Review* 15(2). 426–430.

White, Lidia. 1991. Argument structure in second language acquisition. *French Language Studies* 1. 189–207.

Wong, Wynne. 2005. *Input enhancement*. Boston: McGraw-Hill.

Yin, Bin & Elsi Kaiser. 2011. Chinese speakers' acquisition of telicity in English. In Gisela Granena, Joel Koeth, Sunyoung Lee-Ellis, Anna Lukyanchenko, Goretti Prieto Botana & Elizabeth Rhoades (eds.), *Selected proceedings of the 2010 second language research forum: Reconsidering SLA research, dimensions and directions*, 182–198. Sommerville: Cascadilla Proceedings Project.

Zurlo, Francesco. 2009. Fenomeni d'interferenza nell'apprendimento dell'italiano da parte di parlanti spagnolo. *Italiano LinguaDue* 1.

IV **Constructing a constructicon for L2 learners**

Bert Cappelle and Natalia Grabar
Towards an n-grammar of English

Abstract: In this chapter, it is shown how we can develop a new type of learner's or student's grammar based on n-grams (sequences of 2 or 3, 4, etc. items) automatically extracted from a large corpus, such as the Corpus of Contemporary American English (COCA). The notion of n-gram and its primary role in statistical language modelling is first discussed. The part-of-speech (POS) tagging provided for lexical n-grams in COCA is then demonstrated to be useful for the identification of frequent structural strings in the corpus. We propose using the hundred most frequent POS-based 5-grams as the content around which an 'n-grammar' of English can be constructed. We counter some obvious objections to this approach (e.g. that these patterns only scratch the surface, or that they display much overlap among them) and describe extra features for this grammar, relating to the patterns' productivity, corpus dispersion, functional description and practice potential.

Keywords: ESL/EFL; POS n-grams; frequency; construct-i-con; grammar teaching

1 Introduction: Words, words, words, but where's the grammar?

Linguists these days are being spoiled with increasingly large corpora. There is for instance Oxford University's popular British National Corpus (BNC), which contains 100 million words and which is freely available from Mark Davies's website, among other online services.[1] Davies's bigger and more up-to-date Corpus of Contemporary American English (COCA) contains 450 million words (Davies 2008-) and his more recently added Global Web-Based English (GloWbE) allows us to search through 1.9 billion words (Davies 2013). This web corpus is now dwarfed by others, such as ENCOW14, which contains almost 17 billion tokens.[2] And then there is the biggest 'corpus' of all, the indexable part of the World Wide Web itself, which as long ago as June 2006 was estimated to contain 14.3 billion web pages and to increase in size by 280 million web pages a day (De

---

[1] http://corpus.byu.edu/, last accessed on 2 February 2015.
[2] http://corporafromtheweb.org/encow14/#more-72, last accessed on 28 February 2015.

Kunder 2006). Whether we use a search engine such as Google or query a comparatively much smaller but still very large corpus designed for linguistic research, what we have at our finger tips in each case is a venerable treasure trove of data about real language use.

The availability of frequency-based word lists compiled from such large corpora of varied texts (e.g. Davies and Gardner 2010) may be of great benefit to practitioners in the field of teaching English as a second or foreign language (ESL/EFL). And indeed, for several decades, corpora have already served as a valuable aid in developing vocabulary teaching materials (see, e.g., McCarthy and O'Dell 2001 for a well-known product). Corpus-based vocabulary teaching prevents certain 'pet' expressions in ESL/EFL, such as *raining cats and dogs*, from being taught too vigorously, and common but less favorite ones, such as *right up your* (or *his*, *her*, etc.) *alley*, from being ignored altogether.

In sharp contrast to the teaching of lexis, grammar teaching does not involve much attention to frequency and focuses instead on, for example, how to construct interrogative or passive structures from canonical (declarative, active) ones. Very often, though, grammar is not even taught that explicitly, since this is felt to go against the prevailing functionally-oriented approach to language learning. It is our impression that when grammar is taught at all, explicitly or in task-based learning settings, the sequence and selection of grammar patterns is mostly a matter of convention and convenience.

Lexis and grammar, as we shall have the opportunity to see, are two sides of the same coin, in that concrete lexical items (words and collocations) belong to more abstract categories (word classes and phrasal structures). One might therefore assume that teaching specific words and expressions automatically results in teaching rules of grammar. Moreover, as there are patterns which combine concrete and more abstract pieces, a distinction between lexis and grammar is often claimed to be illusionary (cf. Ellis and Cadierno 2009). Nevertheless, abstract structures also have an existence which is not wholly reducible to the collocations and idioms that they represent. This is because grammar patterns are generalizations not just over idioms but over lexically rather mundane combinations as well. For instance, the passive construction is not 'just' used in expressions such as *to be cast in stone* or *to be caught between a rock and a hard place*. It is a structure which can be applied productively and it should therefore be taught as such. So, since abstract phrasal constructions do not only underlie frequently used lexical sequences but also provide blue-prints for creative combinations, they need to be focused on in their own right. A purely lexical approach cannot suffice in language teaching.

Most importantly, we need to know which abstract structures are most frequent in the language, because as it is, ESL/EFL is still in dire need of a reliable, ordered inventory of the most frequently used grammatical patterns in English. Material developers would much appreciate linguists to provide them with a list of common grammar structures for active mastery, to be distinguished from less common patterns that learners can acquire more incidentally. This is, in any case, what the first author of this paper has heard first-hand from an educational advisor for Flemish secondary school teachers (Johan Delbaere, personal communication). The result of this lack of an objective standard of frequent patterns is that constructions that are typically taught may not actually be that frequent and, conversely, that frequent constructions may go unnoticed by material developers. The aim of this paper, therefore, is to show that we can exploit corpus data not just to identify frequent lexical items and lexical patterns of co-occurrence but also to find frequent grammar patterns. That is, just as lexicographers have been successful in detecting common words and collocations, grammarians should really start using corpora to find the most common structural patterns in a language.

To be fair, some existing grammars do take corpus frequencies into account. A prime example is the *Longman Grammar of Spoken and Written English* (Biber et al. 1999), which is entirely corpus-based and provides detailed frequency information (across registers), as well as the *Longman Student Grammar of Spoken and Written English* (Biber, Conrad, and Leech 2002), which is based on the latter. Another example of a corpus-based grammar is Cobuild's two-volume *Grammar Patterns* (Francis, Hunston, and Manning 1996, 1998), whose lexicogrammatical approach, outlined in Hunston and Francis (2000), is heavily influenced by work by Halliday and Sinclair (e.g. Halliday 1978; Sinclair 1991). Other early studies that comment on frequency of use are referenced in Celce-Murcia and Larsen-Freeman (1999). However, despite these valuable works, linguists so far have not yet produced any *ranking* of frequent grammar patterns for the benefit of EFL/ESL teachers, students and material developers.

We will show that this can be achieved by using *n-grams* – continuous sequences of *n* (i.e. any specified number of) items. Our demonstration will be restricted to n-grams extracted from the COCA corpus. This is entirely for practical reasons, as will become clear.[3] We believe that common lexical and grammatical n-grams are constructions, in a Construction Grammar sense: they are form-

---

[3] Apart from COCA, there are other corpora which allow n-gram-based grammar studies. For instance, as shown in Cappelle (2014), using Google's *Ngram Viewer* (Michel et al. 2010), we can exploit the n-grams extractable from Google Books for (diachronic) research into grammar patterns, since this corpus has been tagged and allows part-of-speech searches (Lin et al. 2012). The COW corpora also provide n-gram data sets (http://hpsg.fu-berlin.de/cow/ngrams/, last accessed on 28 February 2015).

function pairings which native speakers have memorized (and which learners of a language should acquire) as a result of their high frequency. For Construction Grammarians, frequency is only one of the criteria to identify constructions, another possible criterion being the unpredictable nature of the link between a unit's form and its function (e.g. Goldberg 2006). Yet, a great number, perhaps even a majority, of Construction Grammarians these days seem to take a usage-based approach to the study of patterns, which means that they consider a unit as a construction as soon as it has sufficient frequency (as evidenced by corpus data), regardless of whether or not that unit displays any sort of arbitrariness in the way its form links up with its function. This is also the approach taken here. We are less concerned with the potential unpredictability of a pattern's form or function than with its high frequency.

The structure of our paper is as follows. In Section 2, we will introduce the concept of n-grams. In Section 3 we will propose an application of n-grams to English language learning. Section 4 is devoted to some possible criticisms that could be levelled at this approach and to our rebuttal of them. Section 5 presents some further features of an envisaged n-gram-based grammar, or 'n-grammar', of English, which is a project-in-progress. Our conclusions can be found in Section 6.

2 What are n-grams, and what are they typically used for?

N-grams are sequences of n items, where *n* stands for any natural number (1, 2, 3, 4, etc.) of linguistic units. For example, the word string *the fool on the hill* contains five 1-grams (usually called 'unigrams'), namely *the*, *fool*, *on*, *the* and *hill*, four 2-grams (or 'bigrams'), namely *the fool*, *fool on*, *on the* and *the hill*, three 3-grams (or 'trigrams'), namely *the fool on*, *fool on the* and *on the hill*, two 4-grams, namely *the fool on the* and *fool on the hill*, and also one 5-gram, namely the string *the fool on the hill* itself. There are not just word-based n-grams but also character-based n-grams. Thus, the letter sequence *chat* consists of four unigrams (*c*, *h*, *a* and *t*), three bigrams (*ch*, *ha* and *at*), two trigrams (*cha* and *hat*) and one 4-gram (*chat*). The items in question that an n-gram has *n* adjacent instances of could be of any category. For instance, in Section 3, we will make use of n-grams whose items are word classes (determiner, noun, verb, etc.).

N-grams can be automatically extracted from spoken and/or written corpora and primarily play a role in computational linguistics, where they are used for statistical language modelling. By 'language model', computational linguists understand a set of probabilities (P's) which reflect, as accurately as possible, real language use. As Jurafsky (2012) puts it, "[i]t might have been better to call this 'the grammar'. I mean, technically, what this is, is telling us something about how [well] [...] words fit together, and we normally use the word 'grammar' for that, but it turns out that the word 'language model' [...] is standard". Based on n-grams extracted from a large corpus, a language model may compute the likelihood of an entire string of n items ('joint probability') and/or the likelihood of a single upcoming item given n-1 previous items ('conditional probability'). Estimates of these probabilities generated by an n-gram-based language model are used in a variety of practical applications. Table 1 gives some examples, drawn from Jurafsky (2012).

Table 1: Some applications of an n-gram-based probabilistic language model (based on Jurafsky 2012)

Application	Task	Example
Machine translation	Distinguishing between 'good' and 'bad' translations by their probabilities	*High winds tonight* may be a better translation than *large winds tonight*, based on: P(*high* winds tonight) > P(*large* winds tonight)
Spell correction	Detecting likely mistakes based on the probabilities of word sequences	*The office is about fifteen minuets from my house* likely contains a misspelling from *minutes*, based on: P(about fifteen *minutes* from) > P(about fifteen *minuets* from)
Speech recognition	Deciding between two sequences that sound phonetically similar by comparing their probabilities	*I saw a van* is likely to be a more accurate transcription than *eyes awe of an*, based on: P(*I saw a van*) >> P(*eyes awe of an*)

There are many other everyday applications. Word-based and character-based n-grams underlie features such as word suggestion and word completion available on search engines and on our smartphones' text messaging function.

While extracting n-grams from corpora is a common method of identifying recurrent formulae in discourse, other types of sequences are sometimes used apart from n-grams, such as so-called p(hrase)-frames (Römer 2010) and skip-grams (Guthrie et al. 2006). Word-based n-grams have also been referred to as "lexical bundles" (Biber, Conrad, and Cortes 2004; Hyland 2008; Chen and Baker 2010).

3 Using COCA n-grams for a new kind of grammar

3.1 The problem of ubiquitous constructions

Finding out what the most frequently used constructions are in a short text may sound like an easy enough task. In fact, it is not. To begin with, we would have to decide on an appropriate definition of 'construction'. Secondly, suppose that we adopt a quite open definition of 'construction', as is common in Construction Grammar (e.g. Goldberg 2006), and count as construction every learned form-function pairing, ranging from individual words and morphemes to larger syntactic structures, it would then be hard not to overlook any of them, as any single sentence typically may contain one or several dozen constructions. This will become clear if we consider an example taken from Goldberg (2003):

(1) *What did Liza buy the child?*

This short sentence contains all of the following constructions:

(2) a. the *buy, child, did, Lisa, the* and *what* constructions (i.e. words)

    b. the Ditransitive construction (i.e. double-object construction)

    c. the Question construction (which is a fairly abstract construction, involving a certain intonation contour)

    d. the Subject-Auxiliary Inversion construction (which is not only used in questions)

    e. the VP construction

    f. three cases of the NP construction (namely, *What, Liza* and *the child*)

For the time being, it is technically very hard, if not impossible, to detect and tally all these kinds of constructions automatically, which is what would be required if we wanted to count constructions in a whole corpus.

    We propose to bypass the problem of scripting such a construction-detecting program by relying on readily available part-of-speech (POS) n-grams, which we will treat as constructions (or major parts thereof). This decision, of course, needs proper justification, which we will attempt to give in Section 4.1. At present, we are focusing on describing the methodology used.

3.2 The general idea

Via the website www.ngrams.info, one can download free lists of the most frequent 2-, 3-, 4- and 5-grams from COCA. Each list contains about 1,000,000 lexical n-grams. The lists are ordered from the most frequent to the least frequent n-grams. Table 2 gives some examples from the top of each list.

Table 2: N-grams from COCA, with some of the highest-frequency examples

N-grams	Examples
2-grams	*of the, is a, going to, I think,* ...
3-grams	*one of the, a lot of, the United States, as well as,* ...
4-grams	*I do-n't know, for the first time, on the other hand,* ...
5-grams	*I do-n't think so, the rest of the world, by the end of the,* ...

Observe, by the way, that the contracted negator (*-n't*) is treated as a separate word by the tagger.

Via the website mentioned above, it is also possible to download lists of n-grams where part-of-speech tags are presented together with the actual words making up each n-gram. What we claim here is that one can exploit this information to find common grammar structures in the corpus (and hence, to the extent that COCA is a representative corpus, in a major variety of the English language). For the purposes of illustration, Figure 1 shows the top section of the list of 4-grams containing part-of-speech information.

The left-most column gives us the number of occurrences ('tokens') of the lexical n-gram ('type') in question in COCA. Thus, *I don't know* is the most frequent 4-gram in COCA, occurring 54,632 times in the corpus, followed by *I don't think*, with 43,760 occurrences.

The four columns to the right contain the part-of-speech information, based on the CLAWS 7 tagset.[4] Thus, the tag *ppis1* stands for 'singular personal pronoun, first person, subjective case' (i.e. the word *I*), *vd0* for '*do* as a finite form (in declarative and interrogative clauses)', *xx* for '*not*' or its contracted form, and *vvi* for 'the base form of a lexical verb used as an infinitive'. As can be noticed, the first two n-grams have the same part-of-speech tags. They share this part-of-speech tagging with *I don't want*, a little further down the list (see the boxes with dotted lines). Similarly, the 4-grams *the end of the* and *the rest of the* (in 4th and 6th position) share their part-of-speech labelling (see the boxes with full lines). The idea now is to order all these POS 4-grams by their frequency,

---

4 http://ucrel.lancs.ac.uk/claws7tags.html, last accessed on 28 February 2015.

54632	I	do	n't	know	ppis1	vd0	xx	vvi
43760	I	do	n't	think	ppis1	vd0	xx	vvi
33968	in	the	United	States	ii	at	np1	np1
29848	the	end	of	the	at	nn1	io	at
27119	do	n't	want	to	vd0	xx	vvi	to
21537	the	rest	of	the	at	nn1	io	at
19864	at	the	end	of	ii	at	nn1	io
19165	for	the	first	time	if	at	md	nnt1
18632	I	do	n't	want	ppis1	vd0	xx	vvi
18115	at	the	same	time	ii	at	da	nnt1
16809	in	the	middle	of	ii	at	nn1	io
16681	one	of	the	most	mc1	io	at	rgt
16626	of	the	United	States	io	at	np1	np1
15857	is	one	of	the	vbz	mc1	io	at
14392	to	be	able	to	to	vbi	jk	to
...								

Figure 1: Most frequent lexical 4-grams ('types') from COCA, together with their number of corpus occurrences ('tokens') and their part-of-speech tags

that is, by the number of different lexical 4-grams (lexical types) that instantiate them. What this reordering results in is shown in Figure 2.

The most frequent POS 4-gram in COCA is the one instantiated by *at the end of*, *in the middle of* and 6,984 other sequences of a preposition (other than *of*), the definite article, a singular common noun and the preposition *of*. In contrast to the list of lexical 4-grams (Figure 1), this list gives us direct information about what the most common syntactic structures are for 4-word sequences in COCA. We could use such a frequency list as the basis for an n-grammar of English. As an added bonus, we could combine this syntactic information with lexical information about the most common actual 4-grams (see also Section 3.4). Indeed, Construction Grammar assumes that both lexical chunks and the more general patterns they instantiate have their role to play in (first and second) language

6986	ii at nn1 io
5382	nn1 io at nn1
4645	ii at jj nn1
4235	nn1 ii at nn1
4177	at jj nn1 io
3847	at nn1 io at
3609	ii at1 jj nn1
3569	at1 jj nn1 io
3313	to vvi at nn1
3249	at nn1 ii at
3028	ii at nn1 nn1
2848	at nn1 io nn1
2797	ii at nn1 cc
2684	at1 nn1 ii at
2573	at1 jj nn1 ii

...

Figure 2: Most frequently instantiated POS 4-grams in COCA with number of lexical instantiations ('types') for each POS 4-gram

acquisition (cf. Ellis 1996, 2003, 2013; Tomasello 2003; see also Lewis 1993, the papers in Cowie 1998 and Wray 2002, inter alia, on the role of chunks in acquisition). Learners can be said to master a target language all the more accurately the more they manage to use lexical items in their preferred constructional environment (Wulff and Gries 2011).

Rather than using 2-, 3- or, as just demonstrated, 4-grams, we suggest using 5-grams as the basis of our n-grammar of English, which are the longest n-grams available from COCA's n-gram website. Traditional grammars tend to focus on shorter units, but if we want to target intermediate to advanced students, we believe that strings of 5 segments present an adequate size – neither too short, nor too long. While even longer n-grams could in principle have been used, if they had been available from COCA, we do not think such longer strings would have provided many more relevant constructions, since longer strings are likely to be made up of shorter component structures, which we will show to be the case for 5-grams already. Moreover, in those cases in which a 5-gram does not coincide with a complete syntactic phrase, it can still be extended 'by hand' with a phrasal category, something which will also be illustrated below. In short, our choice of using complete or extended 5-grams is thus motivated by the aim to use units that are as long and complete as possible, but which at the same time still allow manipulation and combination to form even larger structures in the language.

3.3 The method in detail

We restrict our selection to the 100 most frequent POS 5-grams based on the COCA list of lexical 5-grams containing part-of-speech information. In an n-gram-based grammar of English, each such pattern could and should be presented together with some of its frequent lexical instantiations, so as to show how the skeletal structures can be fleshed out in actual language use. Why 100 patterns? This is a somewhat arbitrary choice, motivated less by linguistic factors than by reasons related to learner motivation: learners might consider 100 patterns an achievable target. Needless to say, one could also select 200 patterns, 500 patterns, etc., or alternatively 365 patterns, one for each day of the year.

The list of lexical 5-grams with part-of-speech tags that can be downloaded from Mark Davies's website mentioned above (www.ngrams.info) contains exactly 1,293,537 types of lexical strings. The list is cut off at 5-grams with a minimum frequency of 5 occurrences in the corpus (presumably because the list was meant to contain ca. one million types). Remember from Table 2 that this list contains such sequences as *I don't want to* or *the rest of the world*. We grouped these lexical strings according to the syntactic patterns they instantiate (i.e., their part-of-speech tag sequence). We thus obtained a total of 325,552 POS 5-grams. The number of lexical strings ('types') per POS 5-gram varies from 7,272 for *at nn1 io at nn1*, a structure shared by *the rest of the world*, *the side of the road* and thousands more (where *at* stands for *the*, *nn1* for a singular common noun and *io* for *of*), to just 1, for instance in the case of *appge cc appge jjt nn1* for *his or her best interest* (in which *appge* stands for a possessive determiner, *cc* for a coordinating conjunction and *jjt* for a superlative adjective).

We then took the 100 most frequent POS 5-grams as main content for the n-grammar. By 'most frequent' POS 5-grams, we mean those that represent the highest number of types, that is, the highest number of different lexical 5-grams that have the structure specified by them. These patterns (for which we also made the part-of-speech labels more transparent) now range in frequency from still 7,272 types for the sequence [*the* X_{noun} *of the* Y_{noun}] to 499 types for the sequence made up of a complex 3-word preposition followed by *the* and an adjective (e.g. *in front of the whole*).

As is clear from this last example, a 5-gram does not necessarily form a complete constituent, since n-grams are 'blind' to constituent structure. Sometimes, an n-gram does not contain enough (or one might say, it may contain too much) to make up what we would intuitively consider an ordinary linguistic sequence. We therefore added an element to the right in those cases where the right-most boundary of a 5-gram does not coincide with a closing bracket, so to speak. Thus, in the case of the pattern [*at/in/to/… the* X_{noun} *of the*], we just add an element to the right of the determiner. This element could be a noun, but it could also be an adjective which precedes a noun, among other possibilities. Technically, the grammatical category covering all of these is what is called a 'nominal' (nom) in Huddleston, Pullum et al.'s (2002) grammar, or an 'N-bar' (N$^{\prime}$) in X-bar theory (Chomsky 1970; Jackendoff 1977) – that is, a noun phrase minus the determiner. We always completed with a category label that stands for the widest range of possible continuations. Additions are between parentheses in what follows. Table 3 shows the result of the procedure for the ten most common POS 5-grams, along with an example of each.

Table 3: Ten most frequent syntactic (completed) 5-grams in COCA

Syntactic pattern	Example
the X_{noun} *of the* Y_{noun}	*the rest of the world*
at/in/to/… the X_{noun} *of the* (Y_{nom})	*at the end of the (day)*
X_{noun} *at/in/to/… the* Y_{noun} *of* (Z_{NP})	*increase in the number of (students)*
the adj X_{noun} *of the* (Y_{nom})	*the other side of the (room)*
to verb the X_{noun} *of* (Y_{NP})	*to improve the quality of (life)*
at/in/to/… the adj X_{noun} *of* (Y_{NP})	*on the other side of (the room)*
a(n) adj X_{noun} *at/in/to/… the* (Y_{nom})	*a far cry from the (original proposal)*
at/in/to/… the X_{noun} *of one's* (Y_{nom})	*at the top of his (lungs)*
the X_{noun} *of the adj* (Y_{nom})	*the end of the Cold (War)*
at/in/to/… the X_{noun} *at/in/to/… the* (Y_{nom})	*on the way to the (hospital)*

We never added any symbol to the left of the 5-gram, as the left-most symbol always constitutes the first element of a constituent. However, in some cases, a lexical instantiation of a POS n-gram might benefit from one or more added elements at the left. For instance *the benefit of the doubt* is a syntactically complete unit – it is an NP – but it typically occurs in lexically larger environments, involving verbs such as *give*, *get* or *deserve*.

3.4 The medium-level and hybrid nature of the POS n-grams

As the reader will have noticed, the syntactic information associated with the n-grams from COCA consists of quite specific part-of-speech tags. While there are only eight or nine word classes traditionally recognized in English, the CLAWS 7 tagset, which was used for tagging COCA, distinguishes between 137 different categories. For instance, the preposition *of* is treated not as any preposition but as the word *of*, all the forms of the verb *be* are treated differently from each other, singular nouns are treated as different from plural nouns, common nouns as different from proper nouns, and so on. As a result, the POS n-grams are not maximally general, as would have been the case if they were of the type 'Det N Prep Det N'. Nor of course are these POS n-grams maximally specific, which is the case only for purely lexical n-grams such as *the name of the motel*, where each item is an actual word. While it would be possible for us to come up with more general patterns based on the specific part-of-speech tags and to calculate their frequencies, our POS n-grams as they are may in fact come close to having the ideal grain size of a construction: neither too schematic nor too concrete. We do not want to claim here that there are no such things as very general constructions or that some specific lexical strings cannot have the status of stored language units; indeed, a standard assumption of Construction Grammar is that generalizations over exemplars and the (sufficiently frequent) exemplars themselves are stored in the speaker's mind (cf. Section 4.1). Yet, while it is obvious that specific items *have to* be stored if they are formally or semantically unpredictable – storage is required for words and idioms – there is no equally compelling reason why we would need to store the most schematic rules of language. As Croft (1998: 168) formulates it, "[s]peakers do not necessarily make the relevant generalizations, even if clever linguists can".[5]

---

5 In actual fact, Croft's (1998) quoted sentence is lifted from an article that deals more with semantics (polysemy and homonymy) than with the level of generality at which speakers store constructions. However, these issues are not unrelated and lie at the heart of the difference between a Goldbergian (1995) approach to argument structure constructions (i.e. one in which they are treated as highly schematic form-meaning patterns) and a Boas-style (2003) or Iwata-style (2008) approach to them (i.e. one in which so-called 'mini-constructions' or specific lexical constructions are associated with individual verbs or even individual verb senses). See also Levshina and Heylen (2014) for related findings about the optimality of medium-level granularity in the context of semantic classes of predicates governing the choice between competing constructions.

Apart from, or as a corollary of, being somewhat below the maximum level of generality, our POS n-grams are also somewhat hybrid in nature, that is, they are *partially* rather 'syntactic' and *partially* rather 'lexical'. The mixing of levels results purely from the rich, fine-grained tagset that is used for the COCA corpus, but there are computationally more sophisticated methods for automatically generating linguistically 'interesting' n-grams which combine lexical items and formal categories: see Wible and Tsao (2010), Lyngfelt et al. (2012) and Forsberg et al. (2014). Again, by mixing more general and more specific items in a single template, we may approximate the ideal of constructions viewed as language units that actually operate in the mind of speakers. For instance, in our top hundred POS n-grams, we find the following hybrid structures:[6]

(3) a. *the* X_{noun} *of the* Y_{noun} (pattern No. 1), e.g. *the rest of the world*

b. *the* X_{noun} *of a(n)* Y_{noun} (pattern No. 20), e.g. *the son of a bitch*

c. *a(n)* X_{noun} *of the* Y_{noun} (pattern No. 30), e.g. *a thing of the past*

The trained linguist may need some convincing to see that these are distinct patterns and not *just* different realizations of a single more general pattern. But notice, first of all, the difference in frequency. The POS n-gram in (3a), as we noted above, covers 7,272 lexical types (with at least five tokens, i.e. corpus occurrences, each), while the ones in (3b) and (3c) only cover 1,448 and 968 lexical types, respectively. The pattern [*a(n)* X_{noun} *of a(n)* Y_{noun}], with two indefinite articles, does not even rank among the hundred most frequent POS 5-grams. Secondly, while each pattern provides open slots for nouns, they do not allow the same nouns in these slots. For instance, we would not find ?*the son of the bitch*, ??*the thing of the past* or ??*a rest of the world*. This suggests that each pattern has its own particular properties, causing it to attract certain nouns and to repel certain others. We will come back to this in Section 5.3.

Because of a pattern's close association with *some* lexical items and not with others, we feel that it is worthwhile to provide this information to learners. This is fully in line with a constructionist and usage-based approach to language learning, which stresses the importance of exemplars in acquisition (Abott-Smith and Tomasello 2006; Ellis 2006, 2013). So, ideally, an n-grammar should present not just semi-schematic and hybrid patterns but also some of

---

[6] The first segment is not always the determiner *the* but could also be the quantifier *no*, as in *no mention of the fact (that...)*. Because this determiner is used far less frequently than *the*, we use the latter as a transparent substitute for the tag 'at'. A rare example in which the quantifier *no* is used before the second noun is *the point of no return*.

the frequent lexical instantiations that they generalize over. In the case of the pattern [*the* X$_{noun}$ *of the* Y$_{noun}$], this would mean that the learner also gets to see some fully lexical sequences, possibly even with corpus frequencies (number of tokens) added to them, as shown in Table 4.

Table 4: Most frequent lexical realizations of the pattern
[*the* X$_{noun}$ *of the* Y$_{noun}$] in COCA

the rest of the world (3,618)	*the benefit of the doubt* (547)
the side of the road (1,217)	*the edge of the bed* (530)
the rest of the country (1,174)	*the center of the room* (526)
the fact of the matter (825)	*the State of the Union* (495)
the end of the world (764)	*the back of the room* (463)
The fact of the matter (717)	*the back of the head* (450)
the end of the war (670)	*the middle of the room* (448)
the rest of the way (597)	...

Note, incidentally, that *the fact of the matter* appears twice. This is due to the fact that the downloadable lexical n-grams with POS information are case-sensitive, which means that a word with a capital letter and the same word without a capital letter are treated as belonging to different n-grams. This may seem like a nuisance, but it actually provides useful information about where that n-gram is found in the sentence (sentence-initially or not).

4 Possible points of criticism and their rebuttal

We are aware of some immediate objections that one might raise against the approach we take to selecting patterns to be included in a new, radically usage-based grammar. We can think of at least the following four points of criticism:
(i) Not all of these POS 5-grams are constructions.
(ii) There is a lot of (and perhaps too much) overlap between them.
(iii) The top hundred POS 5-grams are but the tip of the iceberg.
(iv) By restricting ourselves to 5-grams, we may miss out on interesting 2-, 3- and 4-grams.

In the following subsections, we will defend our approach against this possible criticism.

4.1 Not all of them constructions?

One might wonder what is so special about, for example, the pattern [*the* X_{noun} *of the* Y_{noun}], which appears to be formed on the basis of some general phrase-structure rules, namely the ones listed in (4), combined with the knowledge that *the* is a determiner and *of* a preposition:

(4) a. NP → det nom

   b. nom → noun (PP)

   c. PP → prep NP

It is true that on Goldberg's (1995: 4) original definition of the term, this first pattern and many (if not most) of the other patterns in our top hundred POS 5-grams would not qualify as constructions. This definition stated that a form-function pairing is a construction only if there is something about its form or function that is not strictly predictable from what is already available in the grammar. However, in Goldberg's (2006: 5) later work, this requirement is loosened: "Any linguistic pattern is recognized as a construction as long as some aspect of its form or function is not strictly predictable from its component parts or from other constructions recognized to exist. *In addition, patterns are stored as constructions even if they are fully predictable as long as they occur with sufficient frequency*" [emphasis ours]. The view that constructions are psychologically entrenched form-function pairs is also expressed by Croft and Cruse (2004: 288), Langacker (2005: 140) and Bybee (2006: 715).

Given their high frequency, which is the basis of their selection in the first place, there is no doubt that all of the hundred POS 5-grams meet this definition of 'construction': even if some of them are compositional, their sheer frequency makes it unlikely that they are formed anew each time they are used. It is much more plausible that these patterns are directly retrieved from what construction grammarians, using a term coined by Jurafsky (1991), call the 'construct-i-con'.

4.2 Too much overlap between them?

It will have been noted that many of the patterns shown in Table 3 look like variations on a theme. That is, they do not all represent fully distinct constructions. For example, the two most frequent POS 5-grams ([*the* X_{noun} *of the* Y_{noun}] and [*at/in/to/... the* X_{noun} *of the* (Y_{nom})]) share four fifths of their component elements (namely '*the* X_{noun} *of the*').

As we see it, however, this overlap is not a problem. On the contrary, it allows us to integrate in this new type of learner's and student's grammar an important feature of language: the possibility of reusing parts of structures over and over again in slightly different environments or with slight modifications. In other words, one of the main properties of language is that it involves structures that are partially reusable and adaptable. This feature can be visualized in chart form, which for each pattern shows its relatedness to some of the other patterns in the grammar. Figure 3 is an example of what such a chart could look like for the first pattern in the n-grammar.

No. 1		the		X_{noun}	of	the		Y_{noun}
No. 2	at/in/to/…	the		X_{noun}	of	the		Y_{nom}
No. 4		the	adj	X_{noun}	of	the		Y_{nom}
No. 9		the		X_{noun}	of	the	adj	Y_{nom}
No. 13		the		X_{noun}	of	one's		Y_{noun}
No. 18		the		X_{noun}	at/in/to/…	the		Y_{noun}
No. 20		the		X_{noun}	of	a		Y_{noun}

Figure 3: 'Chop and change' chart for the first pattern in the n-grammar (top row)

The chart shows how a pattern can be chopped up to allow for the insertion of elements in the right position (e.g. adjectives before nouns) and be changed by replacing elements in a structural position by alternatives in that position (e.g. an indefinite article or a possessive determiner instead of a definite article). As such, this 'chop and change chart' (a term whose rights of use in grammar instruction we hereby reserve) directly represents the syntagmatic and paradigmatic relations between structural elements in the grammar. The overlap between patterns reflects the fact that grammar is a combinatorial system, which operates on classes of discrete string segments such as adjectives or nouns. This is not just how linguists see it, but how the human brain treats grammar (Pulvermüller and Knoblauch 2009; Pulvermüller, Cappelle, and Shtyrov 2013).

The n-grammar proposed here is thus not a maximally parsimonious system to generate word sequences. Instead, it represents structural information in a way that is full of redundancy. This redundancy may be helpful for learners to master the structures: though they could have been captured more economically, this would have been at the expense of a range of learning opportunities spread out through time, which is needed for consolidated acquisition. This is as true for humans as it is for the simplest of organisms. To cite the Nobel prize winning neuroscientist Eric R. Kandel: "Conversion of short-term to long-term memory storage requires spaced repetition – practice makes perfect, even in snails" (Kandel 2001: 1031).

4.3 Just the tip of the iceberg?

Remember that for the n-grammar proposed here, we retained a mere 100 POS 5-grams out of 325,552 such patterns in COCA (themselves generalizing over more than a million lexical 5-grams with at least 5 occurrences each in the corpus). In other words, our top hundred most frequently occurring syntactic templates only represent 0.03% of all possible POS 5-grams based on lexical 5-grams with at least 5 tokens in COCA. Put differently still, our selection does not seem to count for much. Using familiar imagery, if the part of an iceberg that appears above water is only one tenth of its total volume, then our selection does not represent the proverbial tip of the iceberg, and not even the tip of the tip of the tip of the iceberg.

If we disregard POS 5-grams that are instantiated by fewer than 5 different lexical 5-grams ('types'), there are no longer 325,552 POS 5-grams in COCA, but 36,617 of them. Our selection then represents 0.27% of these. This is admittedly still a very small portion, which is barely visible in the left-most stacked bar in Figure 4. However, if we now look at the types represented by these 36,617 POS 5-grams, we find that there is a total number of 823,683 different lexical 5-grams in COCA. Our top hundred POS 5-grams represent a non-negligible portion of these: 105,184 types, which is 12.77% (cf. middle stacked bar in Figure 4). In terms of tokens (individual occurrences), there are 11,248,178 sequences of 5 words corresponding to the 36,617 POS 5-grams. Our top hundred POS 5-grams cover 1,615,199 tokens. This high number represents 14.36% of the total number of tokens for all 36,617 POS 5-grams (cf. the stacked bar on the right in Figure 4). What we find here is something akin to what Zipf (1935) noted for lexical items, namely that the most frequent items (types) cover a large part of the occurrences (tokens) in usage. In the Brown corpus, for instance, half of the word volume is accounted for by only 135 vocabulary items (Fagan and Gençay 2010).

In sum, even our very small set of POS 5-grams (just one hundred out of more than thirty thousand in the corpus) appears to have quite large coverage in terms of number of lexical strings (both the types and their tokens) that correspond to these syntactic templates. It exceeds the percentage of an iceberg that extends above the water surface.

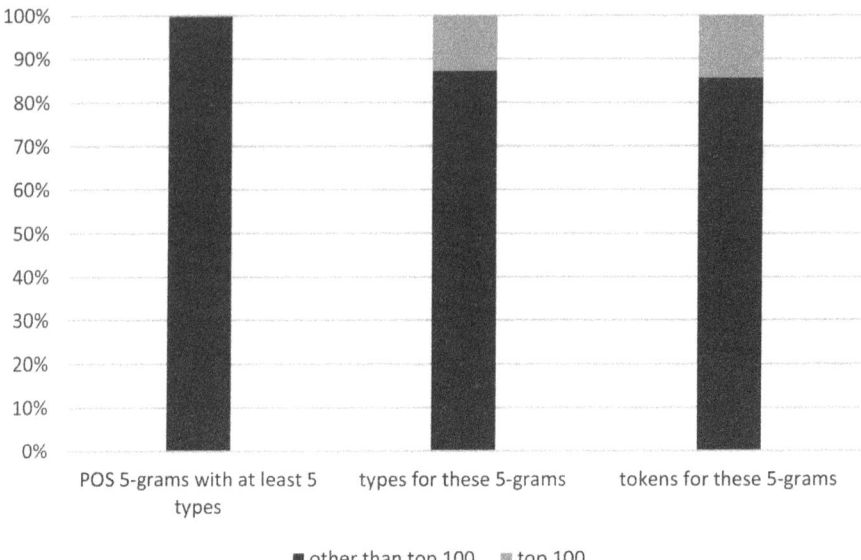

Figure 4: Share of the selected highest-frequency POS 5-grams in COCA and its coverage in terms of types and tokens

4.4 Neglecting important 2-, 3- and 4-grams?

It may seem an odd choice to take 5-grams as our basis for a grammar of English. Even quite apart from the fact that some constructions are longer than five words or may involve discontinuities and hence cannot be captured as 5-grams, there is the risk of overlooking interesting grammar patterns that are shorter than 5 words. For instance, among the top ten most frequently used 2-grams, we found the pattern [X_{noun} $Y_{noun\ plur}$], that is, a noun-noun compound in the plural, such as *family members*, *interest rates*, *phone calls*, *college students*, *side effects*, and several thousands more. Unfortunately, the two-word POS sequence [X_{noun} $Y_{noun\ plur}$] is not a part of any of our top hundred POS 5-grams. Does this example not suggest that we may fail to integrate some vital grammar patterns by focusing on 5-grams only?

While any common lower-n-gram pattern that is not included in any of our 5-gram patterns is surely a missed opportunity to capture all that is essential in grammar, the actual situation does not give reason for too much concern. Table 5 shows that the five highest-frequency POS 2-grams taken together are included 102 times in our selection of POS 5-grams, and that the five highest-frequency POS 3-grams and POS 4-grams are still also included 64 times and 35 times, respectively. (Obviously, shorter sequences have a higher likelihood of being included than longer ones.)

Table 5: Inclusion of high-frequency POS 2-, 3- and 4-grams from COCA in the hundred most frequent POS 5-grams from COCA

N-grams with n < 5	Top 5 most frequent POS n-grams	Number of inclusions in top 100 POS 5-grams
2-grams	1. adj X_{noun}	19
	2. X_{noun} Y_{noun}	3
	3. adj $X_{noun\ plur}$	2
	4. X_{noun} {at/in/to/...}	20
	5. the X_{noun}	58
3-grams	1. {at/in/to/...} the X_{noun}	27
	2. a(n) adj X_{noun}	9
	3. the adj X_{noun}	7
	4. X_{noun} {at/in/to/...} the (X_{nom})	14
	5. {at/in/to/...} an X_{noun}	7
4-grams	1. {at/in/to/...} the X_{noun} of (Y_{NP})	17
	2. X_{noun} of the Y_{noun}	6
	3. {at/in/to/...} the adj X_{noun}	3
	4. X_{noun} {at/in/to/...} the Y_{noun}	6
	5. the adj X_{noun} of (Y_{noun})	3

Clearly, it is not the case that by looking at 5-grams only, we ignore <5-grams. As explained in Section 2, a 5-gram by its very nature simultaneously harbors two 4-grams, three 3-grams and four 2-grams. As a consequence, if we study a hundred 5-grams, we actually get to see a thousand n-grams, not even counting the individual words. This is not to say that we get nine hundred *different* 2-, 3- and 4-grams for free with our 5-grams, as many of these lower-n-grams will be included several times. This is not a problem, in light of our discussion of redundancy and repetition in Section 4.2.[7]

---

[7] To look at this from a somewhat different perspective, we might say that the high frequency of certain 5-grams accounts to some extent for the frequency of some of its included <5-grams. This is what O'Donnell (2011) points out to be the case for lexical n-grams: for instance, at the top of the list of lexical 5-grams in COCA we find *I don't want to*. This occurs 12,659 times in the corpus and thereby contributes in no small way to the high frequency of its multiple component parts (*I*, *do*, *n't*, *want*, *to*, *don't*, *want to*, *I don't want*, etc.). Therefore, by studying high-frequency 5-grams, the learner is given a glimpse into some of the reasons why smaller combinations are so frequent. This is true, we feel, for both n-gram templates of the sort discussed in our text and lexically 'filled-in' n-grams, of the sort O'Donnell (2011) focuses on.

By selecting 5-grams, we automatically retrieve more complex structures. This is why a '5-grammar' of English may be more ideally suited for intermediate to advanced learners of English than for absolute beginners. For lower-level learners, n-grams other than 5-grams (namely, 2-grams, 3-grams and 4-grams) might be a better way to start. In other words, we do not want to claim that using 5-grams is the only valid way of constructing an n-grammar of English.

5 Further features of the n-grammar

5.1 Adding a visual measure of productivity

Pedagogical grammars do not generally contain any statistical information about frequency, unlike modern dictionaries, many of which provide an indication of how common a word is, or in which genre or register it is typically used. Our proposed n-grammar can easily include such information. In Sections 3.2 and 3.4 we already suggested that individual lexical n-grams associated with the more schematic POS n-grams may be shown with their actual corpus frequencies, thus giving the learner some idea of their usefulness as chunks in the target language. We believe that if learners see, for example, that *The fact of the matter* at the beginning of a sentence is used more than 700 times in a corpus of native-speaker English, this kind of knowledge may cause them to take note of this expression more consciously and stimulate them to use it themselves (cf. e.g. Schmidt (1990) and Robinson (2006) on the 'noticing' hypothesis and the role of conscious attention in second language acquisition). But the patterns themselves could also be provided with frequency information. Thus, the most frequent POS 5-gram, [*the* X_{noun} *of the* Y_{noun}], might be stated explicitly to have 7,272 types (with at least 5 tokens each). In addition, we might mention that these types together represent 126,077 tokens in the corpus.

Such figures may not mean much by themselves to the learner. Though such high numbers might of course be impressive and therefore encourage the learner to devote due attention to the pattern, they will vary from corpus to corpus. A more general indication of frequency, similar to what can be found in certain dictionaries (e.g. high-frequency, medium-frequency, low-frequency) could be sufficient, if it were not for the fact that the top hundred most frequent POS 5-grams are naturally all at the high end of the frequency scale anyhow. It would probably be more beneficial to the learner to have a direct visual indication of a pattern's *usefulness*. If by 'useful' we mean how many different lexical realizations the pattern allows the learner to form, we should include a measure of the pattern's productivity. Productivity can be defined in terms of the ratio of types per tokens: the more types per number of tokens, the more productive a pattern is. This is clear if we consider the other extreme case: if all the corpus occurrences of a pattern were instances of only one lexical string, that 'pattern' would have no productivity at all. Alternatively, productivity can be expressed in terms of the ratio of unique corpus occurrences ('hapax legomena', i.e. types with only one token) to tokens (cf. Baayen 1989): the more such single-occurrence types, the higher the probability that also 'outside' the corpus the pattern will be used to form novel creations and so the more productive the pattern. We propose here to combine the two measures (type-to-token ratio and hapax-to-token ratio) in a single graph.

There is one slight problem to overcome. Remember that all the lexical n-grams used for our n-grammar have at least five corpus occurrences, so that, strictly speaking, there are no hapax legomena among them. Therefore, we need to rely on a related statistic, which we could call 'pentakis legomena', that is, sequences that occur only five times in the corpus. The ratio of these, too, just like the ratio of hapax legomena, can give us an idea of how readily novel combinations are formed based on a given pattern. The cut-off of five occurrences per type (cf. Section 3.3) also results in a somewhat skewed type/token ratio: above this cut-off point, there is a smaller type/token ratio (as here we find types with comparatively many tokens) than below that cut-off point (where we find types with relatively few tokens). Our solution to compensate for this skewing is to multiply the type/token ratio by 5. This makes mathematical sense: suppose all the lexical types had just five occurrences, then the unadjusted type/token ratio would be 0.2, and by multiplying this by 5, we would obtain the maximal productivity score of 1, which would be just what we would like to find in that situation. Likewise, the pentakis/token ratio is also skewed compared to the more commonly used hapax/token ratio, since for any pattern, if there are many 'pentakises', one could expect there to be even more hapaxes. So, there is naturally a smaller 'pentakis'/token ratio given a cut-off restriction of 5 occurrences than there would be a 'hapax/token' ratio if the cut-off restriction was removed (and this is so even if the total number of tokens would of course also increase if we removed the cut-off restriction). The solution, here too, exists in multiplying the pentakis/token ratio by 5. The formula for the combined and adjusted type/token and pentakis/token measure of productivity of a pattern is given below, whereby n stands for the total number of lexical types instantiating the pattern with at least five occurrences, N the total number of tokens for all these types and p the number of lexical types with just five occurrences:

$$Productivity = \frac{\left(\frac{n}{N}\right).5 + \left(\frac{p}{N}\right).5}{2}$$

What this says is that the productivity of a pattern can be calculated by taking the average of its type/token ratio multiplied by five and its pentakis/token ratio multiplied by five. Thus, for the pattern [the X_{noun} of the Y_{noun}], the number of lexical types n is 7,272 types, the total number of corpus occurrences N is 122,685 and the number of pentakis legomena p is 1,670. If we feed these numbers in the formula above, we get the following result:

$$Productivity = \frac{\left(\frac{7,272}{122,685}\right).5 + \left(\frac{1,670}{122,685}\right).5}{2} = 0.186$$

This result can be represented in graph form on a scale from 0 to 1. A theoretical zero value of productivity would be obtained for a pattern where all types are prefabricated chunks. The value 1, for full productivity, would be the score for a pattern where all types are novel creations (or at least, where they are all pentakises). For ease of visual interpretation and comparison with other patterns, we use a logarithmic scale of 10, with the minimum value approximating zero and the maximum value 1.

Figure 5 charts the productivity of the first and second most frequent POS 5-gram in COCA. The lower productivity of [at/in/to/... the X_{noun} of the (Y_{nom})] is explained by the fact that the part (Y_{nom}) is not actually included in the 5-gram and so plays no role in the type and token data used for the calculation. This 'extended' 5-gram thus contains only two open slots, for a preposition and a noun, only the latter of which is an open word class. In the first pattern, there are two slots for an open word class, so the productivity of this pattern is obviously much higher. One might wonder whether it makes sense to add items that are not taken into account when counting the number of occurrences. The reason why we did this is that we want to show learners how a POS 5-gram can be used grammatically. If a POS 5-gram ends in a determiner or an adjective, we find it useful to state what the next element will be (a nominal). It should be obvious, though, that this element cannot be taken into consideration when we want to compare POS n-grams for frequency, as there is no easy way to list up all the possible instantiations of this element, which could be a bare noun, a noun preceded by one or more adjectives, a noun followed by a prepositional phrase of any length, and so on.

It is important to make the learner see that a low-productivity pattern does not necessarily equal an uninteresting one. The lower the productivity, the greater the role of strongly entrenched sequences, which are responsible for the high token frequency. Thus, while this second pattern is clearly less productive, its most common type ([at the end of the Y_{nom}]) has 10,663 occurrences in COCA, against only 3,618 occurrences for the most frequently used lexical sequence

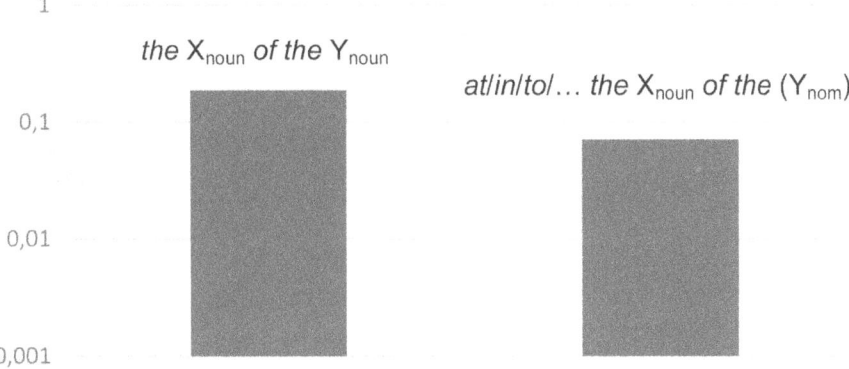

Figure 5: Productivity of two grammar patterns, visualised on a logarithmic scale

instantiating the first pattern (*the rest of the world*). To avoid the automatic association of higher with 'better', a suitable alternative visual representation might be one that plots the productivity score on a horizontally-oriented scale, where patterns towards the left margin are more 'chunkified' or 'lexical' and patterns towards the right margin are more 'gridlike' or 'syntactic'.

5.2 Adding a visual measure of dispersion

5-grams may not appear as frequently in some genres or registers as they do in others. To indicate how evenly or how skewed a language item appears in different sections of a corpus, we can (or even should) use measures of dispersion (cf. Gries 2008a). Figure 6 illustrates a visually attractive way of showing which of the large components of COCA make use of the pattern [*the* X_{noun} *of the* Y_{noun}] the most and the least. The data were obtained by entering the query 'the [*nn1*] of the [*nn1*]' in the COCA search interface and looking up how many hits we retrieve in each of the main components of the corpus (spoken, fiction, magazine, newspaper and academic). This is information which the COCA search interface provides at a click of the mouse. Note that this search retrieves results for types whose token frequency is also lower than five. As could be expected of a rather complex NP, we find this grammatical structure used least frequently in spoken English and most frequently in academic writing. The spread through the corpus is clearly uneven.

Besides making immediately clear the uneven frequency of the pattern across broad corpus components, the graph can be adapted to indicate in which of these components, if any, the pattern in question occurs *much* more/less fre-

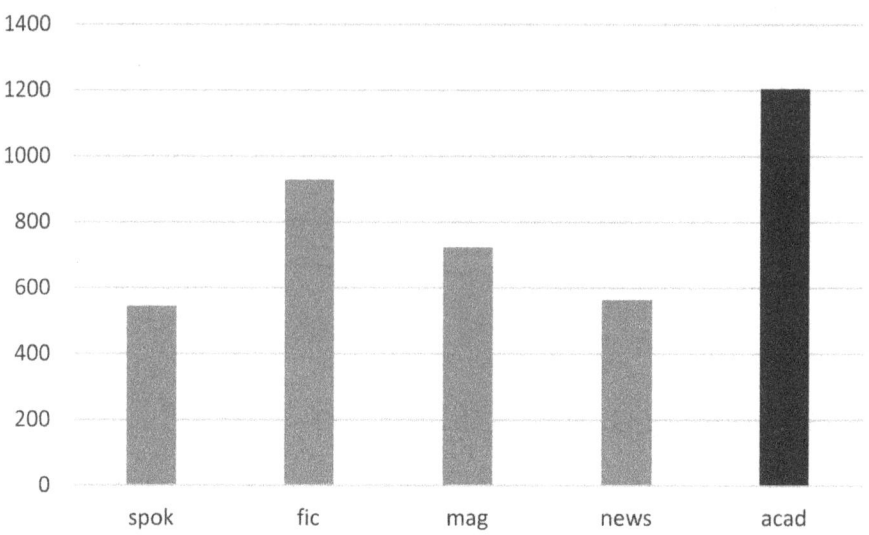

Figure 6: Dispersion of *the* X$_{noun}$ *of the* Y$_{noun}$ across COCA components. Bars indicate number of tokens per million words.

quently than expected (given an average). Specifically, we can use darker grey and lighter grey for markedly higher or lower frequency, respectively. This allows the learner to quickly identify the genre(s) in which the pattern is more conspicuously present or absent than what could have been expected under the assumption that it had an equal chance of occurrence in each component. We here define a markedly higher or lower frequency as a difference of at least 50% (for a positive difference, i.e. a surplus) or at least 33.33% (for a negative difference, i.e. a shortage) compared to the expected frequency. In this case, the expected frequency is 790 hits per million words (a figure obtained by dividing the total number of occurrences by the total corpus size multiplied by one million). Only in academic written discourse does the pattern display a marked difference (namely, an overuse of 53%) between what is observed and what is expected. In spoken discourse, the pattern is not sufficiently underrepresented – there is an underuse of (only) 31% – for its relative infrequency in this component to be considered of significance to the learner. This is why only the bar corresponding to academic writing has been given a different grey shade in Figure 6.

This uneven dispersion suggests that if we had used another corpus (containing for instance no academic writing at all), the frequency ranking of our POS n-grams might have been very different. The same may be true if we had used a corpus representing another variety of English. Obviously, corpus results depend on (and vary with) the corpus used. This is also valid for the tagset (see Section 3.4), whose choice will have an important influence on the patterns that are extracted, as well as for the settings (e.g. case sensitivity, mentioned also in Section 3.4). There is no such thing as *the* n-grammar of English.

5.3 Providing a functional description

The quantitative measures discussed in Sections 5.1 and 5.2 may be interesting to the numerically-minded learner. However, especially if we want to adopt a constructionist approach to language pedagogy, we should also attempt to show how each pattern has its own functional properties, unless one is prepared to argue for "the legitimacy of semantically null constructions" (Fillmore et al. 2012: 326; see Hilpert 2014: Chapter 3 for discussion). Providing a semantic or functional characterization of a POS n-gram may need some inventiveness on the part of the grammarian. Yet, by looking at the most frequent lexical n-gram instantiations, we often get a clue as to what the pattern is predominantly used for. In the case of the by now familiar pattern [*the* X_{noun} *of the* Y_{noun}], we could formulate its function along the lines shown in (5):

(5) [*the* X_{noun} *of the* Y_{noun}]
This pattern allows speakers to link two entities: the noun phrase following *of* (e.g. *the road*) and the noun preceding it (*side*). Among the most frequent instantiations of this pattern, there are quite a few sequences where the first noun denotes a portion (e.g. *rest*) or a position or dimension in space or time (e.g. *end, side, edge, center, middle, back, top*) which 'zooms in' on a part of the larger whole expressed by the noun phrase after *of*. Not surprisingly, this pattern overlaps with the next most productive one, namely [*at/in/to/... the* X_{noun} *of the* Y_{noun}] (pattern No. 2), which adds a preposition to indicate a relation to this spatial or temporal portion or location, e.g. <u>at</u> *the end of the Y*, <u>in</u> *the middle of the Y*, <u>at</u> *the top of the Y*, <u>by</u> *the end of the Y*.

Note that this pattern's functional description is not only informed by its frequent lexical instantiations; it also brings out the formal and functional relatedness of this pattern with another one.

5.4 Providing opportunities for practice

Finally, let us offer some thoughts on how the selected grammar patterns can be integrated into language learning activities aimed at consolidating the syntactic structures and their common instantiations. We hope that developers of language learning materials might come up with a full range of concrete ideas, but one obvious possibility of a practice activity for a given pattern is to encourage learners to use suitable lexical instantiations in particular usage contexts. This could be implemented as a simple fill-in exercise, which may or may not take the form of a multiple-choice task whereby, given a particular sentence, learners have to use the most suitable lexical n-gram from a set. These lexical n-grams themselves, too, could be presented with gaps, which learners have to fill in with contextually suitable items. Ideally, the sentences to be completed should be taken from carefully selected authentic spoken or written discourse (although one may have to clean up and/or simplify attested examples if learners are to benefit from them optimally; cf. Gries 2008b); the fillers should be chosen from the set of high-frequency sequences provided with the pattern (cf. Table 4).

Another sort of exercise could take the form of a role play between pairs of students, who in a particular usage situation have to use a number of preselected n-grams. For instance, two students could be asked to act as people of influence in international politics, such as the Secretary of State of the US and the British Prime Minister, discussing one or other rogue state's presumed possession of weapons of mass destruction. Student A has to use *(give X / get / deserve) the benefit of the doubt, the rest of the world, the State of the Union* and *(on/off/from) the face of the earth*. Student B has to use *the end of the world, the fact of the matter, (reach) the end of the line* and *(just) the tip of the iceberg*. The teacher should not stop the role play until he or she is satisfied these sequences have been used accurately and naturally (i.e. in a correct syntactic environment and, whenever relevant, taking account of the idiomatic or encyclopedic meaning of an expression, which of course should first have been illustrated by means of authentic examples).

Once such common sequences have been mastered, a further exercise could consist in using n-grams flexibly. For instance, teams could compete against each other to produce the highest number of phrases that instantiate a POS n-gram. This would allow them to learn the language by thinking in more general categories, to exploit the combinatorial flexibility of grammar and use and reuse at best available linguistic chunks. Other creatively-oriented exercises could be to use patterns to form rhymes (for more advanced students), but of course, such an exercise should not replace tasks that appeal more directly to functional needs. As an alternative focusing again more on realistic language use, students could be asked to detect instantiations of a set of POS n-grams, say 5 different ones provided to them, in an authentic text. Some of these POS n-grams, and accordingly their instantiations, may overlap (e.g. *with the tip of the* and *the tip of the tongue*), demonstrating how n-grams can incrementally combine to form full sentences. An easy related exercise could be to ask learners which lexical 5-grams in a text form complete constituents and which lexical 5-grams do not. Such an exercise would raise students' awareness of language structure and might enhance linguistic insight.

For students of linguistics, the 'linear' approach to grammar proposed here could be offset by digressions on how the seemingly purely sequential structure of grammar patterns is actually hierarchically organized. An n-gram-based approach to grammar need not be incompatible with a more traditional linguistic reflection about constituent structure. For instance, we may explain to students that the sequence *the rest of the world* has the structure shown in Figure 7.

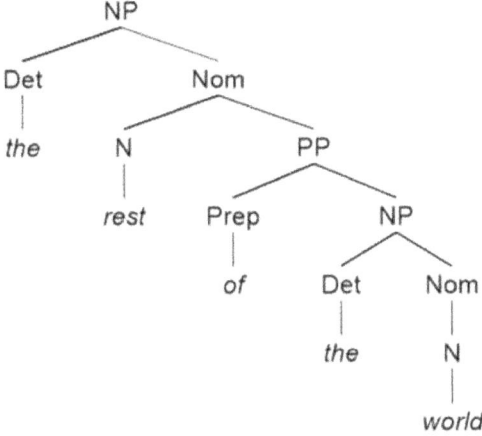

Figure 7: Tree diagram showing the hierarchical structure of a linear sequence

Such a tree diagram could lead to a discussion of recursion – the fact that a noun phrase can contain a noun phrase, for instance – or of why a preposition should not be simplistically defined as a word which comes before a noun – since in that case, a determiner would also be a preposition. An exercise could be to form complex trees by means of tree fragments constituting a toy grammar, such as one in which NP branches into Det and Nom, another in which Nom branches into N and PP (or just N), and yet another in which PP branches into Prep and NP.

6 Conclusion

These are exciting times. We have access to online corpora, specifically designed for linguistics or otherwise, containing staggering amounts of words. Corpora have opened our eyes to lexical frequencies, collocations, and so on, but they need not close our eyes to syntactic patterns. With the help of automatic taggers that reach high precision rates, we can now hold our descriptions of grammar to the same empirical standard as our descriptions of the lexicon.

Espousing a radically usage-based approach to grammar, we have shown here how we can make use of relatively schematic templates derived from the Corpus of Contemporary American English as the basis of an 'n-grammar' of English. The selection of patterns to be included in such a grammar is based on the corpus frequency of part-of-speech 5-grams, which we consider to be constructions. We have demonstrated that a small number of high-frequency 5-grams – just one hundred out of several tens of thousands – can cover quite a large portion of actually used 5-word strings (as well as strings of 2, 3 and 4 words). This leads to a rather revolutionary approach to developing a pedagogical grammar: it breaks with traditional sequencing in grammars, which often deal first with everything related to the verb, then the noun, etc. – in this or another convenient (for largely conventional) order. Our motivation for following the order suggested by corpus frequencies is that it seems to us only common sense that those patterns that underlie the highest number of concrete word sequences should be presented before any others. While Leech (2011) may be right in taking a somewhat more considered stance regarding the principle "more frequent = more important to learn", this is mainly because some researchers (cf. De Cock and Granger 2004) have noted that learners may overuse vocabulary items, such as *big* or *nice*. It is true that there are very common words which learners will soon come across, use themselves successfully and as a result start feeling rather too comfortable with. Leech's reservation, however, applies less to more complex grammar patterns of the sort we have considered here, consisting of as many as five segments.

Our proposal to rank frequent and productive n-gram templates may help EFL/ESL material developers to select form-function patterns for active mastery. We hope to have illustrated or at least suggested how the construction of a book-length construct-i-con, discussing the hundred most frequent 5-gram templates, can lead to a fresh, empirically based and ultimately perhaps more relevant approach to teaching grammar.

Acknowledgements

Earlier versions of this paper were presented not just at the international conference Constructionist Approaches to Language Pedagogy (CALP, 8-9 November 2013, Brussels, Belgium) but also at the University of Erlangen-Nurnberg,

Germany (1 July 2014) and the University of Tsukuba, Japan (8 July 2014). We thank the organizers of these occasions for giving us a stage, as well as members of the audience whose questions helped us formulate our ideas more clearly. We are also especially grateful to the editors of this volume and the anonymous reviewers for their constructive comments. All remaining inadequacies are ours alone.

References

Abott-Smith, Kirsten & Michael Tomasello. 2006. Exemplar-learning and schematization in a usage-based account of syntactic acquisition. *The Linguistic Review* 23. 275–290.

Baayen, R. Harald. 1989. *A corpus-based approach to morphological productivity: Statistical analysis and psycholinguistic interpretation*. Ph.D. dissertation, Free University of Amsterdam.

Biber, Douglas, Susan Conrad & Viviana Cortes. 2004. If you look at...: Lexical bundles in university teaching and textbooks. *Applied Linguistics* 25(3). 371–405.

Biber, Douglas, Susan Conrad & Geoffrey Leech. 2002. *Longman student grammar of spoken and written English*. London: Longman.

Biber, Douglas, Stig Johansson, Geoffrey Leech, Susan Conrad & Edward Finegan. 1999. *Longman grammar of spoken and written English*. London: Longman.

Boas, Hans C. 2003. *A constructional approach to resultatives*. Stanford: CSLI Publications.

Bybee, Joan L. 2006. From usage to grammar: The mind's response to repetition. *Language* 82 (4). 711–733.

Cappelle, Bert. 2014. Review of Stefan Thim, *Phrasal verbs: The English verb-particle construction and its history*. Berlin & New York: Mouton de Gruyter. *English Language and Linguistics* 18(3). 572–586.

Celce-Murcia, Marianne & Diane Larsen-Freeman. 1999. *The grammar book: An ESL/EFL teacher's course*. Boston, MA: Heinle & Heinle.

Chen, Yu-Hua & Paul Baker. 2010. Lexical bundles in L1 and L2 academic writing. *Language Learning & Technology* 14(2). 30–49.

Chomsky, Noam. 1970. Remarks on nominalization. In Roderick A. Jacobs & Peter S. Rosenbaum (eds.), *Reading in English transformational grammar*, 184–221. Waltham: Ginn.

Croft, William. 1998. Linguistic evidence and mental representations. *Cognitive Linguistics* 9(2). 151–173.

Croft, William & D. Allen Cruse. 2004. *Cognitive Linguistics*. Cambridge: Cambridge University Press.

Cowie, A.P. (ed.). 1998. *Phraseology: Theory, analysis, and applications*. Oxford: Oxford University Press.

Davies, Mark. 2008–. *The Corpus of Contemporary American English: 450 million words, 1990–present*. Available online at http://corpus.byu.edu/coca/.

Davies, Mark. 2013. *Corpus of Global Web-Based English: 1.9 billion words from speakers in 20 countries*. Available online at http://corpus2.byu.edu/glowbe/.

Davies, Mark & Dee Gardner. 2010. *A frequency dictionary of contemporary American English: Word sketches, collocates, and thematic lists*. London/New York: Routledge.

De Cock, Sylvie & Sylviane Granger. 2004. Computer learner corpora and monolingual learners' dictionaries: The perfect match. *Lexicographica* 20. 72–86.

De Kunder, Maurice. 2006. *Geschatte grootte van het geïndexeerde World Wide Web* [Estimated size of the World Wide Web]. MA dissertation. Tilburg University.

Ellis, Nick C. 1996. Sequencing in SLA: Phonological memory, chunking, and points of order. *Studies in Second Language Acquisition* 18. 91–126.

Ellis, Nick C. 2003. Constructions, chunking, and connectionism: The emergence of second language structure. In Catherine J. Doughty & Michael H. Long (eds.), *Handbook of second language acquisition*, 63–103. Malden, MA: Blackwell.

Ellis, Nick C. 2006. Cognitive perspectives on SLA: The Associative-Cognitive CREED. *AILA Review* 19: 100–121.

Ellis, Nick C. 2013. Second language acquisition. In Thomas Hoffmann & Graeme Trousdale (eds.), *Oxford handbook of construction grammar*, 365–378, Oxford: Oxford University Press.

Ellis, Nick C. & Teresa Cadierno. 2009. Constructing a second language: Introduction to the special section. *Annual Review of Cognitive Linguistics* 7. 111–139.

Fagan, Stephen & Ramazan Gençay. 2010. An introduction to textual econometrics. In Aman Ullah & David E. A. Giles, *Handbook of empirical economics and finance*, 133–153. Boca Raton: Chapman & Hall/CRC.

Fillmore, Charles J., Russell R. Lee-Goldman & Russell Rhodes. 2012. The FrameNet Constructicon. In Hans C. Boas & Ivan A. Sag (eds.), *Sign-Based Construction Grammar*, 283–299. Stanford: CSLI.

Forsberg, Markus, Richard Johansson, Linnéa Bäckström, Lars Borin, Benjamin Lyngfelt, Joel Olofsson & Julia Prentice. 2014. From construction candidates to constructicon entries: An experiment using semi-automatic methods for identifying constructions in corpora. *Constructions and Frames* 6(1). 114–135.

Francis, Gill, Susan Hunston & Elizabeth Manning. 1996. *Collins COBUILD Grammar Patterns 1: Verbs*. London: HarperCollins. Available online at http://arts-ccr-002.bham.ac.uk/ccr/patgram/.

Francis, Gill, Susan Hunston & Elizabeth Manning. 1998. *Collins COBUILD Grammar Patterns 2: Nouns and adjectives*. London: HarperCollins.

Goldberg, Adele E. 1995. *Constructions: A construction grammar approach to argument structure*. Chicago: University of Chicago Press.

Goldberg, Adele E. 2003. Constructions: A new theoretical approach to language. *Trends in Cognitive Sciences* 7(5). 219–224.

Goldberg, Adele E. 2006. *Constructions at work: The nature of generalization in language*. Oxford: Oxford University Press.

Gries, Stefan Th. 2008a. Dispersions and adjusted frequencies in corpora. *International Journal of Corpus Linguistics* 13(4). 403–437.

Gries, Stefan Th. 2008b. Corpus-based methods in analyses of second language acquisition data. In Peter Robinson & Nick Ellis (eds.), *Handbook of Cognitive Linguistics and second language acquisition*, 406–431. New York: Taylor & Francis.

Guthrie, David, Ben Allison, Wei Liu, Louise Guthrie & Yorick Wilks. 2006. A closer look at skip-gram modelling. *Proceedings of the fifth international conference on language resources and evaluation (LREC'06)*, 1222–1225. Genoa, Italy.

Halliday, M.A.K. 1978. *Language as social semiotic: The social interpretation of language and meaning*. London: Arnold.

Hilpert, Martin. 2014. *Construction Grammar and its application to English*. Edinburgh: Edinburgh University Press.
Huddleston, Rodney, Geoffrey K. Pullum et al. 2002. *The Cambridge grammar of the English language*. Cambridge: Cambridge University Press.
Hunston, Susan & Gill Francis. 2000. *Pattern Grammar: A corpus-driven approach to the lexical grammar of English*. Amsterdam: John Benjamins.
Hyland, Ken. 2008. As can be seen: Lexical bundles and disciplinary variation. *English for Specific Purposes* 27(1). 4–21.
Iwata, Seizi. 2008. *Locative alternation: A lexical-constructional approach*. Amsterdam: John Benjamins.
Jackendoff, Ray S. 1977. *X-bar syntax: A study of phrase structure*. Cambridge, MA: MIT Press.
Jurafsky, Dan. 1991. *An on-line computational model of human sentence interpretation: A theory of the representation and use of linguistic knowledge*. Ph.D. Dissertation, University of California, Berkeley.
Jurafsky, Dan. 2012. Language modeling: Introduction to n-grams. Lecture slides of Stanford University's online course Natural Language Processing. https://class.coursera.org/nlp/lecture/14 (last accessed on 7 August 2014).
Kandel, Eric R. 2001. The molecular biology of memory storage: A dialogue between genes and synapses. *Science* 294. 1030–1038.
Langacker, Ronald W. 2005. Construction grammars: Cognitive, radical, and less so. In Francisco J. Ruiz de Mendoza Ibáñez & M. Sandra Peña Cervel (eds.), *Cognitive Linguistics: Internal dynamics and interdisciplinary interaction*, 101–159. Berlin: Mouton de Gruyter.
Leech, Geoffrey. 2011. Frequency, corpora and language learning. In Fanny Meunier, Sylvie De Cock, Gaëtanelle Gilquin & Magali Paquot (eds.), *A taste for corpora: In honour of Sylviane Granger*, 7–32. Amsterdam: John Benjamins.
Levshina, Natalia & Kris Heylen. 2014. A radically data-driven Construction Grammar: Experiments with Dutch causative constructions. In Ronny Boogaart, Timothy Colleman & Gijsbert Rutten (eds.), *Extending the Scope of Construction Grammar*, 17–46. Berlin: Mouton de Gruyter.
Lewis, Michael. 1993. *The Lexical Approach: The State of ELT and the Way Forward*. Hove, UK: Language Teaching Publications.
Lin, Yuri, Jean-Baptiste Michel, Erez Lieberman Aiden, Jon Orwant, William Brockman & Slav Petrov. 2012. Syntactic annotations for the Google Books Ngram Corpus. *Proceedings of the 50th annual meeting of the Association for Computational Linguistics, Volume 2: Demo papers (ACL '12)*, 169–174. Stroudsburg, PA: Association for Computational Linguistics.
Lyngfelt, Benjamin, Lars Borin, Markus Forsberg, Julia Prentice, Rudolf Rydstedt, Emma Sköldberg & Sofia Tingsell. 2012. Adding a Constructicon to the Swedish resource network of Språkbanken. *Proceedings of KONVENS 2012 (LexSem 2012 workshop)*, 452–461. Vienna, September 2012.
McCarthy, Michael & Felicity O'Dell. 2001. *English vocabulary in use: Upper-intermediate*. Second Edition. Cambridge: Cambridge University Press.
Michel, Jean-Baptiste, Yuan Kui Shen, Aviva Presser Aiden, Adrian Veres, Matthew K. Gray, William Brockman, The Google Books Team, Joseph P. Pickett, Dale Hoiberg, Dan Clancy, Peter Norvig, Jon Orwant, Steven Pinker, Martin A. Nowak & Erez Lieberman Aiden. 2010. Quantitative analysis of culture using millions of digitized books. *Science* 331(6014). 176–182.

O'Donnell, Matthew Brook. 2011. The adjusted frequency list: A method to produce cluster-sensitive frequency lists. *ICAME Journal* 35. 135–169.

Pulvermüller, Friedemann & Andreas Knoblauch. 2009. Discrete combinatorial circuits emerging in neural networks: A mechanism for rules of grammar in the human brain? *Neural Networks* 22. 161–172.

Pulvermüller, Friedemann, Bert Cappelle & Yury Shtyrov. 2013. Brain basis of meaning, words, constructions, and grammar. In Thomas Hoffmann & Graeme Trousdale (eds.), *Oxford handbook of construction grammar*, 396–416. Oxford: Oxford University Press.

Robinson, Peter. 2006. Attention, memory, and the "noticing" hypothesis. *Language Learning* 45(2). 283–331.

Römer, Ute. 2010. Establishing the phraseological profile of a text type: The construction of meaning in academic book reviews. *English Text Construction* 3(1). 95–119.

Schmidt, Richard W. 1990. The role of consciousness in second language learning. *Applied Linguistics* 11(2). 129–158.

Sinclair, John. 1991. *Corpus, concordance, collocation: Describing English language.* Oxford: Oxford University Press.

Tomasello, Michael. 2003. *Constructing a language: A usage-based theory of language acquisition.* Cambridge, MA: Harvard University Press.

Wible, David & Tsao, Nai-Lung. 2010. StringNet as a computational resource for discovering and investigating linguistic constructions. *Proceedings of the NAACL HLT workshop on extracting and using constructions in computational linguistics*, 25–31. Los Angeles, CA: ACL.

Wray, Alison. 2002. *Formulaic language and the lexicon.* Cambridge: Cambridge University Press.

Wulff, Stefanie & Stefan Th. Gries. 2011. Corpus-driven methods for assessing accuracy in learner production. In Peter Robinson (ed.), *Second language task complexity: Researching the cognition hypothesis of language learning and performance*, 61–88. Amsterdam: Benjamins.

Zipf, George K. 1935. *The psychobiology of language: An introduction to dynamic philology.* Cambridge, MA.: MIT Press.

Hans C. Boas, Ryan Dux, and Alexander Ziem
Frames and constructions in an online learner's dictionary of German[1]

Abstract: What types of lexical and grammatical information should a learner's dictionary cover? How can the architecture of an online language resource take account of these requirements? This paper introduces the so-called German Frame-Based Online Lexicon (G-FOL), a frame- and construction-based language resource for English-speaking learners of German that aims at overcoming the general disconnect between vocabulary and grammar in most pedagogical resources. First, to illustrate the problem, we take grooming verbs as a 'test case'. They exhibit subtle semantic and grammatical differences, which are rarely obvious to the average foreign language learner. On the basis of these findings, we demonstrate how G-FOL employs the principles of FrameNet to solve major didactic challenges identified in the case study. Finally, the third part shows how G-FOL is also capable of presenting constructional information in the same format.

Keywords: frames; constructions; vocabulary teaching and learning; G-FOL; FrameNet; constructicon

1 Introduction

The goal of this paper is to explore what types of lexical and grammatical information should be contained in an online learner's dictionary of German intended for speakers of English, and what the architecture of such a resource should look like. Even though we focus on language learning issues from a linguistic rather than a didactic perspective and thus address first and foremost linguists interested in the pedagogical potential of Frame Semantics and Construction Grammar, the architecture of the German frame-based online lexicon builds on the idea that language is always embedded in cultural experiences and practices. From a linguistic point of view, there are two main motivations for our study. The first is that foreign language learning requires the acquisition of vocabulary. Without proper knowledge of what words mean and how they are

---

[1] We would like to thank two anonymous reviewers as well as the editors of this volume for their helpful comments on an earlier draft of this paper. Their comments helped to substantially improve our paper.

used, it is impossible to adequately learn a foreign language. At the same time, however, there are time constraints on the average foreign language syllabus as well as certain cognitive demands for foreign language learning (see Ellis 1997; Nation 2001). Second, there is often a disconnect between the types of information presented by lexical resources such as dictionaries and syntactic resources such as grammars. More importantly, although there is already a plethora of online lexical and grammatical resources available (see, e.g., Heid 2006), very few, if any, provide answers to the demands of foreign language learners.

To illustrate, consider an English speaker trying to learn the German translation equivalent of *to take a shower*, which does not consist of a corresponding support verb construction **eine Dusche nehmen* ('to take a shower'). Instead, German requires the use of a reflexive verb *sich duschen* ('to shower oneself'). Even though a beginning English-speaking learner of German using traditional instructional resources such as textbooks and dictionaries might think that this lexical difference is an isolated exception, it is in fact an instantiation of the more general support verb construction [*to take a(n) N*] that is well attested across different semantic domains in the English lexicon, such as *to take a shower*, *to take a swim*, *to take an exam*, *to take a leave of absence*, and *to take a nap*.

However, not all of these specific support verb constructions have corresponding German counterparts that consist of reflexive verbs. While *to take a shower* has a reflexive verb translation equivalent in German, *sich duschen* (lit. 'to shower oneself'),[2] the scenario described by *to take a swim* does not, and its German translation equivalent is the non-reflexive verb *schwimmen (gehen)* ('to (go) swim(ming)'). In contrast, some of the German translation equivalents of the support verb construction [*to take a(n) N*] are also support verb constructions, but with different support verbs. Compare *ein Nickerchen machen* ('to take a nap', lit. 'to make a nap') and *sich frei nehmen* ('to take a leave of absence', lit. 'to take oneself free'). These examples illustrate that German translation equivalents of specific instantiations of the English support verb construction [*to take a(n) N*] do not follow a coherent pattern that would allow an English-speaking learner of German to learn any specific (or abstract) strategies that would help him/her systematically predict German translation equivalents of such English support verb constructions even in cases where s/he has never heard them before.

At the same time, there appear to be some regularities among German verbs in certain semantic domains. Consider, for example, body grooming verbs such

---

2 However, to make things more complicated, even, for example, in a present or past tense use there is a non-reflexive verb equivalent, namely if it surfaces as a so-called indefinite null instantiation (Ruppenhofer et al. 2010, 24–25; cf. *er duscht* 'he showers').

as *sich waschen* ('to wash oneself'), *sich die Zähne putzen* (lit. 'to brush oneself the teeth'), and *sich die Haare bürsten* (lit. 'to brush oneself the hair'). These examples show that German grooming verbs appear to have a systematic preference for reflexive patterns.

The differences between apparently unsystematic and systematic verbal behavior raises a number of important questions for foreign language learning. (1) How do we capture both the idiosyncrasies and the general grammatical patterns in a way that is easily understandable to the foreign language learner? (2) How do we represent the relationship between form and meaning in such a way that it allows the foreign language learner to easily remember systematic differences between the foreign language and his/her native language? (3) How can we use the foreign language learner's existing knowledge of his/her own language to help him/her learn words and how to use them in a foreign language? (4) How can we use limited time and resources in an effective way to support the acquisition of both vocabulary items and their associated grammatical constructions outside the classroom so that classroom instruction can focus on using the foreign language?

In the remainder of our paper, we aim to provide answers to these questions by showing how an online lexical resource for English-speaking learners of German can support the acquisition of new vocabulary and grammatical constructions. Section 2 first presents the basic concepts of Frame Semantics (Fillmore 1982), a theory of lexical semantics that forms the basis for FrameNet, a lexicographic database for English (Baker, Fillmore, and Lowe 1998; Fillmore and Baker 2010). We then discuss how the concept of semantic frames has been extended to languages other than English. Next, we present the architecture of the German Frame-based Online Lexicon (G-FOL; Boas and Dux 2013) by describing how words pertaining to body grooming are presented to the foreign language learner. In Section 3, we discuss the need to include additional syntactic information about grooming words that goes beyond the scope of grammatical information typically provided by learner dictionaries and grammars. Section 4 summarizes our findings and discusses points to be addressed by future research.

2 Introducing the German Frame-based Online Lexicon (G-FOL)

2.1 Frame Semantics and FrameNet

Frame Semantics (Fillmore 1982, 1985) is based on the idea that "a word's meaning can be understood only with reference to a structured background of experience, beliefs, or practices, constituting a kind of conceptual prerequisite for understanding the meaning" (Fillmore and Atkins 1992: 76–77).[3] In this view, word meanings are understood in terms of semantic background frames that motivate the concept encoded by a word. Since the late 1990s, Frame Semantics has been applied to the construction of a corpus-based lexical database of English, FrameNet, which is built around the concept of semantic frames that can be evoked by lexical units (a lexical unit is a word in one of its senses) (Baker, Fillmore, and Lowe 1998; Fillmore and Baker 2010). Semantic frames are taken as structuring devices to model the types of knowledge necessary for interpreting utterances in the language (see Petruck 1996; Boas 2005a; Ziem 2014a).

The FrameNet database consists of lexical entries for several thousand words taken from a variety of semantic domains. Based on corpus data, FrameNet identifies and describes semantic frames and analyzes the meanings of words by appealing directly to the frames that underlie their meanings. In addition, it documents the syntactic properties of words by asking how their semantic properties are given syntactic form (Fillmore, Johnson, and Petruck 2003a: 235). Since 1997, FrameNet has defined 12,777 lexical units (LUs) in 1,180 frames (status as of July 7, 2014).

FrameNet describes LUs in terms of the semantic frames they evoke and presents for each LU a lexical entry that lists different types of interconnected information (see Ruppenhofer et al. 2010 for details). Consider the verb *load*, which has multiple senses, and is thus represented in terms of multiple LUs in FrameNet. One such LU evokes the Filling frame,[4] which is also evoked by other verbal LUs such as *fill, glaze, smear, spatter, spray,* and *tile*, among many others. The lexical entry of the LU *load* in the Filling frame consists of three parts: (1) the frame description, (2) an exhaustive inventory of how frame elements are realized syntactically, and (3) annotated example sentences from the British National Corpus (BNC). Each frame description consists of frame elements (FEs) that are essential for a full understanding of the associated situation type. For example, the frame description of the Filling frame is defined as

> words relating to filling CONTAINERS and covering AREAS with some thing, things or substance, the THEME. The AREA or CONTAINER can appear as the direct object with all these verbs, and is designated GOAL because it is the goal of motion of the THEME. Corresponding to its nuclear argument status, it is also affected in some crucial way, unlike goals in other frames. The AGENT is the actor who instigates the filling. (FrameNet; Ruppenhofer et al. 2010)

---

3 This section is based on Boas (2009a, 2011). The FrameNet data can be accessed online at http://framenet.icsi.berkeley.edu (last accessed on August 4, 2014).
4 Names of semantic frames are in Courier New font. Names of frame elements are in small caps. Frame Elements differ from traditional universal semantic (or thematic) roles such as Agent or Patient in that they are specific to the frame in which they are used to describe participants in certain types of scenarios.

The frame description also contains detailed definitions of all FEs as well as a list of all LUs that evoke the frame (see Ruppenhofer et al. 2010). For each LU, FrameNet provides a Lexical Entry Report, which provides a definition for that LU (cf. *to load*: fill a container-like entity with something, often in abundance), a list of FEs and their syntactic realizations, and the valency patterns (see Figure 1), illustrating how frame element configurations are realized syntactically by that LU.

Number Annotated	Patterns			
1 TOTAL	**Agent**	**Goal**	**Manner**	**Theme**
(1)	NP Ext	NP Obj	AVP Dep	PP[with] Dep
15 TOTAL	**Agent**	**Goal**	**Theme**	
(4)	CNI --	NP Ext	PP[with] Dep	
(1)	CNI --	NP Obj	PP[with] Dep	
(1)	NP Ext	DNI --	INI --	
(1)	NP Ext	DNI --	PP[with] Dep	
(2)	NP Ext	NP Obj	INI --	
(6)	NP Ext	NP Obj	PP[with] Dep	

Figure 1: Valency information for *load* in the Filling frame[5]

Each lexical entry also contains the Annotation Report, which provides annotated corpus sentences from the BNC exemplifying how the FEs are realized in context. Compare, for example, the following sentences illustrating how the FEs of the Filling frame are realized syntactically:

(1) a. [Two girls]_AGENT are loading^tgt [the donkeys]_GOAL [with water containers and sacks]_THEME.

    b. Did you know that [Cecil Beaton]_AGENT couldn't even load^tgt [his own camera]_GOAL?

    c. We'd have [our packs]_GOAL loaded^tgt [with various weights]_THEME ...

---

[5] Cf. the Filling frame retrievable through the "Frame Index" in the FrameNet database (https://framenet.icsi.berkeley.edu/fndrupal/, last accessed on August 4, 2014).

The examples in (1) illustrate how semantic frames are structuring devices that help linguists to identify verb classes based on their ability to describe similar types of scenes or situations. While identifying frames and contrasting them with others may raise a number of problems (for details see Petruck et al. 2004; Ruppenhofer et al. 2010), frame-semantic definitions are nevertheless advantageous because they are intuitive and can be checked against corpus evidence.

2.2 Multilingual FrameNets

The concept of semantic frame has also been applied to the analysis of languages other than English (Lambrecht 1984; Petruck 1986; Matsumoto 1989; Baker 1999). Over the past decade, several studies have investigated how semantic frames developed on the basis of English data such as Commitment (Subirats 2009), Communication (Subirats and Petruck 2003; Boas 2005b), Revenge (Petruck 2009), Risk (Fillmore and Atkins 1992; Ohara 2009), and Self_motion (Fillmore and Atkins 2000; Boas 2001; Iwata 2002) can be applied to the analysis of other languages such as Spanish, German, Japanese, French, and Hebrew. The consensus emerging from these studies is that frame-semantic information allows us to characterize semantically coherent classes, both within a single language and cross-linguistically (see Boas 2009a and 2009b for details). At the same time, however, these studies also point out that the range of syntactic frames occurring with a given LU is to a certain degree idiosyncratic and cannot always be automatically deduced from semantic information.

In addition, several research teams started constructing FrameNets for a variety of other languages. Following proposals by Heid (1996) and Boas (2002), the basic idea is to reuse semantic frames from the original Berkeley FrameNet for English and apply them to the analysis of other languages to see whether the semantic frames can also be used to describe the lexicons of these other languages. While these multilingual FrameNets all aim to reuse English FrameNet frames, they differ from each other in their goals, workflow, corpora, and tools. Projects such as the German 'Saarbrücken Lexical Semantics Acquisition Project' (SALSA; see Burchardt et al. 2009) are interested in full-text annotation of an entire corpus instead of finding isolated corpus sentences to identify lexicographically relevant information as is the case with the Berkeley project, Spanish FrameNet (see Subirats 2009), or Swedish FrameNet (Borin et al. 2009). In addition, these FrameNets use different types of resources as data pools. That is, besides exploiting a monolingual corpus, as is the case with Japanese FrameNet (see Ohara 2009), projects such as French FrameNet (Pitel 2009) also employ multilingual corpora and other existing lexical resources (see Fontenelle 2009).

FrameNets for other languages also differ in the tools for corpus searches and annotation. While the Japanese and Spanish FrameNets choose to adopt the Berkeley FrameNet software (Baker, Fillmore, and Cronin 2003) with slight modifications, others such as SALSA develop their own to conduct semi-automatic annotation on top of existing syntactic annotations, or they integrate off-the-shelf software packages as is the case with French FrameNet or Hebrew FrameNet (see Pitel 2009; Petruck 2009). Different FrameNets also focus on different semantic domains. While the majority of non-English FrameNets aim to create databases with broad coverage, other projects focus on specific lexical domains such as soccer language (see *Kicktionary*; Schmidt 2009) or terminology from bio-technology (see Dolbey, Ellsworth, and Scheffczyk 2006). Finally, to produce parallel lexicon fragments for other languages, projects utilize different methodologies. While German FrameNet (Boas 2001, 2002) and Japanese FrameNet (Ohara 2009) rely on manual annotations, French FrameNet and BiFrameNet (Fung and Chen 2004) use semi-automatic and automatic approaches to create parallel lexicon fragments for French and Chinese, respectively.

English FrameNet and the FrameNets for other languages are rich lexical resources constructed primarily for professional linguists interested in conducting research particularly in the realm of (computational) lexicography and semantics. While the frame descriptions and the information contained in the lexical entries are extremely detailed and useful for both linguistic research and natural language processing applications, they are not helpful for foreign language learners, because (1) they contain too much information, (2) they are too detailed, (3) the linguistic concepts are too difficult to understand for non-linguists, and (4) learners of foreign languages often have limited pre-existing knowledge of the language they are learning (cf. also Atzler 2011).

2.3 The German Frame-based Online Lexicon

Insights of the FrameNet project led to the development of a prototype frame-based online lexical resource for learners of German at the University of Texas at Austin (UT Austin): the German Frame-based Online Lexicon (G-FOL; Boas and Dux 2013; http://www.coerll.utexas.edu/frames/), a project headed by Hans Boas. Currently, G-FOL is designed for English-speaking learners of German in the first or second year of college-level German courses.[6] However, as the database is continuously extended and refined, we aim to provide frames and constructions for more advanced learners as well.

---

[6] The first phase of the G-FOL project focuses on vocabulary in the semantic domains typically taught in first- and second-year university German courses. The next phases will cover more vocabulary and grammar, and will also provide information about different registers (as well as language variation more broadly).

The basic idea was to use existing English FrameNet frames for the description of those German words that beginning and intermediate learners of German have to learn during the course of their language studies. Achieving this goal required several steps. First, programmers at UT Austin's Center for Open Educational Resources and Language Learning (COERLL) downloaded the FrameNet database for English from the International Computer Science Institute in Berkeley. The English FrameNet database was then installed on local servers at UT Austin and subsequently stripped of all English-specific information, leaving only the frames and the frame-to-frame relations intact (in addition to the frame identification numbers so that the German frame information can be linked to frame information in the Berkeley FrameNet database for English).

Next, a team of Germanic linguists at UT Austin examined the vocabulary lists of the textbook used for the first year of German instruction at UT Austin in order to identify sets of relevant words evoking the same semantic frame. Using a variety of online corpora, the team of linguists extracted simple German example sentences and annotated them with frame-semantic information. The team created user-friendly lexical entries to be stored in the stripped FrameNet database on local servers. The result is a set of easy-to-use contrastive German-English entries with notes on contrastive differences between German and English, culture-specific information, collocational information, and information about basic grammar usage. Finally, a team of web-designers created an easy to use website to present the resulting information to learners of German. The following sections provide more details on the individual steps underlying this process.

The first step in developing the G-FOL involved choosing which frames to include in the resource. We decided to begin with didactically useful frames that deal with topics included in most introductory foreign language textbooks. We especially wanted to begin with frames that may pose problems for English-speaking students of German, either due to one-to-many translations resulting from different word meanings or due to grammatical differences in how the FEs are expressed. We decided to begin with the Personal_relationships, Eating_and_drinking, Education, and Grooming frames. The Grooming frame, for instance, is particularly suitable for the resource, as it contains common words that are typically taught in introductory language courses and are necessary for describing one's everyday activities. There are some instances of translational difficulties (see also Section 1): for instance, while English uses the same verb, *brush*, for brushing one's hair and one's teeth, German employs different verbs for the different body parts (*bürsten* 'to brush' for hair, and *putzen* 'to clean/scrub' for teeth). The Grooming frame is also grammatically interesting from a cross-linguistic perspective, as English sentences realize the possessor of the BODY_PART with a possessive determiner (*to brush my teeth*), whereas German expresses this participant as a reflexive dative object with a definite article preceding the BODY_PART (*putze mir die Zähne*, lit. 'brush myself the teeth'). The G-FOL is particularly suited for such verb sets, as it gives explicit information on differences in both the lexical and grammatical expression of such events across the two languages.

For each frame, we created a "Frame Description" page, which includes the definition of the frame and each of the FEs. For the Grooming frame, these definitions were taken directly from FrameNet. However, for other frames, such as Personal_relationships, we modified the FrameNet definitions slightly if they involved linguistic jargon which may be too technical for language learners. Figure 2 shows a screenshot of the Frame Description page for Grooming, including the Frame Definition, a picture depicting the frame's meaning, and the list of core FEs for the frame,[7] whose definitions can be viewed by dragging the mouse over the FE name.

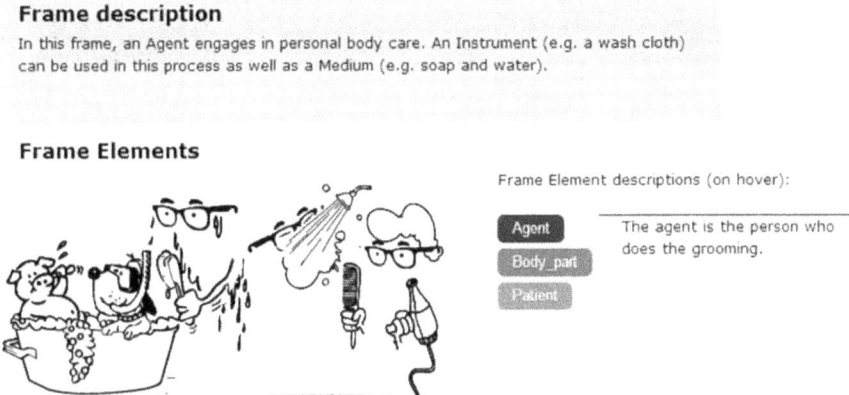

Figure 2: Frame Description for Grooming frame in G-FOL[8]

At the bottom of the Frame Description page, we provide a list of all the relevant LUs, and more detailed information about the individual LUs can be accessed by clicking on the appropriate circle next to the LU. Figure 3 shows a portion of the LU list for the Grooming frame, as well as the "Details" for the

---

[7] In accordance with FrameNet (e.g. Ruppenhofer et al. 2010: 35), we distinguish between non-core and core FEs whereby the latter, but not the former, are supposed to be conceptually essential elements of the respective frame.

[8] Please see http://coerll.utexas.edu/frames/frames/grooming (last accessed on August 4, 2014).

LU *bürsten* ('to brush'). Before populating the list, we chose which LUs to include in the G-FOL. We began by searching the English LUs on FrameNet to identify the most important and interesting ones. To simplify the experience for the users, some LUs were excluded if they were particularly infrequent, such as *ablution* and *moisturize* in the Grooming frame.

For the chosen LUs, we identified any German equivalents using bilingual dictionaries and native speaker intuitions. It is important to note that German-English word pairs are rarely true translation equivalents, thus necessitating a cross-listing of English LUs to multiple German LUs, or vice versa, or a further specification of meaning in the entry title. For instance, the second item on the list of LUs on the left of Figure 3 shows not just the verb *bürsten*, but also the common collocation *die Haare bürsten* ('to brush the hair'), and the English counterpart is also listed with the collocating noun *hair*.

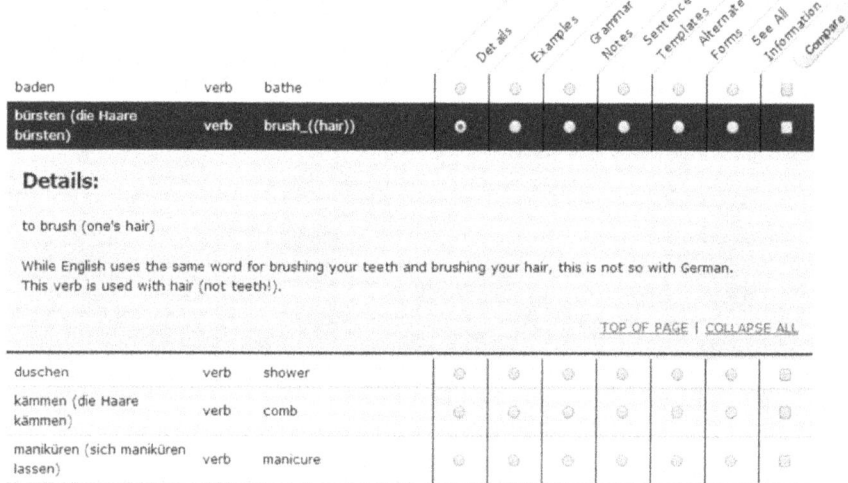

Figure 3: Portion of LU list for Grooming frame and Details for the LU *bürsten* ('to brush')[9]

For the Details page, we provide brief instructions in prose about how the LU may differ from English and cause translation difficulties for learners. For this LU, we pointed out that the verb *bürsten* is only used for brushing one's hair and not for brushing one's teeth.

Another useful piece of information provided for LUs in the G-FOL is the "Grammar Notes", which describe how individual LUs or sets of LUs differ from

---

[9] The "compare" button in the top right corner in Figure 3 allows G-FOL users to check any number of verbs for comparison of their properties in an external pop-up window.

their English counterparts in the grammatical expression of FEs. Figure 4 shows a portion of the "Grammar Notes" relevant for the verb *sich duschen* ('to take a shower'). In particular, it points out that *sich duschen* is used as a transitive verb (with the direct object frequently appearing as a reflexive pronoun when one showers oneself), whereas English speakers use the noun *shower* in combination with the light verb *take*, as in *take a shower*.[10] In Section 3, we describe how we plan to expand the grammatical coverage of the G-FOL to address the constructional behavior of LUs more systematically.

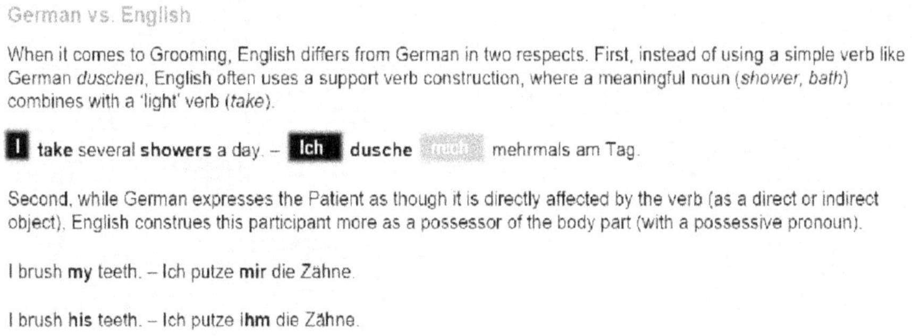

German vs. English

When it comes to Grooming, English differs from German in two respects. First, instead of using a simple verb like German *duschen*, English often uses a support verb construction, where a meaningful noun (*shower*, *bath*) combines with a 'light' verb (*take*).

I take several **showers** a day. – **Ich** dusche *mich* mehrmals am Tag.

Second, while German expresses the Patient as though it is directly affected by the verb (as a direct or indirect object), English construes this participant more as a possessor of the body part (with a possessive pronoun).

I brush **my** teeth. – Ich putze **mir** die Zähne.

I brush **his** teeth. – Ich putze **ihm** die Zähne.

Figure 4: Portion of "Grammar Notes" for *sich duschen* ('to take a shower')

To show users how a given LU is used in context, G-FOL provides for each LU a list of three to six example sentences along with English translations. Most of the examples were hand-selected from online corpora, such as the DWDS corpus (*Digitales Wörterbuch der deutschen Sprache*; www.dwds.de), with the criteria that the sentence should be brief and clear and exemplify a common use of the LU in question. In some cases, examples were made up by a native speaker to more clearly demonstrate the meaning and grammar of the LU. The example sentences are also annotated for FEs using color-coding in order to show users how individual participants are realized grammatically and point

---

10 Note that individual verbs may differ with respect to their occurrence in reflexive valency patterns. This is likely the case with *duschen* ('to shower') and *baden* ('to bathe'). Specifically, one reviewer points out that (s)he prefers verbs such as *baden* without a reflexive object over its reflexive counterpart *sich baden*. This might be due to regional variation. It could also reflect the fact that some native speakers associate the non-reflexive *baden* more with an activity interpretation, whereas the reflexive *sich baden* evokes more directly the actual Grooming frame, because the PATIENT FE is explicitly mentioned. To account for this variation, the G-FOL co-indexes such LUs with a Grammar Note stating that the reflexive object may be omitted in certain contexts in modern colloquial German.

out differences between the two languages. Figure 5 shows the example sentences for the verb *baden* ('to bathe') in the Grooming frame, with the German on the left side and the English translations, provided by the UT Austin linguists developing the G-FOL, on the right. The AGENT FE is colored purple (here, dark gray), the PATIENT FE is pink (here, light gray), and the BODY_PART FE is green (here, normal gray).

Figure 5: Example sentences for *baden* ('to bathe')

In addition to "Details", "Grammar Notes", and "Example Sentences", G-FOL also provides a list of "Alternate Forms" for each LU, which lists various tense forms for verbs (preterite, participle, etc.) or plural forms for nouns. Finally, G-FOL provides "Sentence Templates" which are simple sentence "skeletons" that show how a verb combines with various configurations of its FEs. For example, the templates for *baden* include "AGENT badet", "AGENT badet PATIENT", and "AGENT badet BODYPART".[11] The German sentence templates also appear with English translation equivalents on the right side.

This section has described the development and layout of the G-FOL, which provides detailed information about German LUs for English-speaking learners. While the G-FOL also provides grammatical information as it is relevant for the documented vocabulary items, a more systematic and comprehensive treatment

---

[11] As the sentence templates serve to show what FEs a given verb may appear with, they only include the simple FE name but not any grammatical information on how the FE is realized (e.g. PATIENT as a reflexive object).

of how constructions are related across German and English is desired. The following section sketches how constructional information can be integrated into the G-FOL.

3 From frames to constructions

3.1 Completing the learner's dictionary: why constructions matter

What does a language learner need to know in order to correctly use and understand LUs in a given language, such as German? To what extent can, or should, the design of an online dictionary adjust to the learners' linguistic competence? The answer we offered so far is: s/he needs to know the frame an LU evokes, including its FEs, and their syntactic realization patterns. Note, however, that an approach solely built on frames runs into serious problems if it deals with grammatical structures that are not fully transparent (Fillmore 2008; Fillmore, Lee-Goldman, and Rhodes 2012; Ziem, Boas, and Ruppenhofer 2014; with reference to didactic issues: Ziem 2015a). Such grammatical structures include, for example, grammatical idiosyncrasies that cannot be explained by valency reduction or augmentation, that is, the addition or omission of valents, alone. Hence, opaque grammatical and semantic structures are true challenges for language learners. To illustrate, consider (2):

(2) a. In the afternoon we organized a small bridal shower for Lydia who is getting married soon.[12]

   b. ?In the afternoon we organized a cold shower for Lydia who is getting married soon.

(2a) only differs from (2b) with respect to the direct object's adjectival attributes, with *small bridal* specifying the noun *shower* in (2a) and *cold* specifying it in (2b). However in (2b), but not in (2a), the LU *shower* (noun) evokes the Grooming frame. This is because in (2a) *shower* is part of an [Adj N] construction displaying regular syntax while exhibiting semantic idiosyncrasies, in that its meaning is not compositional, but rather meaningful as a whole. In other words, *bridal shower*, but not *cold shower*, is semantically intransparent, since it is not produced through regular adjective-noun modification as specified in a

---

12 http://www.danielhause.com/usa/february/english.html (last accessed on August 4, 2014).

grammar. In line with Berkeley Construction Grammar (Fillmore 2013), we refer to such complex linguistic units as constructions, defined as linguistic signs licensed on the basis of other linguistic signs.

How, then, does a language learner know that the NP *bridal shower* in (2a) is interpreted in such a way that the whole unit evokes a frame? And why is it, on the other hand, that in (2b) both lexical constituents of the NP *cold shower* evoke a frame of their own in such a way that the Temperature frame tied to the LU *cold* specifies the Grooming frame evoked by the noun *shower*? Even worse, how does a language learner know that the linguistic unit *bridal shower* evokes the Social_event frame instead? Obviously, *bridal shower* is an instance of a lexically specified [Adj N] construction that requires its own entry in a dictionary for language learners. Due to the non-compositional nature of such idiomatic expressions, their syntactic and/or semantic properties cannot be captured in a purely lexical approach relying on valency alone, such as the Berkeley Frame-Net project, although the project accounts for many multi-word units acting as frame-evoking units, including, for example, [Adj N] constructions like *given name*, compound adjectives such as *light-fingered*, and particle verbs like *take off* (Ruppenhofer et al. 2010: 7, 53).

One of the key insights of Construction Grammar, the sister theory of Frame Semantics (cf. Ziem 2014b), is that constructions (pairings of form and meaning) are the basic building blocks of language (see the contributions in Hoffmann and Trousdale 2013). As such, constructions also concern the very foundations of a learner's dictionary (Holme 2010; Ziem under review). However, despite their prevalence, constructions are often quite elusive and difficult to address for language learners. Consider even more complex constructions subsuming *shower* as its lexical constituent:

(3) a. Finally, simply shower off the remaining salt residues with cold or warm water.[13]

   b. These power brokers regularly dine with their congressman, accompany him on vacations and shower him with gifts.[14]

Compare (3a) with (3b). The meaning of the prepositional verb *shower off* in (3a) is structured by the Grooming frame. However, if the lemma *to shower* (verb) enters the construction [subject + VERB + direct object + prepositional

---

[13] http://goo.gl/xknZg9 (last accessed on August 4, 2014).
[14] http://www.washingtonpost.com/wp-dyn/content/article/2006/02/07/AR2006020701736_Technorati.html (last accessed on August 4, 2014).

object with *with*], as exemplified in (3b), then it evokes a different frame, namely Giving. Here, it is the construction, and not the meanings of the sentence's LUs compositionally combined with the sentence's meaning, that defines the meaning. More precisely, once *shower* enters into the construction exemplified in (3b), it undergoes a semantic shift yielding a metaphoric reading. Also, in this case, learning frames evoked by LUs does not suffice; a language learner must also know in which constructions LUs form a lexical constituent. In other words, lexical meanings may vary depending on the constructions in which they are embedded. Bearing the examples given above in mind, there is no way constructional information can be kept out of a learner's dictionary. In (3b) it is the construction that gives rise to a metaphoric interpretation of *shower*. Metaphors of this kind also need to be covered by a learner's dictionary (cf. Ziem 2015b for integrating metaphors in G-FOL).

Fortunately, constructional information can easily be incorporated into the infrastructure of G-FOL. Note that LUs and constructions share basic properties. Most importantly, both are linguistic signs, that is, conventionalized pairings of form and meaning. Hence, rather than forming distinctive entities, there is a continuum between lexicon and grammar (Boas 2010; Broccias 2012; Fillmore, Lee-Goldman, and Rhodes 2012; for an overview see Ziem and Lasch 2013: 90–95). Just like words, constructions are learned by associating forms with meanings. Goldberg (2006: 5) thus argues that words are also constructions; lexical constructions only differ from grammatical ones in that they are neither schematic nor abstract. As a result, the same mechanisms should apply to the presentation of both words and constructions, including idioms and grammatical patterns, in a learner's dictionary. Furthermore, not only do the structural similarities of words and constructions allow for unified empirical descriptions, including homogenous annotations; they also call for integrating constructional information in G-FOL, as we demonstrate in the following sections.

3.2 Annotating and analyzing constructions in FrameNet

Over the past two decades, the Berkeley FrameNet community has become increasingly aware of the necessity to extend the lexical resource of frames to a FrameNet constructicon. As a natural extension of the lexical FrameNet resource, the FrameNet constructicon is designed to be a repository of grammatical structures peculiar to a language (Fillmore 2008; Fillmore, Lee-Goldman, and Rhodes 2012; Ziem 2014b). As Fillmore notes, a sophisticated valency dictionary such as FrameNet provides the following advantages to aid in sentence interpretation:

a set of articulated lexical descriptions of each (frame-bearing) word, awaiting compositional principles based on simple patterns of grammatical organization to integrate the meanings provided by each word into reasonable formulation of the meaning of the sentence. (Fillmore 2013: 1)

He adds, however, that a full account of the syntactic and semantic structures a sentence instantiates also requires the inclusion of grammatical constructions that have meanings and functions on their own (Fillmore 2013: 17). Similar to examples such as *bridal shower, meteor shower,* and *to shower somebody with something,* many syntactic and semantic structures "cannot be fully explained in terms of the kind of structures recognized in FN's [= FrameNet's] annotation database, or simple conjoinings or embeddings of these" (Fillmore, Lee-Goldman, and Rhodes 2012: 312). Nevertheless, the FrameNet database already contains a good deal of constructional information including, most importantly, so-called realization constructions, or valency patterns in which an LU could be realized (Ziem 2014b: 279–280). Realization constructions provide constraints on the combinatory potential of an LU by defining patterns in which FEs can be syntactically combined.

By using the same formalisms and annotation criteria for both frame-bearing words and grammatical constructions, Fillmore demonstrates how to integrate the latter into the FrameNet database (Fillmore 2008; Fillmore, Lee-Goldman, and Rhodes 2012). Table 1 summarizes similarities of the annotation work yielding detailed descriptions of frames and constructions.

Table 1: Annotation of Lexical and Grammatical Units (cf. Fillmore 2008: Chapter 5.1)

Lexical Units (in FrameNet)	Grammatical Units (in the FrameNet-Constructicon)
Identification of frame-evoking LUs	Identification of construction-evoking elements (CEE)
Description and annotation of frames, FEs, frame-to-frame relations	Description and annotation of constructions, their constructional elements (CEs), construction-to-construction relations
Naming of FEs according to their function in a frame	Naming of CEs according to their function in a construction
Annotation of FEs according to their grammatical function and phrase type	Annotation of CEs according to their phrase type, annotation of lexical head of the construction (if applicable) according to its grammatical function
Providing sample sentences for illustrating a frame	Providing sample sentences for illustrating a construction
Identifying and illustrating valency patterns	Identifying and illustrating realization patterns of constructions

Similar to frame-evoking LUs, the linguistic unit evoking a construction is called a 'Construction Evoking Element' (CEE). To illustrate, consider the construction [subject + *shower* + direct object + prepositional object with *with*] exemplified in (3b). For convenience, we shall call this the *shower-sb-with-sth* construction. In this construction, *shower* acts as the CEE, and the actually realized expression, the so-called construct, licensed by the construction comprises (a) the subject instantiating the FE DONOR, (b) the direct object *him* instantiating the FE Recipient, and (c) the prepositional object *with gifts* instantiating Theme. Since the meaning of the construction is determined by the Giving frame, its Constructional Elements (CEs) can be annotated with recourse to the FEs inherent to the Giving frame. CEs are those constituents of sentences that instantiate parts of a construction. Consequently, the definition of the *shower-sb-with-sth* construction is very similar to that of the Giving frame in FrameNet:[15]

> A DONOR transfers a THEME from a DONOR to a RECIPIENT. Just like the Giving frame, this construction includes only actions that are initiated by the DONOR (the one that starts out owning the THEME). Sentences (even metaphorical ones) must meet the entailment that the DONOR first has possession of the THEME. Following the transfer, the DONOR no longer has the THEME and the RECIPIENT does. (FrameNet, Ruppenhofer et al. 2010)

Constructional annotations help describe and define a construction appropriately. First, the CEE is identified. Note that in contrast to frame annotation, many grammatical constructions are not associated with an explicit target LU that provides a link to the construction. We then name those parts of sentences that form the constituents of the constructs licensed by the construction. Finally, these components are labeled as elements of the construction. Following this procedure, (4) exemplifies the annotation of (3b) with regard to (i) the CEE, (ii) the CEs and their functions within the construction, and (iii) the construct that is licensed by the construction. Sticking to FrameNet conventions, we tag CEs with square brackets and constructs with curly brackets, while labeling the meanings or functions of these elements with the help of subscripts.

(4) [$_{\text{DONOR}}$These power brokers] regularly dine with their congressman, accompany him on vacations and {$_{\text{SHOWER-WITH-STH}}$[$_{\text{CEE}}$<shower>] [$_{\text{RECIPIENT}}$him] [$_{\text{THEME}}$with gifts]}.

(4) does not include annotations of the grammatical function and phrase structure of each of the CEs. In line with the descriptions of the respective FEs in the Giving frame, the CEs realized in (4) can be defined as follows:

---

15 https://framenet.icsi.berkeley.edu/fndrupal/index.php?q=luIndex (last accessed on August 4, 2014).

- DONOR is the person that begins in possession of the THEME and causes it to be in the possession of the RECIPIENT.
- RECIPIENT is the person that receives the THEME from the DONOR.
- THEME is the object that changes ownership.

All of this information is relevant for designing a proper constructional entry in a learner's dictionary. The following section shows how this information can be neatly integrated into the G-FOL database.

3.3 Integrating constructional information into G-FOL

We now demonstrate how to integrate constructional information into G-FOL on the basis of the *shower-sb-with-sth* construction introduced above. Currently, G-FOL is limited to words that evoke a frame; it does not yet contain constructions. However, just as FrameNet may be extended to a FrameNet constructicon (cf. Ziem 2014b: 283–285), we may expand the G-FOL database to a repository of grammatical constructions relevant for language learners' needs when consulting a dictionary.

The most basic information to include in the database concerns the "Construction Description" subsuming definitions of the CEs. With respect to the *shower-sb-with-sth* construction, the data are similar to the descriptions and definitions given in the prior section. Analogous to the "Frame Description", which provides a list of all frame-evoking LUs (cf. details in Section 2.3), the "Construction Description" will comprise a list of CEEs. The list will encompass verbs such as *overwhelm* or *flood*, which also serve as CEEs once they enter into the construction.

Regarding the information provided for each CEE and the respective constructions, we will also stick to the data structure developed for each frame-evoking LU wherever possible. To be precise, the following categories will be adopted, which are illustrated by the German equivalent of the *shower-sb-with-sth* construction (see previous sections above).
- *Details*: If a German construction differs from its English equivalent, it is elaborated to what extent this is the case. Even though the German *jdn. mit etwas überschütten* ('to shower-sb-with-sth') construction does not exhibit grammatical properties peculiar to this unit, there are constraints concerning the realization of the CEs: first, in a declarative active sentence DONOR must be realized in subject position; second, RECIPIENT is required to be realized as a direct object; third, THEME must take the form of a PP whose nominal constituent might well be abstract (*joy, love*); finally, all three CEs

must be realized. Furthermore, it is worth mentioning that in the standard translation *shower-sb-with-sth*, the verb *shower* undergoes a metaphorical shift, just like *überschütten* ('to shower-sb-with-sth' or 'to shower-sth-on-sb') in the German equivalent. Since this metaphorical meaning is conventionalized, it should also show up in the "Details" portion of the entries for *shower* and *überschütten* respectively.

- *Examples*: This rubric will include annotated sample sentences instantiating the grammatical construction addressed, such as (3b). To keep the examples for language learners as simple and accessible as possible, the annotations only cover CEs and their functions within a construction. Thus, in (3b) the NP *these power brokers* is labeled as DONOR, the NP *him* as RECIPIENT, and the noun *gifts* within the PP *with gifts* as THEME.
- *Grammar Notes*: As a more specific instance of the abstract construction [VERB + direct object + prepositional object with *with*], *jdn. mit etwas überschütten* ('to shower-sb-with-sth') displays regular syntactic properties and it inherits the prototypical meaning of ditransitive constructions, namely that the "[a]gent successfully causes recipient to receive patient" (Goldberg 1995: 38), and more specific information from the Giving frame as defined in FrameNet.[16] However, note that in written discourse verbs such as *überfluten* and *überschwemmen* ('to flood') are limited to rather informal registers; as a matter of fact, they are common in spoken discourse but also occur in narrative texts including newspaper articles.
- *Sentence Templates*: Neither the English *shower-sb-with-sth* construction nor its German equivalent *jdn. mit etwas überschütten* varies in terms of the realization and configuration of CEs. The sentence template is thus restricted to 'DONOR shower/s RECIPIENT with THEME'.
- *Alternative Forms*: As mentioned in Section 2.3, the G-FOL database also provides a list of alternate verb forms (preterites, participles, etc.) for each frame-evoking LU. For constructional entries, these pieces of information are equally relevant in that many constructions either comprise irregular verbs or allow for a variety of CE configurations.

In order to make G-FOL as user-friendly as possible, we intend to allow users to access constructional information in two ways. In addition to providing a repository of basic constructions relevant for language learners, or a mini-constructicon, constructions should also be accessible through the entries of those LUs that act as CEEs.

---

16 https://framenet.icsi.berkeley.edu/fndrupal/index.php?q=frameIndex (last accessed on August 4, 2014).

4 Conclusions and outlook

This paper reported on the conceptual development and implementation of a frame- and construction-based online dictionary for language learners. Specifically, we introduced G-FOL, a bilingual lexical resource developed first and foremost for English-speaking university students in first- and second-year German courses. Given that G-FOL is based on Berkeley FrameNet data revised for pedagogical purposes, we discussed how constructional information could be integrated into the database established so far.

Our aim to build a didactic resource such as G-FOL, designed for supporting foreign language teaching and learning, is motivated by three observations. First, there is a practical need for rich vocabulary instruction within the constraints of an average US college syllabus and in line with our knowledge about the cognitive demands for foreign language learning (Ellis 1997; Nation 2001). Second, there is a general disconnect between vocabulary and grammar in most pedagogical resources, yielding enormous difficulties for language learners. Third, there is typically not enough time in foreign language class periods to also teach the detailed aspects of word meaning and grammar that are necessary for proper usage.

To illustrate these challenges for a modern learner's dictionary, we showed how verbs in the Grooming frame exhibit semantic and grammatical differences, which are rarely obvious to average language learners. Based on findings in this case study, we described the general structure of the G-FOL database, including a "Frame Description" for each frame, "Details" about annotated sentences, grammar notes, sentence templates, and alternative forms for each frame-evoking LU. In this context, it was our goal to demonstrate how G-FOL employs and expands on principles of FrameNet (Fillmore and Baker 2010) and to what extent the methodological framework could be applied to more complex frames and constructions.

To this end, G-FOL is designed to enable language learners to learn the meaning and usage of new words outside of the classroom, using contrastive examples and semantic frames to make vocabulary acquisition more effective. This learning can take place at any time with the help of any device connected to the internet (e.g. computer, tablet, smartphone), thereby allowing learners to individually tailor their learning process.

In the future, we intend to implement grammatical constructions in the G-FOL database systematically. An important part of this endeavor is to set up an even richer pedagogical resource, documenting the entire range of constructions for each LU. Not only does such a "mini-constructicon" for language learners reveal relations between various constructions in German and English, but, more importantly, implementing annotated exercise texts (such as cloze and multiple choice tests) into the dictionary also facilitates interactive vocabulary and construction learning. In addition, we plan on developing accompanying pedagogical materials such as online exercises (e.g. fill-in-the-blank, multiple choice, writing tasks) and classroom activities specifically designed for different learner levels. For detailed ideas about what such materials may look like, see Boas and Dux (2013).

References

Atzler, Judith 2011. *Twist in the list: Frame Semantics as a vocabulary teaching and learning tool*. Austin, TX, The University of Texas at Austin dissertation.
Baker, Collin F. 1999. *Seeing clearly: Frame Semantic, psycholinguistic, and cross-linguistic approaches to the semantics of the English verb* see. Berkeley, CA, University of California, Berkeley dissertation.
Baker, Collin F., Charles J. Fillmore & John B. Lowe. 1998. The Berkeley FrameNet Project. In *COLING-ACL '98: Proceedings of the Conference*. Montreal, Canada.
Baker, Collin F., Charles J. Fillmore & Beau Cronin. 2003. The structure of the FrameNet database. *International Journal of Lexicography* 16. 281–296.
Boas, Hans C. 2001. Frame Semantics as a framework for describing polysemy and syntactic structures of English and German motion verbs in contrastive computational lexicography. In Paul Rayson, Andrew Wilson, Tony McEnery, Andrew Hardie & Shereen Khoja (eds.), *Proceedings of Corpus Linguistics 2001*, 64–73. Lancaster: University Centre for Computer Corpus Research on Language.
Boas, Hans C. 2002. Bilingual FrameNet dictionaries for machine translation. In M. González Rodríguez & C. Paz Suárez Araujo (eds.), *Proceedings of the Third International Conference on Language Resources and Evaluation, Vol. IV*, 1364–1371. Las Palmas, Spain.
Boas, Hans C. 2005a. Semantic Frames as interlingual representations for multilingual lexical databases. *International Journal of Lexicography* 18(4). 445–478.
Boas, Hans C. 2005b. From theory to practice: Frame Semantics and the design of FrameNet. In S. Langer & D. Schnorbusch (eds.), *Semantik im Lexikon*, 129–160. Tübingen: Narr.
Boas, Hans C. 2009a. Semantic frames as interlingual representations for multilingual lexical databases. In Hans C. Boas (ed.), *Multilingual FrameNets in computational lexicography: Methods and applications*, 59–100. Berlin & New York: Mouton de Gruyter.
Boas, Hans C. 2009b. Recent trends in multilingual computational lexicography. In Hans C. Boas (ed.), *Multilingual FrameNets in Computational Lexicography: Methods and Applications*, 1–26. Berlin & New York: Mouton de Gruyter.
Boas, Hans C. 2010. The syntax-lexicon continuum in Construction Grammar: A case study of English communication verbs. *Belgian Journal of Linguistics* 24. 57–86.
Boas, Hans C. 2011. Constructing parallel lexicon fragments based on English FrameNet entries: Semantic and syntactic issues. In Hanna Hedeland, Thomas Schmidt & Kai Wörner (eds.), *Multilingual resources and multilingual applications. Proceedings of the German Society*

for *Computational Linguistics and Language Technology*, 9–18. Hamburg: University of Hamburg: Center for Language Corpora.

Boas, Hans C. & Ryan Dux. 2013. Semantic frames for foreign language education: Towards a German frame-based dictionary. *Veredas* 17(1) [special issue on Frame Semantics and its technological applications]. 82–100.

Borin, Lars, Dana Dannélls, Markus Forsberg, Maria Toporowska Gronostaj & Dimitrios Kokkinakis. 2009. Thinking green: Toward Swedish FrameNet++. *Proceedings of FrameNet Masterclass*, University of Milan. http://tlt8.unicatt.it/allegati/Session_I_3.pdf (last accessed on August 4, 2014).

Broccias, Christiano. 2012. The syntax-lexicon continuum. In Terttu Nevalainen & Elizabeth C. Traugott (eds.), *The Oxford handbook of the history of English*, 735–747. Oxford: Oxford University Press.

Burchardt, Aljoscha, Katrin Erk, Anette Frank, Andrea Kowalski, Sebastian Pado & Manfred Pinkal. 2009. Using FrameNet for the semantic analysis of German: Annotation, representation, and automation. In Hans C. Boas (ed.), *Multilingual FrameNets in computational lexicography: Methods and applications*, 209–244. Berlin & New York: Mouton de Gruyter.

Dolbey, Andrew, Michael Ellsworth & Jan Scheffczyk. 2006. BioFrameNet: A domain-specific FrameNet extension with links to biomedical ontologies. Paper presented at the International Workshop Biomedical Ontology in Action, Baltimore, MD, November 8.

Ellis, Nick C. 1997. Vocabulary acquisition: Word structure, collocation, grammar, and meaning. In Norbert Schmitt & Michael McCarthy (eds.), *Vocabulary: Description, acquisition and pedagogy*, 122–139. Cambridge: Cambridge University Press.

Fillmore, Charles J. 1982. Frame Semantics. In Linguistic Society of Korea (ed.), *Linguistics in the morning calm*. 111–137. Seoul: Hanshin.

Fillmore, Charles J. 1985. Frames and the semantics of understanding. *Quaderni di Semantica* 6. 222–254.

Fillmore, Charles J. 2008. Border Conflicts: FrameNet Meets Construction Grammar. In Elisenda Bernal & Janet De Cesaris (eds.). *Proceedings of the XIII EURALEX International Congress*, 49–68. Barcelona: Universitat Pompeu Fabra.

Fillmore, Charles J. 2013. *Frames, constructions, and FrameNet*. Berkeley, CA. Unpublished paper.

Fillmore, Charles J. & Beryl T. S. Atkins. 1992. Towards a frame-based organization of the lexicon: The semantics of RISK and its neighbors. In A. L. E. Kittay (ed.), *Frames, fields, and contrasts: New essays in semantics and lexical organization*, 75–102. Hillsdale, NJ: Erlbaum.

Fillmore, Charles J. & Beryl T. S. Atkins. 2000. Describing polysemy: The case of 'crawl'. In Y. Ravin & C. Laecock (eds.), *Polysemy*, 91–110. Oxford: Oxford University Press.

Fillmore, Charles J., Chris R. Johnson & Miriam. R. L. Petruck. 2003. Background to FrameNet. *International Journal of Lexicography* 16(3). 235–251.

Fillmore, Charles J. & Collin F. Baker. 2010. A frames approach to semantic analysis. In B. Heine & Heiko Narrog (eds.), *The Oxford handbook of linguistic analysis*, 313–339. Oxford: Oxford University Press.

Fillmore, Charles J., Russell Lee-Goldman & Russell Rhodes. 2012. Sign-based construction grammar and the FrameNet constructicon. In Hans C. Boas & Ivan A. Sag (eds.), *Sign-based construction grammar*, 309–372. Stanford: CSLI Publications.

Fontenelle, Thierry. 2009. A bilingual lexical database for Frame Semantics. In H. C. Boas (ed.), *Multilingual FrameNets in computational lexicography: Methods and applications*, 37–58. Berlin & New York: Mouton de Gruyter.

Fung, Pascale and Benfeng Chen. 2004. BiFrameNet: Bilingual frame semantics resource construction by cross-lingual induction. *Proceedings of the 20th international conference on computational linguistics.* Association for Computational Linguistics.

Goldberg, Adele. 1995. *Constructions. A construction grammar approach to argument structure.* Chicago: Chicago University Press.

Goldberg, Adele. 2006. *Constructions at work. The nature of generalization in language.* Oxford: Oxford University Press.

Heid, Ulrich. 1996. Creating multilingual data collection for bilingual lexicography from parallel monolingual lexicons. *Proceedings of Euralex 1996.* Gothenburg: University of Gothenburg.

Heid, Ulrich. 2006. Valenzwörterbücher im Netz. In Petra Steiner, Hans C. Boas & Stefan J. Schierholz (eds.), *Contrastive studies and valency. Studies in honor of Hans Ulrich Boas,* 69–90. Frankfurt: Peter Lang.

Hoffmann, Thomas and Graeme Trousdale (eds.). 2013. *The Oxford handbook of construction grammar.* Oxford: Oxford University Press.

Holme, Richard. 2010. A construction grammar for the classroom. *International Review of Applied Linguistics* 48(4). 355–377.

Iwata, Seizi. 2002. Does MANNER count or not? Manner-of-motion verbs revisited. *Linguistics* 40(1). 61–110.

Lambrecht, Knud. 1984. Formulaicity, frame semantics, and pragmatics in German binomial expressions. *Language* 60(4). 753–796.

Matsumoto, Yoshiko. 1989. Politeness and conversational universals – Observations from Japanese. *Multilingua – Journal of Cross-Cultural and Interlanguage Communication* 8(2–3). 207–222.

Nation, Ian S. P. 2001. *Learning vocabulary in another language.* New York: Cambridge University Press.

Ohara, Kyoko. 2009. Frame-based contrastive lexical semantics in Japanese FrameNet: The case of *risk* and *kakeru.* In Hans C. Boas (ed.), *Multilingual FrameNets in computational lexicography: Methods and applications,* 163–182. Berlin & New York: Mouton de Gruyter.

Petruck, Miriam R. L. 1986. *Body part terminology in Hebrew: A study in lexical semantics.* Berkeley, CA: University of California, Berkeley dissertation.

Petruck, Miriam R. L. 1996. Frame Semantics. In Jef Verschueren, Jan-Ola Östman, Jan Blommaert, and Chris Bulcaen (eds.), *Handbook of pragmatics.* 1–13. Philadelphia: John Benjamins.

Petruck, Miriam R. L. 2009. Typological considerations in constructing a Hebrew FrameNet. In Hans C. Boas (ed.), *Multilingual FrameNets in computational lexicography: Methods and applications,* 183–208. Berlin & New York: Mouton de Gruyter.

Petruck, Miriam, Charles J. Fillmore, Michael Ellsworth & Josef Ruppenhofer. 2004. Reframing FrameNet data. *Proceedings of the 11th EURALEX International Congress,* 405–416. Lorient, France.

Pitel, Guillaume. 2009. Cross-lingual labeling of semantic predicates and roes: A low-resource method based on bilingual L(atent) S(emantic) A(nalysis). In Hans C. Boas (ed.), *Multilingual FrameNets in computational lexicography: Methods and applications,* 245–286. Berlin & New York: Mouton de Gruyter.

Ruppenhofer, Josef, Michael Ellsworth, Miriam R. L. Petruck, Christopher R. Johnson & Jan Scheffczyk. 2010. FrameNet II: Extended theory and practice. Manuscript. University of Berkeley. https://framenet2.icsi.berkeley.edu/docs/r1.5/book.pdf (last accessed on August 4, 2014).

Schmidt, Thomas. 2009. The Kicktionary – A multilingual lexical resource of football language. In Hans C. Boas (ed.), *Multilingual FrameNets in computational lexicography: Methods and applications*, 101–134. Berlin & New York: Mouton de Gruyter.

Subirats, Carlos. 2009. Spanish FrameNet: A frame-semantic analysis of the Spanish lexicon. In Hans C. Boas (ed.), *Multilingual FrameNets in computational lexicography: Methods and applications*, 135–162. Berlin & New York: Mouton de Gruyter.

Subirats, Carlos & Miriam R. L. Petruck. 2003. Surprise: Spanish FrameNet! In Eva Hajičová, Anna Kotěšovcová & Jiří Mírovský (eds.), *Proceedings of the 17th International Congress of Linguists*, CD-ROM. Prague: Matfyzpress.

Ziem, Alexander. 2014a. *Frames of understanding in text and discourse: Theoretical foundations and descriptive applications*. Amsterdam & Philadelphia: John Benjamins.

Ziem, Alexander. 2014b. Von Kasusrahmen zum FrameNet: Frames, Konstruktionen und die Idee eines Konstruktikons. In Alexander Lasch & Alexander Ziem (eds.), *Grammatik als Netzwerk von Konstruktionen: Sprachliches Wissen im Fokus der Konstruktionsgrammatik*, 351–388. Berlin & New York: Mouton de Gruyter.

Ziem, Alexander. 2015a. Fußball für Anfänger: Sieben Thesen zur Konzeption eines elektronischen Wörterbuches für den Sprachunterricht. In Joachim Born & Thomas Gloning (eds.), *Sport, Sprache, Kommunikation, Medien: interdisziplinäre Perspektiven* (Linguistische Untersuchungen 8), 381–410. Gießen: GEB.

Ziem, Alexander. 2015b. *Metaphors meet G-FOL*: Zur Integration von Metaphern in eine Lehr- und Lernplattform für DaF. In Martin Dalmas & Elisabeth Piirainen (eds.), *Figurative Sprache*, 201–220. Tübingen: Stauffenburg.

Ziem, Alexander. Under review. Towards a frame- and construction-based dictionary for language learners.

Ziem, Alexander, Hans C. Boas & Josef Ruppenhofer. 2014. Semantische Frames und grammatische Konstruktionen für die Textanalyse. In Jörg Hagemann & Sven Staffeldt (eds.), *Syntaxtheorien. Vergleichende Analysen*, 297–333. Tübingen: Stauffenburg.

Ziem, Alexander & Alexander Lasch. 2013. *Konstruktionsgrammatik. Konzepte und Grundlagen gebrauchsbasierter Ansätze* (Germanistische Arbeitshefte 44). Berlin & New York: de Gruyter.

Lisa Loenheim, Benjamin Lyngfelt, Joel Olofsson,
Julia Prentice and Sofia Tingsell
Constructicography meets (second) language education: On constructions in teaching aids and the usefulness of a Swedish constructicon

Abstract: This chapter addresses the need for better coverage of semi-general linguistic patterns in (second) language pedagogy, which is currently biased towards general rules on the one hand and concrete expressions on the other. Arguably, this reflects the descriptive resources available: grammars and dictionaries. Hence, we propose that L2 education should benefit from a constructionist approach, which is less restricted to distinct linguistic levels and therefore better suited to handle, in particular, patterns combining lexical and grammatical properties.

We review some of the leading Swedish L2 textbooks and study aid materials, and illustrate how they tend to neglect semi-general patterns and fail to capture the productivity and variability of constructions. For future L2 education to achieve better coverage in this regard, access to constructionist descriptive resources should be helpful. As an example of such a resource, we present the Swedish constructicon (SweCcn), an electronic database of Swedish construction descriptions, and discuss its usefulness for developing construction-based teaching materials, as a complement to the grammar and dictionary approach.

Keywords: language pedagogy; second language learning; constructicon; constructicography; construction grammar; Swedish

1 Introduction[1]

Teaching materials in (second) language pedagogy obviously have to account for concrete expressions as well as general rules. What tends to be overlooked,

---

[1] The Swedish constructicon project is funded by the Bank of Sweden Tercentenary Foundation (grant agreement P12–0076:1). We are grateful to the editors and two anonymous reviewers for valuable comments on an earlier version of this paper.

however, are semi-general patterns (such as *the X-er the Y-er* or resultative constructions), even in cases where this is the relevant level of generalization (e.g. Littlemore 2009). This bias in textbooks is a natural reflection of the types of linguistic resources available: grammars and dictionaries. The common conception of language as consisting of a grammar and a lexicon invites a corresponding treatment of linguistic units as general (grammatical) rules on the one hand and lexical idiosyncrasies on the other.

There are, however, many linguistic patterns that are too specific to be considered general rules, yet too general to be restricted to particular lexical units. As studies in construction grammar have shown time and again (see e.g. Fillmore, Lee-Goldman, and Rhomieux 2012; Hoffmann and Trousdale 2013), these are by no means just a few borderline cases but actually a large and significant part of the language. Furthermore, semi-general constructions of this kind have been shown to be much more frequent in first language usage than in second language usage, even at fairly advanced levels (e.g. Ekberg 2013), and (second) language education should benefit from paying more attention to them (see further below).

Since many constructions combine lexical, grammatical and other features, they are hard to capture from either a purely grammatical or a purely lexical perspective, instead requiring some other mode of representation. Such a perspective is provided by construction grammar (henceforth CxG; Fillmore, Kay, and O'Connor 1988; Fillmore and Kay 1993; Croft 2001; Goldberg 2006; Hoffmann and Trousdale 2013; and others), where the traditional grammar-lexicon dichotomy is rejected and "peripheral", "borderline" constructions are treated on an equal footing with other language patterns. From a CxG point of view, a language (or at least its lexicogrammar) may be conceived of, not as a modular combination of a grammar and a lexicon, but as a structured inventory of constructions of varying generality and complexity: a constructicon.

As a theoretical construal of language structure, the notion of constructicon has been around since the early days of CxG (at least since Fillmore 1988, although the term *constructicon* appeared later). As corresponding descriptive resources, in the sense of repositories of construction descriptions, constructicons have only recently started to emerge. The first constructicon project was initiated for English, as a complement to FrameNet (Fillmore 2008; Fillmore, Lee-Goldman and Rhomieux 2012), and there are now constructicons under development for Brazilian Portuguese (Torrent et al. 2014), Japanese (Ohara 2013), and Swedish (Lyngfelt et al. 2012; Sköldberg et al. 2013) as well.[2] In practice, constructicon

---

[2] There are also plans for a German constructicon (Boas 2014; Ziem, Boas, and Ruppenhofer 2014).

development combines features of CxG and lexicography in what may be called *constructicography*.

In the Swedish constructicon project, a special concern is to account for constructions that are problematic for second and foreign language acquisition. These are identified from corpora of Swedish as a second or foreign language (L2) among other sources. In the present chapter, we will on the one hand illustrate the treatment of semi-general constructions in some textbooks for L2 Swedish, and on the other hand present the Swedish constructicon (SweCcn) and discuss its potential as a resource for improving Swedish L2 teaching in this regard. First, however, we will briefly introduce a constructionist view of language as a repertory of constructions (Fillmore 1988: 37).

2 A constructionist perspective

Constructions are typically defined as "conventional, learned form-function pairings at varying levels of complexity and abstraction" (Goldberg 2013: 17). They may be anything from entirely schematic patterns like 'noun phrase' to fixed idiomatic expressions like *by and large*, from sentence level constructions to individual words.[3] The crucial property is that a formal pattern is conventionally associated with a certain meaning or function.

Thus, constructions do not make up an intermediate level between lexical items and grammatical rules. Instead, both these kinds of linguistic units may be viewed as types of constructions; they just tend towards different ends of the scale in a continuum of more or less general constructions. There are at least three methodological benefits with this view:
- *coverage*: linguistic patterns with both lexical and grammatical properties are naturally included, instead of being hard to incorporate in either grammatical or lexical accounts;
- *focus*: constructions are treated as actual linguistic entities, instead of merely epiphenomenal products of the interaction between more general principles, on the one hand, or similarities between distinct lexical patterns, on the other;
- *practicality*: linguistic units of different levels are handled in a similar fashion, and, hence, relevant features otherwise associated with different levels may be incorporated in the same analysis.

---

[3] Whether form-meaning pairs smaller than words and larger than sentences should also be considered constructions is a matter of some debate, which we will not go into here.

Consequently, any linguistic pattern is in principle a legitimate object of study in its own right. This does not in any way reduce language to an unordered list of particularities, since the constructions (types) presumably form an ordered network and the constructs (tokens) that instantiate them are combined into utterances in systematic ways. The approach is typically multigrain, and more specific constructions may be treated as instances of more general ones.

As an illustration, consider the Swedish [X *och* X] construction, where a word or phrase from the preceding utterance is repeated twice in a coordinate structure, thereby indicating that the repeated expression is not quite adequate in the present situation (e.g. Lindström and Linell 2007, Norén and Linell 2007). A typical example is given in (1):[4]

(1) – *Har   du   köpt   ny   bil?*
        Have you   buy-SUP   new   car
        'Have you bought a new car?'

     – *Nja,   **ny**   **och**   **ny**,   den   är   från   2008.*
        well   new   and   new   it   be-PRS   from   2008
        'Well, not really *new*, it's from 2008.'

As shown in (1), the [X *och* X] construction consists of the specific word *och* ('and'), the syntactic coordination as such, two occurrences of the variable X, which can be any word as long as it occurs in the previous utterance, and the pragmatic function to renegotiate the relevance of X. Hence, the constraints on [X *och* X] concern several linguistic levels, including particular properties of a preceding sentence. In a network of constructions, [X *och* X] on the one hand belongs to a group of reactive constructions (cf. Linell and Norén 2009), which share the pragmatic property of reacting to an expression in the previous utterance; on the other hand, it is part of a hierarchy of coordination constructions, as shown in Figure 1 (from Lyngfelt and Wide 2014).

---

4 In the glosses and elsewhere, the following abbreviations for grammatical categories are used: Adj (adjective), AP (adjective phrase), DEF (definite), GEN (genitive), INDEF (indefinite), N (noun), NP (noun phrase), Num (numeral), P (preposition), PL (plural), PP (prepositional phrase), PST (past, more specifically preterite), QUANT (quantitative), PRS (present), REFL (reflexive), SG (singular), SUP (supine), VP (verb phrase).

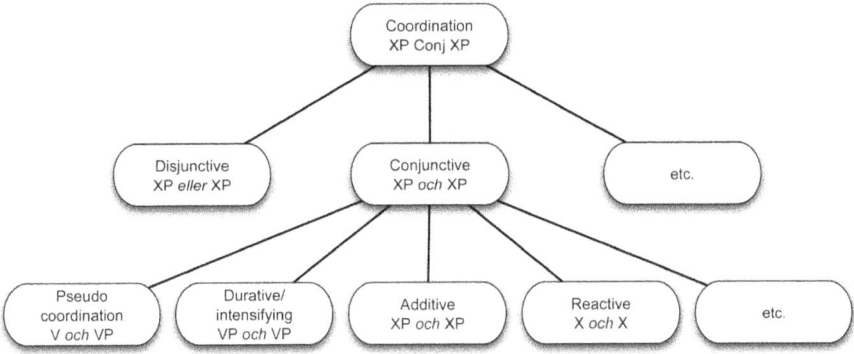

Figure 1: A partial taxonomy of coordination constructions in Swedish (Lyngfelt and Wide 2014)

As illustrated in Figure 1, coordinations may be conjunctive, disjunctive, etc. Zooming in on conjunctive coordination, Swedish employs pseudo coordination (2), durative/intensifying (3) and ordinary additive (4) conjunction, reactive [X *och* X] (1), as well as some other variants.

(2) *Mikael har gått och förlovat sig.*
    Mikael has gone and engage-SUP REFL
    'Mikael has got engaged.'

(3) *Ni bara pratar och pratar.*
    You just talk-PRS and talk-PRS
    'You just talk and talk.'

(4) *Kaffe och konjak, tack.*
    coffee and brandy please
    'A coffee and a brandy, please.'

These constructions may then interact with others. As mentioned above, the specific instantiations of the constructions in an actual utterance are called constructs. Smaller constructs make up larger ones, and all of them represent constructions of different generality and complexity. For instance, the example in (2) instantiates (at least) the following constructions: DECLARATIVE SENTENCE, PSEUDO COORDINATION, PROPER NOUN, VERB PHRASE, PERFECT TENSE, REFLEXIVE, and the lexical constructions MIKAEL, HA, GÅ, OCH, and FÖRLOVA (REFL). By combining the constructions HA, GÅ and PERFECT TENSE (which in turn consists of PRESENT + SUPINE), we get the particular construct *har gått* 'has gone' etc.

The hierarchy in Figure 1 is somewhat redundant in that some of the patterns may be deduced from knowledge of the others (including the relevant lexical items). Such redundancy is considered undesirable according to a longstanding tradition in linguistics to strive for parsimony, in the sense of minimizing the number of assumptions. The idea is basically that the fewer rules a grammar needs to generate the relevant linguistic patterns, the better it is presumably. This parsimony, however, only concerns what is stored and comes at the price of a higher processing load. One may just as well argue that the critical limitations seem to concern the working memory rather than the storing capacity, and that it would therefore be more parsimonious to reduce the processing load by storing more constructions, even if they are predictable from other patterns (e.g. Wray 2008). An indication in this direction is the tendency of first language speakers, who presumably know how to use their language effectively, to use more formulaic expressions than language learners (cf. Ekberg 2013; Wray 2008). This would also suggest that L2 learners should benefit greatly from storing more constructions.

In any case, the issue essentially boils down to the division of labor between storing and figuring out (cf. Croft 2003). Lacking decisive neuro-linguistic evidence for either view, one may at least conclude that a multigrain, more redundant approach should not simply be disregarded on the grounds of parsimony. On the contrary, it is well worth exploring as an alternative to the traditional position.

In an L2 context, it is clear that some of the coordination constructions are typologically unmarked, whereas e.g. pseudo coordination and reactive [X och X] are more idiosyncratic. The particular properties of these patterns do not simply follow from knowledge of coordination in general. Neither can they be reduced to a few lexical exceptions and taught as particular chunks; such a strategy would fail to capture the productivity of these constructions (cf. Lyngfelt and Sköldberg 2013).[5] Instead, they could be taught as individual patterns or in the context of other coordination structures, but either way, they should be recognized as constructions.

Another informative set of examples are time expressions. As in many languages, time adverbials in Swedish are typically oblique, occurring as prepositional phrases. Location in time is often introduced by the preposition *på* 'on', as in (5a). When the location is a date, however, as in (5b), there is no preposition (cf. Prentice 2011).

---

5 Although the concept of productivity is a much debated issue in CxG (see e.g. Barðdal 2008; Kay 2013), we will not enter this discussion here.

(5) a. *Jag är   född på sommar-en   / på kväll-en   / på en torsdag.*
    I   be-PRS born on summer-DEF / on evening-DEF / on a   Thursday
    'I was born in the summer / in the evening / on a Thursday.'

b. *Jag är   född den fjärde juli / *på den fjärde juli.*
   I   be-PRS born the fourth July / *on the fourth July
   'I was born on the fourth of July.'

Neither does Swedish employ prepositions in time expressions regarding the closest preceding or following time unit: *förra veckan* (last week-DEF), *nästa vecka* (next week-INDEF). In this case the lack of a preposition conforms to corresponding constructions in English and other related languages, but there is an added distinction in that the past time units are in the definite form but the future ones are indefinite. This also applies to some related past and future modifiers: *förrförra året* 'the year before last' (definite), *följande måndag* 'the following Monday' (indefinite form).

Furthermore, there is an alternative construction for preceding time units, employing the preposition *i* ('in') followed by a temporal noun in the genitive: *i lördags* (in Saturday-GEN, 'last Saturday'), *i våras* (in spring-GEN, 'last spring'), *i julas* (in Christmas-GEN, 'last Christmas'), etc. It is less productive than *förra* Noun-DEF (for instance, *i kvällas*, in night-GEN 'last night', is ungrammatical), but it is more commonly used.[6]

None of these patterns for time expressions – [*i* $N_{sg,\ gen}$], [*förra* $N_{sg,\ def}$], etc. – may be deduced from general grammatical rules. Neither can they be attributed to lexical properties, with the possible exception of *förra* 'last' and *nästa* 'next'. Even in the latter case, however, a constructional perspective would probably be useful, due to its capacity to smoothly accommodate both the structural features and the productivity of the constructions.

3 Constructions in teaching aids

Previous research has shown that chunks, (semi-general) constructions and related multiword units are important resources for an (advanced) language learner to

---

[6] According to a few quick corpus searches, the structure [*i* $N_{sg,\ gen}$] is more than three times as common as [*förra* $N_{sg,\ def}$]. The comparison was conducted using the corpus tool Korp (http://spraakbanken.gu.se/korp/, last accessed on November 25, 2014), by which more than 150 Swedish corpora can be accessed through the same search interface. The corpora in Korp are annotated for morphosyntactic properties and allow for search strings involving both lexical and grammatical categories (cf. Borin, Forsberg, and Roxendal 2012).

come across as idiomatic or even native-like (e.g. Pawley and Syder 1983; Wray 2008; Ekberg 2013). One may therefore wonder to what extent constructions or multiword units are present in teaching aids in Swedish as a second or foreign language. To investigate this, we have looked into four teaching aids, chosen to represent a broad selection of pedagogical approaches, focusing on a couple of representative examples from each. Our sample includes teaching aids for different target groups, addressing students in Swedish as a foreign language as well as students in Swedish as a second language, at different proficiency levels.[7]

Öppet hus ('Open house') is a traditional textbook meant to teach Swedish as a second language mainly for Swedish for Immigrants (SFI) Courses. It targets beginners at B and C level, corresponding to levels A1-A2 in the European Council's language scales (Common European Framework of Reference for Languages, CEFR; Council of Europe 2001). This teaching aid includes a textbook and a web page with additional exercises and relevant links.

Rivstart ('A flying start') is a traditional textbook that addresses learners of Swedish as a foreign language (but also claims to target learners both in Sweden and abroad), and as such, perhaps, has a more academic approach to learning. Like *Öppet hus*, it is aimed at beginners, explicitly based on the European Council's language scales, levels A1-A2. The textbook is combined with a CD for listening comprehension and a book with grammar exercises.

Skrivhjulet ('The wheel of writing') targets adult students or students in upper secondary school, studying Swedish as a second language. *Skrivhjulet* is a textbook, applying a circle model method to learning, based on genre pedagogical principles (cf. Gibbons 2002).

Form i fokus ('Focus on form') differs from the other teaching aids, not being a textbook but a series of three grammar workbooks intended for adult students studying SFI, Swedish as a second language or Swedish as a foreign language (at universities in Sweden and abroad). *Form i fokus A* – the part examined in this study – starts at a basic level, while *Form i fokus C* addresses more advanced students. The grammar workbooks are complemented with a computer programme with additional exercises and tests.

3.1 *Öppet hus*

As mentioned above, *Öppet hus* is a fairly traditional textbook where the contents are introduced in themes (such as "Shopping for groceries" or "What

---

[7] The teaching aids of the survey are listed last in the reference section.

are you doing for a living/in your spare time?") accompanied by wordlists, grammatical rules and conversation exercises relevant for the theme in question. According to the online book announcement it focuses on the lexicon, i.e. words and phrases in context, rather than grammatical patterns.[8] The expectation is therefore that multiword expressions are typically presented as single phrases usable in certain contexts rather than as variable constructional patterns.

This expectation is met when looking more closely into the presentation of some L2-relevant multiword units in *Öppet hus*. When introducing a theme about someone's fictional calendar and schedule for a week, the phrases *i onsdags* ('last Wednesday') and *i måndags kväll* ('last Monday night') are presented (*Öppet hus* 2004: 40), i.e. two instances of the [*i* N$_{sg, gen}$]-construction (see Section 2 above). This construction occurs twice, alongside a wide range of other time expressions such as *i övermorgon* ('the day after tomorrow') and *på tisdagar* ('on Tuesdays'). Two isolated instances, without comment, and mixed with these other constructions, will probably not lead the student to draw any conclusions about the productivity and variability of the [*i* N$_{sg, gen}$]-construction.

One of the typical topics for conversation exercises in textbooks like *Öppet hus* is "What do you do in your spare time?", including the sentence in (6):

(6) (*jag tycker) det är intressant med mat.*
 (I   think-PRS) it   be-PRS interesting with food.
 '(I think) food is interesting.'

This expression can be described as an instance of the [(*det* VARA) AP *med* NP] construction '[(*it* BE) AP *with* NP]'. In the exercise (*Öppet hus* 2004: 35), the students get to read several short quotations from people about what they like to do in their spare time and the students are then asked to match those quotations to a verb phrase that summarizes the activity (*Öppet hus* 2004: 34). However, the use of idiomatic expressions in the quotations seems quite random, and they are not matched with the contents of a short list of expressions that is previously presented to the students as useful phrases for talking about one's whereabouts (*Öppet hus* 2004: 33). Despite being very productive and idiomatic, the [(*det* VARA) AP *med* NP] construction is not present on that list, and it occurs only once in the exercise, perhaps incorrectly indicating to the student that the construction is not very common.

---

[8] http://turture.abf.se/abfhemsi.nsf/0fef1ab719c1bed2c125659f0055f791/b7ba7d54080ab26d-c1256e6e0045ef4d!OpenDocument (last accessed on November 25, 2014).

In summary, one can say that *Öppet hus* does what it says it does, namely introducing words and multiword units in relevant contexts, mostly leaving grammatical patterns aside. There are good reasons for this, considering, amongst other things, that textbooks for SFI are used by students with various educational backgrounds. Nonetheless, it seems that this kind of contextual approach would probably benefit from adopting more of a constructional perspective, raising students' awareness of the productivity of frequently used and/or language specific, idiomatic linguistic patterns.

3.2 *Rivstart*

The second of the traditional textbooks, *Rivstart*, is also content/theme structured but takes a somewhat different approach to the teaching of context relevant multiword units. In a preface addressing the teacher, the authors state that *Rivstart* is designed to encourage students to figure out linguistic patterns and grammatical rules for themselves. The communicative exercises in the textbook are therefore complemented by so called focus-on boxes that are supposed to illustrate those patterns (*Rivstart* 2007: 3). This approach comes very close to what could be called a constructional one.

Looking at the presentation of some learner-relevant constructions, we find that *Rivstart* is the only teaching aid in our sample that explicitly accounts for e.g. the [i $N_{sg,\ gen}$] construction. The construction is introduced in a short text that deals with past time only. A box next to the text states that this text introduces adverbials of time and the adverb *då* ('then'). The [i $N_{sg,\ gen}$] construction is presented as a list of items including weekdays, "i måndags, i tisdags, osv." ('last Monday, last Tuesday, etc.') and seasons (*Rivstart* 2007: 56). The constructional template is visualized by highlighting the preposition *i* and the recurring genitive-*s* of the noun (see Figure 2).

i måndag<u>s</u>
i tisdag<u>s</u> osv.
i somra<u>s</u>
i vintra<u>s</u>
i våra<u>s</u>

Figure 2: Focus-on box illustrating [*i* $N_{sg,\ gen}$] (*Rivstart* 2007: 56)

The presentation in Figure 2 should make the structural pattern clear for the student, and the list of items implicitly, but clearly, accounts for the productivity of the construction (although the reader is not informed that the construction also includes holidays such as *i påskas* ('last Easter'), as the list does not indicate this possibility).

This strategy for introducing constructional patterns is recurrent in *Rivstart*, and sometimes even generalized beyond single words and wordlists in a way approaching a construction grammar account. A good example of this is (7) (adapted from *Rivstart* 2007: 177), which illustrates a common presentational construction in Swedish:

(7) *det står   / hänger   / ligger   / sitter   / finns* + obestämd form
    it stand-PRS / hang-PRS / lay-PRS / sit-PRS / be-PRS   indefinite form
    'There is + indef. form'

The construction in (7) corresponds to the English phrase [*there* BE NP$_{indef}$] (cf. Lakoff 1987: 462–585 on *there* constructions) but with a variable verb slot. In the *Rivstart* account, *det* ('it') and *obestämd form* ('indefinite form') are highlighted in yellow, explicitly indicating the relevant grammatical information. The book does not, however, go into explicit explanations of how such schematic descriptions are to be understood by the student. There is no information on the degree of variability in the open slots, like the verb slot in (7), nor is anything said about the (non-)variability in the highlighted sections. Such information, along with a short text on the vast number of phrases of this kind within a language, would probably be helpful in drawing the students' attention to these linguistic phenomena and their importance for language learning.

There are also cases where the *Rivstart* ambition to illustrate the relevant linguistic patterns, i.e. the constructions, is less successful – typically due to a focus on particular words in isolation rather than the whole patterns and the functions they express. For example, there is a short text in the form of an sms-conversation that is meant to illustrate the use of certain prepositions (see Figure 3).

The relevant units here are the phrases expressing space and time in answer to the questions *where* and *when*. They are situated in a fairly realistic context, which should make it easy to figure out the basic content of the text. However, as we can see in Figure 3, the highlighting (boldface) only singles out the prepositions rather than accounting for the full adverbial expressions. The focus-on boxes for the two different prepositions are also somewhat unclear regarding the relevant functions. The preposition *om* ('about') is connected to

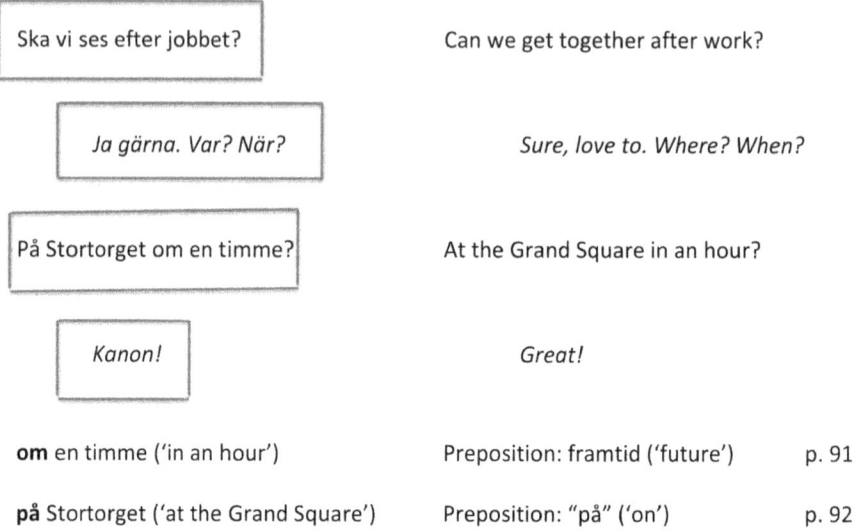

| om en timme ('in an hour') | Preposition: framtid ('future') | p. 91 |
| på Stortorget ('at the Grand Square') | Preposition: "på" ('on') | p. 92 |

Figure 3: Use of the prepositions *på* and *om* in context (from *Rivstart* 2007: 91–92)

'future' (see Figure 3 above), whereas the focus-on box for the place expression merely states that *på* ('on') is a preposition (*Rivstart* 2007: 92).

Prepositions are a well-known difficulty for L2 learners. Part of the problem, though, may be that learning materials (so even *Rivstart*) usually present them as prepositions rather than as parts of the constructions they occur in. A simple presentation of the relevant temporal and spatial constructions, as suggested in Figure 4, would in our opinion improve the chances for students to become aware of the relevant patterns for expressing time and space.

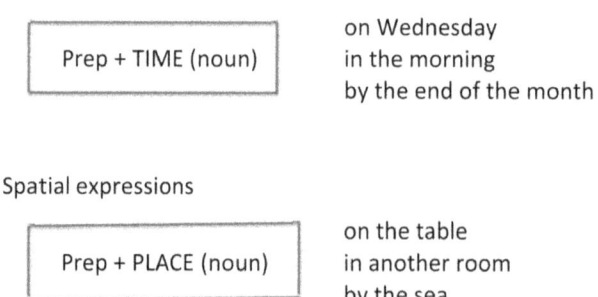

Time expressions

Prep + TIME (noun) on Wednesday
                    in the morning
                    by the end of the month

Spatial expressions

Prep + PLACE (noun) on the table
                    in another room
                    by the sea

Figure 4: Treating prepositional phrases as constructions

Summing up, *Rivstart* can be said to apply what resembles a constructional perspective to some extent and quite successfully so in many cases. The presentation of the [*i* N$_{sg, gen}$] construction, as described above, is a good example of how a constructional perspective can highlight productive linguistic patterns that certain language specific expressions are instances of in a way that is comprehensible for language learners with variable degrees of linguistic knowledge. In other cases the focus-on boxes mainly highlight single lexical or grammatical items – often but not always clearly related to a certain function.

3.3 *Skrivhjulet*

Within the field of second language learning and teaching, the past decade has seen a growing interest in genre pedagogy (cf. Gibbons 2002). Genre pedagogy typically shows the learner how to perform in various genre contexts, e.g. making a description or recounting an event. Teaching materials in Swedish as a second language have been inspired by this paradigm and hence there are learning materials that take textual functions as their point of departure. *Skrivhjulet* is one such teaching aid. Its target group is students in upper secondary school studying Swedish as a second language. Function is the core of interest in these textbooks, and students are taught how to use formulas to start, pursue and close the genre-based texts. Each chapter starts with a text that works as a template for the student. In a second step, the student is asked to fill in the missing forms in a text that closely resembles the template, guided by instructions such as "insert a time expression". Finally, the student is supposed to write his/her own text in the genre.

While describing linguistic characteristics of different genres, *Skrivhjulet* introduces the learner to genre specific ways of structuring the text, and furthermore presents expressions or words useful in that context. The latter is done from a lexical, rather than a constructional, perspective. The learner is introduced to fixed phrases or expressions, even when the expression is an instance of a productive construction, cf. the past time expression in (8), presented in chapter 3 (*Berätta* 'Tell') as a formula to use in narrative text (*Skrivhjulet* 2011: 59, 67).

(8) *för många år sedan*
    for many year ago
    'many years ago'

Even though (8) is an instance of a productive construction where the time unit is variable, the learner is introduced to a fixed phrase, and not provided with any information on how to use this expression productively, cf. (9).[9]

(9) a. [för många N$_{pl}$ sedan]

    b. för många år/månader/veckor/dagar/timmar sedan
       for many TIME-PL ago
       'many years/months/weeks/days/hours ago'

The N slot of this construction (9a) can be filled by different time expressions. However, frequency effects can explain why *Skrivhjulet* chooses to present *för många år sedan* ('many years ago'), i.e. why they combine *många* ('many') with *år* ('years') in the time slot. This is by far the most frequent expression, especially in narrative text (compared to speech). Therefore, it is reasonable to choose this expression if one has to pick out a single one to present. But the point is that the learner probably would benefit from a constructional description that illustrates the variability of the expression (see also Holme 2009).

Furthermore, not only the time slot, but also the quantitative slot (cf. *många*) of the construction is variable, and can include several quantitative adjectives or a numeral (10a–b).

(10) a. [för AP$_{quant}$/Num N$_{time}$ sedan]

    b. för många/flera/två år/månader/veckor/dagar/timmar sedan
       for QUANT TIME ago
       'many/several/two years/months/weeks/days/hours ago'

Since the learners are introduced to the phrase *för många år sedan* ('many years ago') as a fixed expression, rather than an instance of a productive construction with two slots to be filled, they risk being stuck in chunking, not being able to create new instances of the construction, cf. Holme (2009).

Skrivhjulet also introduces another expression of past time, when explicitly teaching the students how to depict a series of past events, in this case telling someone about a trip (chapter 2: *Återge händelser* ('Recounting events')). The only expression for past time given there, in the templates as well as in the exercises, is *förra sommaren* ('last summer'), although the most frequent and

---

9 The English counterpart of this construction is treated by Fillmore and Kay (1993).

most idiomatic expression for a past time period in the current context is to use the [i N$_{sg,\ gen}$]-construction. It is surprising that this frequent, idiomatic expression is left out as an option, cf. example (11) from a fill-in exercise in the book (*Skrivhjulet* 2011: 21).

(11) *Jag och min man åkte till Lettland* _____
till sommar-en / förra sommar-en / i sommar
to summer-DEF / last summer-DEF / in summer
'me and my husband went to Latvia this summer/last summer/in the summer'

The student is supposed to pick out *förra sommaren* ('last summer') as the correct answer in (11). This phrase is, however, somewhat problematic, partly because of it being less frequent and less idiomatic than the [i N$_{sg,\ gen}$] construction (*i somras* ('last summer')), but also because of its ambiguity; *förra sommaren* could mean either the most recently past summer or the summer before that, while the [i N$_{sg,\ gen}$] construction unambiguously points out the most recently preceding time unit. Note that not a single instance of the [i N$_{sg,\ gen}$] construction appears in *Skrivhjulet*, when illustrating how to refer to events in the past.

In summary, *Skrivhjulet* would, in our opinion, benefit from adding more of a constructional perspective, which could fill the gap left by its current approach to deal with either larger textual units or with expressions that are treated as single lexical items. Inspired by the genre pedagogical paradigm, *Skrivhjulet* provides the learners with genre specific templates and formulas – which of course could be helpful. However, there is no note or any other information that could lead a student to the conclusion that there is a template not only for genres, but also for smaller units such as productive phrases or constructions. By mainly focusing on larger textual units and providing the learners with fixed phrases instead of showing their variability, *Skrivhjulet* is likely to pass on too static a perception of linguistic expressions.

3.4 *Form i fokus*

Form i fokus differs from the other teaching aids of this survey in not being a textbook but consisting of three workbooks on grammatical categories. *Form i fokus* is divided into sections where each section introduces a grammatical category and some representatives of that category. After a short introduction on the use of (some members of) a category, an extensive set of worksheets follows.

Staying true to its title, *Form i fokus* introduces time expressions in the context of exploring prepositions. The preposition *i* ('in') is presented as being present in many time expressions, for past, present and future time, e.g. *igår* ('yesterday'), *idag* ('today'), *i kväll* ('tonight') (*Form i fokus* 1996: 229). In the context of past time, the [*i* N$_{sg,\ gen}$]-construction is introduced, and a long list of examples is presented, among them *i somras* ('last summer'), *i vintras* ('last winter'), *i julas* ('last Christmas') (*Form i fokus* 1996: 235). The teaching aid focuses on the preposition when presenting the construction; hence, it does not actually present the construction as such. Rather than emphasising the regularity with which the preposition and the genitive form co-occur for this function, the preposition is singled out in bold type. The students, however, may still be able to use the listed items as a clue to the productivity of the pattern, and may also be able to figure out that the genitive form of the noun is of vital importance, even if this is not explicitly pointed out.

Likewise, instances of the [*för* AP$_{quant}$/Num N$_{time}$ *sedan*] construction only occur in the context of presenting *för ... sedan* ('for ... ago') as a time preposition (*Form i fokus* 1996: 229, 234). Again, the preposition of the expression is singled out in bold type, while the rest of the expression is left uncommented. The presentation of time prepositions is followed by a time preposition exercise that requires the students to fill in the missing prepositions, see (12) (*Form i fokus* 1996: 234).

(12)　*Milan kom till Sverige　　_____ tre år _____.*
　　　　　　　　　　　　　　　När?

　　　'Milan arrived in Sweden　_____ three years _____.'
　　　　　　　　　　　　　　　　'When?'

In exercise (12), the student is supposed to fill in the missing prepositions in the gaps (*för* ('for') and *sedan* ('ago'), respectively), i.e. the constant parts of the construction, while the variable elements, in the quantitative slot and the time slot, are given. Once again, the student is not explicitly introduced to the construction as such, and not provided with information on the variability of the construction or – even less – given an opportunity to use the construction productively, trying to create new instances of it.

Summing up, *Form i fokus* focuses on grammar (in a traditional sense). The learner is introduced to grammatical categories and expressions where these grammatical categories are likely to occur. The lists of example expressions following the introduction of a specific category may, at best, function as an illustration of the variability of certain expressions (cf. *i somras, i vintras, i julas* ('last summer, last winter, last Christmas')), but the learner is left to draw his/

her own conclusions about the relation between form and function of the expressions presented, and to figure out the boundaries, the regularity and the variability of these expressions. We conclude that a more explicit account of the constructions/expressions probably would be of benefit to the learner even in this case.

3.5 Discussion

Regardless of whether the teaching aids we investigated have a very narrow scope of interest and focus solely on form or if they have a broad scope and focus on the function of textual genres, and make use of formulaic language as a means of teaching the production of such genres, they often fail to account for the productivity of constructions and the variability of formulaic expressions or chunks related to a specific function. We believe all four of them would benefit from incorporating a conscious focus on (semi-general) constructions – as a complement to general rules and particular chunks. This applies no less to the one exception in the sample, *Rivstart*; in this case there already is a pedagogical awareness of how to introduce and visualize the constructions that come up in various contexts, but using a collection of L2-relevant constructions and working them into the material would probably take the pedagogical approach a step further.

We will not, in this contribution, enter a discussion on when to introduce a constructional approach in L2 education, but it is reasonable to suppose that access to patterns and constructions becomes more and more important at higher proficiency levels, with an increasing focus on idiomatic language use. Therefore, it is somewhat surprising that *Skrivhjulet*, which addresses more advanced students studying Swedish as a second language in upper secondary school, lacks a constructional approach, while *Rivstart*, targeting beginners, applies such a perspective to quite a large extent. Part of the explanation may be that *Rivstart*, being a teaching aid in Swedish as a foreign language, is used in university courses where previous linguistic knowledge may be expected to some extent.

We have seen above that the teaching aids tend to present fixed phrases commonly used, rather than introduce phrases as variable instances of productive constructions. Langacker (2008: 83) emphasizes that one should, as a pedagogical strategy, start off with prototypical instances of a construction and then move on to more infrequent ones. While often successfully accounting for prototypicality – in presenting commonly used expressions – the teaching aids examined here to a large extent fail to account for the variability and productivity of the constructions these expressions instantiate.

If second language learners do not learn to see individual phrases as variable tokens of a type, they risk being too dependent on chunks (Holme 2009).[10] Therefore, it is important that teaching aids illustrate the variability of expressions, i.e. treat expressions as instances of productive constructions. To overcome the fear of producing an incorrect instance of a construction, learners need deeper knowledge of constructions as well as encouragement to explore the boundaries of certain constructions. Holme (2009: 183, 196–197) suggests that teachers should think more about teaching patterns of variable schematicity and productivity and he suggests exercises to improve students' ability to use constructions productively.

In addition, second language learners could benefit from construction teaching in yet another way. Littlemore (2009: 169) notes that construction grammar is useful in language education, since it "provides a sort of middle ground between the categorical yet inadequate traditional 'grammar rules' approach and the more accurate yet potentially overwhelming 'lexical' approach". She argues that an awareness of the inheritance links between constructions could bring a degree of systematicity to the large number of constructions that need to be learned. Thus, construction grammar is likely to help learners to deal with the problem of data overload. Furthermore, by using construction grammar to explain expressions as instances of a regular pattern, teachers could present phraseology as being a partially motivated, rather than an entirely arbitrary phenomenon (Littlemore 2009: 173–174). It follows that learners are likely to benefit from teaching aids that present a network of constructions, to come to terms with data overload problems and to find systematicity in the phraseology of language.

To enable a constructional approach to teaching and in teaching aids, systematic examination of relevant constructions and their variability is required, based on authentic language use and preferably with a focus on how constructions are linked together in a network. In the following section we present the Swedish constructicon as such a descriptive resource, underlining its potential for developing constructional approaches to (second) language education.

4 The Swedish constructicon

One can hardly expect teaching materials to display a constructionist perspective unless their authors have had access to corresponding descriptive resources. So far, such resources have been largely lacking. Hopefully, the constructicons

---

10 Cf. the discussion in Bybee (2010) on high token frequency leading to chunking, at the expense of a reduced analysability.

currently under development for several languages (Fillmore, Lee-Goldman and Rhomieux 2012; Ohara 2013; Torrent et al. 2014) can remedy this situation, and for the Swedish constructicon (henceforth SweCcn, Lyngfelt et al. 2012; Sköldberg et al. 2013; Bäckström, Lyngfelt, and Sköldberg 2014), this is an explicit aim.

SweCcn is a freely available database of Swedish construction descriptions. While still in its early stages of development, it currently consists of approximately 400 constructions. More constructions are added continuously from a number of different sources, including Swedish learner corpora and automatically generated construction candidates from language technology experiments on L1 corpora (Forsberg et al. 2014). Eventually, SweCcn is meant to be a large-scale electronic resource for linguistics, language technology, and language pedagogy. We especially want to cover constructions that are problematic from a language learner's point of view.

To enable large-scale coverage (and to facilitate adaptation to a wider audience), the construction descriptions need to be relatively simple. Accordingly, we do not strive for the level of detail and precision typical of analyses in construction grammar. The role model is rather the more approximate definitions used in dictionaries. There is, however, an additional level of complexity, since the construction description also has to account for the internal structure of the construction. Hence, the core of a SweCcn construction post consists of a free-text, dictionary-style definition (primarily covering the function or meaning of the construction) combined with a simple structural sketch (accounting for its form) and illustrated by annotated examples. A simplified version of such a post is shown in (13):[11]

(13) Name: *mått_plus_adj* 'Measurement_plus_adjective'

Definition: *Konstruktionen består av en [måttsenhet]$_{Quantitative}$ som tillsammans med ett [relativt adjektiv]$_{Property}$ bildar en adjektivfras.*

'The construction consists of a [unit of measurement]$_{Quantitative}$ forming an AP with a [relative adjective]$_{Property}$'

Form: [Num N Adj]

Example: *En [[tre meter]$_{Quantitative}$ [hög]$_{Property}$]$_{mått\_plus\_adj}$ [bronsstaty]$_{Item}$ föreställande Sir Winston Churchill.*

'A [[three meters]$_{Quantitative}$ [high]$_{Property}$]$_{mått\_plus\_adj}$ [bronze statue]$_{Item}$ of Sir Winston Churchill'

---

[11] The English counterpart of this construction is described in the English constructicon (Fillmore, Lee-Goldman, and Rhomieux 2012: 360–362).

As shown in (13), both the construction elements and the construction as a whole are annotated in the examples and in the definitions as well, if mentioned there. The construction descriptions also contain additional information such as category, inheritance or common words.[12] We will elaborate on some of those features in this section.

The SweCcn database is connected to the Swedish FrameNet and other resources through the lexical infrastructure Karp (Borin et al. 2012) at Språkbanken ('The Swedish language bank'), University of Gothenburg. Through the Karp interface, SweCcn can be explored in a number of ways. After selecting *Konstruktikon* among the Karp resources, one may either target individual constructions directly or filter out groups of constructions. In the following we will present five of the search options: construction, type, category and semantic frame.

a) Construction. It is possible to choose from a list of all the construction entries in SweCcn in alphabetic order, as illustrated in Figure 5. This is an easy way to access individual construction descriptions, at least if the user knows or has a hunch of what the construction might be called.

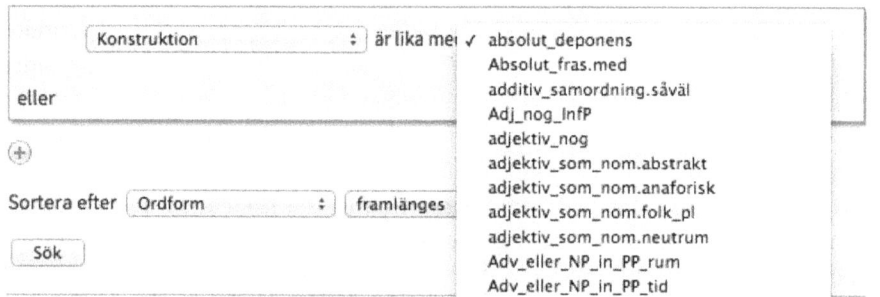

Figure 5: Search option in SweCcn: construction

b) Type. All entries in SweCcn are assigned to one or more types, such as *jämförelse* (constructions of comparison), *underförstådda led* (the construction has implicit elements), *partikel* (the construction includes a verb particle), *bisats* (the construction is a type of subordinate clause), *interaktion* (the construction has an interactional function) or *inlärningsfokus* (the construction is identified as particularly problematic for learners of Swedish).

---

[12] *Common words* is a simple form of collostructional information (cf. Stefanowitsch 2013), where we list words that occur particularly frequently in the construction. In the present example, the following words are listed: {*meter* 'meter': *lång* 'long'}, {*kilo* 'kilo': *tung* 'heavy'}, {*år* 'years': *gammal* 'old'}. The brackets indicate that the words tend to co-occur in the construction. Note, however, that this information is not based on proper collostructional analyses; we have merely noted strikingly frequent occurrences.

This means that if a user wants to identify problematic constructions for L2 learners, it is possible to choose that specific type of constructions and get a list of all entries marked accordingly. One of the constructions with this L2 label is illustrated in (14):

(14) a. **[på NP]**

b. *Hon   sprang   en   mil   [på   45   minut-er].*
   She   run-PST   a   Swedish.mile   on   45   minute-PL
   'She ran 10 km [in 45 minutes]'

The prepositional construction in (14) expresses bounded duration, i.e. the time required to achieve an accomplishment (cf. Eng. *in 45 minutes*). It contrasts with the unbounded durative construction [*i* NP] (cf. Eng. *for 45 minutes*). Time expressions are often difficult for L2 learners (Prentice 2011). As observed in Section 3 above, they also seem hard to account for in a satisfactory way without a constructional perspective.

Likewise, a user who chooses the type *interaktion* would get a set of constructions including the [X *och* X] construction, as described in example (1) above.

c) Category. This refers to the category of the construction, which typically consists of a basic category type such as NP, VP or Adj. For example, choosing 'category' and then 'VP' would yield all verb phrase constructions in SweCcn. Similarly, if we wish to find prepositional constructions, we choose 'PP' from the category list. One such PP construction is illustrated in (10) above (Section 3.3). Another one is shown in (15), a locative construction which was discussed in relation to Figures 3 and 4 (Section 3.2).

(15) a. **[P NP.place]**

b. *Hon   sålde   jordgubb-ar   på torg-et*
   she   sell-PST   strawberry-PL   on market.place-DEF
   'She sold strawberries in the market place'

d) Semantic frame. Many constructions are frame bearing (Fillmore, Lee-Goldman, and Rhomieux 2012: 325), i.e. they have a meaning that corresponds to a semantic frame (Fillmore and Baker 2010; Ehrlemark 2014). This search option targets constructions linked to frames in the Swedish FrameNet (Borin et al. 2010). It could be profitable for the user who wants to find constructions based on concepts, that is, to answer questions of how to express a certain concept in Swedish, such as Time and Motion. When using this option the user actually does not need to know any formal properties of a construction at all.

These are some of the ways currently available to access construction descriptions in SweCcn. In the concluding section, we will offer a few suggestions on what to do with them in a pedagogical setting. For a more comprehensive presentation of SweCcn, see Sköldberg et al. (2013); Bäckström, Lyngfelt, and Sköldberg (2014).

5 General discussion and outlook

In the former sections, we have illustrated how some of the leading Swedish L2 textbooks and study aid materials fall short when it comes to capturing the productivity of constructions. This is not intended as a criticism of these particular teaching aids. They merely reflect the current situation, as described by Littlemore (2009: 173):

> However, in the language teaching profession we have a long way to go before we can produce suitable materials to introduce learners to L2 constructions and the relationships between them in a realistic, systematic and learnable manner. Before this can be done, more research is needed using authentic data to establish the exact nature of constructions, and then pedagogical research is needed to investigate the best ways of introducing them, either explicitly through the use of accessible terminology or implicitly through carefully selected L2 input.

Littlemore thus emphasizes a need for descriptive knowledge of constructions on the one hand, and a need for pedagogical development on the other. One of the main purposes of SweCcn is to fill (at least parts of) the empirical gap Littlemore is referring to. In addition, we hope that SweCcn can be of some help in addressing the need for pedagogical applications as well.

As already mentioned, SweCcn is a systematic collection of construction descriptions. It is a new kind of resource, still fairly modest in size but growing by the day. By combining theoretical insights from construction grammar with practical experience from lexicography, it is hospitable to linguistic patterns that are peripheral in more modular linguistic models and therefore often tend to be neglected. It also provides a format for linguistic description that should be useful for several different purposes. The previous lack of coverage is a problem for language technology (cf. Sag et al. 2002, and others) and other areas as well as for language education, being equally dependent on grammars and lexica, and thus lacking tools to handle patterns that combine lexical and grammatical properties. Through collaboration with constructicon projects for other languages, we also strive for interlingual applications (cf. Bäckström, Lyngfelt, and Sköldberg 2014). Therefore, the database is designed for wide applicability rather than specifically adapted for e.g. L2 education.

Nonetheless, usefulness for (second) language education is a main priority. Regarding the content of SweCcn, this aim is reflected in the selection of constructions, where we focus on patterns that tend to be problematic for language learners. Regarding the presentation, we are working to make the resource more accessible to non-experts, e.g. through a more user-friendly interface, and also to develop classroom exercises and similar aids to illustrate how the database can be applied to a pedagogical setting and hopefully inspire further developments (Prentice et al. in press). In this regard, we seek collaboration with language teachers, who can provide more of a field perspective than we have ourselves and who are able to test the exercises in classroom situations.

It should be stressed that this work is by no means an isolated undertaking. As several researchers have stressed the need for a constructional approach to L2 education, some of them are also working on how to do it. For example, Wee (2007: 29) suggests that the following three questions could form the base when working with constructions in the classroom:

(16) a. What properties of the construction are variable?

b. What properties are invariant?

c. What communicative purposes does the construction serve?

The questions in (16a–b) mainly concern the formal properties of constructions, while (16c) addresses the semantic-pragmatic functions. According to Wee (2007), the teaching of linguistic structures needs to be contextualized, and grammatical properties should constantly be associated with and linked to communicative goals or semantic properties, that is, in what contexts and situations the specific structures are typically used, and what they mean. To illustrate the questions in (16), Wee employs the English [*Yours* ADVERB] construction used to end letters (e.g. *Yours sincerely/truly/faithfully*). Concerning (17a), the adverb slot can vary, even though it is highly restricted; not any adverb will do. The answer to (16b) is that the first part of the construction is lexically filled with the pronoun *yours*, which means that it is not replaceable with another pronoun such as *his* or *hers*. (16c) can be elaborated with questions such as 'Is this construction used in all types of letters or just in certain registers?' and 'Is this construction used in e.g. blog texts and SMS?'. In a classroom situation, such a construction is preferably introduced to the students while reading letters, as well as some authentic blog material. The questions in (16) could easily be used with any of the constructions described in Section 3, like the prepositional time constructions, or with other constructions found in SweCcn.

A related approach is suggested by Holme (2010). He used the sentence in (17) as a foundation for discussing constructional and lexical variation in the classroom (2010: 367).

(17) A new study shows an interesting link between exam success and the number of hours a day that a student studies.

Example (17) is taken from a newspaper article in the section 'popular science'. With the teacher's guidance, the students deduced the following four instances of relevant constructions: 'a new study shows something' (a version of the transitive construction), 'a link/connection between one thing and another thing' (the *between* construction), 'the number of hours a day that somebody does something' (partitive and relative clause construction), and 'hours a day' (ratio construction) (Holme 2010: 367). After the identification and discussion of the constructions in (17), he let the students experiment with lexical variation to see what kind of lexical content would work within the given constructions, the aim being for students to establish constructions as "a productive category" (Holme 2010: 362). Holme (ibid.) summarizes: "Finally it means that we take a form and explore its meaning by looking at where and when it might be used".

Another useful basis for a constructional approach to classroom activities is Atzler's (2011: 13) *components of word knowledge* model (shown in Figure 6), which to some extent can be applied to multiword constructions, as components of constructional knowledge.

Form	spoken	R	What does the word sound like?
		P	How is the word pronounced?
	written	R	What does the word look like?
		P	How is the word written and spelled?
	word parts	R	What parts are recognizable in this word?
		P	What word parts are needed to express the meaning?
Meaning	form & meaning	R	What meaning does the word form signal?
		P	What word form can be used to express this meaning?
	concept & referents	R	What is included in the concept?
		P	What items can the concept refer to?
	associations	R	What other words does this word make us think of?
		P	What other words could we use instead of this one?
Use	grammatical function	R	In what patterns does the word occur?
		P	In what patterns must we use the word?
	collocations	R	What words or types of words occur with this word?
		P	What words or types of words must we use with this word?
	constraints on use (register, frequency, …)	R	Where, when, and how often would we expect to meet this word?
		P	Where, when, and how often can we use this word?

Figure 6: Components of word knowledge according to Atzler (2011: 13)

The figure is divided into the three sections of form, meaning and use, roughly corresponding to the questions listed by Wee (2007) in (16), but Atzler's components cover more detailed questions regarding both receptive (R) and productive (P) matters, such as phonetic properties, collocational relations and usage constraints. When such information constitutes a relevant feature of a construction it is provided in the corresponding SweCcn entry.

A major advantage of a constructional approach to language teaching is that it does not necessarily require students to acquire a set of grammatical terms to be able to discuss constructions. Based on Wee's (2007) three questions in (16), even a primary school class could discuss patterns like the [i $N_{sg,\ gen}$] construction, e.g. by writing a set of examples on the white board and asking which words are used in this pattern. For more advanced exercises, Atzler's (2011) questions might be useful.

Thus, the importance of a constructional approach to second language teaching has been emphasized in the scientific literature, and some practical applications of such an approach have been suggested. One of the many remaining issues, however, is which constructions should be investigated in the classroom, and where adequate information about those can be found. This is one of the ways in which SweCcn should be a useful resource.

To sum up, in this paper we have discussed whether a constructional perspective is present in four leading L2-teaching aids, and found them to be largely lacking in this regard. We have pointed out advantages of a constructional approach to language teaching (and learning), especially regarding linguistic patterns that are difficult to fully describe and understand only in terms of , e.g., parts of speech or when presented as isolated fixed phrases. An increased focus on constructions, as we propose, is, however, to be seen as a complement to the teaching of other aspects of form and meaning in the language classroom and not as a replacement for existing approaches. Focusing on fixed phrases, for example, can be an adequate strategy in certain learning situations and help learners to develop both fluency and idiomaticity in the target language (cf. Skehan 1998; Ekberg 2013). The chapter also introduces constructicography in general and the Swedish constructicon in particular as a promising approach to language description. We have illustrated how construction descriptions can be accessed in the database, both individually and in groups, and tried to indicate how SweCcn could be a resource for bringing a constructional perspective into language teaching aids and language education.

References

Atzler, Judith Kerstin. 2011. *Twist in the list: Frame Semantics as a vocabulary teaching and learning tool*. Dissertation (Doctor of Germanic Studies) – The University of Texas at Austin. Austin, TX.

Bäckström, Linnéa, Benjamin Lyngfelt & Emma Sköldberg. 2014. Towards interlingual constructicography. On correspondence between constructicon resources for English and Swedish. In Lars Borin, Gerard de Melo, Karin Friberg Heppin & Tiago Timponi Torrent (eds.), *Frames, constructions and computation*. Special issue of *Constructions and Frames* 6(1). 9–32.

Barðdal, Jóhanna. 2008. *Productivity. Evidence from case and argument structure in Icelandic*. Amsterdam: John Benjamins.

Boas, Hans C. 2014. Zur Architektur einer konstruktionsbasierten Grammatik des Deutschen. In Alexander Ziem & Alexander Lasch (eds.), *Grammatik als Netzwerk von Konstruktionen? Sprachliches Wissen im Fokus der Konstruktionsgrammatik*, 37–63. Berlin & New York: de Gruyter.

Borin, Lars, Dana Dannélls, Markus Forsberg, Maria Toporowska Gronostaj & Dimitrios Kokkinakis. 2010. The past meets the present in Swedish FrameNet++. In *14th EURALEX International Congress*, 269–281.

Borin, Lars, Markus Forsberg, Leif-Jöran Olsson & Jonatan Uppström. 2012. The open lexical infrastructure of Språkbanken. In *Proceedings of LREC 2012*, 3598–3602. Istanbul: ELRA.

Borin, Lars, Markus Forsberg & Johan Roxendal. 2012. Korp – the corpus infrastructure of Språkbanken. In *Proceedings of LREC 2012*, 474–478. Istanbul: ELRA.

Bybee, Joan. 2010. *Language, usage and cognition*. Cambridge: Cambridge University Press.

Council of Europe. 2001. *Common European Framework of Reference for Languages: Learning, Teaching, Assessment*. Cambridge: Cambridge University Press.

Croft, William. 2001. *Radical construction grammar. Syntactic theory in typological perspective*. Oxford & New York: Oxford University Press.

Croft, William. 2003. Lexical rules vs. constructions: A false dichotomy. In Hubert Cuyckens, Thomas Berg, René Dirven & Klaus-Uwe Panther (eds.), *Motivation in language: Studies in honour of Günter Radden*, 49–68. Amsterdam: John Benjamins.

Ehrlemark, Anna. 2014. *Ramar och konstruktioner – en kärlekshistoria* ['Frames and constructions – a love story']. (GU-ISS 2014-01) Dept. of Swedish, Univ. of Gothenburg. http://hdl.handle.net/2077/35145.

Ekberg, Lena. 2013. Grammatik och lexikon i svenska som andraspråk på nästan infödd nivå ['Grammar and Lexicon in Swedish as a second language at near native level']. In Kenneth Hyltenstam & Inger Lindberg (eds.), *Svenska som andraspråk – i forskning, undervisning och samhälle*, 259–279. Lund: Studentlitteratur.

Fillmore, Charles J. 1988. The mechanisms of 'Construction Grammar'. *Berkeley Linguistic Society* 14. 35–55.

Fillmore, Charles J. 2008. Border conflicts: FrameNet meets construction grammar. In Elisenda Bernal & Janet DeCesaris (eds.), *Proceedings of the XIII EURALEX International Congress*, 49–68. Barcelona: Universitat Pompeu Fabra.

Fillmore, Charles J. & Collin Baker. 2010. A frames approach to semantic analysis. In Bernd Heine & Heiko Narrog (eds.), *The Oxford handbook of linguistic analysis*, 313–339. Oxford: Oxford University Press.

Fillmore, Charles J. & Paul Kay. 1993. Construction Grammar coursebook. Ms. Department of Linguistics, University of California at Berkeley.
Fillmore, Charles J., Paul Kay & Mary Catherine O'Connor. 1988. Regularity and idiomaticity in grammatical constructions: The case of *let alone*. *Language* 64. 501-538.
Fillmore, Charles J., Russell Lee-Goldman & Russell Rhomieux. 2012. The FrameNet Constructicon. In Hans C. Boas & Ivan A. Sag (eds.), *Sign-based construction grammar*, 309-372. Stanford: CSLI.
Forsberg, Markus, Richard Johansson, Linnéa Bäckström, Lars Borin, Benjamin Lyngfelt, Joel Olofsson & Julia Prentice. 2014. From construction candidates to constructicon entries. An experiment using semi-automatic methods for identifying constructions in corpora. In Lars Borin, Gerard de Melo, Karin Friberg Heppin & Tiago Timponi Torrent (eds.), *Frames, constructions and computation*. Special issue of *Constructions and Frames* 6(1). 113-134.
Gibbons, Pauline. 2002. *Scaffolding language, scaffolding learning. Teaching second language learners in the mainstream classroom*. Portsmouth, NH: Heinemann.
Goldberg, Adele E. 2006. *Constructions at work. The nature of generalization in language*. Oxford & New York: Oxford University Press.
Goldberg, Adele E. 2013. Constructionist approaches. In Thomas Hoffmann & Graeme Trousdale (eds.), *The Oxford handbook of construction grammar*, 15-31. Oxford & New York: Oxford University Press.
Hoffmann, Thomas & Graeme Trousdale (eds.). 2013. *The Oxford handbook of construction grammar*. Oxford & New York: Oxford University Press.
Holme, Randal. 2009. *Cognitive linguistics and language teaching*. New York: Palgrave Macmillan.
Holme, Randal. 2010. A construction grammar for the classroom. *IRAL* 48(4). 355-377.
Kay, Paul. 2013. The limits of (construction) grammar. In Thomas Hoffmann & Graeme Trousdale (eds.), *The Oxford handbook of construction grammar*, 32-48. Oxford & New York: Oxford University Press.
Lakoff, George. 1987. *Women, fire, and dangerous things. What categories reveal about the mind*. Chicago and London: The University of Chicago Press.
Langacker, Ronald W. 2008. Cognitive grammar and language instruction. In Peter Robinson & Nick Ellis (eds.), *Handbook of cognitive linguistics and second language acquisition*, 66-88. New York: Routledge.
Lindström, Jan & Per Linell. 2007. Roli å roli. X-och-x som samtalspraktik och grammatisk konstruktion ['*Fun 'n fun*. X-and-x as a conversational practice and grammatical construction']. In Elisabet Engdahl & Anne-Marie Londen (eds.), *Interaktion och kontext*, 19-89. Lund: Studentlitteratur.
Linell, Per & Kerstin Norén. 2009. "Vågar vågar ni väl men..." – en reaktiv konstruktion i svenskan ['"Dare dare you but..." – a reactive construction in Swedish']. *Språk och stil* NF 19. 72-104.
Littlemore, Jeannette. 2009. *Applying cognitive linguistics to second language learning and teaching*. New York: Palgrave Macmillan.
Lyngfelt, Benjamin, Lars Borin, Markus Forsberg, Julia Prentice, Rudolf Rydstedt, Emma Sköldberg & Sofia Tingsell. 2012. Adding a constructicon to the Swedish resource network of Språkbanken. In *Proceedings of KONVENS 2012* (LexSem 2012 workshop), 452-461.
Lyngfelt, Benjamin & Emma Sköldberg. 2013. Lexikon och konstruktikon – ett konstruktionsgrammatiskt perspektiv på lexikografi ['Lexicon and constructicon – a constructionist perspective on lexicography']. *LexicoNordica* 20. 75-91.

Lyngfelt, Benjamin & Camilla Wide. 2014. Introduction: Constructionist approaches to Swedish. In Benjamin Lyngfelt & Camilla Wide (eds.), *Special issue on Swedish constructions. Constructions* 2014. http://www.constructions-journal.com/.

Norén, Kerstin & Per Linell. 2007. Meaning potentials and the interaction between lexis and grammar. Some empirical substantiations. *Pragmatics* 17(3). 387–416.

Ohara, Kyoko Hirose. 2013. Toward constructicon building for Japanese in Japanese FrameNet. *Veredas* 17(1). 11–27.

Pawley, Andrew & Frances H. Syder. 1983. Two puzzles for linguistic theory: Nativelike selection and nativelike fluency. In Jack Richards & Richard Schmidt (eds.), *Language and communication*, 191–221. London: Longman.

Prentice, Julia. 2011. "Jag är född på andra november". Konventionaliserade tidsuttryck som konstruktioner – ur ett andraspråksperspektiv. ['I was born on second November. Conventionalized time expressions as constructions – from a second language perspective']. Course paper on Construction Grammar, Dept. of Swedish, University of Gothenburg.

Prentice, Julia, Lisa Loenheim, Benjamin Lyngfelt, Joel Olofsson & Sofia Tingsell. In press. Bortom ordklasser och satsdelar: konstruktionsgrammatik i klassrummet ['Beyond parts of speech and grammatical functions: construction grammar in the classroom']. In *Svenskans beskrivning* 34. Lund.

Sag, Ivan A., Timothy Baldwin, Francis Bond, Ann Copestake & Dan Flickinger. 2002. Multi-word expressions: A pain in the neck for NLP. In *Proceedings of the 3rd International Conference on Intelligent Text Processing and Computational Linguistics* (CICLing-2002), 1–15.

Skehan, Peter. 1998. *A cognitive approach to language learning*. Oxford: Oxford University Press.

Sköldberg, Emma, Linnéa Bäckström, Lars Borin, Markus Forsberg, Benjamin Lyngfelt, Leif-Jöran Olsson, Julia Prentice, Rudolf Rydstedt, Sofia Tingsell & Jonatan Uppström. 2013. Between grammars and dictionaries: A Swedish constructicon. In *Proceedings of eLex 2013*, 310–327.

Stefanowitsch, Anatol. 2013. Collostructional analysis. In Thomas Hoffmann & Graeme Trousdale (eds.), *The Oxford handbook of construction grammar*, 290–306. Oxford & New York: Oxford University Press.

SweCcn = *Swedish Constructicon*. http://spraakbanken.gu.se/konstruktikon (last accessed on November 28, 2014).

Torrent, Tiago Timponi, Ludmila Meireles Lage, Thais Fernandes Sampaio, Tatiane da Silva Tavares & Ely Edison da Silva Matos. 2014. Revisiting border conflicts between FrameNet and Construction Grammar: Annotation policies for the Brazilian Portuguese Constructicon. In Lars Borin, Gerard de Melo, Karin Friberg Heppin & Tiago Timponi Torrent (eds.), *Frames, constructions and computation*. Special issue of *Constructions and Frames* 6(1). 33–50.

Wee, Lionel. 2007. Construction Grammar and English language teaching. *Indonesian Journal of English Language Teaching* 3(121). 20–32.

Wray, Alison. 2008. *Formulaic language: Pushing the boundaries*. Oxford: Oxford University Press.

Ziem, Alexander, Hans C. Boas & Josef Ruppenhofer. 2014. Semantische Frames und grammatische Konstruktionen für die Textanalyse. In Jörg Hagemann & Sven Staffeld (eds.), *Syntaxtheorien. Vergleichende Analysen*, 297–333. Tübingen: Stauffenburg.

Teaching aids of the survey

Form i fokus = Fasth, Cecilia & Anita Kannermark. 1996. *Form i fokus. Övningbok i svensk grammatik. Del A.* Lund: Kursverksamhetens förlag.
Rivstart = Levy Scherrer, Paula & Karl Lindemalm. 2007. *Rivstart A1 + A2. Svenska som främmande språk. Textbok.* Stockholm: Natur & Kultur.
Skrivhjulet = Asker, Kristina. 2011. *Skrivhjulet. En lärobok om genrer.* Stockholm: Bonnier Utbildning AB.
Öppet hus = Skoglund, Svante & Sandra Heaver. 2004. *Bok-och-webb Öppet hus. Svenska som andraspråk för Sfi och motsvarande kurser, del 1.* Göteborg: Bok & webb i Göteborg AB.

Subject index

abstraction 5, 11, 33, 116, 121–122, 124, 126–127, 136, 138, 141, 144–145, 177, 329
accusative 44, 57, 59, 65, 75, 78, 80
acquisition 3, 5, 7, 138, 177, 204, 226, 238, 244, 263, 283, 286
   acquisition context 11, 14, 115–117, 119, 135, 137, 142, 144–145, 211
   construction acquisition 11, 14, 141, 186, 202, 305
   explicit acquisition 142
   first language acquisition 7, 41, 95, 119, 128, 140–142, 187, 279
   foreign language acquisition 119, 329
   implicit acquisition 142
   input-dependent L2 acquisition 115–116, 119, 125, 127, 132, 134, 136, 139–142
   instruction-based acquisition 142
   L1 acquisition 4, 23, 37, 41, 119
   L2 acquisition 4, 8, 11, 14–15, 37, 41, 115, 119, 137, 140, 144, 177, 197, 211
   second language acquisition 5–8, 13, 15, 90, 96–97, 107, 115, 117, 119, 140–142, 144, 186–188, 199, 204–205, 211, 279, 290, 329, 339
   vocabulary acquisition 153, 303, 305, 322
adjective 31–32, 35, 40, 101, 163, 170, 176, 178, 280–281, 286, 292, 315–316, 330, 340, 345
adverb 22–23, 28–30, 188, 191–192, 200–201, 204, 259, 336, 349
adverbial 27, 32, 39, 332, 336–337
alternation 23
   dative alternation 8–9, 35, 215, 224, 229
annotation 307–309, 317–319, 321
application 7, 9, 24, 37–38, 138, 144, 151–152, 213, 274–275, 309, 348, 351
applied construction grammar 3, 8, 14–15
argument structure (*see also* argument structure construction *under* construction) 66–67, 77, 228, 245
authenticity 44, 79, 108, 117–119, 139, 145, 200, 296, 344, 348–349
avoidance 74, 187, 193, 203–204

bilingualism 72–73, 100, 153, 229, 244, 312, 322

case 56, 59–60, 80
category 5, 32, 44, 70, 108, 155, 194–197, 199, 202, 218, 274, 280–281, 341–342, 346–347, 350
categorization 22, 78, 153
chunk 37, 42, 278–279, 290–293, 296, 332–333, 340, 343–344
clause 27–32, 35, 39–40, 98, 116, 120–121, 125, 132, 134–136, 144, 192–193, 229, 277, 346, 350
coercion 67
cognition 116, 119, 123, 156, 173, 175–176, 214, 230, 237–238, 304, 322
   cognitive approach 12, 33, 238
   cognitive linguistics 7, 9, 14, 21, 24, 32, 38, 78, 115, 152, 180, 185, 237
   cognitive modeling 151, 155–156, 164, 169
   cognitive motivation 172–173, 175
   cognitive pedagogical grammar, *see* pedagogical grammar
   cognitive principles 137, 140, 144, 151, 259
   cognitive process 157, 159, 164, 238, 259, 261
collocation 33–34, 38, 42–43, 45, 55, 139, 272–273, 298, 310, 312, 351
collostructional analysis 5–6, 38, 116, 137–138, 140, 144, 346
   collexeme 5, 138–140, 145
   collostruction 138–139, 346
communicative approach 118, 170, 193, 204
   communicative activities 206, 336
   communicative competence 109, 207
   communicative function 24, 42, 179, 349
   communicative gap 261
   communicative situation 89, 178, 180, 206, 212, 250, 261
competence 90, 109, 152, 180, 207, 315
complementation 4, 29–30, 34–35, 99–100, 112–113, 116, 119–122, 124–125, 134–136, 142, 144, 162, 167, 176, 179, 327–328, 334, 336, 343

composition 12, 89, 99–100, 112–113, 154
  decomposition 126, 140
compositionality 3, 8, 55, 285, 315–318
conceptualization 7, 78, 153, 155–156, 159, 175, 198, 212, 215–216, 221, 238, 305, 322
  conceptual domain 157
  conceptual metaphor 78–80, 238, 243, 258
  conceptual metonymy 78–80, 238
  conceptual similarity 211, 217, 219–222, 225, 228–229
  conceptual structure 157–159, 165, 171–172, 217–218, 228
  conceptual transfer, see transfer
conjunction 22, 28–30, 35, 39, 280, 331
constructicography 13, 327, 329, 351
constructicon 7, 10, 12–13, 303, 317, 320, 328, 345, 348
  German constructicon 13, 303, 328
  Italian constructicon 226
  Swedish constructicon 13, 327–329, 344–345, 351
construction (see also L2 construction, mini-construction)
  argument structure construction 4, 13, 33, 35, 37, 58, 89–92, 95–97, 215–216, 224, 228, 282
  causative construction 5, 8, 11, 38, 115–116, 119–122, 124–132, 135–145
  caused motion construction 3, 8, 10–11, 13, 38, 91, 93, 95, 100, 161, 171, 174–175, 185–193, 201–207
  dative construction 213–214, 218, 221–223, 226–229, 245
  ditransitive construction 3, 8, 13, 37, 53, 55–61, 63–71, 78–80, 89–90, 93, 100, 108, 276, 321
  double-object construction 10, 218–219, 221–223, 226–228, 245, 276
  fulfilling construction 10, 211, 214, 222–229
  gerund construction 5, 27–28
  going to-construction 40
  intransitive motion construction 93, 100
  iterative construction 8, 237–239

partially filled-in construction 237–239, 241, 247, 262
placement caused motion construction 10–11, 185–186, 188–193, 201–205, 207
planned future construction 237–238, 244, 256
prepositional dative construction 214, 218, 221–223, 226–229
prepositional locative construction 218, 220
resultative construction 8, 13, 89–90, 93, 96, 100, 102, 161–162, 168, 171
subjective-manipulative construction 8, 10, 166, 168, 174
the adjective-construction 40
the X_{noun} *of the* Y_{noun} construction 281, 283–285, 290, 292–295
to infinitive-construction 39
V-*ing* construction 38–39, 42
will-construction 39–40
construction-based approach 53–54
construction learning 21, 90, 95–96, 107–108, 175
constructional family 166
constructional transfer, see transfer
containment 185, 187, 196–198, 203, 205, 207
contrastive analysis 10, 14, 151–152, 175, 238, 249
coordination 212, 330–332
corpus 4–5, 9, 12–14, 21, 44, 95, 115–116, 118–119, 121, 123–125, 134–139, 143, 145, 173, 202, 222, 271–278, 283–284, 287, 290–291, 293–295, 297–298, 306–309, 329, 333
  British National Corpus (BNC) 36, 99, 119, 123–124, 129, 143, 271, 306–307
  Corpus of Contemporary American English (COCA) 173, 271, 273, 276–284, 287–289, 292–294, 298
  Digitales Wörterbuch der Deutschen Sprache (DWDS) corpus 313
  International Corpus of English (ICE) 119–120, 123–124
  International Corpus of Learner English (ICLE) 120–121, 123–124

Louvain Corpus of Native English Essays
(LOCNESS) 123
NUS Corpus of Learner English (NUCLE)
119, 123–124
corpus linguistics 4–5, 12, 14, 21, 24, 32–33,
38, 116, 143
corpus-based approach 36, 115, 140,
143–144, 207, 214, 272–273
correspondence principle 56, 58
cross-linguistic 9–10, 151, 153–154, 163,
165–166, 171, 180, 185–187, 189–200,
202, 204, 206–207, 230, 241, 244, 246,
262, 308, 310
curriculum 24, 27, 41, 108, 139, 152–153,
180, 245, 249, 256, 304

Danish 8, 10, 185–188, 190–191, 193–202,
204–205, 207
dative 44, 56–57, 59–60, 66–68, 72, 159,
218, 220–221, 225, 229, 311
dative alternation, *see* alternation
dative construction, *see* construction
double-object dative 217, 245–246
free dative 66–67
prepositional dative 213–214, 217–223,
225–229, 245
decomposition, *see* composition

English as a foreign language (EFL) 22, 25,
89–90, 93, 97–98, 106, 108, 115–119,
121, 123, 125–145, 271–273, 298
English as a second language (ESL) 96, 115–
119, 121, 123, 125–145, 271–273, 298
entrenchment 3, 8, 22, 154, 159, 168, 230,
238, 244, 285, 292
error 22, 98, 120–121, 215, 238, 245, 261
non-standard 60, 122, 124, 129, 134–136,
141, 143–145
ungrammatical 202, 245, 247, 256, 258
experimentation (*see also* task) 4, 7, 9, 12,
14, 64, 68, 95–96, 98, 152, 207, 211–
214, 216, 218–219, 222–225, 228, 237,
246, 345, 350
experimental evidence 34, 38, 211, 246
priming experiment 211, 213, 215
sentence-elicitation experiment 216, 224,
229

sorting experiment 4, 10
exposure 7, 11, 41, 118–119, 132, 134, 139,
141–142, 144–145, 153, 206–207, 216,
228, 230, 237, 240, 245, 247–248, 256,
263

figurative 53, 55–56, 68, 78, 154–155, 157,
161–164, 166, 172–174, 243
figure (*see also* ground) 185, 187, 189–192,
196–198, 203, 205
fluency 146, 153, 178, 180, 230, 351
focus on form 142, 206, 230
force dynamics 185, 190, 196, 198–199,
203–204, 206–207
foreign language (*see also* non-native
language *under* native language) 66,
73, 79, 89–90, 96, 107–109, 115, 117,
119, 152, 202, 204, 228, 230, 238, 272,
304–305, 309, 329, 334, 343
foreign language acquisition, *see*
acquisition
foreign language learning 90, 108, 115,
303–305, 322
foreign language teaching, *see* teaching
form-meaning pair 3, 8, 41–42, 57, 94, 99,
106, 151, 153, 159, 175, 238, 244, 282,
329
Frame Semantics 155, 303, 305–306, 316
frame 13, 97, 155–157, 159, 216, 275, 303,
305–322, 346–347
FrameNet 13, 30, 303, 305–312, 316–322,
328, 346–347
semantic frame 305–306, 308, 310, 322,
347
French 5, 10, 34, 53–56, 60, 62, 68, 71–72,
74–77, 79
frequency 3, 6, 11, 24, 34, 41, 43–44, 68, 91,
95, 99, 107, 115–116, 119, 125–129, 135,
141, 143–145, 194, 201, 207, 271–274,
277–278, 280–281, 283, 285, 288–290,
292–294, 296, 298, 340, 344
fusion 56–58, 62, 68
future tense 26, 38–39, 44

generalization 7, 11–12, 14, 34–35, 37, 55,
132, 151, 153–154, 163–164, 166, 168,

170–171, 174, 180, 211, 241, 272, 282, 328
German 4, 8, 10–11, 13, 21, 26–28, 30, 34, 36–37, 43–45, 53–60, 62, 67–68, 71–74, 79–80, 117, 120, 123, 188, 229, 263, 303–305, 308–315, 320–323, 328
Germanic language 72–73, 229, 263
gerund (*see also* gerund construction *under* construction) 5, 22, 27–29, 31–32, 38, 44
ground (*see also* figure) 185, 187, 189, 191, 196, 203, 238

hierarchical network 13, 89, 92–93, 97, 107–109
hyperbole 151, 157, 164, 170–171

iconicity 163, 216
idiom 5, 33, 35, 55, 66–67, 73–74, 78–79, 154, 215, 272, 282, 317
  idiom principle 38, 43
idiomaticity 53–56, 61–62, 64–66, 74, 76–80, 108, 139, 141, 204, 207, 215, 296, 316, 329, 334–336, 341, 343, 351
inference 152, 156, 160, 163, 168–170
inheritance link 13–14, 92, 344
  instance link 92–93, 97
  metaphorical link 92
  polysemy link 92
  subpart link 92
input 11, 14, 37, 95–96, 101, 107–108, 115–119, 125–126, 135–138, 140–145, 153, 177, 240, 244–248, 256–257, 262–263
instance link, *see* inheritance link
instantiation 7, 30, 69, 71, 79, 279–281, 284, 292, 295–296, 304, 331
instruction (*see also* teaching) 6, 11, 24, 37, 78, 89, 96–99, 101, 103–109, 112, 118–119, 136–137, 142, 207, 230, 240, 247–249, 256, 258–259, 263, 286, 304–305, 310, 322
  construction-centered instruction 12, 89–90, 96–100, 106, 108–109, 112
  effect of instruction 90, 97, 102–104, 106, 240
  explicit instruction 96, 112, 142, 144–145, 151, 176, 247

form-centered instruction 12, 89–90, 97–100, 106, 108, 112
formal instruction 115, 118, 135–136, 139, 141–142, 144, 237, 245, 247–250
processing instruction 206
intentionality 185, 190, 198–199, 204, 206–207, 239
interlanguage 6, 10, 216, 224, 228–230, 238, 240, 243–246, 249, 263
irony 151, 157, 164, 170
Italian 9–11, 53–56, 60, 62, 68, 71–77, 79–80, 120, 123, 211, 216, 224–226, 228–229, 237–244, 246–263

L2 construction 5–6, 11, 14, 152, 172, 174, 186, 202, 230, 263, 348
language acquisition, *see* acquisition
learner
  Chinese learner 4
  Danish learner 10, 186–188, 197, 199–200, 204–205, 207
  Dutch learner 74, 263
  English learner 13, 187, 245, 303–305, 309–310, 314
  French-speaking learner 5, 10, 53, 55–56, 68, 71–72, 74–77, 79, 246, 263
  German learner 4, 37, 43, 117
  Italian learner 9–10, 53, 55–56, 68, 71–73, 75–77, 79, 211, 216, 224, 227–229
  Korean learner 12, 89–90, 93, 97–98, 100, 106–108
  Spanish learner 4, 10, 154, 171, 187, 193, 237, 240, 242–244, 246–249, 257–258, 260–263
learning process 6, 62, 72, 180, 211–212, 230, 322
  unlearning process 10, 237–238, 243–247, 258, 263
lexicography 22, 35, 45, 273, 305, 308–309, 329, 348
  bilingual dictionary 312
  collocation dictionary 45
  dictionary 12–13, 22–24, 30, 38, 45, 117, 120, 290, 304, 315, 327–328, 345
  learner dictionary 30, 43, 45, 303, 305, 315–317, 320, 322–323
  valency dictionary 45, 317

lexicon 12, 33, 41, 215, 247, 258, 298, 303–304, 308–309, 328, 335
lexicon-grammar continuum 79, 317
lexis 13, 32, 35, 40, 121, 145, 171, 213–216, 239, 257, 272–273, 278, 283, 303, 309–311, 317, 327–329, 333, 339, 348, 350
  lexical approach 272, 316, 344
  lexical bundle (*see also* multi-word unit, n-gram) 275, 280, 282, 284, 287, 291–292
  lexical form 42
  lexical unit 306, 318, 328
  lexicalization 64, 190, 196
light verb, *see* verb
literal 10, 13, 53–55, 64–65, 67–68, 70, 78–79, 171, 174, 177, 263

mapping 8, 57–58, 62, 78, 93–94, 99, 157–159, 165–166, 200, 211, 215, 223, 228, 230, 241–243, 256, 261
markedness 108–109, 128, 227–228, 332
meaning construction 151, 159
metaphor 54, 56, 62, 65–66, 74, 76, 78–79, 93, 152, 154–157, 162, 164, 166, 170–171, 241, 243–244, 258–259, 261, 263, 317, 319, 321
  conceptual metaphor, *see* conceptualization
  metaphorical link, *see* inheritance link
metonymy 54, 56, 62, 65–66, 73, 76, 78–79, 154–157, 160–161, 164–165, 170
  conceptual metonymy, *see* conceptualization
mini-construction 282, 322
morphology 27, 33, 60, 79–80, 115, 180, 215, 237, 243, 247, 257
mother tongue, *see* native language
motion event (*see also* motion verb *under* verb) 153, 185–190, 192–193, 204, 206, 245
multi-word unit (*see also* lexical bundle *under* lexis, n-gram) 45, 316, 333–336, 350

n-gram (*see also* lexical bundle *under* lexis, multi-word unit, POS n-gram *under* part of speech) 271, 273–275, 277–284, 287, 289–291, 295–298

native language 37, 116, 118, 123, 125, 185, 207, 305
  mother tongue 5, 7, 9, 62, 73, 78–79, 101, 123, 143, 238, 250, 252
  native speaker 4–5, 9–10, 14, 37, 66, 96, 120, 125, 127–128, 132, 137, 140–141, 171, 180, 186, 188, 197–198, 200, 202–203, 205, 207, 211, 216, 224, 228, 248, 274, 290, 312–313
  non-native language 6, 116–117, 137
  non-native speaker 4–5, 7, 9, 11, 120–121, 127–128, 137, 143
noun 31, 34, 37–40, 80, 115, 165, 177–178, 213, 229, 245, 274, 278, 280–286, 288, 292, 295, 297–298, 312–316, 320–321, 331, 333, 336, 342

overuse (*see also* underuse) 125–128, 141, 145, 202, 204, 294, 298

parsing (*see also* parsing task *under* task) 215–216
part of speech (POS) 277, 280–282, 284, 288
  part-of-speech tagging 124, 271, 273, 277
  POS n-gram 13, 271, 276–285, 287–290, 292–296, 298
participle 22, 27–28, 31–32, 38, 44, 120–121, 124, 132–133, 135–137, 314, 321
particle 5, 10, 29–30, 34, 39, 94, 188–191, 193, 200–205, 316, 346
passive 120–122, 124–125, 127, 131–133, 136–137, 140, 168, 213, 229, 272
pattern
  general pattern 134–135, 142, 278, 282–283
  grammar pattern 272–273, 288, 295, 297–298
  linguistic pattern 34, 91, 239, 285, 328–330, 332, 336–337, 339, 348, 351
  semi-general pattern 12, 327–328
  syntactic pattern 38, 53, 141, 144, 211–212, 218, 228, 243–244, 280–281, 298
pedagogy 3, 12, 24, 53, 109, 152, 154, 206, 216, 237, 240, 260, 263, 295, 327, 339, 345

cognitive pedagogical grammar 151–152, 172, 174–175, 180, 238
pedagogical activities 7, 12, 14, 185, 207, 237–238, 240, 258, 263
pedagogical construction grammar 14, 21, 40–41
pedagogical grammar 12, 39–41, 151–152, 164, 237, 242, 290, 298
pedagogical implication 7–8, 106, 144–145, 154, 163, 171, 180, 186, 188, 205, 207, 237
performance 5, 101, 103, 105, 107, 136, 152, 218–221, 223–226, 228, 230, 249, 252
persistence 211–212
  structural persistence 53, 64, 66, 78
phonology 213, 215, 275, 351
phrasal verb, see verb
phraseology 5, 10, 13, 35, 53–56, 60–61, 63–67, 72, 78–80, 115–116, 119, 121, 137–141, 143–144, 344
  phraseologism 10, 13, 53–56, 60–66, 68–80
placement verb, see verb
polysemy link, see inheritance link
pragmatics 24, 79, 156, 214–215, 330, 349
predictability 34, 42, 53–54, 91, 274, 282, 285, 332
preposition 22–23, 27–30, 39, 59–60, 152, 161, 176–177, 188, 190, 200, 202, 238–239, 259, 278, 281–282, 285, 292, 295, 297, 316, 319, 321, 332–333, 336–338, 342, 347, 349
priming (see also priming task under task) 9, 211–221, 223, 225–228, 230
  constructional priming 211, 216, 224, 228–229
  priming effect 64, 212–215, 222–224, 228–229, 244
  syntactic priming 213–214, 222, 224, 229, 244
processing 3, 64, 68, 206, 212, 214–216, 332
productivity 7, 12, 53, 271–272, 290–293, 298, 327, 332–333, 335–337, 339–344, 348, 350

proficiency 4–5, 98, 106, 146, 154, 175, 188, 207, 211, 224–228, 230, 245–246, 248–249, 334, 343
pronoun 31, 80, 168, 212, 219, 225, 245, 277, 313, 349
prototypicality 35, 53, 56–58, 61–63, 65, 67–68, 70, 77–79, 92, 95–97, 107–108, 117, 130, 132, 134, 136, 185, 189, 203, 205, 226, 321, 343
psycholinguistics 4, 32, 211–212, 214
psychology 4–5, 12, 23, 212, 216, 285
psychotypology 11, 202–203, 243

qualitative approach 247, 252
quantitative approach 5, 141, 247, 258, 295

Romance language 72, 75, 229, 240

satellite 10, 186, 190, 245
satellite-framed language 6, 186, 190
schema 119, 135, 160–161, 226
  image schema 155–157
  schematicity 33, 35, 40, 145, 282–283, 290, 298, 317, 329, 337, 344
second language (see also non-native language under native language) 109, 116–117, 144, 185–186, 202, 205–207, 229, 328, 334, 339, 343–344
  second language acquisition, see acquisition
semantics 7, 32, 37, 42, 44, 53, 55, 57–62, 79, 91–94, 96, 100, 107, 112, 136–137, 139–141, 145, 162–163, 168, 174, 185–186, 191, 194, 198, 200, 204, 207, 211, 213–216, 221–225, 228, 239, 241, 243–244, 282, 295, 303–306, 308–309, 315–318, 322, 349
  semantic category 189–190, 193, 196–198, 200, 203–204, 207
  semantic coherence principle 58–59
  semantic role 57, 59, 217–218, 220, 222–224, 228, 306
simile 157, 164, 166, 170–171
sorting task, see task
Spanish 4, 8, 10–11, 43, 123, 151, 154, 156, 163–172, 174–176, 178, 185–190, 192–

207, 229, 237–249, 252–256, 258–260, 262–263, 308–309
speech (*see also* writing) 5, 95, 146, 187, 189, 197, 206, 213, 215–216, 242, 249–250, 252, 256, 274–275, 293–294, 296, 321, 340
subordination 28, 31, 63, 98, 120–121, 124–125, 135, 346
Swedish 8, 12–13, 123, 187, 308, 327–334, 337, 339, 343–348, 351
syntax 23, 29, 33, 38–39, 53, 56, 59–60, 62, 64, 79, 89, 91, 96, 99–100, 107, 112, 115–116, 119, 121, 125, 128–129, 132, 135, 137, 140–141, 144–145, 162–163, 165, 168, 180, 200, 211–219, 221–225, 228, 237, 239–240, 243–244, 246, 257, 278, 280–283, 287, 293, 296, 298, 304–309, 315–316, 321, 330, 333
  syntactic priming, *see* priming
  syntactic structure 41, 53, 61, 79, 93, 107, 124, 163, 213, 215–217, 219, 222–223, 225, 228–229, 276, 278, 295, 318
  syntactic variation 216

target language 7, 11, 109, 117–119, 136, 142, 200, 204, 238, 244–245, 279, 290, 351
task (*see also* experimentation)
  acceptability judgment task 4–5
  description task 9, 97, 99, 188–189, 206, 225, 229, 237, 240
  fill-in-the-blank task 100, 145, 323, 339, 342
  free association task 6
  grammaticality judgment task 97
  multiple choice task 56, 71, 296, 323
  parsing task 99, 112–113
  picture task 250, 256–257
  priming task 9
  recall task 229, 240, 253–257
  sentence completion task 4
  sentence elicitation task 228
  sorting task 9, 53, 56, 70
  translation task 9, 12, 89–90, 97, 100–107
teaching (*see also* instruction) 4–15, 21, 23–27, 30, 32–33, 36–38, 40–41, 43–45, 54, 56, 78–79, 89–90, 95, 97, 99–100, 106–109, 112–113, 117–118, 136, 141–143, 145, 151–152, 154, 159, 171–172, 174, 180, 203, 206, 224, 229–230, 238, 246–247, 258–263, 272–273, 296, 298, 322, 329, 334, 336, 340, 343–344, 348–351
  foreign language teaching 8, 12, 15, 21, 23–25, 33, 36–37, 40–41, 45–46, 55, 60, 78–79, 90, 108–109, 152, 322
  second language teaching 8, 206, 327–328, 339, 344, 349, 351
  teaching methodology 11–12, 23, 53, 55, 60, 65, 68, 77–78, 80, 152
teaching materials 6, 12–14, 22, 24–25, 38, 41, 44–45, 143, 175, 272, 327, 339, 344
  grammar book 12, 27, 45, 117, 242, 249
  schoolbook 21, 28, 31
  teaching aid 12, 327, 333–334, 336, 339, 341–344, 348–349, 351
  teaching manual 11–12
  textbook 12, 21, 23–26, 28, 31, 38, 40–43, 45, 117, 143, 304, 310, 327–329, 334–336, 339, 348
tense 25–27, 35, 38–39, 44, 154, 179, 244, 256, 304, 314, 331
terminology 12, 23–25, 32, 38, 40, 44, 46, 55, 309, 348
thematic role 214, 217, 220, 306
thinking for speaking 186, 204, 207
  re-thinking for speaking 185–186, 204, 207
traditional grammar 21, 42, 279
transfer 6, 10–11, 14, 46, 74, 77, 204, 237–238, 240–248, 255–258, 261–263
  conceptual transfer 200, 205
  constructional transfer 9, 243, 263
  negative transfer 60, 237, 240, 244
  semantic transfer 10, 200, 204
translation (*see also* translation task *under* task) 42–43, 68, 74, 100, 102, 104–105, 107, 164, 166, 170, 254, 260, 262, 275, 304, 310, 312–314, 321
typology 6, 186, 229, 238, 244, 332
  typological difference 10, 190, 207, 229

underuse (*see also* overuse) 126, 294
usage-based model 3, 7, 9, 11, 14, 21, 32–33, 37, 41, 95, 115–116, 119, 126, 135, 141, 143–144, 151, 153–154, 180, 203, 230, 283–284, 298

valency 29–30, 33–34, 43, 45, 53–54, 57–60, 67, 307, 313, 315–318
  valency theory 3, 30, 67
  verb valency 10, 29, 34, 54–56, 60, 62, 66–68, 78
verb 4–7, 10–11, 23, 26–27, 29–30, 34–35, 37–39, 43, 45, 53–60, 62, 66–71, 75, 78, 91, 93, 95–97, 99–101, 104, 107, 112–113, 119–120, 124–126, 128, 134–141, 145, 162–163, 167–168, 175–177, 179, 186–191, 193–200, 203–205, 213–214, 218, 221–222, 237–239, 241–244, 247, 252–253, 257, 259, 262, 274, 277, 282, 298, 304–306, 310–314, 316, 320–322, 337
  causative verb 116, 121–122, 124, 126, 128–129, 136–137, 145, 167
  caused motion verb 190, 193, 195
  ditransitive verb 56, 63–65, 218
  grooming verb 303–305
  heavy verb 89–90, 93, 100–101, 104
  light verb 11, 89–90, 93, 96–97, 99, 101, 104, 107–108, 304, 313
  manner of motion verb 206, 245
  motion verb 218, 245, 258–259, 263
  non-finite verb 121–122, 124, 128, 131–133, 137–139, 141, 145
  pathbreaking verb 7, 41, 96–97, 136
  phrasal verb 5, 64, 154, 259, 316
  placement verb 10–11, 185–187, 193, 198, 202–203
  posture verb 187
  reflexive verb 304
  stative verb 242, 263
  transitive verb 313
  verb type 10, 89–90, 102, 104, 107, 137, 194, 308
verb-framed language 6, 186, 190
vocabulary 38, 41–43, 45, 140, 152, 193, 272, 287, 298, 303, 305, 309–310, 314, 322–323

writing (*see also* speech) 5, 96–98, 112–113, 123, 128–129, 135, 139, 141, 144, 146, 206, 249, 262, 274, 296, 321, 323, 339, 351
  academic writing 123, 134, 143, 293–294

www.ingramcontent.com/pod-product-compliance
Lightning Source LLC
Chambersburg PA
CBHW050101170426
43198CB00014B/2411